Relativization in Ojibwe

Relativization in Ojibwe

MICHAEL D. SULLIVAN SR.

UNIVERSITY OF NEBRASKA PRESS | LINCOLN

© 2020 by the Board of Regents of the University of Nebraska

All rights reserved
∞

This book is published as part of the Recovering Languages and Literacies of the Americas initiative. Recovering Languages and Literacies is generously supported by the Andrew W. Mellon Foundation.

Library of Congress Cataloging-in-Publication Data
Names: Sullivan, Michael D., Sr., author.
Title: Relativization in Ojibwe / Michael D. Sullivan Sr.
Description: Lincoln: University of Nebraska Press, [2020] | Includes bibliographical references and index. | Summary: "Following previous dialect studies concerned primarily with varieties of Ojibwe spoken in Canada, Relativization in Ojibwe presents the first study of dialect variation for varieties spoken in the United States and along the border region of Ontario and Minnesota"—Provided by publisher.
Identifiers: LCCN 2019015765 | ISBN 9781496214799 (cloth) | ISBN 9781496222268 (paperback) | ISBN 9781496218889 (pdf) | ISBN 9781496218872 (mobi) | ISBN 9781496218865 (epub)
Subjects: LCSH: Ojibwa language.
Classification: LCC PM851 .S85 2020 | DDC 497/.333—dc23
LC record available at https://lccn.loc.gov/2019015765

Set in Merope by Tseng Information Systems, Inc.

For Waadookodaading,
where the dream is in action

CONTENTS

List of Illustrations and Tables xiii
Acknowledgments xv
List of Abbreviations xxi

1. **A Basic Introduction to the Study** 1
   1.1. Purpose and Goals. 4
   1.2. Ojibwe Relative Clauses 5
   1.2.1. What Is a Relative Clause? 6
   1.2.2. Linguistic Preliminaries 8
   1.2.3. Ojibwe RCs 17
   1.2.3.1. Core versus Relative Root Arguments 22
   1.2.4. Variation in SW Ojibwe 25
   1.3. Algonquian Dialectology. 28
   1.3.1. Ojibwe Dialects 29
   1.3.2. Implications of Classifications 31
   1.3.3. Southwestern Ojibwe. 34
   1.3.4. Literature Review: Dialect Studies 37
   1.3.4.1. Rhodes and Todd (1981). 37
   1.3.4.2. Valentine (1994) 38
   1.3.4.3. Nichols (2011, 2012) 41
   1.4. Literature Review: Algonquian RCs 43
   1.4.1. Rhodes (1996). 43
   1.4.2. Johns (1982). 46
   1.4.3. Johansson (2011) 49
   1.4.4. Johansson (2013) 50
   1.4.5. Lochbihler and Mathieu (2013) 52
   1.5. Theoretical Preliminaries 55
   1.5.1. Nonconfigurationality 55
   1.5.1.1. The Pronominal Argument Hypothesis (PAH) 56

1.5.2.	The Mirror Principle and the Minimalist Program 59
1.5.2.1.	Feature Checking 61
1.5.2.2.	Independent versus Conjunct. 62
1.5.3.	Split-CP Hypothesis (Rizzi 1997) 69
1.6.	Conclusion 70
1.6.1.	Concluding Remarks 70
2.	**Ojibwe Morphosyntax**. 72
2.1.	Typological Preliminaries 73
2.2.	The Sound System. 74
2.2.1.	The Vowels 74
2.2.2.	Consonant Inventory. 74
2.3.	Morphology 77
2.3.1.	Nouns 78
2.3.2.	Pronouns 78
2.3.3.	Verbal Morphology 80
2.3.3.1.	Palatalization. 82
2.3.3.2.	Nominalization 85
2.3.4.	Preverbs. 87
2.4.	Inflectional Subsystems 95
2.4.1.	Modes 99
2.5.	Topicality Hierarchy 102
2.5.1.	Obviation 104
2.6.	Initial Change 108
2.6.1.	*Wh*-questions 111
2.6.2.	Participles. 112
2.6.3.	Past/Completive. 121
2.7.	Word Order and Clause Structure 124
2.7.1.	The Noun Phrase 126
2.7.2.	Basic Constituency Order 126
2.7.3.	The Left Periphery. 130
2.7.3.1.	Focus. 132
2.7.3.2.	Topic. 134

3. Methodology................................139

    3.1. Survey Apparatus..........................144

    3.2. Archival Data..............................149

    3.3. Findings..................................151

    3.3.1. *ji-/da-* Complementizer, *jibwaa/dabwaa*............152

    3.3.2. Preterit Peripheral Suffixes....................156

    3.3.3. Neutralization of Inanimate Plural in Conjunct........157

    3.3.4. Number under Obviation......................161

    3.3.5. Restructuring of Dependent Stems..............165

    3.3.6. Core Demonstratives........................167

    3.3.7. Phonological Variation......................170

    3.3.7.1. Nasal Behavior............................171

3.3.7.1.1. Initial /n/..................................171

3.3.7.1.2. Final Nasal in Negation Suffix *-sii(n)*............174

3.3.7.1.3. Final Nasal /n/ Behavior......................180

3.3.7.1.4. Nasal Spreading............................184

    3.3.7.2. Initial /g/................................185

    3.3.7.3. Vowel and Glide Quality......................187

3.3.7.3.1. Labialization and Rounding....................187

3.3.7.3.2. Vowel Height /i/ versus /a/....................189

3.3.7.3.3. Articulation of Glides /y/ and /w/..............192

    3.3.7.4. Other Points of Variation......................196

3.3.7.4.1. Women's Names *-k(we)*........................196

3.3.7.4.2. /t/ Epenthesis..............................198

3.3.7.4.3. Syncope..................................201

    3.3.8. Lexical Variation............................204

    3.3.8.1. Body-Part-Incorporating Suffix *-e*..............205

    3.3.8.2. *-ngwaam(i)* Verbs..........................207

    3.3.8.3. *-aadage/-aadagaa* Verbs......................208

    3.3.9. Animacy Status............................209

    3.3.10. TA *-aw* Stem Contraction....................213

    3.3.11. Initial Vowel Change........................216

    3.3.12. Iterative Suffix............................220

    3.3.13. Participles................................221

3.3.13.1. Southern Strategies.........................224
3.3.13.2. Innovations................................236
3.3.13.3. *gaa-* Participles.........................239

   3.4. Discussion......................................243
   3.4.1. Geographic Variation........................243
3.4.1.1. Leech Lake as a Transitional Area..........245
3.4.1.2. Intelligibility............................249
   3.4.2. Age-Graded Variation........................253
   3.4.3. Free Variation..............................256

4. Relativization in Ojibwe.........................259

   4.1. Ojibwe Relative Clauses.........................259
   4.1.1. Findings: Core Argument versus Relative Root Arguments..263
   4.1.2. Variation in Relativization Strategies......269
   4.2. Theoretical Framework...........................270
   4.2.1. Plain Conjunct Morphosyntax.................270
4.2.1.1. Brittain (2001)............................274
   4.2.2. Split-CP Hypothesis (Rizzi 1997)............276
4.2.2.1. FinP as Host to Conjunct...................277
4.2.2.2. FocP Host to IC............................279
4.2.2.3. ForceP and RCs.............................282
   4.2.3. Cyclicity and Phases (Bruening 2001)........285
   4.3. Refining the Analysis...........................287
   4.3.1. Feature Bundles.............................288
   4.3.2. The Structure of the Ojibwe CP..............292
   4.3.3. Internally versus Externally Headed RCs.....303
   4.3.4. Concluding Remarks..........................306

5. Conclusions......................................308

   5.1. Review..308
   5.1.1. Implications of the Findings................310
   5.2. Limitations.....................................311
   5.2.1. Obsolescence................................312

5.2.2. Access	313
5.2.3. L2 Interference	313
5.3. Comparisons within the Algonquian Family	314
5.3.1. IC	315
5.3.2. Algonquian Participles	317
5.3.2.1. PA Participles	319
5.4. Directions for Future Research	322
Appendix: VTA Paradigms	325
Notes	329
References	341
Index	353

ILLUSTRATIONS AND TABLES

ILLUSTRATIONS
1. The Algic language family tree 29

TABLES
1. Ojibwe verb types 9
2. Initial change (IC) 11
3. Changed conjunct versus participles for *biindige* 's/he enters' 13
4. Inflectional forms of *aabajitoon* 'use it' 14
5. Participial neologisms 15
6. Participles as nominalizations 16
7. North versus south participles 26
8. Featural composition of person arrangement 63
9. Ojibwe vowels 75
10. Ojibwe consonants 75
11. Underlying forms and positions of nominal suffixes 79
12. Peripheral suffixes 79
13. Demonstrative pronouns 79
14. Verb classification *biin-* 'clean' 81
15. Preverb position classes 87
16. pv1: tense-mood 87
17. Locative prefixes 89
18. Relative preverbs 89
19. Orders of verbal inflection *wiisini* 's/he is eating' 96
20. Local theme signs (SAP) independent order 103
21. Local theme signs (SAP) conjunct order 103
22. Nonlocal theme signs (non-SAPs) independent order 103
23. Nonlocal theme signs (non-SAPs) conjunct order 104
24. Plural and obviative suffixes 107
25. *gaa-* prefix in place-names 110

26. Ojibwe A-pronouns (*wh*-questions) 112
27. VTI1 and VAI2 plural participle. 113
28. TI third-person participles 115
29. Findings from Sullivan (2016) 127
30. Word order from narratives. 128
31. Deviations 131
32. Demonstrative pronouns 168
33. Nasal-less VIIs in Odawa 181
34. Loss of final nasal in verb inflection 182
35. Angeline Williams's variation. 190
36. Lexical variation in SW Ojibwe. 205
37. Sample conjunct order verbs 222
38. VTI third-person participles 226
39. Participle innovations: gW- 237
40. SW Ojibwe participle variation. 246
41. A-pronouns and *wh*-questions 280
42. Palatalization in ForceP 291
43. 'Homes'. 298
44. IC patterns for Algonquian languages. 315
45. IC in Pre-PA 316

ACKNOWLEDGMENTS

Akawe niwii-miigwechiwi'aa aw manidoo. Aaniish-naa mii wa'aw gaa-miininang yo'ow bimaadiziwin naa go gaye gidinwewininaan da-gaganoonang. As a spiritually thinking young man I always first give thanks to the *manidoo*. Since I began using my *asemaa* on a daily basis and following the path it leads me on, my life has been filled with joy and experiences I would have never dreamed of. There are countless people that should be named individually that had a hand in the development and completion of this book; they are probably too numerous to name though I will try. From everyone that provided encouragement to those who doubted my academic endeavors, I thank you all from the bottom of my heart for giving me the boost of motivation to carry out this work. The pages that follow are the result of my life's work at this stage in time, the reason for my absence on the powwow trail, and, ultimately, the labor that not only established my ethic as a linguist and a scholar, but also set the direction for my life's path.

I have been blessed with a beautiful family. My wife, Krysten, deserves the most credit and recognition for this publication. Without her and her amazing abilities as a mother and wife, I never would have made it off of the rez to pursue my education. My children also deserve the majority of the credit; Niizhoo, Manidood, Lexie, and Lenny have all had to sacrifice their time with me so I could finish. Their constant questions about what it is I have been working on soon turned into, "When are you going to be done?" This has pushed me down the last stretch of the final chapters and I look forward to more baseball games, 21-tip, and our inevitable and long overdue return to the powwow arena. *Gizhawenimininim!*

I was blessed to have been born to a wonderful mother. In Anishinaabe culture we say that babies choose their parents before they are born. There is no question why I chose my mom. She supported me through the ups and downs of my youth and challenging early adult years, knowing that I would eventually come to my senses and find my path. She treated me like I was smart, even if all of the evidence observable in my attitude, behavior, and demeanor suggested otherwise. *Chi-miigwech*, mom!

I would also like to thank all of my relatives, friends, and professors, way too numerous to name but deserving of recognition nonetheless. My journey as a linguist began long before I ever took classes in linguistics. As a boy on the reservation during a time when just about everyone over sixty spoke Ojibwe regularly, my curiosity and envy were fostered early. I'd like to thank those individuals responsible for providing the first Ojibwe sounds that fell upon my ears. I am especially grateful for the time I spent with the late Harold Frogg—my first fieldwork consultant—long before I had any training or knew what I was doing. There was never a question he didn't appreciate or a moment when he didn't have time for my interest and never-ending barrage of questions. He was so excited and supportive to see me grow in the language. My world changed when you left *niijii*.

Chi-miigwech to all of my first Ojibwe teachers I had as a little boy: Darlene Stockinger, Mary Hart, Beverly Gouge, Monica White, and George O'shogay. I would especially like to thank Thelma Nayquonabe for teaching me Ojibwe when I was in elementary school and encouraging me as a speaker in our community as I grew into a young man. Your support has been crucial to my journey and success. Also, the old-timers I used to listen to at the dances, I say *miigwech* and will always remember Eugene Begay Sr., Bob Merrill, and my *niiyawen'enyiban* Joe Shibiash. I would also like to acknowledge the late Clara Bebe and Ruth Carley for providing us all insight into the classic "LCO dialect." To Jerry Smith and Beverly Bearheart, *miigwech* for everything that you do for the people and the generous and kind nature in which you share your wisdom.

I would not know anything without the teachings of my elders both here and gone. *Chi-miigwech* to Larry "Amik" Smallwood (d. 2017), my principal linguistic consultant and one of my best friends. Much of the data given and conclusions drawn here are a result of his willingness to teach me Ojibwe. His commitment to making sure we "get the humor" and his composure and poise as a public speaker and storyteller have inspired me to do more than just speak Ojibwe. Not a day goes by where I do not remember you with smiles and laughter. Also, *miigwech* to Lee "Chi-obizaan" Staples, who provided much of the classic southern Ojibwe analyzed in this study. Always eager to help with my understanding of the language and our ceremonies, Chi-ob has been instrumental to the completion of this study. I would also like to thank Eddie Benton-Banai for answering my questions and for being willing to share his immeasurable knowledge of the language. There are also two elders who have gone on who contributed greatly to my development as a speaker of Ojibwe and as a linguist—Rose Tainter and Benny Rogers. I got to know both of them very well and many of my first formal field sessions (where I actually had questions about the system of the language itself!) were held with them as my consultants. As those of us in endangered language revitalization know, our best friends are often elders and these two were no exception.

I would also like to honor the memory of many of my elders who have also since walked on: Anna Gibbs, Joe Chosa, Lillian Rice, Geno Bearheart, Rita Corbine, Rose Burns, Mary Jane Frog, Jim Clark, Archie Mosay, James "Pipe" Mustache, Alice Lynk, Dee Bainbridge, Phillip Taylor, Leonard Moose, Jim Bedeau, Marlene Stately, Ray Boshey, and Jimmy Jackson. We are working to ensure that your teachings live on. This book was written about the language of many different elders still living who are graciously supportive of our work. *Miigwech* to Nancy Jones, Mary Moose, Dora Ammann, Maubin Merrill, Tommy Saros, Miskobineshiinh, Dick Smith, Eugene Stillday, Murphy Thomas, Gordon Jourdain, Elfreda Sam, Susan Shingobe, Herb Sam, Maggie Kegg, Ralph and Delores Pewaush, Leona Wakanabo, Geraldine Howard, David Aubid, Rosemarie Debungie, Darryl Kingbird, Dolores Shawinimash, Eugene Goodsky, Ruby Boshey, Frances Songetay, and Joe Nayquonabe. All of you have contributed to my journey in your own way.

As a tribal college graduate, I could not go without thanking everyone at Lac Courte Oreilles Ojibwe Community College for believing in me and providing the foundation on which I would grow. *Chi-miigwech* to David Bisonette (my first Ojibwe grammar teacher!), Dr. Eric Reddix (now professor at University of Minnesota Duluth), Tom Antell, Dan Gretz, Dr. Deb Anderson, Jenny Schlender, Annette Wiggins, and Vernon Martin. All of you witnessed the journey of a troubled rez kid transform into a super nerd! *Miigwech!*

I can't forget all of the folks at my undergraduate alma mater, University of Wisconsin–Superior. Thanks to Dr. Marsha Francis, Sue Holm, Deb Provost, Dr. Marshall Johnson, Dr. Deborah Augsburger (my first linguistics teacher!), Dr. Michael Ball, Dr. Eri Fujeada, Ivy Vaino, Chip Beal, and Gary Johnson. All of these people had a hand in making graduate school a reality for me.

When arriving at the University of Minnesota to embark on my graduate studies, I had trouble at first in finding my place. I am so grateful for the folks in linguistics for being my friends, confidants, and advisers. I would like to acknowledge University of Minnesota professors Dr. Brenda Child, Dr. Mary Hermes, Dr. David Schueler, Dr. J. P. Marcotte, Dr. Brian Reese, Dr. Nancy Stenson, Dr. Martha Bigelow, Dr. Kendall King, Dr. Elaine Tarone, and the entire crew from CARLA. I would also like to thank my Malagasy consultants, Tsitsy and Daniel, for their help during my field methods course. I also started a journey learning the Dakota language while at the U and would like to say *chi-miigwech* to Dakota Joe Bendickson. Being a student in Joe's classes inspired many of my teaching methods and I am forever grateful. I also can't forget Dennis Jones, who always welcomed me in whatever was happening at the U. His gracious way and kind nature has opened the door to many students who have dedicated themselves to learning Ojibwe. *Chi-miigwech niijii.* I also feel inclined to acknowledge my fellow grad students at the U, Nora Livesay, Paul Tilleson, Dr. Muhammad Abdurrahman, and Yolanda Pushetonequa.

I'd also like to thank the language table crew from Minneapolis: Dr. Rick Gresczyk, one of the most kind and welcoming instructors I've ever known, Laurie Harper, Laura Cloud, Yulia Bjorgen, Louise Erdrich, Hope Flannagan, and many others too numerous to name. I'd also like to say *miigwech* to the *OOGikweg*: Lucia Bonnaci, Michelle Goose, and Robin Hanks. I also owe a lot to Chuck Fiero for always being willing to share his data and for taking an interest in my work.

I would not have been able to attend graduate school nor finish without the gracious support given by the D.O.V.E. Fellowship Program, the Community of Scholars, and the D.O.V.E. Summer Dissertation Fellowship program. I specifically thank Noro Andriamanalina from the Office of Diversity in Graduate Education. Mighty fine work you do. I also say *chi-miigwech* to the Lac Courte Oreilles Higher Ed. Office for their support, the American Indian College Fund, the American Indian Graduate Center, and the Education Office of the Forest County Potawatomi.

I'd especially like to express my thanks to my doctoral dissertation committee: Dr. Hooi Ling Soh, whose patience with me as I grappled with syntactic theory sustained my sanity while I tried to make sense of Ojibwe syntax. Also, thanks to Dr. Claire Halpert for being the fresh air needed when I was selecting my committee. Her assistance and guidance to the theoretical analysis provided here is immeasurable. I am also forever grateful for Dr. Jeanette Gundel, my adviser through graduate school and co-chair of my dissertation committee. Dr. Gundel's commitment to seeing me through and believing in me has carried me to the finish line. Last but certainly not least, I'd like to say *chi-miigwech* to Dr. John D. Nichols. John has helped me in so many ways. I cannot thank him enough. From bringing me on board the Ojibwe People's Dictionary project to sharing his vast knowledge and resources pertaining to Ojibwe and the Algonquian family, my work never would have even begun without John. His attention to detail and meticulous ethic is something I will always strive to replicate in my own work. I will forever be fortunate in being his student.

I'd also like to acknowledge my colleagues from the College of St. Scholastica. They have shared many words of wisdom as I crawled down the home stretch of this volume. *Chi-miigwech* to Dr. David Scheuttler, Valerie Tanner, Dr. Jill Dupont, Dr. Elyse Carter-Vosen, Dr. Martin Phlug, Dr. Tammy Ostrander, Mary Lee, Pat Greenwood, Christina Woods, Dr. Thomas Morgan, and Dr. Karen Rosenflanz. Also, my language students at CSS have been incredible. I say *miigwech* to Tressa Erickson, Miigis Gonzalez, Misty Peterson, Winona Ojanen, Vic Huju, and Ricki Mesna.

In Ojibwe country, you can't mention Ojibwe language revitalization without reference to the Waadookodaading Ojibwe Language Immersion School. The pioneers of this effort are the ones who originally inspired me to become fluent in Ojibwe and use it daily with my children. *Miigwech* to Keller Paap and Lisa Laronge. The work that goes into the immersion effort is unsurpassed. *Chi-miigwech* Michelle Haskins, Lisa Clemons, Dustin Burnette, Brooke Mosay Ammann, Katy Butterfield, Andrea Debungie, Nick Hanson, Brooke Simon, Cathy Begay, Carla Miller, Persia Erdrich, Rosie Gonzalez, Willis Ford, and Bezhig Hunter, the school board (past and present), and the LCO Tribal Governing Board.

I also owe a great deal to the language warriors who inspired my work.

Dr. Anton Treuer has been a constant supporter throughout my journey and has contributed in more ways than I could ever repay. Dr. Brendan Fairbanks helped convince me to go into linguistics and was a mentor to me through the coursework and the rigor of the program. Throughout my travels I have made many friends and have been inspired by their work on language in their areas. *Miigwech* to Paul Demain, Jim Miller, Meg Noodin, Henry Flocken, Leon Valliere, Wayne Valliere, Mary Pyawasit, Sierra Merrill, Wes Pagel, Wesley Connors, Dr. Alton Sonny Smart, Mark Pero, Dr. David Truer, Alex Decoteau, Dr. Brian McGinnis, Dan Jones, Melissa Boyd, Kim Anderson, Rebecca Boyd, Rebecca Countryman, Dawn Frost-Gokee, Bill and Edye Howes, Charlie Smith, Jim Northrup, John Slick Benjamin, Sam Pete, Aanakwadoons Aubid, Jada Montano, Jason Jones, Leslie Harper, Adrian Liberty, Monique Paulson, Manidoo-bines, Alex Kmett, Summer Gokey, Miskwaanakwad Rice, Monty McGahey, Jessica Benson, and my Menominee bros Ron Corn and Joey Awanahopay.

I also have to express my utmost appreciation to my brothers Jay, Justin, Jimmy, and Nick. Our conversations kept me sane as I evolved into something I don't think any of us were expecting. I'd also like to acknowledge my nephews Donavan, Jonah, and Isaiah for providing inspiration. Life can be tough if we try to blaze our own trail. Also to my childhood best friend, Chato Gonzalez, who later would allow me to crash at his place while I finished the last couple of years of coursework—*miigwech niijii*. Chato's work contributed immensely to my own understanding of Ojibwe. Last but not least I'd like to thank my powwow brothers from the drum, Pipestone. *Miigwech* George Budman Morrow III, Johnny Morrow, Ahsinees Larson, Mike Demain, Mat White, Nick Hanson, Jerome Powless, Tommy Cain, Jason Pettibone, Wanbli Williams, Dylan Jennings, and Opie Day-Bedeau for your patience and support while I stepped away to do this academic work. Now let's hit the road!

ABBREVIATIONS

The following abbreviations are used in the interlinear morpheme glossing and elsewhere in the text:

0s	inanimate singular	DIR	direct
0p	inanimate plural	DM	distributed morphology
1	first person	DP	determiner phrase
1s	first-person singular	Dpart	deictic particle
1p	first-person plural exclusive	DUB	dubitative
		EPEN	epenthetic
2	second person	EMPH	emphatic
2s	second-person singular	EXCL	exclamative
2p	second-person plural	EXT	extension
21p	first-person plural inclusive	FUT	future
		h/	him/her or his/her
3	third person	IC	initial change
3s	third-person singular	IMP	imperative
3p	third-person plural	INAN	inanimate
3'	obviative third person	INCORP	incorporated
ADVP	adverb phrase	IND	independent
AM	aspectual marker	INV	inverse
AN	animate	ITER	iterative
AUG	augment	L	locative oblique (argument)
CJ	conjunct		
CMN	Cree-Montagnais-Naskapi	LCA	linear correspondence axiom
COMP	complementizer	LOC	locative
CONJ	conjunct	MAT	matrix
CP	complementizer phrase	MOD	modal
DEM	demonstrative pronoun	NEG	negative
DET	determiner	NEGP	negation phrase
DIM	diminutive	NOM	nominal

OBJ	object	RR	relative root
OBV	obviative	SG	singular
PA	Proto-Algonquian	S/HE	she/he
PAH	pronominal argument hypothesis	SUBJ	subject
		TA	transitive animate
PEJ	pejorative	TI	transitive inanimate
PL	plural	TI1	transitive inanimate theme marker -*am*
PM	participle marker		
PN	proper name	TI2	transitive inanimate theme marker -*oo*
POSS	possessive		
POT	potential	TI3	transitive inanimate theme marker -*i*
PP	prepositional phrase		
PPN	pausal pronoun	TP	tense phrase
PRET	preterit	VAI	verb animate intransitive
PROX	proximate		
PRT	participle	VII	verb inanimate intransitive
PST	past		
PV	preverb	vP	light verb phrase
QP	question particle	VTI	verb transitive inanimate
RC	relative clause		
REDUD	reduplicative	VTA	verb transitive animate
REL	relative	X	indefinite actor

Examples collected in primary fieldwork sessions are glossed with the speaker's initials, date (year, month, day), and the context of collection. For examples obtained from the Ojibwe People's Dictionary, the lemma for the word in which the example appears is given. For examples obtained from unpublished sources, the speaker's initials are given along with an abbreviated title of the article or story. Abbreviations for contexts are as follows:

BT	back-translation	OPD	Ojibwe People's Dictionary (followed by the head word)
BT-C	back-translation correction		
C	conversation	TM	text message
E	elicitation		
N	narrative		

Speakers' initials are as follows:

AL	Alice Lynk	JB	Jim Bedeau
AM	Archie Mosay	JC	Joe Chosa
AS	Larry "Amik" Smallwood	JN	Joe Nayquonabe
BR	Benny Rogers	LB	Lillian 'Ruby' Boshey
CB	Clara Bebe	LS	Lee Staples
DB	Dee Bainbridge	LW	Leona Wakanabo
DS	Dolores Shawinimash	NJ	Nancy Jones
EB	Eddie Benton-Banai	PM	Pipe Mustache
EG	Eugene Goodsky	PT	Phillip Taylor
ES	Eugene Stillday	RB	Ray Boshey
GH	Geraldine Howard	RC	Ruth Carley
GJ	Gordon Jourdain	RD	Rosemarie Debungie
GO	George O'shogay	RT	Rose Tainter

Community codes used here are as follows:

LCO	Lac Courte Oreilles, Wisconsin	NL	Nett Lake (Sugarbush), Minnesota
LDF	Lac du Flambeau, Wisconsin	nLL	northern Leech Lake, Minnesota
LL	Leech Lake, Minnesota	RG	Red Gut (Nigigoonsiminkaaning), Ontario
LLC	Lac La Croix, Ontario		
LV	Lake Vermilion, Minnesota	RL	Red Lake, Minnesota
		SC	St. Croix, Wisconsin
ML	Mille Lacs, Minnesota	sLL	southern Leech Lake, Minnesota

Dialect codes here are as follows:

GO	General Ojibwe
WO	Wisconsin Ojibwe
BL	Border Lakes Ojibwe

Relativization in Ojibwe

ONE

A Basic Introduction to the Study

The focus of this study is on *relative clauses* (RCs) in Ojibwe and the variation in morphosyntactic form of participial verbs used in relative clauses. Strategies for the formation of these participial relative clauses differ in regard to number agreement and appear to be a defining parameter in geographical subdialect variation for the larger grouping popularly known in the Algonquian literature as Central Southern Ojibwa (Goddard 1996a), Southwestern (SW) Ojibwe, or Chippewa (Valentine 1994, Rhodes and Todd 1981). Although the language has a high level of mutual intelligibility across the Southwestern communities of Wisconsin and Minnesota, there is a significant break in homogeneity in some of the more northern reservations in Minnesota. Variation should come as no surprise since, as Valentine indicates, "from earliest contact, Ojibwe has existed in recognizable linguistic dialects" (1994, 106). Perhaps the most extreme point of difference is the formation of participial verbs and the composition of relative clauses.

Participial verbs, hereafter referred to as *participles*, are derived by a series of morpho-phonological processes, minimally an ablaut process of the first vowel in the verbal complex, along with the relevant agreement suffixes. These agreement suffixes appear only in the varieties of Ojibwe spoken from the southern side of the Leech Lake reservation in northern Minnesota and further south through Minnesota, throughout Wisconsin, and the Upper Peninsula of Michigan. These suffixes are analyzed as agreement markers that only surface when third-person plural or obviative noun phrases (NP) serve as heads of the relative clause. As will be shown, varieties spoken on the northern side of Leech Lake and all points north in the SW region do not employ the relative agreement markers on participles. I argue that participles, verb forms derived by an additional layer of inflection on an already complex morphological system, appear to have been morphologically leveled in the northern communities, in a form of paradigm leveling bringing them closer in shape to another inflectional form of the verb, making the system more regular.

The main goal of this study is to document and address regional dialect variation in Southwestern Ojibwe, providing an empirical resource for researchers and others involved in its documentation and revitalization effort. With revitalization occurring in many reservation and urban areas, speakers are interacting with individuals from other dialect regions. Similarly students engaged in second-language (L2) study of Ojibwe are often instructed by individuals from different dialect areas. In addition to the focus on the varieties spoken in the United States, a portion of the Border Lakes region of Ontario will also be included. Valentine states that the Border Lakes region is a "transitional area" between northwestern Ojibwe and southwestern, closely related to Saulteaux (Valentine 1994, 45). Particular attention in this region is paid to the speech of speakers from the communities of Lac La Croix, Ontario, and Nigigoonsiminikaaning (Red Gut), Ontario. Based on the results of primary fieldwork with many speakers throughout the southwestern territory, along with archived sources from many of the same areas, I show that the two strategies of RC formation differ in agreement and appear to align with a north-south geographical distribution.[1] Taking a microparametric approach, in addition to RCs, I also document many other features that vary from community to community.

In regard to linguistic variability, all of the SW Ojibwe communities discussed in this study form a mutually intelligible grouping, but as I will show in chapter 3, a breakdown occurs with speakers from the northern communities in their ability to interpret some of the more morphologically marked southern RCs. There is also the issue of internal variation in this area determined by ancestry and linguistic socialization in assuming that where a speaker comes from is represented in their speech. Ojibwe people have a long nomadic history, with various paths of migration leading them to each of their respective present-day locales. These historical groupings represent historical linguistic communities that are still relevant in accounting for observable variation in the speech of present-day speakers. Contrary to popular belief, there has been a considerable degree of language change, to be expected of a linguistic community undergoing rapid acculturation and external societal pressures. As a result, language shift has occurred in a number of Ojibwe communities and is near completion in all others. By comparing archived materials from previous generations to data from modern speakers, we see that there is a substantial degree of age-graded variation. With lifestyle and cultural changes experienced within the past hundred years, there has been an increasing loss of terminology and discourse surrounding more traditional activities and ways of life.

Through the collective Ojibwe experience, there appears to have been an emergence of two major groupings or subdialects in the SW Ojibwe territory. The division is inextricably linked to settlement patterns and historical ties with other communities. For instance, northern communities in the SW area such as Red Lake, Leech Lake, and Nett Lake have a long history of interaction and intermarriage with each other as well as with communities to their north, who are often regarded as Saulteaux-speaking bands of Manitoba and the Border Lakes region of Ontario, as well as the Cree to the immediate north. Southern communities, however, including White Earth, Mille Lacs, Fond du Lac, St. Croix, Lac Courte Oreilles, and Lac du Flambeau have very extensive ties with one another dating back to precontact times as well as a connection and history of interaction with their neighbors to the east including the Potawatomi and Odawa.

Interestingly, spiritual and religious practices can be linked to a division (see Valentine 1994, 416) that is relevant for the SW Ojibwe linguistic situation. In the southern communities there has been a long-standing tradition of traveling to attend specific ceremonies with other bands, including for services of the Big Drum society, the Grand Medicine, or Midewiwin, lodge, and other gatherings of traditional Ojibwe spirituality. This connection between places is still observed to some degree today. Similarly the influence of Christianity in the south has been much more far-reaching than in the north, an influence I credit with language loss in the south. It is no coincidence that, in the United States, communities with a higher percentage of reservation Christians are, more often than not, communities with no or few remaining speakers of Ojibwe. Communities that have fared better in regard to the maintenance of spiritual beliefs in light of missionary and colonizing forces have maintained an Ojibwe speech community (such as Mille Lacs and Ponemah).[2] Until fairly recently, with the revitalization effort and emergence of a strong L2 movement, speaking Ojibwe provided no real social status or economic benefit outside of traditional ceremony. With English viewed as the language of opportunity and with constant pressures to assimilate, the Ojibwe language began to decline.

In the sections that follow, I first provide the purpose and goals of this study. In 1.2, I define RCs and give a brief description of Ojibwe grammar necessary for the introduction to relativization in Ojibwe, including the variation observed. In 1.3, I give some background on the Algonquian language family, Ojibwe dialects, and a review of the literature on Ojibwe dialectology. A review of the Algonquian relative clause literature is given in 1.4. In section 1.5 I discuss the theoretical preliminaries for the subsequent discussion of the syntax of RCs provided in chapter 4, with 1.6 being a summary and conclusion of the chapter.

1.1. PURPOSE AND GOALS

The main purpose of this study is to identify and describe the two strategies of RC formation in Southwestern Ojibwe and to establish the geographical distribution of the forms. Additionally I provide descriptions of the other features that define subdialect variation in this area. Ojibwe in some communities has not been documented at all; some have lost their last speakers before ever making an effort to document their language. This research is of the utmost urgency as many communities have dwindled down to a handful of speakers; many of those who remain are extremely elderly and somewhat inaccessible.[3]

Almost twenty years ago Goddard stated, "80% of the extant native languages were no longer spoken by children and were facing effective extinction within a single lifetime or, in many cases, much sooner." We are all aware of the immense loss of cultural knowledge and identity that follows language loss, which is also a "great potential setback to the development of general theoretical accounts of human language" (Goddard 1996a, 3). The most recent (informal) survey lists 720 total speakers in the United States, primarily concentrated at Ponemah on the Red Lake reservation in northern Minnesota (Treuer and Paap 2009, 1). The same survey provides a generous estimate of 150 speakers at Mille Lacs, while only 42 speakers are estimated for the entire state of Wisconsin. Treuer and Paap found no living speakers left at Fond du Lac; since their survey was published, the remaining speakers at Red Cliff and Bad River have since passed on. Treuer (2010, 51) attributes significant language loss to the massive numbers of Ojibwe children adopted into non-Ojibwe-speaking homes. All native speakers of Ojibwe in the United States are bilingual; as a result of the lack of opportunity to use Ojibwe, they are often more proficient in English.

In response to the dire state of the language in most areas, certain SW Ojibwe communities have launched large-scale revitalization efforts in an attempt to produce Ojibwe-speaking school-age children. Communities in Wisconsin and Minnesota have developed immersion schools and classrooms of varying age levels, the two most notable being Niigaane at Leech Lake, serving K–5th grade, and Waadookodaading at Lac Courte Oreilles in Wisconsin offering pre-K–7th grade immersion instruction. The schools have seen tremendous academic success and produced highly proficient school-age children. In addition to the community revitalization efforts, Ojibwe is also offered as a course at many colleges and universities, especially those in close proximity to reservation areas. Many of the immersion school and college-level instructors are imported from Canadian communities, bringing with them their native dialect. Many instructors at all levels are aware of the importance of regional variation and its correlation with linguistic and ethnic identity, though, more often than not, most are unaware of what exactly it is that makes their variety distinct from another.

Ultimately the goal of this research is to provide a resource not only for linguists and researchers on language, but especially for language teachers, students, and activists concerned with local variety. I have attempted to obtain data from every possible source, both primary and secondary. Although I have succeeded in making a contribution to the gaps in documentation, much work remains in this area, as individuals involved in language revitalization have new questions every day that are worthy of research and exploration.

1.2. OJIBWE RELATIVE CLAUSES

In the sections that follow I first provide the definition of RCs and their definitive characteristics. I then introduce the reader to some preliminary and pertinent points of Ojibwe grammar.[4] In 1.2.3 I provide an overview of Ojibwe RCs, outlining some of the issues to be treated in chapter 4. Crucial to this discussion is the distinction between core arguments and relative root arguments, introduced in 1.2.3.1. This section concludes with an introduction to variation observed in the SW Ojibwe territory in regard to RC strategies and the morphosyntactic shape of participles in RCs.

1.2.1. What Is a Relative Clause?

Before presenting the relevant data concerning relative clauses (hereafter RCs) and participles, I offer the definitive characteristics of RCs as well as approaches to their analysis. Relative clauses are essentially subordinate clauses that modify an NP. For my purposes here, I follow the definition provided by Andrews (2007, 206) given below:

(1) Relative clause

 A relative clause (RC) is a subordinate clause which delimits the reference of an NP by specifying the role of the referent of that NP in the situation described by the RC.

The NP that is modified or relativized is the head of the RC. In Andrews's notation, the head is treated as NP_{mat}, or the noun phrase of the matrix clause "whose reference is being delimited" (2007, 206). The subordinate clause itself responsible for the delimitation of NP_{mat} is treated with the notation S_{rel} (Keenan 1985; Andrews 2007), and is the "defining feature of RCs" (Keenan 1985, 142). Within S_{rel} is the relativized noun phrase itself, or the "element within the restricting clause that is coreferential with the head noun" (Payne 1997, 325–26). The notation used is NP_{rel}, which Keenan describes as the position "which refers to the elements in the domain of relativization" (1985, 146). More specifically, NP_{rel} indicates the grammatical function of S_{rel} (Andrews 2007), essentially the head of the RC. The final element of a relative clause to be discussed here is the actual relativizing component, which identifies S_{rel} as a restricting clause. Often termed the "relativizer," it can appear as a relative pronoun, morpheme, particle, or other language-specific indicator.

The English example provided below in (2) shows the components of a relative clause as discussed above:

(2) English RC[5]
   I chased the **dog** ᴿᶜ[**that** ∅ bit the child].
   'dog'_NPmat ['that'_relativizer 'O'_NPrel 'bit the child'_Srel]

In addition to the structure above in (2), the form of the verb in S_{rel} (V_{rel} in Keenan 1985) may occur in what is typically called a participial or gerund form (-*ing*) for English. English makes use of "*that*-relatives"—as shown above in (2), where *that* functions as a relative clause complementizer—and pronominal relatives employing relative pronouns; essentially, *wh*-expressions that have undergone *wh*-movement. RCs are commonly analyzed crosslinguistically as involving one or more of the following strategies shown in (3), where (3a.) consists of a relative pronoun *who(m)*, and (3b.), which involves a complementizer *that*:

(3) RC strategies
   a. Pronominal RCs
   She saw the child [ᴿᶜ **who(m)** the dog bit]

   b. Complementizer 'that' RCs
   She saw the child [ᴿᶜ **that** the dog bit]

As will be seen, both types of RCs shown above can be found in Ojibwe.

In accounting for the syntax of RCs, it is necessary to examine the relationship between the RC and its head (the modified element). Another common focus in RC typology and analysis concerns the relation between this relative head and the site where relativization occurs. In terms of syntactic structure, this implies, as Benţea (2010, 165) suggests, "one should determine whether the relative clause is a complement or an adjunct of the DP [determiner phrase] that contains it and whether the relativized element originates inside the clause or is base-generated in a position external to the clause." For the pronominal type shown above in (3a.), overt pronominals are coindexed with an NP that may be null, whereas standard analyses for the complementizer strategies like (3b.) above involve a null or relative operator that undergoes movement out of its internal position within the RC to become the head of the RC (Henderson 2006, 41).

Prior to introducing the specifics of RCs in SW Ojibwe, I provide some preliminary background on Ojibwe grammar.

1.2.2. Linguistic Preliminaries

Ojibwe is a head-marking, agglutinative language with a complex inflectional agreement-marking morphological system. Nouns come in one of two grammatical genders, animate or inanimate. The animacy status of a noun referent agrees in gender with associated verbs and determiners. Plural forms of a noun indicate animacy status, where all animate nouns take the plural suffix with a final /g/, while inanimate plural nouns take the plural suffix with a final /n/, as seen below in (4):

(4) Animacy status in plural
    a. Animate
    Singular   Plural
    inini   *ininiwag*
    'man'   'men'

    b. Inanimate
    Singular   Plural
    ziibi   *ziibiwan*
    'river'   'rivers'

As a highly synthetic language with complex derivational and inflectional morphology, the verbal morphology of Ojibwe deserves discussion here. The verb's core can often be internally complex. Verb stems are composed of at least an *initial*, which is often prepositional, adverbial or adjectival in character, and a *final*, which determines the valency and verb type based on the verb's arguments. Finals can also denote the means by which an action is carried out and are often complex in cases where verbs are derived from other verbs via morphological valence-changing operations. In addition to initials and finals, verbs can also contain a *medial*, which adds classificatory noun-like character to the verb either through incorporation of a full noun or specialized noun-medials. The example below in (5) shows how the initial, medial, and final are parsed in a verb stem.

Table 1. Ojibwe verb types

Verb type	Example	Gloss
VAI	agaas**hiinyi**	's/he is small'
VII	agaas**aa**	'it is small'
VTA	agaa**si'**	'make h/ small'
VTI	agaa**sitoon**	'make it small'

(5) Derivational morphology: initial, medial, final
    noojikwewe

nood=	=kwew=	=e
INITIAL	MEDIAL	FINAL
'pursue; hunt'	'woman'	INCORP

's/he actively pursues the company of women'

Ojibwe verbs are also subject to extensive inflectional morphology including a modal system, participant reference, complex stacked roots (preverbs), directional (path preverbs), and relative preverbs, among others to be discussed in chapter 2.

In regard to the classification of Ojibwe verbs, valency and animacy status are the criterion for classification, determined by their final. Like all Algonquian languages, Ojibwe has four verb types. Intransitive verbs are classified on the animacy status of the subject. For intransitive verbs with animate subjects, the type is Animate Intransitive (VAI). For intransitive verbs with inanimate subjects, the type is Inanimate Intransitive (VII). Transitive verbs, however, are classified based on the animacy status of their object. When the object is animate, the verb type is Transitive Animate (VTA) and when the object is inanimate, the type is Transitive Inanimate (VTI). Table 1 illustrates this dichotomy.

As the examples in table 1 suggest, the words are all related to one another in that they all contain the same initial element *agaas=* 'small.' The words are differentiated by their finals (shown in bold), where the intransitive verbs contain a stative final particular to the animacy status, and the transitive verbs each involve a causative final, respective to the animacy status of the object.

Another important aspect of the grammar for the current discussion is obviation, the system used to keep track of multiple third-person referents in the discourse. A well-known feature of the Algonquian languages, third-person arguments occur as either proximate (focal) or obviative (backgrounded). Proximate arguments involve no overt morphological marking in the singular, while obviative arguments are marked with an obviative suffix that agrees with the verbal inflection and determiners. If only one third-person argument (regardless of singular or plural number) is specified in the discourse, that argument is proximate (6a.). If multiple third-person arguments co-occur in the same clause, one is obligatorily marked for obviation (6b.):

(6) Proximate vs. obviative

a. *ingii-noondawaag **ingiw** abinoojiin**yag***
in-gii-noondaw-aa-**g**   **ingiw**   abinoojiinh-**yag**
1-PST-hear.h/-DIR-**3p**$_{PROX}$ DET$_{PROX}$ child-**3p**$_{PROX}$
'I heard the children'

b. *ogii-noondawaa**n** iniw abinoojiin**yan***
o-gii-noondaw-aa-**n**   iniw   abinoojiinh-**yan**
3-PST-hear.h/-DIR-**OBV**   DET$_{OBV}$ child-**OBV**
'S/he heard the child(ren)'

As the glossing indicates, verbs, determiners, and nouns all agree with respect to this proximate/obviative distinction. Also, the glossing of (6b.) indicates the ambiguity regarding the number of the obviative argument. For most varieties of SW Ojibwe, the number of obviative arguments is neutralized, with no morphological distinction made between the singular and the plural. The syntax of obviation is discussed below in 1.5.2.1. A more descriptive account is given in 2.5.1 and the variation regarding number under obviation observed over the course of this study is treated in 3.3.4.

The Ojibwe verb comes in three distinct orders of inflection: the *independent*, in which verbs are "predicative"; the *conjunct*, where verbs "generally appear in subordinate clauses"; and the *imperative* (Nichols 1980, 117). The independent order is generally used in main clause constructions with both prefixes and suffixes employed for participant reference. The con-

Table 2. Initial change (IC)

Unchanged form	Changed form
a	e-
aa	ayaa-
e	aye-
i	e-
ii	aa-
o	we-
oo	waa-

junct order is further subdivided between what are typically referred to by Algonquianists as the *plain conjunct* and the *changed conjunct*, where the participant reference is entirely suffixal. Plain conjunct verbs typically occur in dependent, subordinate clauses similar to English conditional clauses introduced by *if*, *when*, or *that*, and in verb complement clauses. They also occur in discourse dependent contexts and when linking extended units of discourse. Changed conjunct verbs undergo an ablaut process that changes the first vowel of the verbal complex according to a fixed pattern and are used primarily in *wh*-agreement contexts, including substantive interrogatives, adjunct relative clauses with manner, temporal, or locative properties, or when indicating "completive aspect" (Fairbanks 2012). The typical "general" Ojibwe pattern of initial change is given in table 2.[6] The imperative order is used in making direct, delayed, or prohibitive commands. The examples shown in (7) illustrate the various orders of inflection.

(7) Orders of inflection *biindige* VAI 's/he enters; goes in'

    a. Independent

biindige	biindigewag	nibiindige
biindige-∅	biindige-wag	ni-biindige
enters-3s$_{IND}$	enters-3p$_{IND}$	1$_{IND}$-enters
'S/he is going in.'	'They are going in.'	'I am going in.'

    b. Plain conjunct

biindiged	biindigewaad	biindigeyaan
biindige-d	biindige-waa-d	biindige-yaan

enters-3$_{CONJ}$	enters-3p-3$_{CONJ}$	enters-1$_{CONJ}$
'if s/he goes in ...'	'if they go in ...'	'when I go in ...'

c. Changed conjunct

baandiged	*baandigewaad*	*baandigeyaan*
IC-biindige-d	IC-biindige-waa-d	IC-biindige-yaan
IC-enters-3$_{CONJ}$	IC-enters-3p-3$_{CONJ}$	IC-enters-1$_{CONJ}$
'when s/he had entered ...'	'when they had entered ...'	'when I had entered ...'

d. Imperative

biindigen!	*biindigeg!*	*biindigedaa!*
biindige-n	biindige-g	biindige-daa
enters-2s$_{IMP}$	enters-2p$_{IMP}$	enters-21p$_{IMP}$
'Come in!'	'Come in!'	'Let's enter!'

As can be seen, the obvious difference between the form of the plain conjunct and changed conjunct is the ablaut of the vowel in the first syllable. A full discussion of the various orders of inflection and their uses is given in 2.4.

Another relevant verb form for the discussion of RCs is the *participle*. Participles are generally treated as verbs with nominal character that are not full nominalizations. Ojibwe participles are similar in form to changed conjunct verbs, showing the same ablaut vowel pattern, but display nominal agreement markers when the head of the participle is either third-person plural or obviative. Valentine (2001, 137–38) treats Ojibwe participles as a "hybrid," somewhere between a noun and a verb, and defines them as "a verb used as a nominal expression ... similarly to the way a noun is customarily used, to identify people and objects." In the majority of Southwestern Ojibwe subdialects, singular participial forms overlap with corresponding changed conjunct forms and are morphologically identical. The contrast is illustrated in table 3.

The singular form in both columns A. and B. appear in identical morphological shape as one another, while the example shown for the plural form of column B. shows the affixation of the participle morpheme /-i-/, along with the animate plural marker /-g/.[7] The bottom row represents the

Table 3. Changed conjunct versus participles for *biindige* 's/he enters'

A. Changed conjunct		B. Participle	
PROXIMATE		PROXIMATE	
Singular	Plural	Singular	Plural
baandiged	*baandigewaad*	*baandiged*	*baandigejig*
IC-biindige-d	IC-biindige-waa-d	IC-biindige-d	IC-biindige-d-i-g
IC-enters-3$_{CONJ}$	IC-enters-3p-3$_{CONJ}$	IC-enters-3$_{CONJ}$	IC-enters-3$_{CONJ}$-PM-3p
'after s/he entered...'	'after they entered...'	's/he who enters'	'they who enter'[a]
OBVIATIVE		OBVIATIVE	
baandigenid		*baandigenijin*	
IC-biindige-ni-d		IC-biindige-ni-d-i-n	
IC-enters-OBV-3$_{CONJ}$		IC-enters-OBV-3$_{CONJ}$-PM-OBV	
'after s/he/they$_{obv}$ entered...'		's/he/they$_{obv}$ who enter/s'	

[a] The third-person morpheme /-d/ shown here is realized as /-j-/ in participles having undergone palatalization triggered by the participial suffix marked tentatively as PM. Palatalization of this sort occurs often in Ojibwe and will be discussed in greater detail in section 2.3.3.1.

obviative forms of changed conjunct and participles as indicated by the subscript notation of the translation. Ojibwe participles also agree in number with relativized plural object arguments, an additional layer of inflection not found in the plain conjunct. This is shown in table 4. Adjectival information in Ojibwe is typically carried in either lexical preverbs, adjectival verbal roots, or via a participle in an adjectival relative clause, often postnominal:

(8) *Daga biidamawishin nimakizinan* **mekadewaagin**.

  daga   biidamaw-ishin   ni-makizin-an   **IC-makadewaa-g-in**
  please   bring.for-2s>1$_{IMP}$ 1-shoe-0p   **IC-is.black-0$_{CONJ}$-PL$_{PRT}$**

  i. Lit.: 'Please bring me my shoes, **those which are black**'
  ii. Free: 'Please bring me my **black** shoes' (AS.13.07.16.E)

Participles are also employed in *wh*-questions 'who' and 'what':

Table 4. Inflectional forms of *aabajitoon* 'use it'

Order	Singular subj.	Gloss	Plural subj.	Gloss
INDEPENDENT	odaabajitoon od-aabajit-oo-n 3-use.it-TI2-0	's/he uses it'	odaabajitoonaawaa od-aabajit-oo-naawaa 3-use.it-TI2-3p$_{IND}$	'they use it'
CONJUNCT	aabajitood aabajit-oo-d use.it-TI2-3$_{CONJ}$	'if s/he uses it/them'	aabajitoowaad aabajit-oo-waa-d use.it-TI2-3p-3$_{CONJ}$	'if they use it/them'
SINGULAR PARTICIPLE/IC	ayaabajitood IC-aabajit-oo-d IC-use.it-TI2-3$_{CONJ}$	's/he who uses it' or 'what s/he uses'/'upon using it'	ayaabajitoowaad IC-aabajit-oo-waa-d IC-use.it-TI2-3p-3$_{CONJ}$	'what they use'
PLURAL PARTICIPLE: REL. OBJ.	ayaabajitoojin IC-aabajit-oo-d-in IC-use.it-TI2-3-PL$_{PRT}$	'those which s/he uses'	ayaabajitoowaajin IC-aabajit-oo-waa-d-in IC-use.it-TI2-3p-3$_{CONJ}$-PL$_{PRT}$	'those which they use'
PLURAL PARTICIPLE: REL. SUBJ.			ayaabajitoojig IC-aabajit-oo-d-ig IC-use.it-TI2-3$_{CONJ}$-PL$_{PRT}$	'those who use it/them'[a]

[a] Object number is neutralized in the participles where the subject has been relativized.

(9) Awenenag negamo**jig**?
    awenen-ag   IC-nagamo-**d-ig**
    who-PL   IC-sings-**3**$_{CONJ}$-**PL**$_{PRT}$
    'Who$_{PL}$ is singing?' (AS.13.07.16.E)

Participles are often loosely treated as nominalizations, or to "express nominal concepts ... to identify people and things on the basis of their behavior or of some quality they have" (Valentine 2001, 210). In some cases, mainly neologisms, specialization or narrowing has occurred, resulting in conventionalized lexicalizations of participles (511). The examples in table 5 show this process, with many terms of more recent coinage involving a conventionalized participle.

Table 5. Participial neologisms

Participle	Literal meaning	Conventionalized meaning
a. *wezaawiminagizijig* IC-ozaawiminagizi-d-ig IC-is.yellow.globular-3$_{\text{CONJ}}$-PL$_{\text{PRT}}$	'those that are yellow and globular'	'oranges'
b. *bemisemagakin* IC-bimisemagad-k-in IC-it.flies-0$_{\text{CONJ}}$-PL$_{\text{PRT}}$	'those that fly'	'airplanes'
c. *ayaawadaasojig* IC-aawadaaso-d-ig IC-hauls.freight-3$_{\text{CONJ}}$-PL$_{\text{PRT}}$	'they who haul'	'semi-trucks'
d. *mayaajiibizojig* IC-maajiibizo-d-ig IC-motors.off-3$_{\text{CONJ}}$-PL$_{\text{PRT}}$	'those that start running (motorized transportation)'	'engines'
e. *gebaakwa'onjig* IC-gibaakwa'w-ind-ig IC-lock.up.h/-X>3$_{\text{CONJ}}$-PL$_{\text{PRT}}$	'they who are locked up'	'prisoners'
f. *mezinaatesegin* IC-mazinaatese-g-in IC-it.is.a.movie-0$_{\text{CONJ}}$-PL$_{\text{PRT}}$	'those that are movies'	'movies'

Participles are especially interesting in that they behave as verbs that can be inflected for person, tense, and number, though the plural/obviative marking resembles that of nominals. Translations of such conventionalized uses seldom suggest relativization but more nominalization treatment, as the examples in table 6 indicate.

This results in a very high frequency of participles in any given discourse, which makes the distinction between the northern and southern forms all the more significant as a parameter for variation. A full discussion of the form of Ojibwe participles is provided in 2.6.2 below and the variation observed in their form is treated in 3.3.13.

With the introductory points of the grammar stated above, we can now move on to the discussion of RCs in Ojibwe. Throughout this study numerous references will be made to the orders of inflection of Ojibwe verbs, that

Table 6. Participles as nominalizations (from Whipple 2015)

Participle	Literal meaning	Conventionalized meaning
a. *wayaabishkiiwejig* IC-waabishkiiwe-d-ig IC-is.white-3$_{CONJ}$-PL$_{PRT}$	'they who are white'	'white people' (Whipple 2015, 42)
b. *bemaadizijig* IC-bimaadizi-d-ig IC-lives-3$_{CONJ}$-PL$_{PRT}$	'they who live; who are alive'	'people' (44)
c. *memaandidojig* IC-mamaandido-d-ig IC-is.big$_{REDUP}$-3-PL$_{PRT}$	'they who are big'	'the bigger ones' (48)
d. *zeziikizijig* IC-zaziikizi-d-ig IC-is.eldest-3$_{CONJ}$-PL$_{PRT}$	'they who are the eldest'	'the oldest ones' (48)
e. *naagaanizijig* IC-niigaanizi-d-ig IC-leads-3$_{CONJ}$-PL$_{PRT}$	'they who lead'	'the head committee' (66)
f. *gaawashkwebiijig* IC-giiwashkwebii-d-ig IC-is.drunk-3$_{CONJ}$-PL$_{PRT}$	'they who are drunk'	'drunks' (74)
g. *weshki-bimaadizijig* IC-oshki-bimaadizi-d-ig IC-young-lives-3$_{CONJ}$-PL$_{PRT}$	'they who are young'	'young people' (84)
h. *menoominikenijin* IC-manoominike-ni-d-in IC-makes.rice-OBV-3$_{CONJ}$-OBV$_{PRT}$	'they$_{OBV}$ who make rice'	'ricers' (68)

is, independent, conjunct, changed conjunct (conjunct verbs with IC), and participles, which are discussed at length in 2.4. The sequence of derivation argued for in this thesis is an obvious one: only conjunct verbs can take IC, and only verbs with IC can be participles. This assumption will bear fruit in the discussion of head movement in chapter 4 and the articulation of the CP layer. In the next section I introduce the phenomena of relativization in Ojibwe.

1.2.3. Ojibwe RCs

One of the main components of the theory proposed in this study is the classification of participles as the verb form in Ojibwe used in RCs. This assumption encompasses all cases of participial verbs, in light of their "nominalized" character as seen above in tables 5 and 6. Descriptions of the function of participles throughout Algonquian languages often involve the nominal nature they display in their usage. However, as argued for in Johansson (2012) for Blackfoot, participles are restricted in their ability to take nominal prefixes and suffixes of prototypical nouns. This is shown in (10) below for the participle *dekaag* 'ice cream' (lit. 'that which is cold'). Participles cannot be inflected as possessive (10a.), locative (10b.), or diminutive (10c.), all typical inflections of nouns in the language:

(10) Participles not nominalizations
   a. Possessive
   nindekaag
   nin-dekaag
   1POSS-ice.cream
   *'my ice cream'

   b. Locative
   dekaaging/dekaagong/dekaagaang
   dekaag-ing/ong/aang
   ice.cream-LOC
   *'in the ice cream'

   c. Diminutive
   dekaagens/oons
   dekaag-ens/oons
   ice.cream-DIM
   *'little ice cream'

Instead of a nominalization analysis, I treat participles instead as the form of the verb used in RCs.

The generalization of participles as RCs has implications for translation, sure to be noted by any reader familiar with Ojibwe. It is not uncommon to find cases, such as (11) below, where what qualifies as an RC in this analysis is not translated as such by speakers:

(11) *Ayi'iin ge wiigwaasi-makakoon iniw*

ayi'ii-n	ge	wiigwaasi-makak-oon	iniw
something-0p	also	birch.bark-box-0p	DET$_{INAN.PL}$

[**gaa-aabajitoowaajin**] *gii-iskigamizigewaad*
[IC-gii-aabajit-oo-waad-in] gii-iskigamizige-waad
[IC-PST-use.it-TI2-3p$_{CONJ}$-PL$_{PRT}$] PST-make.sugar-3p$_{CONJ}$

'They used to use these birch bark boxes when they were sugaring.'
(Whipple 2015, 26)

Adopting the relativization analysis results in the sentence translated instead as 'It was those birch boxes **that they used** when they were sugaring.' This issue of translation goes back, as seen in the example below, with the literal, relative translation added below:

(12) *gaawiin wiin gidakiiminaan, mii sa eta*

gaawiin	wiin	gid-aki-im-inaan	mii	sa	eta
NEG	EMPH	2$_{POSS}$-land-POSS-21p$_{POSS}$	thus	EMPH	only

Biiwaabik [**gegwejimineg**]
Biiwaabik [**IC-gagwejim-ineg**]
mineral [IC-ask.h/-3>2p$_{CONJ}$]

'He does not want to buy your lands, he wants the mineral' (Nichols 1988a, 49) lit. 'Not our land, it is only the mineral **that s/he asks of you**'

With the definition of RCs adopted in this thesis, participles serve as the verb of the clause delimiting the referent of an NP, as shown below in (13), this time with the relativized nature represented in the English translation of the participle:

(13) *Miinawaa aw bezhig ikwezens-gwiiwizens aw*

miinawaa	aw	bezhig	ikwezens	gwiiwizens	aw
and	DET	one	girl	boy	DET

[gaa-niiyo-biboonagizid] ikwezens dash
[IC-gii-niiyobiboonagizi-d]   ikwezens   dash
[IC-PST-four.years.old-3$_{CONJ}$]   girl   but

gii-niso-biboonagizi
gii-nisobiboonagizi
PST-three.years.old

'And another little girl—the little boy **was the one who was four years old**—but the little girl was three years old.' (Whipple 2015, 48)

Ojibwe RCs can contain overt *wh*-pronouns, similar to English *wh*-relatives (14a.), but more commonly occur without an overt pronoun, where IC serves as a sort of complementizer, similar to the so-called English *that* relatives, as shown in (14b.):

(14) Ojibwe RC types

a. Pronominal

aw maajiibatoo idi agaaming da-baa-izhaad

aw	maajiibatoo	idi	agaaming	da-baa-izhaa-d
DET	start.running	over.there	across.lake	COMP-around-goes-3$_{CONJ}$

idi agaamaamashkikii o-nandawaabamaad

idi	agaamaamashkiki	o-nandawaabam-aad
over.there	across.swamp	go-look.for.h/-3>3'$_{CONJ}$

[awenenan idi gaa-ayininamaagojin]
[awenen-anidiIC-gii-ayininamaw-god-in]
[who-OBV-over.there-IC-PST-wave.at.h/-3'>3$_{CONJ}$-OBV$_{PRT}$]

'He starting running, across there along the edge of the lake across the swamp going to look for the person **who was waving at him**' (AS.Aadizooked)

b. Complementizer (IC)

mii iniw [eyininamawaajin]

mii	iniw	[IC-ayininamaw-aad-in]
thus	DET$_{OBV}$	[IC-wave.at.h/-3>3'$_{CONJ}$-OBV$_{PRT}$]

'That is **who he was waving at**' (AS.Aadizooked)

There are many parameters in the typological study of RCs that I will mention only briefly in this introduction. The main point of difference across Ojibwe dialects is in the morphological form of the participle used in the RC. Participles typically occur postnominally, as shown in (15), though they occasionally occur before the NP they modify, as in (16):

(15) Postnominal RC

mii go gii-kiiwanimowaagwen ingiw

mii	go	gii-giiwanimo-waa-gwen	ingiw
thus	EMPH	PST-lies-3p-DUB	DET

chi-ayaa'aag [gaa-nitaawigi'ijig]

chi-aya'aa-g	[IC-gii-nitaawigi'-id-ig]
great-being-3p	[IC-PST-raise.h/-3>1$_{CONJ}$-PL$_{PRT}$]

'then those elders **that raised me** must have been lying too' (Smallwood 2013c, 117)[8]

(16) Prenominal RC

Miish iw gaa-ikidowaad ingiw [waadabimagig]

miish	iw	IC-gii-ikido-waad	ingiw	[IC-wiidabim-ag-ig]
thus	that	IC-PST-says-3p$_{CONJ}$	DET	[IC-sit.with.h/-1>3-PL$_{PRT}$]

ingiw ininiwag akiwenziiyag . . .

ingiw	inini-wag	akiwenzii-yag
DET	man-3p	old.man -3p

'That's what those men said, those old men **that I sat with** . . .' (AS.13.01.31.N)

RCs can also be "headless," or without an overt NP in the higher clause:

(17) Headless RC

*Niminwendaan ganawaabamagwaa [**zhayaazhiibaabagizojig**]*

ni-minwend-an	ganawaabam-agwaa	[IC-zhaazhiibaabagizo-d-ig
1-like.it-TI1	watch.h/-1>3P$_{CONJ}$	[IC-hoop.dances-3$_{CONJ}$-PL$_{PRT}$]

'I like watching **hoop dancers/the ones that hoop dance**.' (AS.13.05.01.OPD)

RCs can also be non-contiguous, dislocated or discontinuous from the NP they modify, shown below in (18). As the example below illustrates, RCs serve a very adjectival-like function modifying the NP of the matrix clause:

(18) Discontinuous RC

*Michijiishinoog [$_{NP}$ **ongow ikwezensag**]*

michijiishin-oog	ongow	ikwezens-ag
lies.with.exposed.stomach-3p	DET	girl-3p

*mazinaakizowaad imaa [$_{RC}$ **gechi-bakaakogaadejig**]*

mazinaakizo-waad	imaa	IC-gichi-bakaakogaade-d-ig
is.pictured-3P$_{CONJ}$	there	IC-great-skinny.legs-3$_{CONJ}$-PL$_{PRT}$

'**These skinny-legged girls** in this picture have their bellies showing.' (AS.12.09.25.P)

lit. 'They lay with bare stomachs, **these girls**, as they are pictured there, **the ones with real skinny legs**'

The most typical Ojibwe ordering of RCs is D-NP-RC or D-RC-NP. The former, as in (15) above, involves an externally headed RC as shown in (19), while the latter consists of an internally headed RC (20), as in (16) above.

(19) External RC

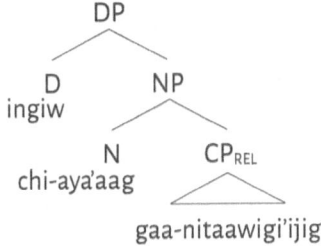

22 Basic Introduction to the Study

(20) Internal RC

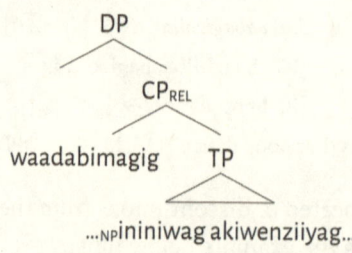

Another important observation is that there appears to be no limitations on which grammatical roles can undergo relativization. Valentine (2001, 584) states:

> There does not seem to be any restrictions on the grammatical relation of a nominal having a relative clause associated with it. Nominals filling the roles of grammatical actors (subjects), goals (objects), recipients (indirect objects), complements of relative roots, and other relations can all freely have relative clauses associated with them.

There is, however, a distinction in how number and case are marked in RCs for different argument types, to which we now turn.

1.2.3.1. Core versus Relative Root Arguments

The previous discussion focused on basic RC properties without considering the role that argument structure plays with the RC. Throughout Algonquian languages a distinction is made between *core arguments*, such as subjects and objects, and oblique *relative root arguments* (RR), which include locative, manner, temporal, and degree properties (Rhodes 1990b, 1996, 2010b). While the core argument RCs have specialized morphological inflections for plural and obviative arguments, RR arguments consist of a relative root or preverb along with the ordinary conjunct inflection. The locative RCs shown below in (21) illustrate how a relative preverb, along with initial change, results in an RC with locative properties, often translated as a nominalization:

(21) Locative RCs

   a. **endazhi**-*minikweng zhingobaaboo*

IC-dazhi-minikwe-ng	zhingobaaboo
IC-REL-drinks-X$_{CONJ}$	beer

   'beer garden'; lit. '**where** beer is drunk' (AS.Flicking)

   b. **endazhi**-*ziiginigeng zhingobaaboo*

IC-dazhi-ziiginige-ng	zhingobaaboo
IC-REL-pours-X$_{CONJ}$	beer

   'the bar (not the building but the bar itself)'; lit. '**where** beer is poured' (AS.Flicking)

The examples given here in (22) exemplify the contrast in morphological form between a locative RR argument (22a.) and a core argument (22b.). Note the parallel of the verb *onjibaa* 's/he comes from there' bearing the RR *ond=* used in both examples:[9]

(22) Relative root argument vs. core argument

   a. Relative root argument

   *Mii imaa Misi-zaaga'iganiing wenjibaa**waad** ingiw ikwewag*

mii	imaa	misizaaga'iganiing	IC-onjibaa-**waad**	ingiw	ikwe-wag
thus	there	at.Mille.Lacs	IC-come.from-3p$_{CONJ}$	DET	woman-3p

   'Mille Lacs is **where** those ladies come from.' (AS.13.05.01.BT)

   b. Core argument

   *Mii ingiw ikwewag Misi-zaaga'iganiing wenjibaa**jig***

mii	ingiw	ikwe-wag	misizaaga'iganiing	IC-onjibaa-**d-ig**
thus	DET	woman-3p	at.Mille.Lacs	IC-come.from-3$_{CONJ}$-PL$_{PRT}$

   'Those are the ladies **who** come from Mille Lacs.' (AS.13.05.01.BT)

As can be seen above, RR RCs, treated as adjunct oblique relatives, which modify temporal and locative relative clauses, are not marked with the nominal agreement inflections typically found in core argument relatives. Valentine (2001) provides a number of examples of RR complements in RCs. These include static locative relatives as in (23a.), locative goal relatives as in (23b.), and manner relatives as in (23c.):

(23) Relative root complements in RCs
   a. Static locative relatives
   endnokiiwaad
   IC-danokii-waad
   IC-works.**there**-3p_CONJ
   '**where** they were working' (Valentine 2001, 586)

   b. Locative goal relatives
   widi waa-ni-**izhaa**yaan
   widi   IC-wii-ani-izhaa-yaan
   there   IC-FUT-along-goes.to.**certain.place**-1_CONJ
   '**where** I was intending to go' (587)

   c. Manner relatives
   maaba jidmoonh **ezhi**nikaazod
   maaba   jidmoonh   IC-izhinikaazo-d
   DET   squirrel   IC-is.called.**certain**.way-3_CONJ
   '**the one called** the squirrel' (587).

Also, he notes the RR *ond-* exemplified earlier in (22) serves as both a source relative (24a.) as well as cause or instrumental relatives (24b.):

(24) RR *ond-* (from Valentine 2001, 587)
   a. Source
   widi Walpole Island gaa-bi-**nji**baayaan
   widi   Walpole Island   IC-gii-bi-**(o)nji**baa-yaan
   there   Walpole island   IC-PST-here-comes.**from.certain**.place-1_CONJ
   'there at Walpole Island **where** I come from' (587)

   b. Cause/instrumental
   iw zhoon'yaa waa-**nji**-mno-yaawaad
   iw   zhooniyaa   IC-wii-**(o)nji**-mino-ayaa -waad
   DET   money   IC-FUT-**RR**-good-is-3p_CONJ
   'the money **by means of which** they live comfortably' (587).

The other RRs work in a similar fashion in RCs, where, when the head of an RC is an RR argument, plural and obviative morphology is identical to that of the conjunct order of inflection. Rhodes (1996) treats these as "adjunct relative clauses," which differ morphologically from his "term relative clauses." This distinction is central to my analysis. A full discussion of RRs is provided in 2.3.4.

Ojibwe fits Andrews's typological classification, where languages can "mark information about the function of NP_{rel} on the verb or complementizer of the relative clause" (2007, 233). Returning to the examples shown above in (22), the marking of the locative function of NP_{rel}, as shown in (22a.), whose head is a singular location, differs from that of the relativized subject in (22b.), whose head is a third-person plural argument.

An important component of the present study is the observation of variation concerning this distinction in morphological marking in RCs. While the examples given thus far of this distinction represent a homogenous inflectional pattern observed among speakers in the southern SW Ojibwe communities, no such distinction exists among speakers of the more northern communities in Minnesota and the Border Lakes region of Ontario. This variation is discussed briefly below and in greater detail in 3.3.13.

1.2.4. Variation in SW Ojibwe

As mentioned above, speakers from the more northern areas of SW Ojibwe do not mark RCs in the same manner as the southern strategy discussed in the previous section. Ultimately, northern speakers in this region do not use the participial inflections discussed above in 1.2.2. Instead, the typical conjunct inflections are used along with one of two possible strategies of IC. For speakers of the varieties of Ojibwe that do not use the additional participial nominal-like inflections, participles are usually constructed in one of two ways. The first involves the same initial change pattern on the first vowel along with normal conjunct inflections.[10] This strategy results in structural ambiguity where a single S_{rel} form is compatible with either a subject or object interpretation. Table 7 below shows how one strategy of the northern varieties differs from that of the southern ones. The participant as head of the RC is bolded in the left column:

Table 7. North versus south participles

Function of NP$_{rel}$	S$_{rel}$ NORTHERN	S$_{rel}$ SOUTHERN	Gloss
subj./actor (sing. prox.) **3s>3'**	gegwejimaad	gegwejimaad	'the one$_{prox}$ that asks h/them$_{obv}$'
obj./theme (obv.) **3s>3'**	gegwejimaad	gegwejimaajin	'the one(s)$_{obv}$ that s/he$_{prox}$ asks'
subj./actor (pl. prox.) **3p>3'**	gegwejimaawaad	gegwejimaajig	'the ones$_{prox}$ that ask h/them$_{obv}$'
obj./them (obv.) **3p>3'**	gegwejimaawaad	gegwejimaawaajin	'the one(s)$_{obv}$ that they$_{prox}$ ask'
obj./theme (prox.) **3'>3s**	gegwejimigod	gegwejimigod	'the one$_{prox}$ that h/$_{obv}$ asks'
subj./actor (obv.) **3'>3s**	gegwejimigod	gegwejimigojin	'the one(s)$_{obv}$ that ask h/$_{prox}$'
obj./theme (prox.) **3'>3p**	gegwejimigowaad	gegwejimigojig	'the ones$_{prox}$ that h/they$_{obv}$ ask'
obj./theme (obv.) **3'>3p**	gegwejimigowaad	gegwejimigowaajin	'the one(s)$_{obv}$ that ask them$_{prox}$'

As the column labeled "northern" indicates, there are many overlapping participial forms in RCs here, whereas the forms provided in the column representing the southern varieties show a unique participial form. However, despite the lack of distinct participial forms in the north, I maintain their treatment as participles since, as Goddard notes, "Like any grammatical category, the participle is fundamentally defined by function rather than by the particular morphological processes that mark it" (1987, 117n19).

The table is representative only of the possible participle forms involving transitive action between third-person arguments. Well known in languages of the Algonquian family is the transitive animate paradigm (VTA), in which each possible combination of first-, second-, and third-person participants along with inflections for inanimate and indefinite actors (sometimes treated as a passive voice) are indicated through the verbal morphology.[11] The participle requires an additional layer of inflection in the south, though it appears to have been leveled in some of the more northern varieties lacking the overt participial morphology. It has been noted in other studies that "conjuncts and participles are no longer formally distinguished due to loss of final syllables by sound law. The Ojibwa dependent paradigm is a blend of both previous paradigms" (Costa 1996, 65n3). Obviously this generalization was made based on data not from the southern subdialects of Southwestern Ojibwe where there remains a formal distinction, at least in the combinations involving third-person plural and obviative arguments.

The other northern strategy of participles and, ultimately, relative clause formation, is with the use of a relativizing prefix *gaa-*, shown in (25a.) below. This prefix is nearly homophonous with the changed conjunct past tense shown below in (25b.):

(25) *gaa-* participles

    a. *minotaagoziwag igiweg **gaa**-nagamowaad*

    minotaagozi-wag   igiweg   **gaa**-nagamo-waad

    sounds.good-3p   DET   **REL**-sings-3p$_{\text{CONJ}}$

    i. Lit.: 'Those ones that are singing sound good.'
    ii. Free: 'Those singers sound good (right now).' (NJ.15.06.08.E)

    b. *gii-minotaagoziwag dibikong **gaa**-nagamowaad*

    gii-minotaagozi-wag   dibikong   **IC-gii**-nagamo-waad

    PST-sounds.good-3p   last.night   **IC-PST**-sings-3p$_{\text{CONJ}}$

    'They sounded good last night when they were singing.' (NJ.15.06.08.E)

Such formation of RCs appears to be the most significant parameter of variation observed in this study; the various strategies for RC formation are described in more detail in the following chapters.

Additionally, a number of other points of variation are discussed in chapter 3 with the intention of this research being twofold. I first identify the variation observed while accounting for the distribution of features of variation. Second, I provide a theoretical analysis for Ojibwe RC morphosyntactic structure, adopting a split-CP analysis, which the data require. Before going into detail on the theoretical explanation of Ojibwe RCs, I provide the background on Algonquian and Ojibwe dialectology, by which the current undertaking was inspired.

1.3. ALGONQUIAN DIALECTOLOGY

It is intuitive to predict that language varies from place to place. The degree of variation that constitutes a variety or dialect of a particular language as opposed to its consideration as a separate language is a complicated and often arbitrary distinction. Widely accepted is the idea that when two varieties are predominantly mutually intelligible, they qualify as dialects or varieties belonging to the same language (Crystal 2000, 8). Undoubtedly the most common type of dialectology is dialect geography, which "seeks to provide an empirical basis for conclusions about the linguistic variety that occurs in a certain locale" (Chambers and Trudgill 1998, 21). Similarities found between many North American Indian languages have long been observed and various classifications have been made as a result of both differences and similarities observed. As reported by Goddard (1996b), Campbell (1997), and Mithun (1999), indigenous languages of North America can be classified into twenty-nine families and twenty-seven isolates, contrary to other "Amerind" approaches (such as Greenberg 1960).[12]

One of those twenty-nine families is the Algic grouping, which includes the Algonquian subfamily.[13] The Algonquian family, at the time of contact, was spoken "widely over the eastern North American continent" (Valentine 1994, 88) and today makes up one of the largest and most widespread language families of North America. Figure 1 opposite illustrates the language family.

Several studies exist on Proto-Algonquian (PA), the theoretical parent language from which the modern languages are derived. The work of Bloomfield (1925, 1946) provided the original reconstruction of PA, to which many references in this study are made. This protolanguage diversified into eleven distinct languages known today as Blackfoot, Cheyenne, Arapahoan, Cree-Montagnais, Ojibwa, Potawatomi, Menominee, Sauk-Fox-Kickapoo, Miami-Illinois, Shawnee, and Proto-Eastern Algonquian, "an ancestor of the eastern languages" (Foster 1996, 99).

The Algonquian language family consists of three major branches: Eastern, Central, and Plains (Goddard 1996a). Eastern Algonquian is applied to those Algonquian languages spoken along the East Coast of North America, "from Micmac in Nova Scotia down the coast to Pamlico in North

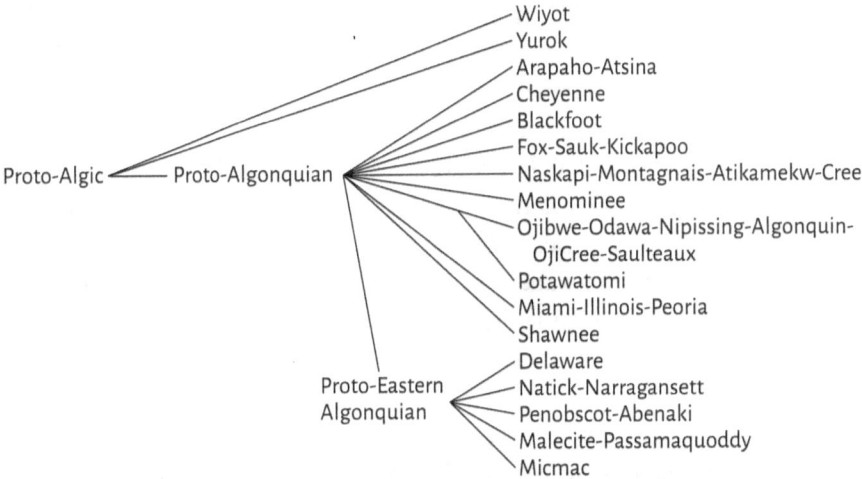

Fig. 1. Algic family tree. Bloomfield 1946; Teeter 1967; Todd 1970; Goddard 1979; Valentine 1994.

Carolina" (Costa 1996, 53). As a result of the East being settled first, the majority of these languages are no longer spoken. Unfortunately there are "no more than a half-dozen Eastern Algonquian languages" for which modern records exist (53–54).

The Plains grouping consists of Blackfoot, Arapaho, and Cheyenne, and are conveniently referred to by their situation on the northern plains. The Central Algonquian languages are the languages spoken around the "Upper Great Lakes and the Canadian North, to the east of the Great Plains" (Goddard 1978, 583). According to Goddard, "the 7 Central Algonquian languages are 7 independent branches descending from the Proto-Algonquian parent language" (585). A further subdivision common in the Algonquian literature is that of the Ojibweyan family; these languages even more closely related to one another within the Central grouping (Rhodes and Todd 1981; Goddard 1978, 1996a; Valentine 1994).

1.3.1. Ojibwe Dialects

According to Goddard (1996a, 4), the Ojibweyan family consists of three major internal subgroupings. They are 1) Northern Ojibwe, 2) Southern

Ojibwe: Saulteaux, Central Southern Ojibwe, Eastern Ojibwe, Old Algonquin, and Ottawa, and 3) Potawatomi. Due to considerable distance between some communities and the vast region in which Ojibwe is spoken, many dialects exist and not all varieties of Ojibwe are mutually intelligible. Valentine declares that the Ojibwe spoken at Walpole Island and that in Big Trout Lake, "standing at the extremes of Ojibwe," are not mutually intelligible though in the area between them exists a "relatively unbroken network of communities and dialects between them forming steps, in which neighboring communities have high measures of lexical similarity" (61).

Eastern Ojibwe is used for many of the communities of southwestern Ontario that consist of the descendants of Ojibwe people fleeing removals from other areas and tribal groups (Valentine 1994, 434). This is reflected in some band designations such as the Chippewas of Sarnia in southern Ontario, often identified as Eastern Ojibwe. Linguistically Eastern Ojibwe is distinguished from Southwestern due to recent innovations including the deletion of vowels in metrically weak positions and the reanalysis of personal prefixes (44).

Odawa (Ottawa) is still spoken by significant numbers at Wikwemikong (Manitoulin Island) and Walpole Island, both in Ontario. The "sister language" of Southwestern Ojibwe (Valentine 2001), Odawa is most distinct in the syncopation of weak, unstressed vowels. Early records of Odawa, however, do not show syncope, suggesting vowel weakening to be an innovation (Goddard 1978, 584). Rhodes and Todd (1981, 58) note age-graded variation in the extent of syncope, further supporting the innovation analysis. It should also be stated that some of the modern differences between the sister languages, Southwestern Ojibwe and Odawa, seem to be recent divergences as some of the signature features of the Odawa dialect can be found in records of Southwestern Ojibwe.[14] Many comparisons will be made to Odawa throughout this study, due to its many similarities with Southwestern Ojibwe and the historical relationship and migration patterns back and forth between Manitoulin Island and Wisconsin. With the exception of the rampant vowel deletion, many of the features found in Odawa can be observed in the speech of many speakers from Wisconsin. In addition to the historical relationship between the Ojibwe and the Odawa, a great deal of literature exists (especially the work of Rhodes and

Valentine) for this dialect; many claims made here can be found in, and are often based on, their work on Odawa.

The last dialect relevant to the discussion here is Saulteaux, sometimes referred to as Plains Ojibwe. This classification often includes the varieties spoken around the Border Lakes region of Ontario, in Manitoba, Saskatchewan, and Alberta. Closely resembling Southwestern Ojibwe (Chippewa) and Border Lakes Ojibwe, Saulteaux is not distinguished by any major parameters of variation, but rather "represents a grading of a few minor features" (Valentine 1994, 41). Most important to the discussion presented here, Red Lake Ojibwe has previously been determined to be a variety of Saulteaux rather than Southwestern Ojibwe (Goddard 1978, 583).

Today Ojibwe is spoken in many different varieties from Quebec to Alberta in Canada, and from the Upper Peninsula of Michigan through Wisconsin and Minnesota. A generation or two ago, Ojibwe speakers could be found as far west in the United States as Turtle Mountain, North Dakota, and Rocky Boy, Montana.[15] The following discussion provides the background for the current study on regional variation observed in SW Ojibwe.

1.3.2. Implications of Classifications

Another issue addressed in this study is how speakers of Ojibwe and other Ojibweyan languages identify themselves and the language(s) they speak. Confusion of terminology and often-misused labels for groups and languages often provide inaccurate designations for tribes and their languages. Rhodes and Todd (1981, 64) identify some of the causes of such confusion:

> There is some confusion about the names of different groups of speakers of Cree and Ojibwa. Government documents list groups by officially assigned band names, while linguists and anthropologists tend to list groups by the name of their settlement and their language affiliation or cultural affiliation. On the other hand, the speakers themselves tend to call themselves by their ancestral affiliation or by political affiliations.

Valentine points out that some languages and dialects have more prestige than others and often speakers will choose to identify with those that they perceive to have the most prestige (1994, 82). Such is the case for many Odawa speakers descended from the Potawatomi and Chippewa, whose ancestors migrated to Walpole Island, Sarnia, and Cape Croker during the period 1830–40. Such individuals say they speak a mixture of Ottawa and Ojibwa "but they call their language Chippewa" (Rhodes 1982, 1–2n3). Most speakers of Ojibweyan languages identify as Anishinaabe and call their language *Anishinaabemowin* 'the Anishinaabe language.' Interestingly some Saulteaux refer to their language as *nakawemowin*, the Cree word for Ojibwe (Valentine 1994, 97).

It is common in the more southern communities of the Southwestern area especially for the language to be referred to as *Ojibwemowin* 'the Ojibwe language'; in these areas *Anishinaabemowin* is used in a broader sense of 'Indian language.' Some speakers of the more northern SW Ojibwe communities reject the Ojibwe classification, as seen in the example below in (26), which occurred during a conversation with a speaker from Nett Lake:

(26) *Gegoo gikinoo'amawindwaa 'ojibwe' gaawiin sha*
something when.they.are.taught Ojibwe no EMPH

giinawind gidoojibwemosiimin, gidanishinaabewimin, bakaan
us we.don't.speak.Ojibwe we.are.Anishinaabe different

inwewag bakaaniziwag ojibweg
they.speak they.are.different the.Ojibwe.people

'When they are taught [they say] 'ojibwe' but we aren't speaking Ojibwe, we are Anishinaabe, they speak a different language; the Ojibwe are different.' (EG.13.08.07.C)

As the quotation illustrates, names provided by linguists can often be at odds with self-designations of the speakers themselves and English terms applied to indigenous populations are problematic as "linguistic realities are often sacrificed on the altar of ethnicity" (Valentine 1994, 79). An example of such is the Maniwaki, Quebec, and Golden Lake, Ontario, sub-dialects, "which are linguistically Eastern Ojibwa (although their speakers call themselves Algonquin)" (Rhodes and Todd 1981, 58). Algonquins, who have the same self-designation *Anishinaabe*, are hardly ever referred to as Ojibwe, though speakers of Odawa, "who can often be just as linguistically divergent as Algonquin," are always referred to as a subgroup of Ojibwe (Valentine 1994, 81).

Such is the case for the term *Chippewa* used to describe the people and language variety of Ojibwe spoken by individuals in the United States. Rhodes and Todd (1981, 66) describe "two variants" of the name *Ojibwe*:

> Ojibwa is the Canadian term (generally spelled Ojibway); Chippewa is the American term. Since there are Ojibwa families in Canada who were moved there from the United States in the late nineteenth century but who still call themselves Chippewa, this terminological distinction must have existed since at least that time.

Schoolcraft stated early on that the term *Chippewa* was derived from *Ojibwe*, which had been "Anglicized by the term Chippewa" (1851, 483n1). Valentine states that *Chippewa* is an English label "reflecting popular usage" (1994, 2), and mentions that it is derived from a European rendering of the word *Ojibwe*, "though its pronunciation is now based on its English spelling" (3). Chippewa is often applied to the speakers known as "American Ojibwas" (Rhodes 1982) as well as the language in the United States (Valentine 1994, 1996). Valentine (1996, 306) refers to the language of Mille Lacs as "Mille Lacs Chippewa" and to the language described in Baraga (1850) as "Michigan Chippewa" (Valentine 1994, 179). Rhodes and Todd (1981, 66) point out that Bloomfield suggested that Ojibwe (spelled *Ojibwa* in his work) is a "technically more correct name for Chippewa," but subsequent work has shown a tendency to favor the Chippewa label.

Many modern speakers reject the Chippewa label (though it is accepted by some as well); the following quotation from 1929 suggests that the term has long been considered inaccurate. In a testimony before the United States Senate subcommittee on Indian affairs, Thomas Leo St. Germaine, a Lac du Flambeau Ojibwe, educated at Wisconsin, Iowa, and Yale universities was asked to serve as an interpreter for George Amos, a chief of the Lac du Flambeau band. Upon being asked by Senator Burton K. Wheeler whether he could speak Chippewa, St. Germaine replied:

> Chippewa! There is no such thing as Chippewa. There is an Ojibway tongue, but no Chippewa. Most of you are too lazy or ignorant to say

Ojibway. So you make it just Chippewa. (unknown staff correspondent, *The Milwaukee Journal*, July 14, 1929)

Similar attitudes are found among speakers today, including many who have contributed to the present study. It should be stated, however, despite the resistance to the term, many federally recognized band designations in the United States and Canada include the Chippewa label. Such is the case for all Wisconsin Ojibwe bands and a few Minnesota bands known as the Lake Superior Chippewa Indians. As a result of the government-imposed designation, some individuals have accepted the label and identify as Chippewa, though there seems to be increasing resistance to the term as more people become aware of its etymology as a corruption of Ojibwe.

The official *Ethnologue* classification of Southwestern Ojibwe, [ciw], reflects the Chippewa label. The classification includes as "dialects" of Chippewa Central Minnesota Chippewa, Minnesota Border Chippewa, Red Lake Chippewa, and Upper Michigan–Wisconsin Chippewa. *Ethnologue* also implies that Red Lake shows similarities with the Ojibwe spoken at Lake of the Woods in Ontario and Nett Lake on the Minnesota side of the Canadian border, being closely related to the dialect spoken at Lac La Croix, Ontario. The *Ethnologue* classification for Ojibwe (Ojibwa), [oji], consists solely of Canadian dialects in Ontario, including Albany River Ojibwa, Berens River Ojibwa (Saulteaux), Lac Seul Ojibwa, Lake of the Woods Ojibwa, and Rainy River Ojibwa.

Throughout this thesis, I will refer to the people and varieties spoken in the United States as Southwestern (SW) Ojibwe when needing to differentiate from other varieties. The territory treated in this thesis, along with a brief historical account of the people and modern description, is provided in the next section.

1.3.3. Southwestern Ojibwe

The area where Southwestern Ojibwe is presently spoken consists of Michigan's Upper Peninsula, the region to the immediate north of Wisconsin's Chippewa Valley, and across the northern half of Minnesota. According to Ritzenthaler the Ojibwe migrated from a more eastern location starting in the seventeenth century, reaching as far west as Saskatchewan and south into present-day Michigan, Wisconsin, Minnesota, and North Dakota, as well as the communities stated above in southern Ontario (1978, 743). A major contributing force behind the westward expansion of the Ojibwe was their role in the fur trade. As the French expanded posts in the western areas, the Ojibwe followed with concentrated populations in close approximation to the new posts (744). During this period Ojibwe was the lingua franca of the fur trade (Treuer 2010, 14); specifically, Southwestern Ojibwe was the trade language of Michigan and southern Ontario as recently as the early nineteenth century, when it was spoken by Menominees, Odawas, and Potawatomis (Rhodes 2012, 359).

During the western expansion of the American territory, the United States government engaged in a series of treaty negotiations with the Ojibwe. This period marked the end of the once seminomadic lifestyle patterns of the Ojibwe. For the Ojibwe of Wisconsin and eastern Minnesota, whose official government designation is the Lake Superior Band of Chippewa Indians, the treaties of 1835, 1837, 1842, and 1854 ceded the majority of Ojibwe country; the Ojibwe were now confined to small reservations. Similarly, in Minnesota, Ojibwe bands entered treaty negotiations in 1826, 1847, 1854, 1855, 1863, and 1864.[16]

The treaty negotiations resulted in the establishment of seven reservations in Minnesota: Fond du Lac, near present-day Cloquet; Grand Portage, near the tip of Minnesota's North Shore, just south of the Canadian border; Leech Lake, between present-day Bemidji and Deer River; Mille Lacs, primarily near Mille Lacs Lake in the eastern region of central Minnesota; Bois Forte, near present-day Tower and Cook; Red Lake, north of Bemidji; and White Earth, the westernmost reservation, just north of Detroit Lakes. In Wisconsin four original reservations were established through the treaty negotiations: Bad River, just east of present-day Ashland; Lac Courte Oreilles, near Hayward; Lac du Flambeau, near Minocqua; and Red Cliff, just north of Bayfield. In 1934 reservations were created at Mole Lake and St. Croix, both in Wisconsin.

The transition to reservations had significant and often traumatizing effects on the Ojibwe, many of which are still observable today.[17] In concert with allotment and tremendous loss of land, the Ojibwe were soon forced to surrender their children to government and missionary boarding schools. With children no longer engaged in the Ojibwe language, the vitality of the language has since continued to decline. Once reservations were established and the Ojibwe became less mobile, local language varieties became more of a concern.

In addition to the subdialect groupings based on the current reservation names, there are also a number of cases where one reservation designation encompasses multiple settlements that prior to the establishment of the reservation were autonomous bands. Such is the case for the Mille Lacs reservation in Minnesota. Before the signing of the treaties and the groupings based on treaty negotiations, independent groups at Sandy Lake, East Lake, Lake Lena, and Isle were lumped together with Mille Lacs as districts (Treuer 2010, 42). Similar situations occurred at St. Croix in Wisconsin, where the southernmost communities, Maple Plain and Round Lake, comprised mainly individuals originally from around Mille Lacs. In many of these cases the separate communities that are now within the borders of one reservation are often a considerable distance apart from one another and show subtle variation in language as a result. The most divergent case is probably found at Leech Lake, where individuals from the northernmost community of Inger show some parallels with other more northern groups, while speakers from the more southern communities such as Onigum show similarities with the southern bands. Furthermore speakers will often identify as being from the more specific communities rather than with the larger reservation title. This is especially the case among speakers from Ponemah, who seldom identify as being from Red Lake, and those from East Lake, Sandy Lake and Aazhoomog (Lake Lena), who are often strongly opposed to being referred to as being from Mille Lacs. Where applicable to the discussion on community variation, I will refer to such varieties by their specific community designations where significant differences can be found between them and the other districts of the same reservation.

Linguistically many of the features that distinguish Southwestern Ojibwe from other dialects are treated in Valentine (1994). The variety of Red Lake briefly investigated by Valentine showed alignment with Saulteaux to the north, though only one speaker at Red Lake was consulted in that work. Among many speakers in the United States there is an apparent sense of cohesiveness regarding the Ojibwe language. Speakers often remark on how "it's all the same," though those with experience in language work consisting of multiband participation can recognize some features of variation between groups. With Valentine's (1994) classification of Red Lake Ojibwe (based on one speaker) as being Saulteaux rather than Southwestern, a re-examination of the American varieties is warranted and more urgent now than ever.

In the next section I provide a review of the literature on Ojibwe dialectology.

1.3.4. Literature Review: Dialect Studies

Until the recent extensive fieldwork for the Ojibwe People's Dictionary (Nichols), variation in Southwestern Ojibwe had not been explored. Though the language over all of the Southwestern areas forms a highly mutually intelligible grouping, a breakdown of intelligibility has been observed among northern speakers regarding the interpretation of RCs provided by southern speakers. Several other relevant features of variation exist; an investigation of those features is provided in chapter 3.

The most recent published dialect study of Ojibwe is Valentine (1994), with the next most recent study being thirteen years prior (Rhodes and Todd 1981). With the exception of these two, as brief as their discussions on SW Ojibwe are, all others (Rhodes 1978; Nichols 1976; Gilstrap 1978; Piggott 1978) have been concerned solely with varieties of Ojibwe as spoken north of the Canadian-American border. For my purposes here I provide a review of only the literature that has at least in some way included Southwestern Ojibwe in the discussion. All dialects involve a certain level of homogeneity; the differences are often very minor when compared to the similarities found throughout the language (Valentine 1994).

1.3.4.1. Rhodes and Todd (1981)

Rhodes and Todd (1981) present a general overview of indigenous languages of the Subarctic Shield. With the exception of the northwest sector, the indigenous languages consist of two branches of the Algonquian family: Cree in the north and, to the immediate south of Cree, a southern branch called "Ojibwa," which includes dialects known locally as

"Chippewa, Saulteaux, Ottawa and Algonquin" (1981, 52). In their classification Ojibwe is spoken in eight distinct dialects: "They are Saulteaux, Northwestern Ojibwa, Southwestern Ojibwa (which does not include all groups treated in 'Southwestern Chippewa,' vol. 15), Severn Ojibwa, Central Ojibwa, Ottawa, Eastern Ojibwa, and Algonquin" (Rhodes and Todd 1981, 56). Besides the general umbrella terms for each dialect and the brief mention of syncope as a parameter for Odawa and SW Ojibwe, Rhodes and Todd offer no real discussion relating to dialect variation that includes SW Ojibwe.

1.3.4.2. Valentine (1994)

By far the most comprehensive Ojibwe dialect study to date, Valentine (1994) is primarily concerned with Ojibwe as spoken in Canada. Funded by Canadian agencies, Valentine's research was limited mainly to Canadian locations. Surveying fifty different Ojibwe communities ranging from eastern Quebec to central Alberta, Valentine included only one US dialect, that of Red Lake, Minnesota, where he had the opportunity to work with one sixty-year-old female. Using just over a hundred texts and lexical and morphological questionnaires designed by Ojibwe dialectologist John Nichols, Valentine was able to focus on many of the already known features of variation across Ojibwe dialects (7). For SW Ojibwe Valentine also compared data from Baraga (1850) and Nichols (1980), citing personal communication with Nichols, who suggested there was "considerable homogeneity to this dialect" (Valentine 1994, 27).

Based on research conducted from 1983 until publication in 1994, Valentine focuses on morphological, phonetic, phonological, and lexical differences as parameters for dialect variation. Since nearly every feature can be shown to vary, even within dialects, Valentine explicitly states that many features characteristic of each area are not necessarily definitive for the respective dialect groupings (283). Valentine (39) found that there are three broad dialectal groupings geographically defined on the basis of northern and southern features:

> First, a northern group, including Severn Ojibwe and Algonquian; secondly, a southern group, including Odawa, Chippewa, Eastern Ojibwe and the Ojibwe of the Border Lakes region between Minnesota and

Ontario, and Saulteaux; and third, a transitional zone between these two polar groups in which there is a mixture of northern and southern features.

Valentine finds that, in the north, few morphological features are "uniformly found in all northern dialects"; instead each dialect represents "more or less a continuum, some more northern others less" (354). The northern dialects are said to have morphemes that are "more phonologically salient and the morphology thereby appears more transparently agglutinative, while southern dialects have corresponding forms that are shorter and less salient" (47). The majority of morphological differences between dialects show a "much stronger divergence on a north/south axis than an east/west, though a few differences characterized by an east/west distribution do occur" (283).

Valentine finds that Saulteaux aligns morphologically with the southern communities (354). His classification of "Border Lakes" represents a "transitional area" between northwestern Ojibwe and southwestern, closely related to Saulteaux (45). "Border Lakes" refers to a group of communities on the Ontario-Minnesota border, including Whitefish Bay and Emo, Ontario (1994, 355–56). When moving south to north, from Valentine's "Chippewa" to Border Lakes and further north to Saulteaux, he finds each dialect is not necessarily marked by "discrete parameters of variation," but rather represent a "grading of a few minor features" (41).

SW clearly aligns with other southern Ojibwe dialects as well. Valentine observes the absence of syncopation in SW, and notes that deletions in SW Ojibwe all involve loss of an initial segment (446). Valentine mentions the loss of initial /n/ in *ingod* 'one,' varying forms of the first-person prefix (1994, 447), *nin-* and *in-* before voiced obstruents (and equivalents with bilabial nasal [448]), which he states extends north to Pikangikum (449). He also recognizes the loss of initial /g/ in words like *(g)akina* (449). Valentine (450) also describes the optional lack of initial /w/, for example in *(w)agij-* versus *ogiji-*, which I have also observed in Minnesota and throughout Wisconsin.

Also relevant to SW Ojibwe spoken in Wisconsin and the historical migration patterns of Ojibwe in that region, Valentine (49) discusses a "seemingly ad hoc but substantial list of lexical items" in Odawa where the initial vowel is lower, such as *anini* 'man' in Odawa (with varying pronunciations at Lac Courte Oreilles and Lac du Flambeau) as opposed to general Ojibwe *inini*, which is pronounced with the initial vowel high and front.

Surveying many more northern communities than southern ones, Valentine recognizes the geographically aligned distinction of participle formation between northern and southern dialects of Ojibwe. For southern varieties, Valentine states, "there are distinct participial forms which are used when verbs function in nominal roles, essentially RCs in the current analysis. Southern participial forms are inflected for the conjunct order, but with nominal endings" (337). In the north, however, Valentine finds varieties with no distinct participial inflection; instead the conjunct morphology alone is employed (338). As mentioned above, morphological features are not necessarily uniform in the north; Valentine mentions instances in Severn Ojibwe where participial forms sometimes occur, such as *gaa-maajaanijin* 'the one$_{obv}$ that left,' though this is more of a rare exception rather than the norm (343). He also mentions a participial suffix *nigamonijih* 'if they sing,' found on the southern edge of Severn, that distinguishes between a singular and plural obviative (344). Valentine notes the northern strategy of participle formation utilizing the relativizing prefix *gaa-*, which he glosses as 'that which.' He indicates the striking similarity in form to the IC past tense marker but reminds us that the *gaa-* relativizer can occur in the same word with a tense marker (267). Lexically Valentine finds a north-versus-south contrast and finds SW Ojibwe, which he regularly refers to as Chippewa, aligns most closely with the Border Lakes varieties in his survey (464).

Recognizing the limitations of his study, he notes that, despite the considerable amount of work on Ojibwe, "unfortunately, no dialect of Ojibwe has received adequate linguistic documentation" (8) and that "much more research needs to be done in the United States" (34). He states that, regarding Ojibwe as spoken in the United States, "we do not have a broad dialectal representation in print" (445). Relying mainly on other published sources for SW Ojibwe, Valentine warns that his American data are "quite tentative" and that he has "designated the entire area as Chippewa" (44).

Importantly, for the purposes of the present study, with certain differences observed in particular communities, Valentine suggests "periods of relative isolation from other varieties of Ojibwe" (43–44). Many of Valentine's findings are discussed and cited throughout this study, particularly in the discussion of SW Ojibwe variation provided in chapter 3, providing a basis for comparison and discussion.

1.3.4.3. Nichols (2011, 2012)

In a recent unpublished presentation (2011) and report (2012), Nichols describes many points of variation serving as parameters for dialect relationships among the American and Border Lakes dialects. He does not mention nor compare all communities but rather notes the differences found among speakers today from Ponemah, northern Leech Lake, and Border Lakes. For the most part Nichols (2012) is based on data collected from one to two speakers for each community and notes that, with the exception of Valentine's (1994) study, "there have been no reports on variation in Ojibwa as spoken in the United States" (2012, 1).

Nichols reports "two overlapping main morphological features that distinguish varieties of Ojibwa in Minnesota ... *initial change* and the use of nominal-type suffixes on the nominalized verbs known as *participles*" (2012, 2). The plain conjunct, changed conjunct, and participle forms are a "three way distinction in conjunct verb forms" that Nichols states is characteristic of "Chippewa [ciw] in Wisconsin and Michigan, and in Ottawa (Odawa), a more eastern southern Ojibweyan language" (3). He indicates that in Minnesota, however, there is variation in the morphological distinction of these forms (3).

He finds the typical pattern of Initial Change (IC) at Mille Lacs, on the south side of Leech Lake, and at least to some extent at White Earth (2012, 3). However, /aa/ and /e/, "the vowels that require breaking in initial change, do not undergo change" on the northern side of Leech Lake, near Inger, and in the speech of some at Ponemah on the Red Lake reservation (4). He also finds no IC on /oo/ by some at Ponemah and among speakers of the Bois Forte band, "which is divided between the Nett Lake reservation and the Lac La Croix First Nation in Ontario" (4). He also mentions one speaker from the northern Leech Lake community Inger, raised by a grandparent from the southern side of Leech Lake, who exhibits the typical patterns of IC (3). The communities that maintain the classic IC pattern (variety A) are designated "pattern 1"; communities that show no change on /aa/ and /e/ (variety B) are classified as "pattern 2"; while those that additionally show no change on /oo/ (variety C) are designated "pattern 3" (4).

The other related morphologically distinguishing feature is the use of nominal third-person plural and obviative suffixes on certain participles: *-ig* 'animate plural,' *-in* 'animate obviative,' or *-in* 'inanimate plural.' Nichols notices the correlation to this feature, which occurs in the historical Lake Superior dialects, in Odawa and in the Minnesota and Wisconsin varieties that all have "pattern 1 initial change" where there is a "full morphological differentiation among the three forms of conjunct verbs in this variety" (4). Not taking into account *gaa-* participles, for varieties B and C, "there is no morphological distinction between changed conjuncts and participles" (4–5).

Another north-versus-south distinction noted by Nichols (2012) is with stem-forming morphemes: *ando-* versus *nando-*. The initial /n/ occurs in southern varieties but seems to have been "lost at Red Lake and Bois Forte," similar to "Canadian Ojibwayan languages to the north and west" (6).[18] Also, Nichols finds that verb-final *-e*, commonly used in the north in body-part-incorporating verbs, is not used in the south with respect to certain body parts, such as *-doon(e)* 'mouth' (7). Additionally Nichols mentions that the animate intransitive *-m* final on certain verbs pertaining to sleeping end with *-ngwaam* in the south but with a final epenthetic vowel, as in *-ngwaami* in the north at Red Lake and Bois Forte (8).[19]

Nichols also describes variation between the north and the south regarding benefactive verbs, where the complex final *-amaw* is productively used in the north, whereas the southern dialects have applied *-amaw* on TI1 verb stems and *-aw* on TI2.[20] As a result, for a TI1 stem such as *ozhit=* 'make it,' the northern dialects have *ozhitamaw* 'make it for h/,' while the southern form is *ozhitaw* (2012, 8). Nichols informs me that Baraga included both *ozhitamaw* and *ozhitaw* and speakers consulted around Mille Lacs showed some of both patterns (pers. comm.). Nichols also mentions the replacement of *-aw* in this form with *-ow* for a "northern speaker at Ponemah" before both the direct theme sign and the zero morpheme (2012, 8). Similar alternations occur in data from southern speakers in my data.

Nichols also finds variation in women's names in the north, where the vocative form appears to have been extended to the general name-giving convention with no special vocative form (2012, 10). In the south, names ending in *-kwe* have a special vocative form *-k* that was documented by Baraga (1850, 40) and Nichols (1980); it seems to have largely replaced the *-kwe* endings in older naming conventions in the northern areas.

Minor lexical variation is also mentioned in Nichols (2012) where such items as 'broom,' 'cradle board,' 'flag,' 'horse,' 'hungry,' 'island,' 'nest,' 'shawl,' 'squash,' 'table,' 'what,' and 'wine' all have slightly different forms in the north from those found in his earlier work in the south. Also, the animacy status of certain nouns such as 'car' and 'potato,' which are animate at Mille Lacs, Leech Lake, and all through Wisconsin, are inanimate at Red Lake and Bois Forte (10). Nichols also mentions the variation found in the dubitative pronoun *namanj/amanj*: he found the nasal-less form *amanj* at Mille Lacs and the nasal-initial form *namanj* in the north. It should be noted that there are many speakers in the south who consistently produce *namanj* and one case where two speakers, both from Aazhoomog, each had one of the forms. Based on comparisons of historical versus modern forms of other examples described above, initial nasals can be subject to deletion.

Much of the variation discussed here is treated in 3.3, where comparisons to Nichols (2011, 2012) form the starting point for the survey employed in this study.

1.4. LITERATURE REVIEW: ALGONQUIAN RCs

In the discussion thus far I have provided the essential background on Ojibwe dialectology and variation in SW Ojibwe concerning the morphological shape of the participles used in RC. Prior to going into further detail in their analysis, I first provide a review of the relevant literature on relativization in Ojibwe and other related Algonquian languages.

1.4.1. Rhodes (1996)

Rhodes (1996) is concerned with relative clauses in Ottawa or Odawa, as previously mentioned, a very closely related Ojibweyan language. Though the languages have their share of differences, RCs seem to be very similar in both languages. Furthermore Odawa is one of the languages that retain the additional, seemingly nominal plural or obviative inflections on participles. Rhodes provides a template for the basic NP structure of Odawa, which serves the purposes of Southwestern Ojibwe:

(27) Templatic ordering of optional elements (Rhodes 1996, 1)[21]

(cat dem)-(cat Q)-(catN)-(cat rel cl)

giw	aanid	binoojiinyag	gaa-zhaajig	widi	gkinoohmaadiiwgamgong
those	some	child	who-will-go	there	school *loc*
dem	Q	n	rel cl		

'several children who were to go to the school' (T8:8, p. 185)

The examples given here in (28) show how each element alone can serve as the NP in and of itself:

(28) Optional element NPs

a. Demonstrative as NP

*aaniin danaa **a'aw** niwii-gagwe-aada'og ganabaj*

aaniin	danaa	**a'aw**	ni-wii-gagwe-aada'w-ig	ganabaj
what	EMPH	**DEM**	1-FUT-try-defeat.h/-INV	I.think.so

'What the heck? I bet **this guy** wants to challenge me!' (AS.Aadizooked)

b. Quantifier as NP

***aanind** ikidowag "giishpin," **aanind** ikidowag "iishpin"*

aanind	ikido-wag	giishpin	**aanind**	ikido-wag	iishpin
some	says-3p	giishpin	**some**	says-3p	iishpin

'**Some** say "giishpin," **some** say "iishpin"' (AS.12.07.11.C)

c. Noun as NP

*ogii-piidoon **wiisiniwin***

o-gii-biid-oo	**wiisiniwin**
3-PST-bring.it-TI2	**food**

'She brought **food**' (RC.Opichi)

d. RC as NP

*gidaa-inigaa'aa **ge-maajaa'ind***

gi-daa-inigaa'-aa	**IC-da-maajaa'-ind**

2-FUT-harm.h/-DIR   **IC-FUT-send.h/.off-X>3**$_{\text{CONJ}}$
'You could hurt **the one being sent off**' (Staples and Gonzalez 2015, 10)

The ability of any one nominal element to stand alone caused Rhodes (1996, 2) to question whether Ojibwe NPs are in fact headed. However, as Bruening (2001, 40) indicates for Passamaquoddy, demonstratives typically occur prior to the noun they modify and "even in such split cases the demonstrative must precede the noun, arguing for some form of constituency." The same pattern holds true for Ojibwe.

As for verbs, Rhodes distinguishes the inflectional orders of verbs based on differences in "the set of person/number markers, by the presence or absence of a morpheme known as the change, and by differences in the way plurality and obviation are marked on the forms in question" (Rhodes 1996, 4). He clearly outlines the distinction by reminding us that only conjunct verbs can undergo IC and only IC verbs can be participles (4). Rhodes defines participle as a "specialized inflectional form of the verb that is used in certain types of relative clauses" (1). For Rhodes, "the sole use of participles is in relative clause constructions" (5).

In Rhodes's analysis Odawa participles are distinguished from changed conjunct verb forms via the plural and obviative markings occurring on plural and obviative participles that are characteristic of nouns. Also, for Odawa specifically, participles are "more conservative with respect to the innovation of treating the change morpheme as a prefix *e-*" (Rhodes 1996, 4). Often dubbed the "aorist" prefix (Valentine 1994; Costa 1996; Goddard 1987) and common in related Algonquian languages, it is almost unheard of in the Southwestern varieties.[22] Like Nichols (1980) and Goddard (1987), Rhodes associates the additional plural and obviative participial markings with the head of the RC and warns that certain singular forms may not resemble participles due to the head not requiring the marking and states that they "look exactly like the corresponding changed conjuncts" (Rhodes 1996, 7). He provides three basic types of RCs, each briefly discussed here.

Type 1, "simple relatives," are RCs that "modify nominals that are coreferential with slots licensed within the relative clause" (Rhodes 1996, 5). These are formed on "any nominal whose grammatical function is licensed by the verb of the clause ... subjects, primary objects, secondary objects, and relative root complements" (5). These include the canonical postnominal RCs composed of participles or, in Rhodes's term, "term relative clauses" (6). For preposed or preverbal RCs, Rhodes states that they must consist of only a single word licensed by a more "general construction" of modifier-head ordering found in adv-v, adv-loc, adv-temp, and adv-q (7–8). Rhodes designates this subtype as "light term relative clauses" (7).

Type 2 RCs are what Rhodes refers to as "non-term relative clauses," relativizing locative and temporal adjuncts of the matrix clause (1996, 5, 8). Formed on relative root complements, or nonterms, "locative and temporal adjuncts are made with verbs that are ambiguous in form between the participle and the changed conjunct" but assumes the nonterm forms are participial (8).[23] The first type treated by Rhodes are those "whose head is licensed within the relative clause by a relative root" (9). These include locative, goal, manner, source, cause or instrumental, and temporal relatives. Rhodes makes a further distinction in the nonterm RCs for a "special case" of "locative adjuncts," which consist of the relative prefix *dazhi-* (10).

Type 3 in Rhodes's classification of Odawa RCs concerns "verbless relatives, which modify nominals but which have no licensor in the modifying phrase" (Rhodes 1996, 5). These consist of temporal, manner, or locative adjuncts, and are distinct from the temporal adjuncts of type 2, which are licensed by a relative root. In type 3 temporal adjuncts, the head of the RC is either adverbial *pii* 'at the time' (*apii* for SW Ojibwe) or what Rhodes calls "bare relatives" indicated by IC (11), similar to the "just past" mentioned in Baraga (1850) and the "single past occurrence" discussed in Nichols (1980). The type 3 locative RCs are "clause fragments" unlicensed in that they lack a locative verb (Rhodes 1996, 10).

The discussion provided by Rhodes (1996) lays out the basic typology of RCs, a typology that is rather consistent for SW Ojibwe and across the Algonquian family. While the data is essentially the same, the approach taken to account for relativization differs in the current study.

1.4.2. Johns (1982)

In her article on RCs and questions, Johns (1982) concentrates on Rainy River Ojibwe (spelled *Ojibwa* in her work), the dialect area referred to here as Border Lakes Ojibwe. As mentioned earlier, northern varieties of Ojibwe tend to use a relativizing prefix *gaa-* along with regular conjunct inflection as opposed to IC and the participial marking. For Johns, in the case of Border Lakes Ojibwe, both the IC verb forms and the relativizing prefix forms are available to speakers. The difference, as Johns claims, is a matter of definiteness (*gaa-* prefix) versus indefiniteness (IC form) (163):

(29) Definite vs. indefinite (Johns 1982, 161–62)

　　a. definite

　　*inini **gaa**-nagamod kinoozi*

　　inini　　　　**gaa**-nagamo-d　　　ginoozi
　　man　　　　REL-sings-3$_{CONJ}$　　　is.tall
　　'**The man** who is singing is tall'

　　b. indefinite

　　ngikenimaa inini negamod

　　n-gikenim-aa　　　inini　　　IC-nagamo-d
　　1-know.h/-DIR　　man　　　　IC-sings-3$_{CONJ}$
　　'I know **a man** who is singing'

Contrary to previous analyses (Lees 1979; Pagotto 1980) that treat the *gaa-* prefix and IC forms as complementizers, Johns's main claim is that they display "properties more characteristic of relative pronouns" (161). Johns notes that the IC form of the past tense marker *gii-* is *gaa-*, nearly homophonous to the relativizing prefix *gaa-* (162–63). This leads to confusion in attempting to elicit certain forms from speakers though Johns provides examples in which the relativizing prefix *gaa-* co-occurs with both past and future tense markers. Similar examples occur in my data from Border Lakes speakers:

(30) Relativizing prefix with tense (Johns 1982, 161–62)

　　a. *ngikenimaa inini **gaa-gii**-nagamod*

　　n-gikenim-aa　　　inini　　　**gaa-gii**-nagamo-d
　　1-know.h/-DIR　　man　　　　**REL-PST**-sings-3$_{CONJ}$
　　'I know the man who sang'

b. *ngikenimaa inini **gaa-wii**-nagamod*

n-gikenim-aa	inini	**gaa-wii**-nagamo-d
1-know.h/-DIR	man	**REL-FUT**-sings-3$_{CONJ}$

'I know the man who will sing'

With respect to participles in interrogative (*wh*-word) constructions, Johns determines their construction to be the same as relative clauses, except they lack the relativizing prefix *gaa-*.[24] She attributes the common IC form in questions rather than the *gaa-* form to be a matter of "pragmatic aspects of questions" in general (166). The "crucial difference" between the two is that, in direct questions, the participle requires "an obligatory lexical antecedent, i.e., an interrogative morpheme" (165). Interestingly, and relevant to the discussion later of the split-CP hypothesis, Johns provides the example shown below in (31) with an intervening NP (shown in bold) between the *wh*-pronoun and the IC verb as evidence for determining that *wh*-pronouns in Ojibwe do not reside in COMP, citing the A/A constraint (Chomsky 1973), where "an element of a category may not be moved unless the maximal string of that category would be moved" (Johns 1982, 166). Rather than treating *wh*-pronouns as such, she refers to them as "interrogative morphemes":

(31) Interrogative morpheme not in COMP (Johns 1982, 165)

*awegonen **inini** bekite'ang*

awegonen	**inini**	IC-bakite'-am-g
what	**man**	IC-hit.it/-TI1-3$_{CONJ}$

'What is the man hitting?'

In summary, Johns determines RCs, indirect questions, focus constructions, and direct questions to all involve a "subordinate sentence containing a WH element" (167). The only difference between them, according to Johns, is that those "generated from an S' (direct questions and focus constructions) require an obligatory antecedent while those generated by an NP (relative clauses and indirect questions) do not" (167). As will be seen in 3.3.13.3, the definiteness distinction between the *gaa-* forms and the IC forms does not typically hold among modern speakers surveyed. In fact the *gaa-* forms seem to be replacing the IC forms with the loss of the productive process of IC in many more northern communities.

1.4.3. Johansson (2011)

Johansson (2011) provides an analysis of two major strategies of RC formation found across the Algonquian language family. The strategies she describes are essentially the same two strategies found in Ojibwe: the SW forms with IC and plural/obviative nominal markings, and the northern forms with the prefixed *gaa-* and regular conjunct inflection. She proposes that the two forms can be accounted for within a single structure while distinctly supporting a "morphologically dependent (affixal) Rel head" (1).

According to Johansson participles are third-person verb stems where the nominal markings are phi-feature inflections. The nominal markings agree in phi-features with the head of the RC (3). Johansson explicitly states that though contrary to native-speaker translations and prior treatments of participles as nominalizations (Frantz 2009), participles are not nominalizations due to the availability of functional heads such as ADVP, NEGP, and TENSE in participle constructions (Johansson 2011, 3–5). To solve the problem of phi-feature marking on verbal complexes, she cites her own work on Blackfoot (Johansson 2010), which states that Blackfoot RCs are verbal complexes marked with phi-feature inflection through phi-feature concord on the head of the RC (2011, 5). She notes similarities found in a number of Bantu languages (Henderson 2006), where the relative clause marker agrees in noun class with the RC head (2011, 5n7).

In light of Goddard's (1987) analysis of Fox (Meskwaki) participles, which defines participles by function rather than form, the *gaa-* prefixed RCs are not participles in Johansson's proposal. Instead, RC is only indicated via the *gaa-* prefix and the verbal complex is "fully verbal" with standard conjunct order morphology. She claims this is the strategy found in Algonquian languages Western Naskapi, Northern East Cree, Plains Cree, and "Rainy River Ojibwa" (Johansson 2011, 6). For Rainy River Ojibwe, she cites the work of Johns (1982) discussed above and sets aside the issue of the IC forms lacking the *gaa-* prefix.

Johansson proposes that, in participial RCs, the verb raises to Rel to support the affix and, due to concord in the Rel head, is marked with the nominal morphology. For *gaa-* prefix constructions, the prefix itself is merged into the Rel head to support the affix. Since there is no verb in Rel for preverb constructions, no nominal morphology appears on the verb (Johansson 2011, 1).

(32) Participle RC (Johansson 2011)

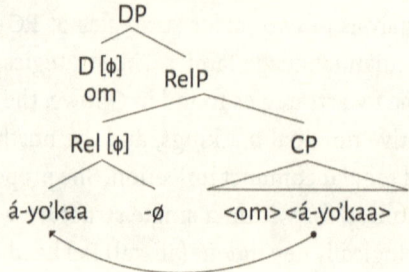

(33) Preverb RC (Johansson 2011)

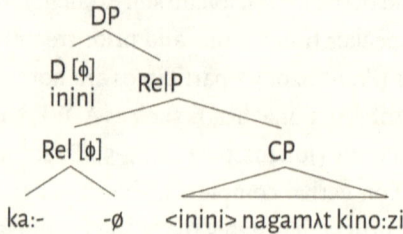

Though the data are very similar to mine, Johansson's (2011) analysis is not ideal in two ways. First, she gives no examples of any word order deviating from the default postnominal RC D+NP+RC or how her account would handle a prenominal RC. Furthermore the preverb RC account she gives is unsustainable from a word order standpoint, where stipulations would need to be made to derive the surface order of constituents.

1.4.4. Johansson (2013)

In her 2013 paper, Johansson is concerned with differentiating participles from nominalizations for Blackfoot RCs. She challenges the claim of Frantz (2009), who provides a "reclassification" analysis where RCs are treated as nominalizations (Johansson 2013, 218). The tendency to treat participles as nominalizations is common in the Algonquian tradition, due to their translation as such (mentioned above in 1.3.1 for conventionalized participles). However, as Johansson argues, RCs "do not have the syntactic characteristics of agent nominalizations.... All clausal functional categories are available in relative clauses" (220). Providing further evidence in support of her analysis, Johansson determines that RCs are not deverbal based on "morphological composition ... non-agentive constructions, and the unavailability of both possessive constructions and adjectival modification" (218).[25]

Johansson follows Baker in his determination of nominal agreement being participle agreement, though highlights a key distinction between the two, in that "participles do share certain characteristics with nouns but are 'less nominal' than nouns or gerunds (see Baker 2011)" (218). In her Bakerian approach, she claims that participles differ from clauses in that, "while clauses project TP and CP, participles project a verbal projection PtplP, followed by a nominal functional projection he calls HP" (233). Johansson departs from Baker in assuming that "there is an InflP projected in relative clauses, as person prefixes are attested in relative clauses," though she assumes that there is no CP projection present in relative clauses (233). Her participle clause structure, modified from Baker (2011), is given in (34).

(34) Participle clause structure (Johansson 2013, 234)

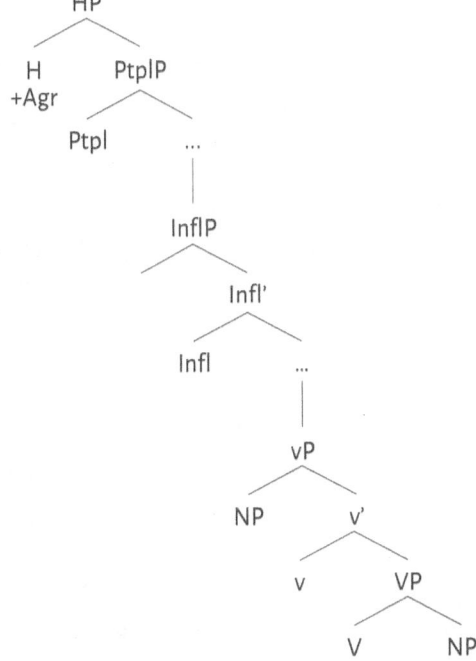

This is essentially the nominal superstructure she puts forth to account for the nominal inflection of participles. In her view, "H agrees with the features of the head noun, which accounts for the nominal agreement morphology within relative clauses" (234). To account for why participles cannot be possessed or modified by adjectives, she proposes a lexical stem-based explanation, where "possessive morphology and attributive roots are morphologically restricted to lexically nominal stems" (235). Johansson's argument is not ideal since what she identifies as "lexically nominal stem" can be similar in shape to verbal stems. Taking a contrary stance I argue that participles cannot be possessed and are restricted in their compatibility with attributive roots because they are not part of a nominal projection.

Other language-specific differences make Johansson (2013) an unattractive approach for Ojibwe RCs. According to Johansson, in Blackfoot, one cannot relativize secondary objects (225); she also claims that "benefactive arguments are not available for relativization in Blackfoot" (227), though they are both possible and attested in Ojibwe. Furthermore Johansson cites Ritter and Wiltschko's (2009) proposal that the inflectional order of a clause "is determined in C; the order of a clause is reflected in verbal inflection. As participles lack verbal inflection, we might say they are 'orderless,' and this could be explained by the missing CP projection" (233). Such an approach is unfeasible for Ojibwe since the verbal nature of participles in RCs is very apparent via number agreement and evidence of verbal quality through the palatalization effects of verbal suffixes (discussed in 2.3.3.1).

Throughout this thesis I use the term *participle* to refer to the form of the verb used in RCs, irrespective of the definitions and phrase structure provided for participles in the sense used by Baker (2011) and Johansson (2013).

1.4.5. Lochbihler and Mathieu (2013)

Lochbihler and Mathieu provide an analysis of Ojibwe RCs, claiming *wh*-agreement on T. Similar to the analysis provided in this study, they treat IC as the morphological realization of *wh*-agreement. Following Chomsky (1977), they discuss the movement of *wh*-elements and operators in different constructions, including interrogatives, relative clauses, and focus constructions. They claim this type of movement is also found in Ojibwe, stating, "relative clauses in Ojibwe involve A'-movement of an operator, and this movement is signaled by initial change on a verb stem" (Lochbihler and Mathieu 2013, 305). Arguing against a nominalization approach, they instead propose RCs as full CP projections where *wh*-agreement occurs on T in Ojibwe not only for interrogatives, but also RCs. They provide evidence that RCs in Ojibwe involve "A-bar movement and projecting full CPs," based on feature inheritance (Chomsky 2005, 2008), which they state is responsible for the realization of *wh*-agreement on T for Ojibwe (Lochbihler and Mathieu 2013, 293). Their claim is that *wh*-agreement features reach T via feature inheritance from C (308).

This analysis rests on several ad hoc types of modifications such as two types of C, each bearing distinct types of features: C for phi-features (independent order) and a different C for discourse features (conjunct) (309). Discourse features are introduced by C in the conjunct but are "transferred down to T where they spell out as *wh*-agreement" (294). Essentially the core of their proposal rests on the featural content of C being determined by clause type (independent versus conjunct) (311). Disregarding the fact that person, tense, and number, the relevant substance of phi-features, can all be realized in the conjunct and across verb types, Lochbihler and Mathieu's proposal of two types of C is based on the lack of "person proclitics" in the conjunct order (309–10).

Proposing that the new locus of *wh*-agreement is T instead of C (293), their approach depends on the relative operator agreeing with T, which spells out the changed form of the past prefix as *gaa*-. They state that the relative pronoun moves to spec, TP to "check the *wh*-features inherited from C to T, and is assumed to A' move to spec, CP to satisfy some EPP or movement feature remaining on C" (298n7). Noting that IC always occurs in *wh*-questions, relative clauses, and certain focus constructions (299), their claim of feature inheritance from C → T is necessary for explaining why no IC occurs on intervening segments such as proper names or emphatics without taking into account that they are not the compatible goals for the feature [change] (314–15). As will be argued in chapter 4, only conjunct verbs can take IC and only IC verbs can be participles in RC.

In line with the current analysis, Lochbihler and Mathieu treat IC as a focusing device:

From another perspective, initial change subordinates a clause to a constituent or to some condition of its context in the discourse. The link between this focusing process (i.e. initial change) and the linguistic notions of operator movement and the use of complementizers is an obvious one. In other words, it is the initial change process—whether in its synchronic use or as an historical process on some underlying morpheme—which is the source of the operator movement. (301n10)

By "synchronic use," they refer to the innovations observed in the variety of Ojibwe they are concerned with (Odawa), where younger speakers employ the *e-* prefix, known in the literature as the aorist (mentioned above in 1.4.1). It should be stated that Lochbihler and Mathieu do not attempt to extend their analysis to other languages of the Algonquian family, citing the nature of IC in Blackfoot and the inconsistency of IC in *wh-*contexts in other languages where they say IC "has a modified underlying function" (305).

In line with my approach in chapter 4, Lochbihler and Mathieu treat temporals with IC as focus constructions involving a *wh-*operator, stating that, "across the board, Ojibwe maintains a correspondence between wh-constructions (i.e., those involving operator movement) and the distribution of initial change, which signals wh-agreement in this language" (308).

Not taking into consideration a split-CP structure, Lochbihler and Mathieu argue against verb raising to C analysis endorsed here. They cite Bruening (2001, 48–49) showing negation and unmarked NPs in Passamaquoddy can occur between *wh-*phrases and the verb, "predicted to be impossible by Campana (1996) and Brittain (1997) if the wh-phrase is in Spec, CP and the verb in C" (Lochbihler andMathieu 2013, 311–12). This is not an issue when adopting a split-CP analysis where specifiers and head positions are available loci for movement. According to them, the difference between the independent and conjunct is the featural content of C-discourse versus phi (312). Both types of conjunct (plain and changed) bear discourse features, though plain in their analysis is a discourse-dependent feature they do not explicitly identify (312–13).

Though many aspects of Lochbihler and Mathieu's analysis are parallel with the current study, I attempt to capture the nature of RCs in a different manner, mainly by accounting for the Ojibwe data in a way that is driven and necessitated by the data.

1.5. THEORETICAL PRELIMINARIES

In the following sections I provide the introductory background on the theoretical assumptions made in this study. In 1.5.1, I discuss nonconfigurationality, first put forth by Hale (1983), and the Pronominal Argument Hypothesis of Jelinek (1984) and Baker (1991, 1996). In 1.5.2, I give a brief introduction to the mirror principle of Baker (1985) and the minimalist program of Chomsky (1993, 1995). The basic tenets of feature checking are provided in 1.5.2.1, with an example of the Ojibwe independent inflectional order. In 1.5.2.2 I show how the conjunct differs from the independent order, adopting a raising analysis for conjunct verbs reminiscent of T-to-C raising in more widely studied languages. In section 1.5.3 I give the background on the split-CP hypothesis of Rizzi (1997) and show how the SW Ojibwe data demand such a structure. More thorough discussions are provided in chapter 4, while arguments and justifications for the theoretical framework are provided throughout the main body of this thesis as the need arises.

1.5.1. Nonconfigurationality

It has been common historically to treat Ojibwe and related Algonquian languages as nonconfigurational, based on Hale's (1983) criterion. According to Bruening (2001, 22), this is the necessary starting point for studies on Algonquian syntax. Nonconfigurational languages generally display the following properties: flexible word order, null constituents, and discontinuous constituents. The first requirement for and hallmark of nonconfigurational languages is flexible word order, which will be discussed regarding Ojibwe in the chapters that follow. Another property of nonconfigurational languages is the existence of null pronouns (*pro*). In this system overt pronouns are not necessary (though they are used primarily for emphasis) and null pronouns are licensed or identified by inflectional morphemes that indicate, person, number, and also the animacy status of the arguments:

(35) *gaawiin anishaa* **pro**$_i$ *ogii-michi-giizhitoosiinaawaa iw*

      gaawiin anishaa   **pro**$_i$ o-gii-michi-   giizhit-oo-sii-naawaa   iw

      NEG for.nothing   **pro**$_i$ 3-PST-bare-   finish.making-TI2-NEG-3p   DET

proᵢ *gaa-tibaajindamowaad* **pro**ⱼⱼ *indebwetawaag* **pro**ᵢ

proᵢ	IC-gii-dibaajind-am-owaad	**pro**ⱼⱼ	in-debwetaw-aa-g	**pro**ᵢ
proᵢ	IC-PST-tell.about-TI1-3p>0	**pro**ⱼⱼ	1-believe.h/-DIR-3p	**pro**ᵢ

'Theyᵢ didn't make up what theyᵢ were telling about, Iⱼⱼ believe themᵢ.' (AS.13.01.31.N)

As the example in (35) exemplifies, overt nominal expressions can be omitted due to the *pro*-drop nature of the language and rich participant reference morphology.

The third condition for nonconfigurationality is concerned with discontinuous constituents. Often these will consist of floating quantifiers and demonstrative pronouns that are not adjacent to the nominal elements they modify. An example of a discontinuous constituent is illustrated below in (36), where the obviate noun *chi-ayaabe-n* 'big buck-OBV' is nonadjacent to the RC that modifies it (both the noun and relative clause are bolded):

(36) Discontinuous constituents

Owiidoomaakizwaan iniw **chi-ayaaben**

o-wiidoomaakizw-aa-n		iniw	**chi-ayaabe-n**
3-pictured.with.h/-DIR-OBV		DET	**big-buck-OBV**

wa'aw inini ***gaa-nisaajin***

wa'aw	inini	**IC-gii-niS-aad-in**
DET	man	**IC.PST-kill-3s>3'**ᴄᴏɴᴊ**-OBV**ᴘʀᴛ

'This man is photographed with the big buck that he killed.' (AS.12.08.15.P)

Indeed the most common cases of discontinuous constituents in Ojibwe are floating quantifiers and determiners nonadjacent to the nominals they modify, or, as in (36) above, a nonadjacent relative clause.

1.5.1.1. *The Pronominal Argument Hypothesis (PAH)*

The aforementioned non-configurational properties noted for many Algonquian languages are captured by the pronominal argument hypothesis (PAH), posited by Jelinek (1984, 1989a, 1989b) and later modified by Baker (1991, 1996). Jelinek's version of the PAH proposes that case and theta-role assignment occur directly in the verbal agreement morphology. In this analysis agreement in the syntactic derivation applies to the "clitic pronouns" (in Jelinek's terms), while overt NPs are coindexed with the appropriate clitic pronoun and are essentially optional adjuncts to TP. The flexibility of overt constituents is merely left or right adjunction to TP, accounting for the flexibility in constituent order.

In Baker's modified version of the PAH, it is null pronominals (*pro*) that occupy argument positions. According to his version of the PAH, the appropriate agreement head (AgrS or AgrO) case-checks *pro* rather than a corresponding agreement morpheme. Brittain adopts this analysis and argues, "phrases are assigned a θ-role by being in a relationship (via agreement or movement) with a morpheme within the verbal complex" (2001, 31–32). For the majority of previous work thus far, overt nominal expressions are analyzed as adjuncts, which occur freely in any order and are licensed by pronominal affixes on the verb. Essentially these analyses treat the morphology of the verbal complex as the syntax. Since the position of the verbal affixes is fixed, there is somewhat of a consensus in the literature that the verbal morphology is analyzed as a syntactic derivation.

The root of this analysis stems from the long-observed reality that a one-word, verbal construction can and often does constitute a grammatical and well-formed sentence. The standard view in the Algonquian tradition is summarized below:

> Every verb constitutes a grammatical sentence by itself and contains pronominal affixes, identified by Jelinek (1984) as syntactic arguments. Full nominals are optional adjuncts. They bear number and gender agreement features which they share with the pronominal affixes on the verb. (Junker 2004, 346)

A variety of other theories and perspectives can be found that account for syntactic representations in the verbal morphology but few are concerned with the syntactic behavior of the overt "adjunct NPs."[26]

Due to the common practice of examining constituent order in textual materials and transcribed narratives, the standard view of "free word order" and Algonquian word-level sentence structure has skewed the view of the role of the NP in more natural, everyday language use. An unavoidable reality when examining any given Algonquian-language narrative is noticing the "paucity of nominals":

> Once the identity of participants has been established in a given discourse, the referring nominals are omitted, reference to them being retained in the verbal complex via an elaborate system of agreement morphology. (Brittain and MacKenzie 2011, 255)

Observed over the course of the current study, there appears to be a systematic ordering of overt NPs occupying syntactic positions. Therefore, for the current analysis of Ojibwe, I adopt a revised version of the PAH where overt NPs are generated in argument positions with *pro* surfacing in argument position only when required, in the absence of an overt NP argument. For structures with overt NP arguments, constituency order is thus configurational, with syntactic projections accounting for discourse-driven movement. This departs from the above-mentioned theories, but follows others such as Mühlbauer, who indicates that the word-level sentence and syntactic approach is unsustainable for a theory of syntax that accounts for Algonquian languages:

> An Algonquian speaker has to start with some overt nominals in order for the subsequent pronominal-only verb structures to be semantically defined. It is also the case that they can't speak for very long in pronouns without massive ambiguity, requiring topic maintenance. Thus sentences made of a single, fully-inflected verb may make for exciting examples in a paper and entertaining dinner conversation, but a theory built on these grounds seeks to account for a language that does not exist. (2003, 22)

I then propose that, for Ojibwe, pronominal clitics and participant reference affixes can either be coindexed with overt nominal expressions or occupied by null *pro* in the argument positions. As will be advocated for in section 2.7.3, flexibility in the linear distributional ordering of NPs can be accounted for given a split-CP structure (Rizzi 1997), with movement to the left periphery for topic and focus interpretations. This approach departs from previous analyses that "set aside nominal adjuncts" that can be either left or right adjoined to TP resulting in the appearance of a "disorganized" clause structure (Brittain 2001, 29). The split-CP framework is also ideal in accounting for the phenomenon of relativization in Ojibwe, which is treated in 4.2.2.

In summary I determine that Ojibwe does have a hierarchical syntactic structure, making use of a revised version of the PAH where null pronouns (*pro*) satisfy verbal agreement in cases with no overt NP arguments. Overt arguments occupy the canonical argument positions and word order is configurational, with the discourse-driven word order variability being a result of syntactic movement. With the basic tenets established regarding the PAH and the direction pursued in this study, we can now discuss the manner in which grammatical relations are established, how features are checked, and the relevant movement operations that occur.

1.5.2. The Mirror Principle and the Minimalist Program

Before discussing the feature-checking operations and the framework followed here, it is critical to consider the relationship between morphology and syntax for a language like Ojibwe. In essence this relationship evokes the consideration of the "mirror principle" first proposed by Baker (1985):

(37) The mirror principle (Baker 1985, 375)
Morphological derivations must directly reflect syntactic derivations (and vice versa).

Baker proposes a theory that can account for both the morphological and syntactic components of verbal constructions in morphologically complex languages with a single process, stating, "what is true of the morphology is true of the syntax as well" (1985, 394). Importantly the mirror principle requires that a constraint in one of the derivations (syntactic or morphological) automatically constitutes a constraint on the other (413). Noting the often dubious distinction between inflectional and derivational morphology, Baker follows Andersen (1982) by saying, "inflectional morphology is what is relevant to syntax" (377).

The mirror principle will be relevant throughout this thesis as I argue that each syntactic phrasal projection can be identified through morphological realizations of functional heads. Baker states that the mirror principle "should not be stipulated as a basic principle of grammar, but rather should be derived from fundamental aspects of the organization of the grammar" (411). This is an ideal approach for a language like Ojibwe, where typically syntactic phenomena are identifiable in the verbal morphology. Though a full syntactic account of the entire inflectional system is well beyond the scope of this study, Baker's mirror principle will bear fruit in the discussion of Ojibwe clause types and the projection of functional heads in the articulation of the CP layer in chapter 4.

I attempt to capture the relevant properties of Ojibwe clause structure using the framework of the minimalist program (Chomsky 1993). The main components of the minimalist program (MP) important to this study are "checking theory" and a universal clause structure, such as the one given in (38). This basic structure accounts for the independent clause in Ojibwe, which will be spelled out explicitly in the sections that follow.

(38) Universal clause structure (from Chomsky 1993,7)

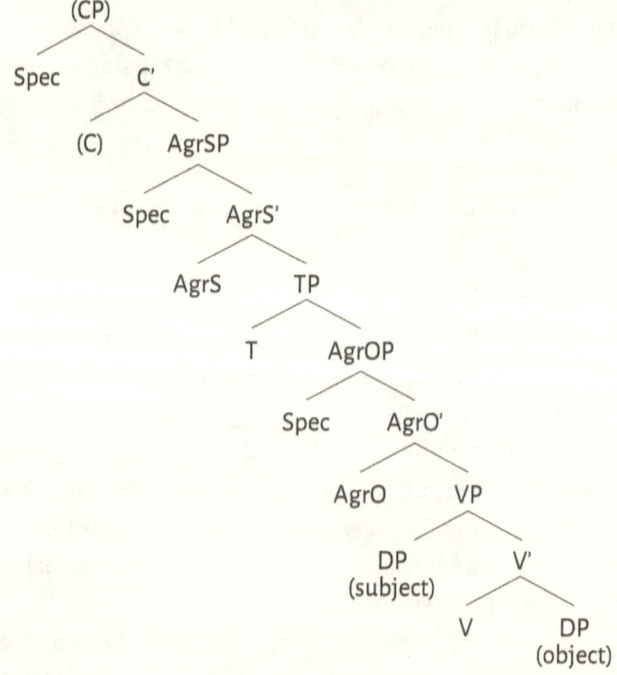

1.5.2.1. Feature Checking

In the minimalist framework, the heads of phrases have features that need to be checked before the spell-out of the derivation. Syntactic licensing and movement occur due to an abstract operation known as Agree. In this system agreement occurs when probes search the structure in the c-command domain for a goal that matches in their featural composition. Features may be valued or unvalued, the latter constituting probes (such as T) with the former serving as goals in the probe-goal system. Features of nominal expressions are those that contribute to their meaning. These include phi-features—essentially gender, person, and number features—which are considered valued when entering the derivation. Case features, however (in the sense used in Bruening 2001), proximate (P) and obviative (O) for Ojibwe, are considered unvalued and need to be checked prior to the derivation being spelled out. In contrast, the T constituent, realized as either an auxiliary or tense marker, enters the derivation with the reverse valuation, where case is a valued feature with phi-features unvalued.

Another important distinction made in the feature-checking theory involves the distinction between interpretable and uninterpretable features. Interpretable features contribute to the semantic interpretation whereas uninterpretable features do not. Interpretable features include those associated here with the T constituent—tense, aspect, and mood (TAM)—while phi-features are uninterpretable on T. Prior to the spellout of the syntactic derivation, uninterpretable features must be deleted. This occurs with a matching or valuation relationship. This matching relationship is the underlying system of agreement.

One final distinction to be made before providing an example of syntactic derivation for a language like Ojibwe involves the difference between strong and weak features. For Ojibwe I assume the T and C constituents contain a strong feature requiring head movement of the V constituent. Only strong features condition movement; such an analysis easily accounts for the basic verb-initial surface constituent ordering found in Ojibwe. With V → T movement, the verb raises to the T constituent, as shown in (39).

(39) V → T movement

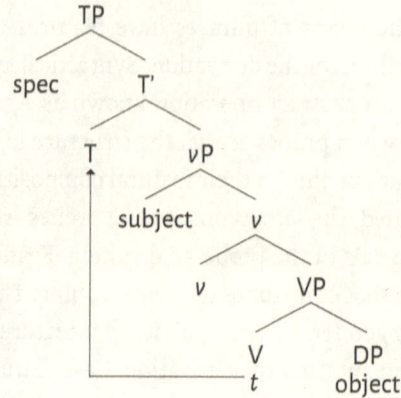

Following Chomsky (1995) among others, I assume the object of the verb is a complement of the verb, with the subject being in the specifier position of the light verb phrase (vP). In the next section I show how the independent order of Ojibwe verbal inflection is accounted for in this system. I also argue for a V → C movement analysis accounting for the conjunct order of inflection as put forth by Brittain (2001) in her C checks V^{CJ} hypothesis.

1.5.2.2. Independent versus Conjunct

Relating back to the PAH discussed above in 1.5.1.1, overt NPs in Ojibwe agree with the agreement morphology of the verbs themselves. In cases where no NPs arise, *pro* occupies the argument position(s). For Ojibwe I assume the following phi-features are available: animate, where NP arguments are either [+animate] or [-animate]; person, where NP arguments are either [person 1], [person 2], or [person 3]; and number [singular] and [plural]. This featural array alone can account not only for the distinction in grammatical gender (animate versus inanimate), but also for the person or participant arrangement, as shown in table 8.

In addition to the phi-features given above, Ojibwe also contains case features. These are especially crucial when considering the interaction between multiple third persons. Aligning with the Algonquian tradition, these features are identified as [P] (proximate) and [O] (obviative). Case features are unvalued and only become valued in cases of agreement. Fol-

Table 8. Featural composition of person arrangement

Person code	Feature bundle	Person	Ojibwe pronoun
1s	[person 1] [+animate] [singular]	1st person singular	*niin*
2s	[person 2] [+animate] [singular]	2nd person singular	*giin*
3s	[person 3] [+animate] [singular]	3rd person singular	*wiin*
1p	[person 1] [+animate] [plural]	1st person plural	*niinawind*
21p	[person 1] [person 2] [+animate] [plural]	21 person plural	*giinawind*
2p	[person 2] [+animate] [plural]	2nd person plural	*giinawaa*
3p	[person 3] [+animate] [plural]	3rd person plural	*wiinawaa*
0s	[person 3] [-animate] [singular]	Inanimate singular	
0p	[person 3] [-animate] [plural]	Inanimate plural	

lowing the analysis in Bruening (2001), an NP's phi-features are syntactically active as an uninterpretable [P] feature. According to Bruening, the principles for valuing [P] result in the Algonquian proximate-obviative distinction essentially being components of a case-marking system (120). Opponents of such an analysis are quick to point out that the proximate and obviative assignment can change across clause boundaries, where Bruening defines the particular Algonquian property of valuation of the uninterpretable feature, on which the current analysis is based:

> What is particular to Algonquian languages is the dependent means of valuing the uninterpretable feature—by context, and by person features. This is the way that the participant hierarchy is encoded in the grammar: in the particular relation between person features and values of the feature [+P]. There is a straightforward mapping between first and second persons and inanimates and the value for [P]: first and second persons are inherently [+P], while inanimates may not be [+P]. Certain third persons in opposition to another third person may be distinguished by giving them the same [+P] value (proximate third persons pattern with first and second persons in agreement morphology). On this theory there is no need for an independent hierarchy of uncertain grammatical status, no need for ranking of violable constraints (e.g., Aissen 1997), or any other mechanism. There is only the fact that cer-

tain persons are inherently valued for [P], while others become valued through pairwise opposition. (2001, 120–21)

With the basic tenets established, we can now account for the derivation of an Ojibwe independent clause. When a verb enters the derivation it selects a theme sign. This is essentially the selection of object agreement (Brittain 2001, 38; Bruening 2001, 118). In Brittain's terms, when appealing to the mirror principle of Baker (1985), object agreement is checked earlier in the derivation than subject agreement, which allows for "subject agreement to be established, by default, relative to the properties of AgrO-mirroring the ordering of syntactic operations" (2001, 38). V → T raising accounts for the spellout of agreement markers upon the assignment of case via Agree.

For transitive verbs the animacy featural specification of the object determines the theme selected ([+animate] versus [-animate]) and ultimately determines the shape of the verb stem in Ojibwe (VTI versus VTA). For the inanimate transitive verbs (VTI), number agreement is checked via the featural specification for number while case features are only valued in cases with a third-person subject.

In the case of transitive animate verbs (VTA), there are five possible scenarios to consider. When a VTA enters the derivation, it has four possible theme options available.[27] The first involves the relationship between first and second persons. When the first person is object and the second person is subject, the theme sign is null, represented here with a zero morpheme (∅):

(40) VTA 2>1 independent
giwiidoopam
| gi- | wiidoopam | -∅ |
| 2- | eat.with.h/ | -2>1 |

'You eat with me.'

When the roles are reversed and the second person is object, the theme sign *-in* surfaces, as shown below in (41):

(41) VTA 1>2 independent
 giwiidoopamin
 gi-   wiidoopam   **-in**
 2-   eat.with.h/   **-1>2**
 'I eat with you.'

When a speech act participant (SAP) is subject to a non-SAP object, the direct theme sign /-aa/ occurs, shown here in (42):[28]

(42) VTA 2/1>3 independent
 niwiidoopamaa
 ni-   wiidoopam   **-aa**
 1-   eat.with.h/   **-DIR**
 'I eat with h/.'

When the roles are reversed and a third-person argument is subject acting on an SAP object, the inverse theme marker /-ig^w/ occurs, given below in (43):

(43) VTA 3>1/2 independent
 niwiidoopamig
 ni-   wiidoopam   **-ig**
 1-   eat.with.h/   **-INV**
 'S/he eats with me.'

The final scenario to consider involves the interaction between third persons and requires the valuation of case features in the derivation. With the co-occurrence of two third persons, one must become [+proximate]. This analysis is in line with other studies of Algonquian languages, mainly following that of Bruening (2001). In Bruening's terms the choice of which third-person argument is valued as [+proximate] is "free," rooted in the context:

> Third persons are not inherently valued (except for inanimates, which cannot be [+P]); they derive a value only from context, and only through opposition between NPs. If two NPs occur in the same local domain (to

be defined below), one will always become [+P], while the other will remain unvalued. Which does which is entirely free; speakers can choose to assign any of two locally co-occurring NPs [+P]. There is one restriction: any animate co-occurring with an inanimate will always become [+P]. This follows from the stipulation that inanimates cannot be [+P]; if one of two third persons must become [+P], it will have to be the animate one. (2001, 119)

What this means is that either the third-person subject or object may be assigned the [+proximate] valuation. In addition to the valuation of the [proximate] case feature described above, whichever third-person argument is not assigned the [+proximate] feature is assigned the other case feature [obviative]. According to Bruening, the [obviative] feature "will be assigned on top of its [P] feature, and will eventually be spelled out as an obviative suffix" (2001, 120). The example given in (44a.) shows the direct theme with the [+proximate] argument as subject, while (44b.) illustrates the inverse theme with the [+proximate] argument as object and the [obviative] argument as subject:

(44) VTA [+proximate] vs. [obviative]

a. [+proximate] as subject (direct theme)

owiidoopamaan iniw ikwewan a'aw inini

o-wiidoopam-**aa**-n	iniw	ikwe-wan	a'aw	inini
3-eat.with.h/-**DIR**-OBV	DET$_{OBV}$	woman-OBV	DET$_{PROX}$	man

'The man$_{PROX}$ eats with the woman$_{OBV}$.'

b. [+proximate] as object (inverse theme)

owiidoopamigoon iniw ikwewan a'aw inini

o-wiidoopam-**igw**-n	iniw	ikwe-wan	a'aw	inini
3-eat.with.h/-**INV**-OBV	DET$_{OBV}$	woman-OBV	DET$_{PROX}$	man

'The woman$_{OBV}$ eats with the man$_{PROX}$.'

Similar to a nominative and accusative case-marking system, Bruening states that the spellout of proximate/obviative arguments "manipulated by speakers to indicate coreference and disjoint is essentially a formal licensing property of NPs" (120–21).

Following crosslinguistic approaches to feature-checking and case-marking analyses, [+proximate] is comparable to nominative case assignment and is checked by T. The unvalued [P] feature resembles accusative case in that it is checked by v. Strengthening the argument for a case approach for Ojibwe is the dichotomy of determiners (demonstrative pronouns) employed for each. Returning to the examples above in (36), [+P] and [+obviative] arguments each have a distinct set of determiners, reminiscent of more well-known case-marking languages of the world. Citing no radical difference between this approach and that of other languages, Bruening determines the only "language-particular" component of this theory is the means in which uninterpretable features of NPs are valued (128). This approach differs from other Algonquian analyses, notably Brittain (2001). Since Brittain has "set aside" the issue of overt nominals as "optional adjuncts," she does not encounter the need for the features [proximate] or [obviative] in her analysis.

Proceeding through the derivation, phi-features are checked in a Spec-head relationship. As stated earlier, movement in the minimalist sense can be explained by the requirement that strong morphological features of lexical items be checked over the course of the derivation or by the particular feature bundle composition of an NP. This requires a match of a particular feature of a lexical item with that of a functional category. Such a match occurs within the probe-goal system. When matching occurs, the relevant feature is thus canceled, at which point the lexical item undergoes no further movement operations.

At the point in which a verb's arguments are established, a strong tense feature on T triggers movement of the verb to the head position of T. In deriving the common surface verb-initial constituent order, the verb raises to T to acquire tense and assign case. Essentially feature checking works in a symmetrical manner where the arguments of a verb (either overt NPs or *pro*) are valued for case by the tense features of T for subjects and v for objects, with the phi-features of the heads T and v valued by the arguments. This is parallel with other studies and accounts for feature checking of languages of the world.[29]

While the above claims easily account for the morphosyntactic derivation of the independent order, further movement is necessary for making the distinction between the independent and the conjunct. As mentioned above in 1.3.1, the conjunct is used in dependent, subordinate clauses similar to English conditional clauses introduced by *if, when,* or *that,* and in verb complement clauses. In accounting for the distinction between the independent and conjunct verbal orders, I follow Brittain (2001) in her C checks V^{CJ} hypothesis.

The association between the syntactic environments in which the conjunct occurs with a complementizer position has long been observed for Algonquian (Valentine 1994; Campana 1996; Brittain 2001, to name a few). While Brittain's C checks V^{CJ} hypothesis deals with Western Naskapi of the Cree-Montagnais-Naskapi (CMN) language complex, she extends the analysis to "members of the Algonquian language family in general" (2001, 3). According to Brittain all verbs inflected for the conjunct order have at least one CP level. Conjunct verbs combine in the lexicon with the formal feature [CJ], which is checked by a non-NEG-C. The dichotomy of verbal inflection for the independent and conjunct orders is handled via feature checking over the course of the derivation. In adopting Brittain's analysis, Ojibwe verbs inflected for the independent order are checked within TP (IP in her terms), motivated by the requirement to check phi-features and case. Simply and minimally, movement to C depends upon the feature [CJ], which is essentially the difference between independent and conjunct inflection (73).

The derivation is essentially the same for conjunct and independent verbs, though the spellout of the morphology differs. While agreement markers in the independent order can be both prefixal and suffixal, in the conjunct, participant reference is entirely suffixal. Following both Brittain and Campana (1996), I assume that the default order is the independent, while the conjunct is employed in more syntactically marked clauses. Since the complementizer position is also associated with [wh] environments, topicalization and focalization, as well as relativization contexts, all morphologically distinct environments of the conjunct order, an articulation of the CP layer is necessitated by the data. This is the subject of the next section.

1.5.3. Split-CP Hypothesis (Rizzi 1997)

Given the range of syntactic phenomena associated with a CP layer, Rizzi determines the X-bar schemata to be "too simplistic" (1997, 281). Similar to the articulation of the traditional IP (TP, AspP, ModeP, etc.), the cartographic approach to clause structure was developed to handle the distinct functional syntactic operations associated with the CP layer. Rizzi determines that the C system expresses at least two kinds of information, "one facing the outside and the other facing the inside" (283). For the "outside," Rizzi follows Chomsky (1995) on the specification of Force in the determination of clause type. For the information facing the inside, Rizzi determines C being concerned with the embedded content underneath it. Ultimately Rizzi determines that the complementizer system needs to be split into distinct heads and syntactic projections. The framework of Rizzi's split CP, essentially an articulated left periphery, is given in (45).

(45)

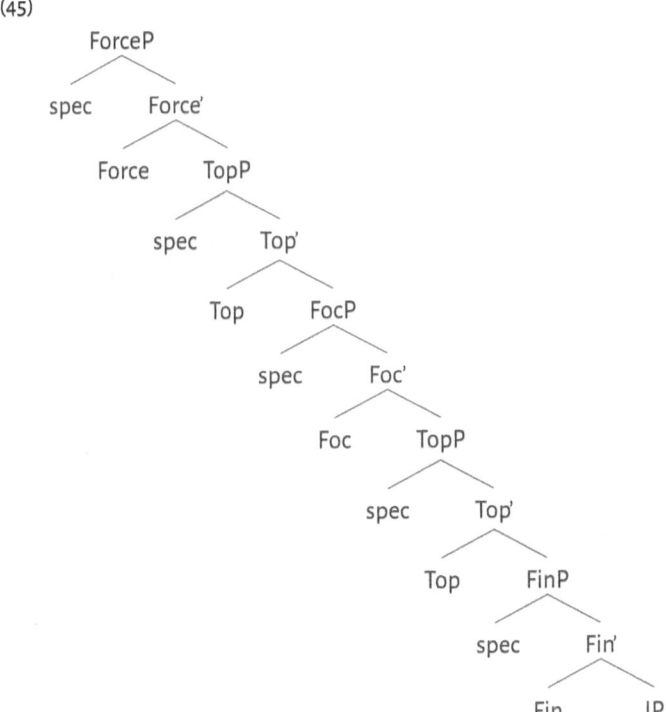

Rizzi's template is ideal for accounting for a language like Ojibwe in two ways. The first and perhaps most obvious is by providing a structure that can accommodate the varying arrangement of constituents within a clause. As will be seen in 4.3.2, any order deviating from the unmarked, most basic, and pragmatically neutral verb-initial order can be accounted for in the split-CP template of Rizzi. The template is also useful in another regard. When considering the differences in the morphological shape of conjunct verbs, changed conjunct verbs, and participles of RCs, I account for the distinctions of each using the Rizzian template in a head movement analysis where the verb raises up the structure in the split CP. A more detailed account and discussion of the various projections of the split CP and how they are exploited in Ojibwe is given in 4.2.2.

1.6. CONCLUSION

In the sections above I have shown how dialectal studies of Ojibwe have neglected detailed exploration in the SW territory, and how this study aims to fill a gap in the research. In defining relative clauses by their function and identifying the two major strategies for RC formation in SW Ojibwe, we can now begin to account for the observable variation found in the data. By recasting the analysis of Ojibwe morphosyntax into a more modern theoretical framework, this thesis presents a starting point for others interested in Ojibwe and the syntax of related Algonquian languages. With the basic overview of the current study established, we can now pursue the discussion of relativization as a key parameter in SW Ojibwe variation.

1.6.1. Concluding Remarks

In the chapters that follow I first offer an overview of the most relevant aspects of Ojibwe morphology and syntax by providing a sketch grammar in chapter 2, necessary for the subsequent discussion. At any point of the thesis where the reader is presented an unfamiliar, language-specific aspect of the grammar, I have made every attempt to direct them to the relevant section of chapter 2. Though a full-blown description of Ojibwe morphosyntax is well beyond the scope of this study, I have strived to provide the necessary information for the reader and their ability to follow the discussion.

Chapter 3 begins with a detailed description of the survey apparatus utilized in this study, providing the context in which the data were obtained. I also include a definition and description of the archived data obtained over the course of this study in 3.2. The findings of the survey are presented in 3.3, with each individual parameter for variation discussed in turn. Section 3.4 includes a discussion of the findings, taking into consideration geographic variation, intelligibility, age-graded variation, and free variation.

Chapter 4 is concerned with the phenomenon of relativization in Ojibwe, with 4.1 illustrating the distinction between core argument and relative root argument relatives, with a discussion of the variation observed. In 4.2 I provide the theoretical framework adopted to account for the various clause types and, ultimately, relativization. Proposing a head movement analysis I show how other studies have exploited the structural framework and what lends itself nicely to the Ojibwe data. In 4.3 I give the theoretical analysis of RCs in Ojibwe, arguing for a feature bundle explanation while articulating the left periphery of a clause in the spirit of Rizzi (1997).

Chapter 5 concludes the thesis with a discussion, comparisons to Proto-Algonquian, acknowledgment of the limitations of the study, followed by some directions for future research.

TWO

Ojibwe Morphosyntax

In this chapter I provide the necessary grammatical information for the subsequent discussion on regional variation and, ultimately, the morphological form of relative clause constructions. I begin with a few general statements about the typological classification of the language in 2.1, followed by the phonetic inventory in 2.2. I then discuss the composition of Ojibwe words in 2.3 with respect to the grammatical categories of the language and the morphophonological process of palatalization, which is pertinent to the study of participles and RCs. In 2.4 I offer a brief description of the verb types along with the relevant subsystems of verbal inflection and a brief discussion of the topicality hierarchy in 2.5. In 2.6 I discuss the ablaut system known as *initial change* (IC), as well as its form and function with reference to Ojibwe and other closely related Algonquian languages. This discussion is most pertinent to the subsequent sections on *wh*-questions and participles. I then provide a brief overview on the syntax of Ojibwe in 2.7.

The Ojibwe discussed in this chapter is essentially what Valentine refers to as "General Ojibwe" (1994, 186). General Ojibwe is essentially a structural description of features of the language that many regional dialects have in common. This is mainly a description of the more standard Ojibwe printed in the most widely used print and web resources (that is, Nichols and Nyholm 1995; Nichols and Price 2002, and so on) and most commonly taught in dialect-neutral settings such as off-reservation colleges and universities. According to Valentine, the Ojibwe recorded at Mille Lacs in the works of John Nichols is more representative of "General Ojibwe" than other dialects such as Severn or Algonquin (204).[1] Exceptions to the paradigm and variation within will be covered in chapter 3 in the discussion of regional variation in Southwestern (SW) Ojibwe.

2.1. TYPOLOGICAL PRELIMINARIES

The Ojibwe language, like all other Algonquian languages, is highly synthetic, or polysynthetic in the Sapirian sense (Sapir 1921). Ojibwe is a head-marking, agglutinative language often characterized as having a "free" or flexible word order. In the Algonquian linguistic tradition, noun gender in Ojibwe is treated in terms of animate and inanimate. According to Goddard, the terminology dates as far back as 1634, in Paul Le Jeune's description of Montagnais, the language of the Innu of Quebec and Labrador (1996b, 20). The animacy status is not immediately recognizable from the singular form of the noun, but is identified by the plural suffix and through agreement with determiners and verbs in the context in which they occur.

The gender distinction is mainly biologically based; however, grammatically animate nouns may be semantically inanimate while grammatically inanimate nouns refer only to semantically inanimate things (Goddard 2002). Despite the largely biologically based distinction, smaller plants and plant products may vary, especially berries, for no real apparent semantic reason (Valentine 1994, 181). Writing on a phenomenon first observed by Bloomfield (1946, 449–50), Valentine (1994, 182) provides some definable collections of grammatical animates, including canoe parts, items of spiritual or religious importance, wheat products, certain natural objects including rocks, ice, snow, sun and moon, as well as a few body parts such as nostrils, shoulder blades, knees, and eyebrows. Discussed in 3.3.9, variation in animacy gender status makes for an important parameter of regional dialect variation.

Animacy agreement, along with person and number agreement, is reflected throughout the language via a system of concord as illustrated below in (46), consisting of three highly inflected verbs and only one overt NP ('their fathers'):

(46) *endaso-onaagoshig ogii-wiijiiwaawaan*
     IC-daso-onaagoshi-g   o-gii-wiijiiw-aa-waa-n
     IC-rel.pv-evening-0$_{CONJ}$ 3-PST-go.with-DIR-3p-3'

> owi-bagida'waanid oosiwaan
> owi-bagida'waa-nid   oos-iwaan
> go-set.nets-OBV   father-POSS$_{3p>3'}$

'Every evening they would go with their fathers when they went to set nets' (Stillday 2013a, 53)

In the remainder of this chapter I will present only the most essential details of the most relevant areas of the language for the subsequent discussion on variation and relativization that concerns primarily morphophonological and morphosyntactic phenomena.

2.2. THE SOUND SYSTEM

While the focus of this study is chiefly morphosyntactic, it is necessary to provide background information on the phonetic and phonological systems that are critical to the discussion of the morphosyntactic forms shaped by morphophonological processes. I begin with the phonetic inventory of the language.

2.2.1. The Vowels

Ojibwe makes use of a seven-vowel system. According to Valentine there are seven phonemic vowels in all contemporary Ojibwe dialects, which vary only at the phonetic level (1994, 132). Vowel length is contrastive, with four long and three short vowels, as shown in table 9.

As pointed out by Piggott, certain initial vowels are tensed and sound long as in the words *amik* 'beaver,' *animosh* 'dog,' and *asab* 'net' (1978, 162). Valentine restricts this tensing to short back vowels such as ***animosh*** having the variant pronunciation of ***aanimosh***. He notes that short vowels are typically phonetically lax except before homorganic glides (1994, 134).

2.2.2. Consonant Inventory

Depending on how the obstruent system is analyzed, Ojibwe contains between eleven and seventeen phonetic consonants (Valentine 1996, 291). The entire consonant inventory is provided in table 10. IPA equivalents are

Table 9. Ojibwe vowels

Orthographic representation	Phonetic approximation
/a/	[ə]-[ʌ]
/aa/	[aː]
/e/	[eː]-[ɛː]
/i/	[ɪ]
/ii/	[iː]
/o/	[o]-[ʊ]
/oo/	[oː]-[uː]

Table 10. Ojibwe consonants (adapted from Valentine 2001, 50)

	Labial	Dental/ Alveolar	Alveopalatal	Palatal	Velar	Glottal
Stops						
Lenis	b	d			g	
Fortis	p	t			k	
Glottal						' [ʔ]
Fricatives						
Lenis		z	zh [ʒ]			
Fortis		s	sh [ʃ]			
Affricates						
Lenis			j [d͡ʒ]			
Fortis			ch [t͡ʃ]			
Nasals	m	n				
Glides	w			y	w	

given in brackets for graphemes and digraphs representing fricatives and affricates, as well as the glottal stop /'/; all other graphemes have their typical value.[2]

All obstruents are differentiated in terms of strength or length. The voiceless member of the pair is said to be stronger and is often referred to as *fortis*; it is pronounced with greater muscular intensity (Valentine 2001, 48). The voiced counterpart is said to be weaker and is referred to as *lenis*. The strong or fortis members of each pair do not occur word-initially unless a vowel is deleted and "may sound long or double, and are voiceless" (Nichols and Nyholm 1995, xxvi). This fortis/lenis distinction is represented in various ways across dialects and, according to Valentine, "arose historically from the simplification of PA obstruent clusters":

> [the fortis/lenis distinction] reflects phonotactic constraints inherited from PA, in that no obstruent clusters were allowed word initially, and hence no distinctive fortis segments occur in this position in any modern Ojibwe dialects, except those that have lost word initial short vowels by a rule of syncope. (Valentine 1994, 121–22)

In addition to this fortis/lenis contrast being realized as a pure voicing distinction (medially), there is also a distinction made regarding length where the fortis segment is geminate. Following Bloomfield (1925), some have chosen to represent this length distinction by doubling the letters used to represent the lenis consonants. Such is the case in some of the transcription systems found in the older works on Algonquian languages, including Ojibwe, for example, Nichols (1980).

This voiced/voiceless, lenis/fortis distinction is characteristic of SW Ojibwe, according to Valentine's data from Minnesota and southeastern Ontario, while the only dialect of Ojibwe where the fortis/lenis distinction is made on the basis of voicing is Algonquin (Valentine 1994, 122). There are lenis obstruents that are phonetically voiceless word-initially; in some communities they may optionally be voiceless word-finally (123–24). In SW Ojibwe, the tense prefixes /wii-/ 'voluntative' and /gii-/ 'past' are followed by a "tensing boundary normally marked by a slight glottal stop or /y/-glide before vowels in careful speech, but by tensing of a following lenis consonant" (Nichols 1980, 129).[3] Valentine (1994) notes the rarity of minimal pairs differentiated by a single phoneme, but offers some in his paper on dialect variation (1996) and in his grammar (2001, 43). With the exception of a few loans and slang expressions, for example, *ochrakiman* 'his truck' (AS) and *majigalipowish* 'good for nothing' (LS), no liquids (/l/ or /r/) exist in SW Ojibwe.[4]

Epenthetic glides are common in the language breaking up undesired adjacent vowel sequences, though these are typically not accounted for in orthographic conventions, i.e., *niwii-izhaa* [nɪwijɪʒa] 'I want to go (there).'

Coincidentally it is common for glides /w/ and /y/ to delete intervocalically in casual speech, for example, *iwidi* → *idi* 'over there.' As mentioned by Valentine, a recent innovation at the time of his study among southern dialects was the coalescence of glide /w/ with /a/ to /o/ in many dialects (1994, 141–42). Such variation is treated in 3.3.7.3.

2.3. MORPHOLOGY

The Ojibwe language is highly synthetic. The language makes use of both a complex inflectional marking system (person, number, tense, and so on) as well as a rich derivational system where, often, each subcomponent can be further dissected into multiple morphemes. Lexical subcomponents of Ojibwe words are typically analyzed in terms of their respective position within a word: initial, medial, and final. In the example below in (47), each of the possible slots are filled:

(47) *bishagigidigweshin* 's/he skins h/ knee'[5]

Initial	Medial	Final
bishag=	=gidigwe=	=shin
'peel'	'knee'	'falls, lies, treads, hits on something'[6]

Whether it is a lexical initial or "root" in the sense used by Nichols (1980) or the "derived initial" for secondary stems (Goddard 1990), the initial element typically carries descriptive adjectival or adverbial information. The medial, the only optional element of an Ojibwe verb, often contains classificatory character, either an incorporated nominal element (such as body parts, as shown in [47] above) or natural landscape and other features or objects. The final can be either abstract or concrete and defines the lexical class of the word by determining the verb stem type, "sensitive to the gender of the goal in transitives, and that of the lone argument in intransitives" (Valentine 1994, 251–52). Despite the straightforward nature of the classification and parsing of Ojibwe morphemes, there remain unanalyzable stems, which most likely reflect older layers of the Algonquian language.

Ojibwe words are typically categorized as nouns, verbs, and particles.[7] Nouns, either animate or inanimate, are inflected for plural number and obviation.[8] Included in this grouping are pronouns and the various subtypes of pronouns. Verbs show complex inflectional morphology and rich agreement with the animacy status and number of its arguments. The third grouping, particles, is the least morphologically complex, as particles are typically not subject to inflection.[9] In addition to the pure nouns and verbs, there are also preverbs, which for nouns usually occur only with stative verbs (Nichols 1980, 101).

2.3.1. Nouns

Nouns are either of the animate or inanimate gender and can be morphologically marked to indicate a range of possibilities, including but not limited to possession, diminution, and pejoration. Prototypical nouns can also take a locative suffix with prepositional qualities such as 'to; toward; at; in.' Table 11 lays out the positions of the possible nominal suffixes while providing their possible surface forms.

The /-i/-initial peripheral suffixes bolded in column F are especially relevant to the present discussion in that the suffixes indicating plurality are included here and will be discussed with participles in 2.5.2. The peripheral suffixes themselves are provided below in table 12, again with the relevant /-i/-initial suffixes bolded. Valentine observes that the peripheral suffixes "indicate nominal categories (gender, number, obviation) of the only or more distant 3rd person participant involved" (1994, 211). This fact will be important for the discussion of participles and variation observed.

2.3.2. Pronouns

Several types of pronouns occur in Ojibwe, including personal pronouns, demonstratives, indefinites, dubitatives, and interrogatives. Pronouns are known to show significant variation across dialects. Perhaps the most variable are demonstratives; "that is how you can tell where a person is from" (Nichols, pers. comm.). Demonstrative pronouns show gender, number, and obviation as well as provide spatial and discourse deixis information. Table 13 illustrates the range of variation found in demonstrative pronouns in SW Ojibwe.[10] A full discussion of their geographical distribution is given in 3.3.6: In addition to the demonstrative pronouns given above, the ob-

Table 11. Underlying forms and positions of nominal suffixes (from Nichols 1980, 15)

A	B	C	D	E	F
Possessed them sign	Pejorative suffix	Nominal central suffixes	Dubitative mode suffix	Preterit mode suffix	Peripheral suffixes
/-m/	/sh/	/-naan/ /-naa/ 'I-ful' /-waa/ 'I-less' /-ni(w)/ 'obviative'	/-go/	/-ban(e)/	/-i/ '0' /-an/~/-**in**/ '0p' /-ag/~/-**ig**/ '3p' /-an/~/-**in**/ '3''
					locative suffix /-ng/
				vocative plural suffix /-dog/	

Table 12. Peripheral suffixes (from Nichols 1980, 185)

Animate singular (3)	0
Inanimate singular (0)	0
Animate plural (3p)	/-ag/, /-**ig**/
Inanimate plural (0p)	/-an/, /-**in**/
Animate obviative (3')	/-an/, /-**in**/
Special singular	/-an/

Table 13. Demonstrative pronouns

	Animate		Inanimate	
Number	CLOSE	FAR	CLOSE	FAR
Singular (GO)	wa'aw 'this'	a'aw 'that'	o'ow 'this'	i'iw 'that'
(WO)	ya'aw 'this'	a'aw 'that'	yo'ow 'this'	i'iw 'that'
(BL)	wa'awe 'this'	a'awe 'that'	o'owe 'this'	i'iwe 'that'
Plural (GO)	ongow 'these'	ingiw 'those'	onow 'these'	iniw 'those'
(WO)	wogow 'these'	agiw 'those'	onow 'these'	aniw 'those'
(BL)	ogowe(g) 'these'	igiwe(g) 'those'	onowe(n) 'these'	iniwe(n) 'those'

viative demonstratives resemble the inanimate forms and show the same spatial distinction:

(48) Obviative demonstrative pronouns (AS.12.01.08.N)

a. *onow asemaan*

onow   asemaa-n
this$_{OBV}$ tobacco-OBV
'this$_{OBV}$ tobacco'

b. *iniw asemaan*

iniw   asemaa-n
that$_{OBV}$ tobacco-OBV
'that$_{OBV}$ tobacco'

As the examples in (48) reveal, the quality of the initial vowel of the obviative demonstratives holds the same spatial distinction as the proximate demonstratives show in table 13.

2.3.3. Verbal Morphology

Ojibwe verbs are often quite complex both in their derivational and inflectional structure. The diagram in (49) illustrates the possibilities and position for verbal composition.

(49) Verb structure (from Nichols 1980, 109)

personal prefix	tense prefixes	locative prefix	relative prefix	verb stem	theme signs	imp. suffixes
initial change						ind. suffixes
						con. suffixes

← PREFIX COMPLEX (6 POSITIONS) →   ← THEME →   ← SUFFIX COMPLEX →

<u>Orders</u>
Imperative
Independent
Conjunct

Table 14. Verb classification *biin-* 'clean'

Gender	Intransitive	Transitive
INANIMATE	*biinad* 'it is clean' *biin-* 'clean' + *-ad* 'stative (inan.)'	*biinitoon* 'clean it' *biin-* 'clean' + /*-t*/ 'causative' + *-oo* 'theme marker' + *-n* 'inanimate'
ANIMATE	*biinizi* 's/he is clean' *biin-* 'clean' + *-izi* 'stative (anim.)'	*biini'* 'clean h/' *biin-* 'clean' + /*-'*/ 'causative'

Many of the distinctions concerning the subtype classification for verbs in Nichols (1980) and Valentine (1994) follow Bloomfield's (1962) classification for Menominee. Verbs are grouped into four types with the transitivity and animacy status of the participants being the determining criteria. There are two subgroupings of transitive, sensitive to the animacy status of the object and two for intransitive verbs, respective to the animacy status of the subject. Each verb type contains a number of subtypes determined by the verb stem's ending. As table 14 illustrates, the initial element can be the same across verb types while either the final element (in intransitive verbs) or theme marker (in transitive verbs) determines the classification of the verb based on the grammatical gender of one of the verbal arguments (subjects of intransitives and objects of transitives). Not discussed in this study is the behavior of the so-called AI+O (VAIs that show object agreement) subtype (Goddard 1979), which differ in inflection from VAIs and TI/TAs in the independent order, though uniform with the VAI paradigm in their conjunct inflections.

In addition to the pure transitives Ojibwe also has morphologically distinct ditransitive, or double-object, verbs. In the Algonquian tradition objects in ditransitive constructions are termed *primary* (equivalent to indirect objects in English) and *secondary* (equivalent to direct objects).[11] Ditransitive verbs only inflect for the primary object. The secondary object is not morphologically indexed in the verbal morphology. The primary object can be the "recipient, goal, beneficiary, maleficiary, etc." (Bruening 2001, 48), while secondary objects are the "semantic direct objects of double object (ditransitive verbs) and certain animate intransitive verbs"

(Goddard 1974, 319). Additionally, detransitive verbs based on ditransitive stems, such as *wiindamaw* 'tell it to h/,' typically follow the inflectional patterns of transitive verbs, though they can take secondary objects, as illustrated below:

(50) Inda-**wiindamaage** yo'ow sa nagamon
    1-FUT-**tell.people** this EMPH song
    'I shall tell about this song.' (BR.12.06.25.N)

However, interesting for the current study of RCs and discussed further in 3.3.13, when the secondary object is the head of a participle, it may be indexed on the verb's plural marking, as shown in the example below concerning the verb *ataw* 'put it there for h/':

(51) *gaa-pi-atawiyeg**in***

IC-gii-bi-	ataw	-iyeg	**-in**
IC-PST-here-	put.for.h/	-2p>1	**-PL**$_{PRT}$

'the **things** you all have put here for me' (JN.13.12.15.N)

Bruening (2001, 48) notes the restrictions on ditransitives for Passamaquoddy, which also hold for SW Ojibwe, pointing out that the secondary object is never first or second person, but it can be either animate or inanimate. Animate objects must also be obviative with respect to the other animate arguments. Similarities in ditransitive agreement occur in other unrelated languages of the world, including Bantu languages (Henderson 2006, 18).

In the next section I discuss the morphophonological phenomenon known as palatalization. This is an especially important component of the grammar for the argument of a cyclic head movement analysis proposed in 4.2.3.

2.3.3.1. Palatalization

Palatalization is a phonological process resulting in the assimilation of place of articulation from one point toward another more palatal. Widespread in Ojibwe, palatalization occurs at several different levels, all of which provide the same morphophonological environment.[12] Known in the literature as T-palatalization (Kaye and Piggott 1973), dental or alveolar stops assimilate to alveopalatal affricates before a high front vowel /i/ (/ii/ in the double-vowel orthography). This alternation can occur at the root boundary with an epenthetic /i/ inserted (52a.); as the initial sound of the following morpheme at the morpheme boundary in finals and complex finals with the addition of a passive (52b.); or as a detransitive suffix (52c.):[13]

(52) Palatalization

    a. Root boundary /biid=/ 'hither; toward' + epenthetic /-i/

No palatalization	Palatalization
bii*d*aasamose	bii*j*ibatoo
biid-aasam-ose	biid-i-batoo
toward-facing-walk	toward-EPEN-run
's/he is walking this way'	's/he is running this way'

    b. *biinit*= 'make clean' + *-igaade* 'passive'

No palatalization	Palatalization
biini*t*oon	biini*ch*igaade
biinit-oo	biinit-igaade
make.clean-TI2	make.clean-PASS
'clean it'	'it is clean'

    c. *gikend*= 'know' + *-ige* 'detransitive'

No palatalization	Palatalization
gikendan	gikenjige
gikend-am	gikend-ige
know.it-TI1	know.it-DETRANS
'know it'	's/he knows things'

The relevance of this process applies especially to participles, either plural or obviative. When one of the core arguments is head of the construction (shown below in [53a.] and [53c.] below), the normal third-person marker /d/ is palatalized to /j/ before the participle plural or obviative marker.[14] When the third-person marker *-g* is used for AI2 and TI1 stems (53b.) or the head of the construction is a relative root (RR) argument (53d.), no palatalization occurs:

(53) Plural/obviative participle
 a. Plural participle (palatalization)
 gekendaasojig

IC-gikendaaso	-d	-ig
IC-is.educated	-3$_{CONJ}$	-PL$_{PRT}$

 'they who are educated'

 b. Plural participle (no palatalization)
 gekendangig

IC-gikend-	-am	-g	-ig
IC-know.it-	-TI1	-3$_{CONJ}$	-PL$_{PRT}$

 'they who know it'

 c. Obviative participle (palatalization)
 endaanijin

IC-daa	-ni	-d	-in
IC-dwells	-OBV	-3$_{CONJ}$	-OBV$_{PRT}$

 's/he/they$_{OBV}$ who live there'

 d. Obviative RR participle (no palatalization)
 endaanid

IC-daa	-ni	-d
IC-dwells	-OBV	-3$_{CONJ}$

 'where s/he/they$_{OBV}$ live(s)'

The examples above in (52)–(53) exemplify the most relevant aspects of palatalization for the purposes of this study. However, the astute Ojibwe student will notice that the d → j alternation before the high front vowel /i/ (IPA /ɪ/) does not always occur, as in the example below:

(54) No palatalization
 biidinan

biid	-in	-am
toward	-w/hand	-TI1

 'hand it over'

The accepted explanation is a historical one; ultimately, Proto-Algonquian distinguished between short *i and *e, but they have since merged to /i/ in Ojibwe, "so that there is no short /e/" (Valentine 1996, 291).[15] It is claimed that the /i/s that come from PA *i are the vowels that condition the preceding segment to palatalize (Valentine 2001, 88).[16] Since the double-vowel orthography does not capture this distinction, there are certain orthographic /i/s that trigger palatalization and others that do not.[17]

In a few roots, assibilation occurs, where the /d/ will intermittently result in an alveolar fricative, as illustrated by the examples below:

(55) naad- 'fetch; go get; approach'

    naadasabii   *naajidaabii*   *naazikan*

    naad-asab-ii   naad-i-daabii   naad-i-k-am

    fetch-net-AI   fetch-EPEN-drag; pull   fetch-EPEN-foot;body-TI1

    'goes after nets'   'fetches things by sled/wagon'   'go up to it'

Other phonemes also show a palatalization process, though they are not necessarily relevant for the present discussion.[18]

2.3.3.2. Nominalization

Ojibwe makes use of a few processes for deriving nouns. The first is by compounding, where a noun stem combines with a modifying prior member—either a noun stem, a nonstative intransitive verb, or a pronoun (Nichols 1980, 92). The first element can be an existing noun stem, as shown in (56) below, or a verb, as given in (57):

(56) *wiigwaasi-jiimaan* 'birch-bark canoe'
    wiigwaas 'birch-bark' *jiimaan* 'boat/canoe'

(57) *mazina'ige-mazina'igaans* 'credit card'
    mazina'ige 'gets on credit' *mazina'igaans* 'card'

Adjectival initials can also combine with noun stems, as shown here in (58), where the adjectival initial *des=* 'flat' combines with a noun-final *=iiwakwaan* 'hat,' resulting in a new noun stem as shown below:

86 *Ojibwe Morphosyntax*

(58) *wiiwakwaan* 'hat' *desiiwakwaan* 'flat-brimmed hat'
  des= 'flat' *=iiwakwaan* 'hat'

For deverbal nouns, one of two nominalizing suffixes is employed. The first, *=n*, (often perceived as a suffix, *-gan*), is used in cases where the noun referent is some concrete object, usually an instrument or product from verb stems (Nichols 1980, 78).[19] The derivation of one such noun is given in (59).

(59) Nominalizing suffix -n (from Valentine 1994, 258)

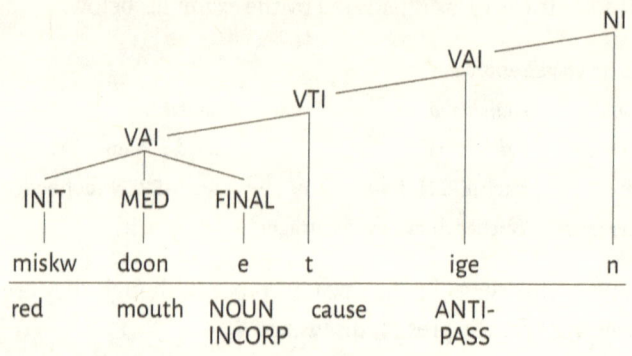

miskodoonechigan 'lipstick'

The other common nominalizing suffix is *=win*, typically used to derive abstract nouns (Valentine 1994, 259) and less frequently resulting in "concrete nouns of instrument and product" (Nichols 1980, 80).

(60) Nominalizing suffix =win (from Valentine 1994, 259)

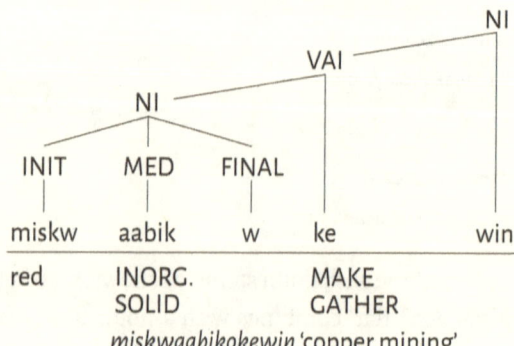

miskwaabikokewin 'copper mining'

The examples in (59) and (60) show the derivations of typical nominalizations in Ojibwe. These derive prototypical nouns capable of the usual inflections for locatives, possessives, diminutives, and pejoratives. These differ from the participial "nominalizations" treated in other studies.

2.3.4. Preverbs

As part of the overall verb structure laid out in (49) above, preverbs are relevant to the discussion of participles and relative clauses, warranting a brief overview here. Table 15 illustrates the position of preverbs. The first type, pv1, is laid out in table 16, based on the linear position in which they occur. The future preverb *da-* occurs in independent verbs only when no personal prefix is present.[20] If a personal prefix is present, the future definite marker is *ga-*. The modal tense marker *daa-* "indicates obligation, permission, possibility (especially with an implied or stated condition), or characteristic activity. Translations normally employ English modals 'should,' 'would,' 'could,' and 'can'" (Nichols 1980, 134). The past tense marker *gii-* indicates completion of the event or activity in the past and has a regular

Table 15. Preverb position classes (modified from Nichols 1980, 128)[a]

	pv1	pv2	pv3	pv4
personal prefixes[b]	tense-mood preverbs	directional preverbs	relative preverbs	lexical preverbs

[a] Not including lexical preverbs, Nichols's (1980, 128) original treatment only recognizes four "categories of verbal prefixes."

[b] Not treated as preverbs, personal prefixes occur in the leftmost slot and are employed only in the independent order. As part of the participant reference system, personal prefixes are essentially the same as those used with possessed nouns indexing the noun possessor.

Table 16. pv1: tense-mood (from Nichols 1980, 133)

B	C	d
aano- 'in vain'	*gii-* past	*wii-* voluntative
da- ga- future	*gii-₂* potential	
daa- modal		
ji- future, modal	c-d	
	bwaa- 'lest'	

changed form *gaa-* under initial change (IC). Nichols also provides /gii-/₂ as "potential." Differing from the past tense *gii-*, /gii-/₂ "occurs in text sentences where the meaning is potential rather than past ... it does not cause tensing of the following lenis consonant and it appears, in at least one example, to have no changed form." Nichols notes the difficulty in accurately describing the preverb, stating, "it has not been possible to elicit examples of the potential so its full range of meaning and occurrences is not known" (1980, 136). The example in (61) below illustrates this "potential" meaning and the lack of tensing of the following lenis consonant:

(61) *gaawiin ominwendanziin giboodiyegwaazon **gii**-biizikang*

gaawiin	o-minwend-am-ziin	giboodiyegwaazon	**gii-**₂-biizik-am-g
NEG	3-like.it-TI1-NEG	pants	**POT**-wear.it-TI1-3_CONJ

'She doesn't like wearing pants' (RD.14.06.11E)

Future "volitional" marker *wii-* of the d position "indicates intention or clear possibility in contrast to the simple future of the b position future prefixes" (137).[21]

Tense preverbs are also found to co-occur, stacking in the order shown above in table 16, as seen in the examples below with a hypothetical, modal perfective function in (62a.) and the past perfective in (62b.):

(62) Tense (pv1) stacking

a. *in**daa-gii**-kiziibiigazhe onzaam idash ingii-ojaanimiz.*

in-**daa-gii**-giziibiigazhe	onzaam	idash	in-gii-ojaanimizi
1-**MOD-PST**-bathes	too.much	but	1-PST-is.busy

'I **should have** showered but I was too busy.' (RT.12.04.03.E)

b. *mii sa minowaa naano-biboon apane niiyogiizhik **gii-wii**-ayaad*

mii	sa	minowaa	naano-biboon	apane	niiyogiizhik	**gii-wii-**ayaa-d
thus	EMPH	and	five-year	always	four.days	**PST-FUT-**be.there-3

'And for 5 years **he had** always **wanted** to be there for four days' (CB.Manoomin)

The second type, directional preverbs or pv2, also formerly known as "locative prefixes" (Nichols 1980, 138), index the direction of a movement

Table 17. Locative prefixes (from Nichols 1980, 138)

Prefix form	Changed prefix form	Verb root form	Meaning
bi-	ba-*	biid-	hither/toward
ani-, ini-	eni-	anim-	thither/away
bimi-	bemi-	bim-	along; by
baa-[a]	—	baam-	locally distributed
babaa-	bebaa-	babaam-	freely distributed
o-, a'o-	we'o-*	—	go over to

* irregular initial change
[a] Nichols (pers. comm.) points out that *baa-* may very well be a truncated form of *babaa-*, given the lack of IC.

Table 18. Relative preverbs (Nichols 1980, 142)[a]

Unchanged form	Changed form	Root	Category	Gloss
ako-	eko-	akw-	distance	'so long; so far; since'
apiichi-	epiichi-	apiit-	extent	'such intensity; such extent'
izhi-	ezhi-	iN-	manner; goal	'thus; thither'
onji-	wenji-	ond-	source; cause	'thence; therefore'
daso-	endaso-	dasw-, das-	frequency; number	'so many'
dazhi-	endazhi-	daN-, da(a)-	place	'there'

[a] Depending on the morphophonemic derivational environment in which they enter, relative roots are subject to palatalization.

or location. Direction and location can be temporal as well as physical. The directional preverbs are laid out in table 17. As the table indicates, many of the directional preverbs have corresponding verbal root forms.

Perhaps most relevant to the present study, relative preverbs play a central role in relative clauses. Each relative preverb is given in table 18.

Central to the current study is the distinction made in argument structure between core arguments (subjects, objects, and secondary objects) and relative root arguments. Addition of a relative root or preverb to the verbal complex typically results in a locative, extent (distance or frequency), manner, or source adjunct argument.

The relative preverb *ako-* pertains to distance and often includes 'so long,' 'so far,' or 'since' in native-speaker translations. It can indicate a physical linear distance:

(63) Linear distance

a. *Aaniin **eko**onagak jiimaan?*

aaniin	IC-**ako**onagad-g	jiimaan
how	IC-**it.is.so.long**-0_{CONJ}	boat

'**How long** is the boat?' (NJ.OPD.akoonagad)

b. ***eko**-gikendamaan gii-abinoojiinyiwiyaang*

IC-**ako**-gikend-am-aan	gii-abinoojiinyiwi-yaang
IC-**REL**-know.it-TI1-1_{CONJ}	PST-be.a.child-1p_{CONJ}

'**what I know about it** when we were kids' (Whipple 2015, 47)

It can also indicate a temporal linear quality when used in the past tense and is translated as 'since':

(64) 'since'

a. *mii ishkwaaj gii-minikwed gaa-**ako**-ayaawaad abinoojiiyan*

mii	ishkwaaj	gii-minikwe-d	IC-gii-**ako**-ayaaw-aad	abinoojiinh-yan
thus	last	PST -drink	-3	IC-PST-**since**-have-3s>3'	child-OBV

'She doesn't drink **since** she had kids' (ES.12.03.28.E)

The relative preverb *apiichi-* relates to the particular extent or degree of an event or action, indicating the extent of quality, quantity, or time (Nichols 1980, 142):

(65) Extent

a. *mii iw **epiichi**-gashkitooyaan ji-apagizomag aw asemaa*

mii	iw	IC-**apiichi**-gashkit-oo-yaan	ji-apagizom-ag	aw	asemaa
thus	DET	IC-**extent**-able-TI2-1s	FUT-throw.w/ voice-1>3	DET	tobacco

'That is the **extent of my ability** to speak for the tobacco.' (JN.13.12.15.N)

b. *waa-**apiichi**gamideg i'iw ziinzibaakwad*
IC-wii-**apiichi**gamide-g   i'iw   ziinzibaakwad
IC-FUT-boils.**just.so**-0_{CONJ}   DET   sugar
'to get the sugar **to the right consistency**' (Whipple 2015, 30)

The manner prefix *izhi-* and root *iN* indicate goal, place, or manner. As Nichols observes, "motion verbs require this prefix if they do not already contain a relative root." When the manner prefix or root occurs, as in (66a.) and (66b.), "the antecedent is an adverb or adverb phrase when manner is indicated" and that "quoted discourse requires /iši-/ on the verb introducing the quotation unless it already contains an appropriate relative root" (1980, 143), as in (66c.):

(66) Manner

a. Manner

*gaa-**izhi**-wiinaawaajin inow Anishinaaben*
IC-gii-izhi-wiinN-aa-waad-in   inow   anishinaabe-n
IC-PST-REL-name.h/-DIR-3p>3'-OBV_{PRT}   DET_{OBV}   indian-OBV

gaa-kabe-bimaadizinijin
IC-gii-gabe-bimaadizi-nid-in
IC-PST-throughout-lives-OBV_{CONJ}-OBV_{PRT}

'The Anishinaabe_{OBV} that were called, *gii-kabe-bimaadizi*' (LS.Ambesanoo)

b. Goal

*ingii-**in**ose iwidi*
in-gii-**in**ose   iwidi
1-PST-**walks.there**   over.there
'I walked there.' (AS.12.03.19.TM)

c. Quotative

"*Gibi-andawataagoom gichi-bikwaakwad,*"
gi-bi-anda-w-ataw-igoom   gichi-bikwaakwad
2-here-seek-EPEN-bet.h/-1p>2p   basketball

izhi-nakwetam awe Migiziins

izhi-nakwetam	awe	Migiziins
REL-answers	DET	PN

'"We've come to challenge you in a game of basketball" answered *Migiziins*' (Stillday 2014, 58)

Also, pervasive in narratives, the manner prefix *izhi-* "links clauses or sentences sequentially," translated commonly as 'then' and 'and so' (144):

(67) *izhi-* 'so then'

mii dash ezhi-giiwed

mii	dash	**IC-izhi**-giiwe -d
thus	and	**IC-manner**-go.home-3

'**So then** he went home' (CB.Manoomin)

Common when relating actions in the past tense, *gaa-izhi-* links clauses sequentially, as in the example below:

(68) **Gaa-izhi**-*debibidood gichi-bikwaakwad awe Bizhikiins*

IC-gii-izhi-debibid-oo-d	gichibikwaakwad	awe	Bizhikiins
IC-PST-REL-get.it-TI2-3$_{CONJ}$	basketball	DET	PN

gaa-izhi-apagidamawaad iniw Maanishtaanishensan

IC-izhi-apagidamaw-aad	iniw	Maanishtaanishan
IC-REL-throw.to.h/-3s>3'$_{CONJ}$	DET$_{OBV}$	PN

'**So then** *Bizhikiins* got the ball **and then** she threw it to *Maanishtaanishens*' (Stillday 2014, 59)

The source or cause prefix *onji-* has an antecedent of a "locative phrase, particle, or noun" as a source (145), as illustrated below in (69), a speaker's response to the question, 'Where are you calling from?':

(69) *onji-* as source

*indooning ind**oonji**-giigid*

in-doon-ing	ind-**onji**-giigido
1-mouth-loc	1-**source**-talks

'I'm calling **from** my mouth' (AS.12.11.18.C)

As a cause its antecedent is a clause or noun phrase (145):

(70) *onji-* as cause

*mii gekinoo'amaageyaan noongom mii **wenji**-gikinoo'amaageyaan **wenji**-*

mii	IC-gikinoo'amaage-yaan	noongom	mii	**IC-onji**-gikinoo'amaage-yaan	**IC-onji**-
thus	IC-teach-1$_{CONJ}$	today	thus	**IC-cause**-teach.h/-1$_{CONJ}$	**IC-cause-**

gikinoo'amawagwaa ingiw gikinoo'amaaganag

gikinoo'amaw-agwaa	ingiw	gikinoo'amaagan-ag
teach.h/-1>3P$_{CONJ}$	DET	student-3p

'That is what I teach today, the **reason** I am teaching, the **reason** I am teaching those students' (Smallwood 2013a, 14)

The frequency or number prefix *daso-* 'so many,' normally refers to either a numeral or quantity phrase, but also functions as an iterative (145–46). Nichols provides *endaso-ziigwaninig* 'every spring' (146) and the example in (71) below:

(71) Iterative with *daso-*

*indayaa imaa **endaso**-naano-giizhigak*

ind-ayaa	imaa	**IC-daso**-naanogiizhigad-k
1-am	there	**IC-every**-Friday-0$_{CONJ}$

'I'm there **on Fridays**.' (AS.12.01.08.E)

However, another iterative strategy is possible in the language, given in the examples below in (72a.) and (72b.):

(72) Iterative suffix
   a. *nayaano-giizhigakin gida-abwezo-inanjigemin*
   IC-naanogiizhigad-g-**in**   gi-da-abwezo-inanjige-min
   IC-Friday-0$_{CONJ}$-**ITER**   2-FUT-sweats-eats.certain.way-21p
   'We'll go eat Thai food **on Fridays**.' (LS.14.11.23.C)

   b. *apane nayaano-giizhigakin naa eyishkwaajanokii-giizhigakin*
   apane   IC-naanogiizhigad-g-**in**   naa   IC-ishkwaajanokiigiizhigad-g-**in**
   always   IC-Friday-0$_{CONJ}$-**ITER**   and   IC-Saturday-0$_{CONJ}$-**ITER**

   apii gaa-niimi'idiwaad
   apii   IC-gii-niimi'idi-waad
   when   IC-PST-dance.together-3p$_{CONJ}$

   'The ceremonial dances held **every** Friday and Saturday' (LS.Aaniindi)

The common use of the relative root or preverb *daso-* is exemplified in the example shown below in (73), where the relative *daso-* is built into the verb as a relative root:

(73) *amanj gaa-**tashi**waagwen ingiw ikwewag*
   amanj   IC-gii-**dashi**-waa-gwen   ingiw   ikwewag
   DUB   IC-PST-**how.many**-3p-DUB   DEM   women
   'I don't know **how many** women there were.' (Whipple 2015, 46)

The relative prefix *dazhi-* 'there' indexes place and "has as antecedent a locative phrase particle or noun" (Nichols 1980, 146). Nichols states its usage denotes emphatic connotations, which coincides with an explanation one of my speaker consultants provided, explaining that it indicates a more specific or precise location, as suggested below in the exchange between the speaker and the author:

(74) *dazhi-* specifically/precisely 'where'
   AS: *Aaniindi gii-waabamad?*
   aaniindi   gii-waabam -ad
   where   PST-see.h/-2>3$_{CONJ}$
   'Where did you see him?'

MS: *Gakaabikaang ingii-waabamaa*
gakaabikaang   in-gii-waabam-aa
Minneapolis   1-PST-see.h/-DIR
'I saw him in Minneapolis'

AS: *Aaniindi gaa-**tazhi**-waabamad?*
aaniindi   IC-gii-**dazhi**-waabam-ad
where   IC-PST-**REL**-see.h/-2>3$_{\text{CONJ}}$
'Where (**exactly**) did you see him?'

MS: Walmart.

Lexical preverbs (pv4) carry the meaning of otherwise independent words. They function as the roots of compounds and are always affixed closer to the verb stem than other preverbs:

(75) *Gaawiin indaa-gashkitoosii ji-izhaayaambaan ind**oondami**-anokii*
    gaawiin   in-daa-gashkit-oo-sii   ji-izhaa-yaam-baan   ind-**ondami**-anokii
    NEG   1-MOD-able-TI2-NEG   to-go-1s-PRET   1s-**busy**-works
    'I can't go because I'm **busy** working.' (ES.12.03.28.E)

The following example in (76) shows all four pv slots filled:

(76) *mii-sh i'iw **gaa-ani-izhi-mino**-ayaad*
    mii   dash   iw   IC-**gii-ani-izhi-mino**-ayaa-d
    thus   then   DET   IC-**pv1-pv2-pv3-pv4**-be.there-3$_{\text{CONJ}}$
    'But then he got better.' (Whipple 2015, 58)

With the basics of internal lexical composition introduced, we can now discuss the systems of inflection for Ojibwe verbs.

2.4. INFLECTIONAL SUBSYSTEMS

Following the conventions established by Bloomfield (1946), Ojibwe verbs are analyzed as occurring in one of four modes or orders of inflection: independent, conjunct, changed conjunct, and imperative. A subcategory of the changed conjunct is the participle, the form of the verb used in RCs.

Table 19. Orders of verbal inflection *wiisini* 's/he is eating'

Number	Order				
	INDEPENDENT	CONJUNCT	CHANGED CONJUNCT	PARTICIPLE	IMPERATIVE
Singular	wiisini 's/he is eating; eats'	wiisinid 'if/when s/he eats'	waasinid 'after s/he eats'	waasinid 's/he who is eating; s/he who eats'	wiisinin! 'eat!'
Plural	wiisiniwag 'they are eating; they eat'	wiisiniwaad 'if/when they eat'	waasiniwaad 'after they eat'	waasinijig 'they who are eating; they who eat'	wiisinig! 'eat!' (plural command)

The syntactic function of a clause and participant reference is determined by the verb's order (Nichols 1980, 106). The imperative order is used in direct commands and hortatives, both positive and negative. Imperative verbs are not relevant to the present topic and will not be further discussed here.[22] Table 19 illustrates the different orders of inflection for a VAI verb.

Often described as serving as "the main predication of a sentence" (Valentine 1994, 177), independent verbs are predicative in the sense that they may serve alone as a complete and well-formed sentence. The independent order is the only inflectional order in which personal prefixes are used; all other participant reference is suffixal.

The conjunct order is further dissected into a *plain conjunct* and a *changed conjunct*. The plain conjunct, sometimes referred to as the "dependent" or "unchanged conjunct" (Bruening 2001, 46), is typically used in verb complement clauses, conditionals, and other subordinate clause types. Glosses of conjunct verbs usually include 'when' or 'if' and 'that' as verbal complements. In generative terms, verbs inflected in the conjunct order have a structural configuration of having a filled COMP (Valentine 1994, 177). The example shown below in (77) illustrates the distinction between the independent, matrix-type clause and the conjunct, or dependent, complement-type clause:

(77) Independent vs. conjunct[23]

[$_{IND}$ niminwendam] [$_{CONJ}$ gii-wiisiniwaad]
ni-minwendam   gii-wiisini-waad
1-am.happy   PST-eats-3p$_{CONJ}$
'I'm glad they ate' (AS.15.07.15.BT)

The conjunct order inflections can be triggered by "conjunctive particles" that create subordinate clauses, requiring verbs in the conjunct order (243). One such particle is the ever-pervasive *mii*, often glossed as 'thus.' Often, *mii* is predicative and requires the conjunct inflection. However, as Nichols points out, "In a number of cases *mii* forms a clause with a noun or locative phrase and the main verb is independent" (Nichols 1980, 118).[24] As a glance over any running narrative will reveal, clauses containing conjunct verbs may be linked with any predicative element and "are simply strung along indicating temporal sequence" (119).

Fairbanks cites Rhodes (1979) in describing the use of conjunct verbs in an independent context as "independent thematic verbs" (Fairbanks 2009, 202). In the example below in (78) (first appearing in Rhodes 1979, 110–11), the conjunct verbs shown in bold serve the expected purpose of verbs inflected for the independent order:

(78) Plain conjunct as independent verbs (Fairbanks 2009, 202)

a) *Gii-pagdosed*   *iidig*   *gaa-dbikak.*
   that s/he walked/CONJ must have   after it got dark

b) *Mkoon*   *iidig*   *gaa-zhi-nkweshkwaad.*
   bear   must have   IC.and so met him/her/CONJ

c) *Aabii-sh ezhaayan?*   *wdigoon-sh ge.*
   where are you going   s/he tells him/her also

d) *Ann Arbor,*   *odinaan ge.*
   Ann Arbor   s/he tells him/her also

e) *Gga-ni-waawiidsemi,* *kido*   *giiwenh wa mko.*
   we will walk together s/he says   apparently this bear

f) *Bbaamsewaad*   *giiwenh nshaawi-dbik.*
   that they walk around/CONJ apparently through the night

a) After it had gotten dark, **he set out walking**.
b) That's how he came to meet this bear.
c) Where ya headed? the bear asked him.
d) Ann Arbor, he replied.
e) Let's walk together, the bear suggested.
f) So **they walked around** through the night.

Pointing out the typical, sentential functions of the conjunct, including subordinate clauses, complements, embedded clauses, and adjunct clauses, Fairbanks (2009) also follows Rhodes (1979) in his analysis of the use of conjuncts in "temporal immediacy," where conjunct clauses do not fall into one of the aforementioned categories of use but instead function as independent clauses. The example below is one such case:

(79) Conjunct as temporal immediacy

*aaniishnaa apane gii-pakade Wenabozho, apane **babaamosed** ingoji*

aaniishnaa	apane	gii-bakade	Wenabozho	apane	babaamose-d	ingoji
well	always	PST-hungry	PN	always	walks.about-3$_{CONJ}$	somewhere

'After all, Wenabozho was always hungry, **he was always walking around somewhere**' (AS.Aadizooked)

Perhaps related to this "temporal immediacy" is what Fairbanks treats as "situational immediacy," where conjunct verbs "are uttered in isolation." Common in conversation, "speakers usually make these comments or remarks in response to an event, action, or situation which has just occurred, either in real time, or within a conversation" (Fairbanks 2009, 211). The situation of their utterance, in Fairbanks's terms, provides the discourse context for such usage, that is, the immediacy, noting that, out of context, speakers typically provide examples inflected for the independent order (212).[25] The following example shows one such case. After dropping his ice cream, one speaker provided the example, inflected for the conjunct order in the "situational immediacy" treated by Fairbanks (2009):

(80) Hay!   **Gii-paninamaan**   iwe   dekaag
     dang   **I.dropped.it**~CONJ~ that   ice.cream
     'Dang, I dropped my ice cream.' (12.03.28.ES.C)

Similarly, for Plains Cree, Cook (2008) makes a distinction between indexical clauses (independent) and contextually rooted anaphoric clauses (conjunct), essentially a lumping of the various functions of the inflectional orders into two categories.

Changed conjunct verbs are verbs with the typical conjunct suffixes but that occur with a word-initial ablaut process "of special focus," referred to as *initial change* (Nichols 1980, 107). Changed conjunct verbs are used in most *wh*-questions, in indicating certain "completive" aspectual information (Fairbanks 2012), and in oblique relative clauses. Costa treats "dependent verbs" in Algonquian as occurring in two subtypes: participles and conjunct verbs. Participles, in this classification, include changed conjunct verbs and form relative clauses in "most Algonquian languages" (1996, 39).

In Rhodes's (1996) analysis, Odawa participles are distinguished from changed conjunct verb forms via the plural and obviative markings occurring on the plural and obviative participles characteristic of nouns. Similarly, Nichols's analysis treats participles as "nominalized verbs" (1980, 106). Rhodes defines a participle as a "specialized inflectional form of the verb that is used in certain types of relative clauses" (Rhodes 1996, 1). For Rhodes, "the sole use of participles is in relative clause constructions" (5). Like Nichols (1980) and Goddard (1987), Rhodes associates the additional plural and obviative participial markings with the head of the RC and warns that certain singular forms may not resemble participles due to the head not requiring the marking; he states that they "look exactly like the corresponding changed conjuncts" (1996, 7). Participles are discussed further in 2.6.2.

2.4.1. Modes

In addition to the subsystems of inflection the Ojibwe verbal system (nonimperative orders) is analyzed as four distinct aspectual or evidential modes: neutral, dubitative, preterit, and preterit dubitative. The neutral mode is the most frequently used and is "unmarked for mode in both meaning and form" (Nichols 1980, 121). The preterit mode is less frequent and contains some variant of the suffix *-ban*. It is a type of irrealis mood that either indicates a past action or event that no longer occurs, or some hypothetical future action or event that is typically "an unlikely" future occurrence (122). The examples given below in (81) show the use of the preterit in the hypothetical future:

(81) Preterit future

a. *Bwaanawichige a'aw inini ji-anokii**pan**.*
bwaanawichige   a'aw   inini   ji-anokii-**pan**
is.unable   that   man   to-**work-3**$_{\text{PRET.CONJ}}$
'That man is unable to work' (ES.OPD.anokii)

b. *Aaniin akeyaa ge-aanikanootamam**ban**?*
aaniin   akeyaa   IC-da-aanikanoot-am-an-**ban**
how   direction   IC.-FUT-translate.it-TI1-2$_{\text{CONJ}}$-**PRET**
'How **would** you translate it?' (AS.11.12.07.C)

The use of the preterit in the past tense is given here in (82):

(82) Preterit past

a. *gichi-mewinzha gii-waabamagi**ban***
gichi-mewinzha   gii-waabam-ag-**iban**
great-long.ago   PST-see.h/-1>3$_{\text{CONJ}}$-**PRET**
'I **haven't** seen her in a long time' (RT.12.04.03.E)

b. *ingii-anokiinaa**ban** iwidi*
in-gii-anokii-naa-**ban**   iwidi
1-PST-works-EXT-**PRET**   over.there
'I **used to** work there' (AS.15.12.20.TM)

Nichols adds that the preterit mode "contrasts with subsequent non-occurrence of that or another event or state. A negative preterit verb marks the inverse: prior non-occurrence contrasted with subsequent occurrence" (121). An example is given below in (83):

(83) Negative preterit
*indaa-gii-minwendaan bi-izhaasigo**ban***
in-daa-gii-minwend-am   bi-izhaa-si-g-**ban**
1-MOD-PST-like.it-TI1   here-go-NEG-3-**PRET**
'I would have been glad if she **hadn't** come' (AS.14.03.14.C)

The preterit is also suffixed to nouns, resulting in a noun referent that 'used to be' or no longer is in existence or use:

(84) Preterit noun
*akiwenziiyi**iban**eg*
akiwenziiy   -**iban**   -eg
old.man   -**PRET**   -3p
'the old men who have since gone on' (PM.Dewe'igan2)

The dubitative mode represents doubt or uncertainty and is used in contexts in which the speaker is not committed to the truth conditions of an utterance. Dubitative verbs often include in the translation 'must be' or 'I wonder':

(85) Dubitative
*mazhiwe**dogenag***
mazhiwe   -**dogenag**
has.sex   -**DUB**$_{3p.IND}$
'**they must be** poonjin' (AS.14.06.26.TM)[26]

The preterit dubitative mode is marked for both preterit and dubitative and indicates both completed action and uncertainty; according to Valentine (1994, 229), it is common in traditional narratives. Preterit dubitative verbs are increasingly rare but can still be found in the speech of older, more conservative speakers:

(86) Preterit dubitative
*ninaanaagadawendaanan ge-gii-kiizhiikam**owaambaanen***
ni-naanaagadawend-am-an   IC-ga-gii-giizhiik-am-**aan-ban-en**
1-contemplate.it-TI1-0p   IC-FUT-PST-finish.it-TI1-**1-PRET-DUB**
'I'm thinking about what I **possibly could have** finished' (LS.14.04.03.C)

Having given the basic introduction to Ojibwe inflection and the various modes recognized in the relevant literature, we turn to a discussion of the participant morphology of the transitive paradigm, organized in terms of a topicality hierarchy.

2.5. TOPICALITY HIERARCHY

The direction morphology of Algonquian languages has traditionally been discussed in terms of direct and inverse in relation to a person or animacy hierarchy, sometimes referred to as an agency or empathy hierarchy (Comrie 1989). Hockett states that there is no morpheme in Algonquian languages equivalent to 'subject' or 'object', but rather these languages possess a morpheme that signals such relations (1966, 69). In transitive animate (TA) verbs and some intransitive verbs based on transitive stems, a morpheme responsible for the direction of a particular action occurs, indicating the syntactic roles of the participants involved (Valentine 1994, 214). Referred to as "theme signs" in the Algonquian literature, these morphemes have been grouped according to their relative function. The first grouping concerns local or speech-act participants (SAP) and the second grouping refers to nonlocal or non-SAP. The local theme signs are given in table 20 for the independent order and table 21 for the conjunct. The nonlocal theme signs are provided in table 22.[27] With TA verbs, three rankable categories exist: person ranking, animacy ranking, and proximate/obviate ranking. Nonlocal theme signs are treated in terms of direct and inverse in accordance with the rankable categories. Valentine collapses all three rankable categories into one hierarchy, which he refers to as the "*Nishnaabemwin* Topicality Hierarchy" (2001, 268), given here in (87):

(87) *Nishnaabemwin* Topicality Hierarchy (Valentine 2001)
  $2 > 1 > X > 3 > 3' > 0$

Basically, when an actor who is either an SAP or a non-SAP is a more highly ranked participant further left on the hierarchy from a non-SAP goal, the direct theme marker /*aa*/ appears. When the action is initiated by an actor ranked lower (further right) than the theme, the inverse morphology /*igw*/ is employed.[28] The notion of whether the second person outranks the first

Table 20. Local theme signs (SAP) independent order[a]

Form	Gloss	Actor	Goal	Theme	Prefix
giwaabam	'you$_{sg}$ see me'	2s	1s	i	gi-
giwaabamim	'you$_{pl}$ see me'	2p	1s	i	gi-
giwaabamimin	'you$_{sg/pl}$ see us'	2	1p	i	gi-
giwaabamin	'I see you$_{sg}$'	1s	2s	iN	gi-
giwaabamininim	'I see you$_{pl}$'	1s	2p	iN	gi-
giwaabamigoo	'we see you$_{sg}$'	1p	2s	igw	gi-
giwaabamigoom	'we see you$_{pl}$'	1p	2p	igw	gi-

[a] The shaded rows in tables 20 and 21 are morphologically identical to the indefinite actor forms and can be translated as 'they (indef.) see you$_{sg}$; you$_{sg}$ are seen' and 'they (indef.) see you$_{pl}$; you$_{pl}$ are seen.' This is the "passive" construction identified by Bloomfield (1958).

Table 21. Local theme signs (SAP) conjunct order

Form	Gloss	Actor	Goal	Theme	Goal suffix	Actor suffix
waabamiyan	'if you$_{sg}$ see me'	2s	1s	I		(y)an
waabamiyeg	'if you$_{pl}$ see me'	2p	1s	I		(y)eg
waabamiyaang	'if you$_{sg/pl}$ see us'	2	1p	I	(y)aang	
waabaminaan	'if I see you$_{sg}$'	1s	2s	iN		Aan
waabaminagog	'if I see you$_{pl}$'	1s	2p	in	Agog	
waabamigooyan	'if we see you$_{sg}$'	1p	2s	Igw	(y)an	
waabamigooyeg	'if we see you$_{pl}$'	1p	2p	Igw	(y)eg	

Table 22. Nonlocal theme signs (non-SAPs) independent order

Form	Gloss	Actor	Goal	Theme	Prefix
niwaabamaa	'I see h/'	1s	3s	aa	ni-
niwaabamig	's/he sees me'	3s	1s	igw	ni-
giwaabamaa	'you$_{sg}$ see h/'	2s	3s	aa	gi-
giwaabamig	's/he sees you$_{sg}$'	3s	2s	igw	gi-
owaabamaan	's/he sees h/$_{obv}$'	3s	3'	aa	o-
owaabamigoon	's/he/they$_{obv}$ see h/'	3'	3s	igw	o-

Table 23. Nonlocal theme signs (non-SAPs) conjunct order

Form	Gloss	Actor	Goal	Theme	Goal suffix	Actor suffix
waabamag	'if I see h/'	1s	3s			Ag
waabamid	'if s/he sees me'	3s	1s	i		D
waabamad	'if you_sg see h/'	2s	3s			Ad
waabamik	'if s/he sees you_sg'	3s	2s	iN		G
waabamaad	'if s/he sees h/_obv'	3s	3'	aa		D
waabamigod	'if s/he/they_obv see h/'	3'	3s	igw		

has been contested with no real evidence of a ranking relationship observed (Bruening 2001; Hockett 1966; Nichols 1980). Bruening describes this arrangement with the independent prefixes marking the proximate argument whereas the theme signs determine if this argument is the subject or object (2001, 43). This is an important feature of the system of agreement endorsed in this study.

The conjunct transitive (TA) inflections are much more fusional than those of the independent order and the themes are "irrespective of localness" (Valentine 1994, 223). This is illustrated in table 23. Ultimately, theme signs are the morphological realizations of agreement and are important for the discussion of feature checking and case assignment earlier in 1.5.

2.5.1. Obviation

Another interesting aspect of Ojibwe grammar (and Algonquian languages in general) necessary for the present discussion is the notion of obviation: "the obviative is an inflectional category of Algonquian languages that marks one third-person referent as different from some other third-person referent in the immediate context" (Rhodes and Todd 1981, 57). As seen in 1.4.2 I follow Bruening (2001) in the treatment of obviation as a type of case marking. All animate nouns in Ojibwe are either proximate, essentially the focal participant in a given discourse, or obviative, a backgrounded participant. Traditionally considered to be a "syntactic/discourse feature of relative prominence," obviation is similar to case-marking systems employed to keep track of multiple participants within a clause. Both verbs and noun phrases may bear the morphological obviative markings, the absence of which represents the proximate argument:

(88) Obviation

a. *ogii-ashaamaan **iniw** akiwenzii**yan** gii-pakade**ni**d a'aw ikwe*

o-gii-asham-aa-**n**	**iniw**	akiwenzii-yan	gii-bakade-**ni**-d	a'aw	ikwe
3-PST-feed.h/-DIR-**OBV**	**DET**_{obv}	old.man-**OBV**	PST-hungry-**OBV**-3	DET_{prox}	woman

'The woman_{prox} fed the old man_{obv} when he was hungry' (AS.16.02.03.GJ)

b. *ogii-ashaamaan **iniw** akiwenzii**yan** gii-pakaded a'aw ikwe*

o-gii-asham-aa-**n**	**iniw**	akiwenzii-yan	gii-bakade-d	a'aw	ikwe
3-PST-feed.h/-DIR-**OBV**	**DET**_{obv}	old.man-**OBV**	PST-hungry-3	DET_{prox}	woman

'The woman_{prox} fed the old man_{obv} when she was hungry' (AS.16.02.03.GJ)

As the examples above indicate, the only difference between (88a.) and (88b.) is the conjunct obviative morpheme /-ni/ suffixed to *bakade* in (88a.). The 'woman' of the examples is said to be proximate, or the "entity at the focus of interest" (Hockett 1966, 60). The system of concord can differentiate proximate participants not only by affixes on verbs and nouns, but also by way of proximate/obviative determiners, for example, *a'aw* versus *iniw* above (treated as demonstrative pronouns in 2.3.2). Valentine points out that number is neutralized under obviation in many dialects of Ojibwe (1994, 184). So, for many dialects, the examples shown in (88a.) and (88b.) above could also be translated as having plural obviative arguments: 'The woman fed the old men when they were hungry' (88a.) and 'The woman fed the old men when she was hungry' (88b.). The number distinction under obviation is an important dialect parameter and is discussed in 3.3.4.

Word order is quite flexible in Ojibwe, eliminating the possibility for ambiguity through this system of obviation. Shifts in proximate/obviative participants can and often do occur over the span of a given discourse, dependent upon which particular participant is considered most focal at any given point, as seen in the example provided here in (89):

(89) Obviative/proximate shift
Gii-maaminonaabamaad Bizhikiinsan anzhikegaabawinid[29]

Gii-maaminonaabam-aad	bizhikiins-**an**	anzhikegaabawi-**ni**-d
PST-notice.h/-3s>3'	PN-**OBV**	stand.alone-**OBV**-3

apagidamowaad
apagidamaw-aad
throw.to.h/-3s>3'

gii-ni-biinjwebinang Bizhikiins

gii-ani-biinjwebin-am-g	bizhikiins
PST-away-throw.in-TI1-3	PN

'When **he**_prox_ saw **Bizhikiins**_obv_ standing alone, **he**_prox_ threw it to **her**_obv_ and **she**_prox_ went and threw it in.' (Stillday 2014, 63)

Bruening points out that "obviation can change within a sentence. It must be set within a clause, between co-arguments, but it is not necessarily maintained across clause boundaries" (2001, 38–39). Once a nominal is marked obviative, especially as a possessed argument, it may become proximate:

(90) *Mii dash **iniwen odikweman iniwen** chimookomaan-ikwen*

thus	then	DET_OBV_	h/woman_OBV_	DET_OBV_	whiteman-woman-**OBV**

mii awe bebaa-wiindaawasod iwidi ayi'iing Gaa-zagaskwaajimekaag

mii	awe	IC-babaa-wiindaawaso-d	iwidi	ayi'iing	Gaazagaskwaajimekaag
thus	DET_PROX_	IC-around-give.names-3_PROX_	there	PPN	Leech.Lake

'And **his woman**_obv_ is a **white woman**_obv_, that's **who**_prox_ is going around giving names in Leech Lake' (RD.14.06.11.C)

While the third-person argument is always indexed as proximate (zero morpheme), Valentine points out that "all other animate third persons associated with the predication either in complements or adjuncts are either obligatorily or optionally marked with overt obviate marking" (1994, 183).

Table 24. Plural and obviative suffixes

Animate nouns			AI verbs		
SINGULAR	PLURAL	OBVIATIVE	SINGULAR	PLURAL	OBVIATIVE
amik 'beaver'	amik**wag** 'beavers'	amik**wan** 'beaver(s)'	dajise 's/he is late'	dajise**wag** 'they are late'	dajise**wan** 's/he/they$_{obv}$ are late'
akik 'kettle'	akik**oog** 'kettles'	akik**oon** 'kettle(s)'	dagoshin 's/he arrives'	dagoshin**oog** 'they arrive'	dagoshin**oon** 's/he/they$_{obv}$ arrive'

The obviative argument is often referred to as "second third person" (Baraga 1850; Wilson 1870, 35) or "fourth person" (Fairbanks, pers. comm.).[30]

Third-person dependent kinship terms (91) and all other third-person animate possessed terms (92) are obligatorily marked for obviation:

(91) =sayenhy 'older brother'

  nisayenh(yag)   gisayenh(yag)   osayen**yan**   osayenyiwaan
  ni-sayenh (yag)   gi-sayenh (yag)   o-sayenh-**yan**   o-sayenhy-iwaa-**n**
  1-brother (PL)   2-brother (PL)   3-brother-**OBV**   3-brother-3p-**OBV**
  'my older   'your older   'h/ older   'their older
  brother(s)'   brother(s)'   brother(s)'   brother(s)'

(92) odaabaan 'car'

  indoodaabaan(ag)   gidoodaabaan(ag)   odoodaabaan**an**   odoodaabaaniwaan
  ind-odaaban (ag)   gid-odaabaan (ag) od-odaabaan-**an** od-odaaban-iwaa-**n**
  1-car (PL)   2-car (PL)   3-car-**OBV**   3-car-3p-**OBV**
  'my car(s)'   'your car(s)'   'h/ car(s)'   'their car(s)'

The pattern of obviative marking for nouns generally follows that of the proximate plural form. Rather than the final /g/ represented in the animate plural form, final /n/ occurs in the obviative forms. For independent AI verbs, the same pattern (with /n/ in place of /g/) holds, as given in table 24.

In the following section I provide a discussion of initial change, first its form and then its multiple functions.

2.6. INITIAL CHANGE

Initial change (IC) is the traditional term used among Algonquianists to refer to the first-syllable ablaut process verbs may undergo in certain focus constructions, most *wh*-questions, completive aspect, and participles used in RCs. It is a single ablaut process that applies to the initial vowel of the "verb complex" (Valentine 1994, 179) or the first vowel of the "extended verb," in Bruening's (2001, 46) terms. As described above in section 2.3.4, preverbs occurring in the verb complex are also subject to IC. As stated above, IC can only occur on conjunct verbs. As noted by Valentine (1996, 309–10), the form of IC varies across dialects; the variation in SW Ojibwe is provided in 3.3.11. The pattern of IC in general Ojibwe is given here again:

(93) Initial change in General Ojibwe

Unchanged vowel	Changed vowel
a	*e-*
i	*e-*
o	*we-*
aa	*ayaa-*
e	*aye-*
ii	*aa-*
oo	*waa-*

As the pattern given in (93) indicates, all short vowels are lengthened while long vowels /aa/ and /e/ take a prefixed /ay-/ in their changed forms.[31] According to Valentine, IC is a "very ancient process no longer derivable by any phonological mechanism of feature change," but he mentions evidence that suggests it involved "a principal phonological mutation." He also points out that all vowels resulting from IC are non-high and do not include round short vowels (1994, 136).

In addition to the typical change presented in (94) above, there are certain relative roots and preverbs that show a specialized pattern of IC. Relative preverbs *daso-* 'amount' and *dazhi-* 'place' from table 18 in 2.3.4 prefix *en-* rather than the typical /a/ → /e/ vowel change. This exception is common across Algonquian languages in general; verbs that undergo this process are referred to as "t-verbs" (Costa 1996, 41).³² Nichols also notes the irregular IC pattern on certain directional prefixes such as the *bi-* 'hither; here,' which changes to *ba-* as opposed to the normal i- → e- pattern of IC. Also, the directional prefix *o-* 'go over to' changes to *we'o-* as opposed to the expected *we-* of IC (1980, 138, 147–48). Certain preverbs such as *aano-* 'in vain' show no IC form, though Baraga provides *ayaano-* (cited in Nichols 1980, 133). Similarly, I have been unsuccessful in eliciting an IC form for the lexical preverb *wenda-* 'especially,' which varies between *enda-* and *waanda-*.

Variation in IC is an interesting subject not only for Ojibwe, but for the Algonquian language family in general. The pattern for IC shown in both Baraga (1850) and Wilson (1870, 35) is the same pattern still found today at Lac du Flambeau, Lac Courte Oreilles, St. Croix and Mille Lacs, accounting for all seven vowels. Nichols points out that the form of IC he found in use for the Mille Lacs dialect was the "same as that described by Bloomfield (1958, 4.2) although this is not universal for Ojibwe dialects" (1980, 146–47). Also, for Odawa specifically, participles are "more conservative with respect to the innovation of treating the change morpheme as a prefix *e-*" (Rhodes 1996, 4). Often dubbed the "aorist" prefix (Valentine 1994; Costa 1996; Goddard 1987), and common in related Algonquian languages, it is rare in the Southwestern varieties. One speaker from Onigum provided the following examples under elicitation:

(94) Aorist prefix *e-* (JB.13.07.17.E)

a. *Awenen **e**-nagamod*

awenen   e-nagamo-d
who   **AOR**-sings-3$_{CONJ}$
'Who is singing'

b. *Awenenag **e**-nagamowaad*

awenen-ag   e-nagamo-waad
who-3p   **AOR**-sings-3p$_{CONJ}$
'Who$_{PL}$ is singing?'

Valentine (1994, 324) also notes the prefix used in complement clauses in Odawa in seemingly unrelated IC contexts.³³ Although it is common in Al-

Table 25. *gaa-* prefix in place-names

Ojibwe name	Place	Gloss
Gaa-miskwaawaakokaag	Cass Lake, Minn.	'Place of the red cedars'
Gaa-zagaskwaajimekaag	Leech Lake, Minn.	'Place of many leeches'
Gaa-zhiigwanaabikokaag	Hinckley, Minn.	'Place of the grindstone'
Gaa-waabaabiganikaag	White Earth, Minn.	'Where there is an abundance of clay'
Gaa-zhingwaakokaag	Pine Grove Leadership Academy, Sandstone, Minn.	'Place of the white pine'
Gaa-mitaawangaagamaag	Sandy Lake, Minn.	'Place of the sandy bottom'
Gaa-niizhogamaag	Twin Lakes, Minn.	'Place of two lakes'
Gaa-waawiyegamaag	Round Lake, L.C.O., Wisc.	'Where the lake is round'

gonquian languages, Brittain (2001, 84) makes a distinction between what she calls IC infixation (ablaut) and IC prefixation (*e-* prefix or *gaa-*) in Western Naskapi, with the prefixation strategy "increasingly favored." Such innovation is also reported by Wolfart (1973) for Plains Cree. Costa (1996) provides a thorough description of IC in several Algonquian languages; many innovations have been shared across the Algonquian family.[34]

Mentioned in Costa (1996) is the cross-family tendency to innovate IC strategies with the aorist prefix mentioned above and the prefix *gaa-*, often referred to as a relativizer or nominalizer.[35] Introduced above in 1.3.3 and attested in a number of the more northern SW Ojibwe communities, the *gaa-* prefix is employed in a number of *wh-*environments, where IC is expected. It is plausible to associate the prefix with the homophonous *gaa-*, common in old naming conventions found throughout the language. Shown in table 25, many proper names of places bear the prefix, often translated as 'place of,' 'that which,' or 'where'. The variation observed concerning the *gaa-* prefix in complementary distribution with IC is discussed in 3.3.11 and 3.3.13.3, while the argument for *gaa-* being a morphological realization of *wh-*movement and innovative strategy for IC is provided in 4.2.2.2 and 4.1.2.

The multiple functions of initial change have not adequately been described in the literature. Nichols (1980) follows Rogers in her analysis of the function of IC, in which she vaguely states that IC indicates explicit focus "on a participant, or the circumstance, or some other aspect of the verb complex" (Rogers 1978, 168; quoted in Nichols 1980, 128). Rogers also expresses the difficulty in characterizing the meaning of IC:

> Attempts to predict the occurrences of changed as opposed to simple conjunct forms on formal syntactic or specific lexical grounds-that is, in certain types of constructions or with particular lexical items-reveal no more than tendencies, to which exceptions can nearly always be found. (Rogers 1978, 175; cited in Nichols 1980, 148)

Nichols also points out that many verbs with IC have either relative roots or preverbs which "generally have explicit focus on the circumstance of the event, in the technical sense of the term introduced by Rogers (1978, 169), "self-centered predications" (Nichols 1980, 149).

In the current analysis I determine IC to be a morphological realization of *wh*-movement, discussed further in chapter 4. This is applies to *wh*-questions (2.6.1), participles used in RCs (2.6.2), and changed conjuncts with past/completive interpretations (2.6.3).

2.6.1. Wh-questions

An important aspect of the grammar in which IC occurs is with *wh*-questions triggered by *wh*-pronouns or A-pronouns for Ojibwe. Sometimes referred to as "interrogative particles" (Valentine 1994, 250) or "interrogative adverbs" (Nichols, Ojibwe People's Dictionary), interrogative pronouns generally trigger IC and always require conjunct verbal morphology. Table 26 illustrates *wh*-questions in Ojibwe.

As the table indicates, the mere presence of the A-pronoun triggers IC. This is the case for all A-questions in Ojibwe, with the exception of location questions with *aaniindi*. For location, IC is only required on verbs with relative roots, questions with goal or source, and dubitative clauses with *dibi* (Nichols 1980, 150). Previous confusion concerning IC with A-questions was documented early on, with Baraga (1850) including in his rule 4 of the change that "the *Change* is made sometimes; but ordinarily it is not used" (1850, 137). *Wh*-questions inquiring about source, cause, or reason generally have either a relative root *ond-* or prefix *onji-*, as discussed above in 2.3.4.

Table 26. Ojibwe A-pronouns (*wh*-questions)

A-pronoun	Varying forms	Gloss	Example	Gloss
aaniin	aaniish; aansh	'how; what (abstract)'	Aaniin ezhichigeyan?	'What are you doing?'
aaniin apii	aaniin wapii; aaniin wapiish; ampiish; aaniish apii; aansh apii	'when; what time'	Aaniin apii gaa-pi-dagoshinan?	'When did you get here?'
aaniin dash	aaniish; aansh	'why; what for'	Aaniish wendiyan?	'What is the matter with you?'
aaniindi	aandi; aandish	'where'	Aaniindi wenjibaayan?	'Where are you from?'
awegonen	awegonesh; wegonen; wegonesh	'what (concrete)'	Awegonen waa-miijiyan?	'What do you want to eat?'
awenen	awenesh; wenen; wenesh	'who'	Awenen gaa-piidood?	'Who brought it?'

ª Nichols includes an example where the "appropriate question word" for relative root *onji-* is *wegonen* and gives *wegonesh gaa-onji-biidood?* 'Why did he bring it?' (1980, 145). One example occurs in Jones (2013c, 51): *Wegonen dash wenji-miinigooyaan waabikwaanan?* 'Why did they give me white hairs?'

As I propose in chapter 4, *wh*-questions in Ojibwe involve head movement of the verb to a FOCUS position of the split-CP structure. IC in this approach is the morphological realization of this movement.

2.6.2. Participles

Participles are nominal-like verbs that have undergone IC and often bear special nominal plural or obviative markings. They can be used in place of nouns or with nouns where they serve as modifying, relative clauses. Participles differ from full nominalizations such as those discussed above in 2.3.3.2. They lack many of the categories of prototypical nouns such as possessives, diminutives, and locatives, and they can carry verbal inflections not found on other kinds of nominals, such as tense and direction (Valentine 2001, 177). Participles may be formed from any verb subtype (TA, TI, AI, II) in both positive and negative polarities.

Importantly for the current study, I treat participles as the verb of rela-

Table 27. VTI1 and VAI2 plural participle

mikwendan *vti1* 'remember it'		mikwendam *vai2* 's/he remembers'	
mikwendang 'that s/he remembers it'	plain conjunct mikwend-am-g remember-TI1-3	*mikwendang* 'that s/he remembers'	plain conjunct mikwendam-g remember-3
mekwendang 'the one who remembers it; what s/he remembers'	changed conjunct IC-mikwend-am-g IC-remember-TI1-3	*mekwendang* 'the one who remembers'	changed conjunct IC-mikwendam-g IC-remember-3
*mekwend***angig** 'those who remember it'	plural participle IC-mikwend-am-g-ig IC-remember-TI1-3-PL$_{PRT}$	*mekwend***angig** 'those who remember'	plural participle IC-mikwendam-g-ig IC-remember-3-PL$_{PRT}$

tive clauses. Nichols treats participles as "nominalized conjunct verbs" and though for every conjunct verb there is at least one corresponding participle, only certain participles with third persons as heads differ in morphological form from their corresponding changed conjunct verbs (1980, 148). Participles are often treated as a sort of hybrid, "consisting of verbal bases, showing much verbal inflection, but having some noun-like inflectional features, and functioning as nouns in sentences" (Valentine 2001, 510). Similar to the authors before him, Wilson noticed the frequency of participles in Ojibwe and remarked on their use as a "relative pronoun, and answering for both noun and adjective" (1870, 7).

Due to the frequency of the plural participle formed on vowel-ending verb stems, participles are often conceptualized and discussed as *-jig* forms by some speakers, teachers, and students alike. The third-person conjunct suffix is selected based on the final segment of the verb's stem; vowel-final stems select a final *-d* for the third person, while *-g* occurs elsewhere. The unit *-jig* then consists of a participial morpheme *-i* that forces $d \rightarrow j$ palatalization along with the animate plural marker *-g*. As shown in (53) above, for TI1 and AI2 verbs, the *-g* is selected over the *-d* for the third-person conjunct, resulting in *-angig* for the plural participle form. As the data in table 27 indicate, the third-person conjunct marker assimilates to the place of articulation for the stem-final nasal and no palatalization occurs.

Nichols explains the peculiarity of participle plural marking where "peripheral suffixes appear and the use of /waa/ differs." Number and obviative marking peripheral suffixes index the "nominal category of the head of the construction," while /-waa/ only indexes the third-person participant, which is not the head of construction (Nichols 1980, 200). For example an AI verb's participial peripheral suffix -*ig* replaces the regular conjunct pluralizer -*waa*. This difference is illustrated here in (95):

(95) Plural -*waa* vs. participial -*ig*

a. *waa*- pluralizer

*mii iw gekinoo'amawag**waa***

mii	iw	IC-gikinoo'amaw-ag-**waa**
thus	DET	IC-teach.h/-1>3$_{CONJ}$-**3p$_{CONJ}$**

'That's what I teach them' (AS.12.01.08.N)

b. -*ig* participle marker

*mii ingiw gekinoo'amawag**ig***

mii	ingiw	IC-gikinoo'amaw-ag-**ig**
thus	DET	IC-teach.h/-1>3$_{CONJ}$-**PL$_{PRT}$**

'Those are the ones I teach' (AS.12.01.08.E)

This is the main difference in participles as they occur in the southern varieties as opposed to those found in the north. As will be discussed in chapter 3 most speakers of more northern communities do not use the nominal participial markings found across the south.[36]

Also, obviative participles are doubly marked since "the thematic obviative suffix -*ni* is used as in the conjunct verb, but a peripheral suffix also indexes the obviation of the participant" (Nichols 1980, 200). The example given below in (96) shows this:

(96) Obviative participle

ayaakozinijin

IC-aakozi	**-ni**	-d	**-in**
IC-sick	**-OBV**	-3$_{CONJ}$	**-OBV$_{PRT}$**

'the sick one(s)$_{OBV}$; the one(s)$_{OBV}$ who are sick'

Table 28. TI third-person participles (from Nichols 1980, 201–2)

Subject head		Object head	
3-O, Op	-ang	3-O	-ang
		3-Op	-angin
3p-O, Op	-angig	3p-O	-amowaad
		3p-Op	-amowaajin
3'-O, Op	-aminijin	3'-O	-aminid
		3'-Op	-aminijin

Here we have the normal conjunct obviative marker *ni-* with a third-person marker *-d*. The *-d* undergoes palatalization with the affixation of *-in*, a nominal inflectional marker for obviation (Valentine 2001, 510). Containing one verbal inflection for obviation and another "external" nominal inflection for obviation, this is a "peculiarity" of the obviative participle (Rhodes 1996, 5).

Nichols indicates that for each transitive verb with two third-person participants, there are two possible participial forms for each possible participant relationship, "one with the subject as the head of the construction and one with the object as head of the construction" (1980, 201). Valentine mentions "de-participlized nouns" that have lost their conjunct verbal inflection and been lexicalized as nouns and can take a locative suffix; he also mentions "participial nominals" that show IC but no other formal features of participles (2001, 514–15).[37] One such example is given below in (97):

(97) Participial nominal
gekaanyag
IC-gikaa   -yag
IC-s/he.is.elderly   -3p$_{NOM}$
'old people' (LS.14.03.24.C)

The example above shows initial change on the verb *gikaa*, which takes a normal noun plural suffix rather than the participle plural marker. Such examples are rare but occur occasionally in conversation. Another seemingly related example involves the neologism for 'wheel,' shown here in (98):

(98) *detibise*
 IC-ditibise
 IC-it.rolls
 'wheel' (Clark and Gresczyk 1991)[38]

The example above does not show a conjunct suffix, expected with IC. Furthermore, the plural, given below in (99), takes a normal nominal plural rather than the participial plural, which is also attested among southern speakers:[39]

(99) *detibiseg*
 IC-ditibise   -g
 IC-it.rolls   -PL$_{NOM}$
 'wheels' (Clark and Gresczyk 1991)

Another peculiarity of participles is their ability to focus on the theme or secondary object of the ditransitive verb (mentioned above in 2.3.3). Typically, for ditransitive verbs in Ojibwe, only the primary object is overtly accounted for in the verbal morphology; the secondary object is not represented. The verbal morphology of ditransitive verbs reveal no animacy or number distinction for secondary objects, as shown in (100a.) and (100b.). The participle, however, reveals number when the head of the participle is plural. Compare the singular participle in (100c.) to the plural participle in (100d.):

(100) Secondary object inflection
 a. Singular secondary object
 bezhig dibaajimowin ingii-miinaa
 bezhig   dibaajimowin   in-gii-miiN-aa
 one   story   1-PST-give.h/-DIR
 'I gave her one story' (AS.13.07.16.E)

 b. Plural secondary object
 niizh odaabaanan ingii-miinaa
 niizh   odaabaan-an   in-gii-miiN-aa
 two   car-OBV   1-PST-give.h/-DIR
 'I gave her two cars' (AS.13.07.16.E)

c. Singular participle

gaa-pi-atawiyeg

IC-gii-bi-ataw-iyeg

IC-PST-here-put.for.h/-2p>1$_{\text{CONJ}}$

'what (sing.) you (pl.) have put here for me' (JN.13.12.15.N)

d. Plural participle

gaa-pi-atawiyegin

IC-gii-bi-ataw-iyeg-**in**

IC-PST-here-put.for.h/-2P>1$_{\text{CONJ}}$-**PL**$_{\text{PRT}}$

'the thing**s** you (pl.) have put here for me' (JN.13.12.15.N)

Crucial to the current study, participles are often used in place of nouns as a headless relative clause (101) or as relative clauses modifying existing noun phrases (102):

(101) Headless RC

*niminwendaan ganawaabamagwaa **zhayaazhiibaabagizojig***

ni-minwend-am	ganawaabam-agwaa	IC-zhaazhiibaabagizo-d-ig
1-like.it-TI1	watch.h/-1>3p	IC-hoop.dances-3-PL$_{\text{PRT}}$

'I like watching **hoop dancers/the ones that hoop dance**.' (AS.13.05.01.OPD)

(102) Postnominal RC

*mii go gii-kiiwanimowaagwen ingiw chi-ayaa'aag **gaa-nitaawigi'ijig***

mii	go	gii-giiwanimo-waa-gwen	ingiw	chi-aya'aa-g	IC-gii-nitaawigi'-id-ig
thus	EMPH	PST-lies-PL-DUB	DET	great-being-3p	IC-PST-raise.h/-3>1-PL$_{\text{PRT}}$

'then those elders **that raised me** must have been lying too' (Smallwood 2013c, 117)

As mentioned above in 2.6.1, the distinct plural participles are also employed in *wh*-questions (interrogative mode) with *awenen(ag)* 'who (pl.)' and *awegonen(an)* 'what' and in the dubitative mode where the head of the construction is plural. The plural (neutral mode) participles differ in form from the plural dubitative participles, as the examples below in (103) and (104) indicate:

(103) Plural participle (neutral mode) (from Nichols 1980, 120)
awenenag nebaajig

awenen-ag	IC-nibaa-**d-ig**
who-3p	IC-sleeps-3_{CONJ}-**PL**$_{PRT}$

'Who (pl.) is sleeping?'

(104) Plural participle (dubitative mode)
*awegwenag nebaagwen**ag***[40]

awegwen-ag	IC-nibaa-gwen-**ag**
I.wonder.who-3p	IC-sleeps-3_{DUB}-**PL**$_{PRT}$

'I wonder who (pl.) is sleeping?'

Participles are also theoretically possible in both polarities, positive and negative. Negative participles have a "the ones that aren't X" interpretation, as the examples below illustrate:

(105) Negative participles[41]

a. VAI

*gii-pi-izhaawag akina ingiw oshkinaweg **waadigesigog***

gii-bi-izhaa-ag	akina	ingiw	oshkinawe-g	IC-wiidige-**sigw-ig**
PST-here-go-3p	all	DET	young.men-3p	IC-marry-**NEG-PL**$_{PRT}$

'All of the young men came **that weren't married**' (JS.unknown.date.N)

b. VII

*ogii-mamoonan iniw waawanoon **gaa-michaasinogin***

o-gii-mam-oo-an	iniw	waawan-oon	IC-gii-michaa-**sinog-in**
3-PST-take-TI2-0p	DET	egg-0p	IC-PST-is.big-**NEG-PL**$_{PRT}$

'He took the eggs **that weren't big**' (AS.14.01.01.C)

While plural participles (where the head of the participle is plural) are quite easy to identify due to their additional nominal markings, participles where the head is singular have overlapping morphological shape. Nichols remarks on this overlap and contrast in the mixed set and provides the examples shown here:

(106) Contrast in mixed set (from Nichols 1980, 201)

    a. overlap
    wayaabamag
    IC-waabam-ag
    IC-see.h/-1>3
    'I who see him; he who I see'

    b. contrast

wayaabamagwaa	*wayaabamag**ig***
IC-waabam-ag-waa	IC-waabam-ag-**ig**
IC-see.h/-1>3-PL$_{CONJ}$	IC-see.h/-1>3-**PL**$_{PRT}$
'I who see them'	**'they who** I see'

He goes on to state:

> In transitive verbs with two third person participants, there are two forms for each possible participant relationship; one with the subject as head of the construction and one with the object as head of the construction. As the singular suffixes are both zero in form, there is some overlap. The TA examples below use direct themes but there are parallel forms with the inverse theme. With the subject as head:
>
> *wayaabamaad* 'he who sees the other'
> *wayaabamaajig* 'they who see the other'
>
> With the object as head:
>
> *wayaabamaajin* 'the other who he sees'
> *wayaabamaawaajin* 'the other who they see'
>
> There is also contrast in the mixed set where there is overlap:
>
> *wayaabamag* 'I who see him'; 'he who I see'
> *wayaabamagwaa* 'I who see them'
> *wayaabamagig* 'they who I see'
> (Nichols 1980, 201)

The question, then, lies in distinguishing a participle from a changed conjunct verb. Third-person forms are phonetically identical in the singular though distinguished in the plural. Syntactic evidence shows that word order can play a role in the differentiation, as the examples reveal in (107a.), where the changed conjunct occurs clause-initially, whereas in (107b.) it is interpreted as a participle in a relative clause:

(107) Changed conjunct vs. participle[42]

    a. Changed conjunct
gaa-aabajitood ogii-azhe-atoon
IC-gii-aabajit-oo-d   o-gii-azhe-at-oo-n
IC-PST-use.it-TI2-3   3-PST-return-put.it-TI2-0
'**After he used it** he put it back' (AS.14.06.24.BT)

    b. Singular participle
ogii-azhe-atoon gaa-aabajitood
o-gii-azhe-at-oo-n   IC-gii-aabajit-oo-d
3-PST-return-put.it-TI2-0   IC-PST-use.it-TI2-3
'He put back **what he used**' (AS.14.06.24.BT)

Similar examples are frequent in textual examples, as seen here in (108) with plural arguments with the plural third-person argument head of the relative clause donning the participial inflection *-ig* (108a.) while the changed conjunct in (108b.) shows the plain conjunct third-person plural marker *-waa(d)*:

(108) 3p participle vs. changed conjunct (from Whipple 2015, 8)

    a. *mii giiwenh ingiw bemi-nishwanaajichige**jig***
mii   giiwenh   ingiw   IC-bimi-nishwanaajichige-**d-ig**
thus   supposedly   DET   IC-along-does.damage-**3-PL**$_{PRT}$
'**the ones who** make tornadoes as they go by'

    b. *bemi-gichi-nishwanaajichige**waad** ingiw aaningodinong*
IC-bimi-gichi-nishwanaajichige-**waad**   ingiw   aaningodinong
IC-along-great-does.damage-**3p**   DET   sometimes
'sometimes they go by and raise hell'

Following Rhodes, I treat participles as being associated with the head of the RC. Rhodes adds, "thus in transitive clauses with singular inanimate primary object heads the verb forms may not look like participles simply because the head does not require the marking of either the plural or obviative" (1996, 5). More often than not the identification and distinction between a singular or plural participle can be made through concord, where number agreement is carried out throughout the clause. Number agreement morphology can be observed in the examples below in (109), with the singular represented with a zero morpheme in (109a.) and the plural marked in (109b.):

(109) Number agreement

   a. Singular agreement

   *niwii-ayaan **iw** aabajichigan ayaabajitood aw inini*

ni-wii-ay-aa-0	**iw**	aabajichigan-**0**	IC-aabajit-oo-d	aw	inini
1-FUT-have-TI4-**0s**	**DET**$_{SG}$	tool-**0s**	IC-use.it-TI2-3	DET	man

   'I need the **tool** that man is using' (AS.13.07.16.E)

   b. Plural agreement

   *niwii-ayaan**an** **iniw** aabajichigan**an** ayaabajitoo**jin** aw inini*

ni-wii-ay-aa-**an**	**iniw**	aabajichigan-**an**	IC-aabajit-oon-d-**in**	aw	inini
1-FUT-have-TI4-**0p**	**DET**$_{PL}$	tool-**0p**	IC-use.it-TI2-3-**PL**$_{PRT}$	that	man

   'I need the **tools** that man is using' (AS.13.07.16.E)

A full discussion of participles and the variation of their forms are presented in 3.3.13. Their role in relative clauses is discussed in chapter 4. In the next section I provide a brief discussion of the past/completive function of changed conjuncts.

2.6.3. Past/Completive

Another function of initial change is to indicate the completion of an event (Fairbanks 2012), past tense with *(a)pii* (Valentine 2001), actions "just past" (Baraga 1850), or focusing on a "single past occurrence" (Nichols 1980). In his "9 rules of the change," Baraga states, "The Change is likewise employed in sentences which express actions or events as *just past*, and contain in English the words when, as soon as, etc." (1850, 136):

(110) "Just past" (Baraga 1850, 136)

gaa-maajaad goos, gii-ikidowag iw

IC-gii-maajaa-d	goos	gii-ikido-wag	iw
IC-PST-leave-3	your.father	PST-says-3p	DET

'when thy father had gone away (or, after he went away) they said that.'

Nichols describes this use of IC as a "focus on single past occurrence, especially when relevant to setting the time of another event or state" (1980, 153). He provides the examples shown below in (111), which support Fairbanks's "completive aspect" analysis:

(111) From Nichols (1980, 153)

a. *miish nebonid noomayaa ko . . . mii iniw onaabeman aw*

miish	**IC**-nibo-ni-d	noomayaa	ko	mii	iniw	o-naabem-an	aw
thus	**IC**-die-3'-3	recently	ko	thus	DET	3-husband-3'	DET

mindimooyenh mawid

mindimooyenh	mawi-d
old.lady	cries-3

'thus when her husband **died** not long after, that old lady cried'

b. *miish iidog gweshkoziwaad, . . . a'aw ikwe o-gwaaba'ang . . .*

mish	iidog	**IC**-goshkozi-waad	a'aw	ikwe	o-gwaaba'-am-g
thus	DUB	**IC**-wakes.up-3p	DET	lady	go-scoop-TI1-3

'when they **woke** in the morning, that lady went to get water . . .'

As the examples above show, IC occurs when referring to what Nichols calls a "single past occurrence." However, when a specific event is not reported, IC does not occur, as illustrated below on the preverb *ishkwaa-*:

(112) No IC (Nichols 1980, 153)[43]

miish giiwenh ishkwaa-maamigipiniiwaad iwidi . . . ,

miish	giiwenh	ishkwaa-maamigipinii-waad	iwidi
thus	so.it.is.said	after-pick.potatoes-3p	there

mii ba-izhi-maajaawaad

mii   IC-bi-izhi-maajaa-waad
thus IC-come-manner-leaves-3p

'When they finish picking potatoes over there, they leave for here'
(Nichols 1980, 153)

Fairbanks is concerned with shedding light on what he treats as an additional function of IC used to indicate what he calls completive aspect. He writes that "changed conjuncts may be used to express completive aspect within subordinate clauses, resulting in meanings similar to the English *after X happens, once Y occurs*" (Fairbanks 2012, 2). This is common in narratives in relating a series of events in the past tense. Often, the completive IC form comes initially in a clause, and speaker translations often contain "after X" or "upon X-ing," as illustrated in the following excerpt from a text collected from a speaker from the Aazhoomog community of the Mille Lacs Band in Minnesota:

(113) IC as completive aspect (from *Gii-paashkijiisijigeyaan*, Larry Smallwood)

a. ***gaa**-keshawa'amaan, mii kina gaa-izhi-ombaakwa'wag weweni.*

IC-gii-geshawa'-am-aan	mii	kina	IC-gii-izhi-ombaakwa'w-ag	weweni
IC-PST-loosen.it-TI1-1s	thus	all	IC-PST-REL-raise.h/-1>3	carefully

'**After** loosening them up, I then carefully jacked the car up all the way.'

b. ***gaa-**ombaakwa'wag,*	*mii*	*dash*	*gii-pakwajibidooyaan*	*iniw*	*biimiskonigaansan*
IC-gii-ombaakwa'w-ag	mii	dash	gii-bakwajibid-oo-yaan	iniw	biimiskonigaans-an
IC-PST-raise.h/-1>3	thus	and	PST-pull.it.off-TI2-1	DET	lug.nut-0p

'**After** jacking up the car, I took off the lug nuts and ...

c. *gii-mamag a'aw ozid gaa-paashkijiishing.*

gii-mam-ag	a'aw	ozid	IC-gii-baashkijiishin-g
PST-take.h/-1>3	DET	tire	IC-PST-bursts-3

took off the tire that had blown.'

The IC forms bolded in lines a. and b. show this use of IC as an 'after X' strategy, as discussed in Fairbanks (2012). In line c. of the example shown above in (115), the unchanged tense marker (*gii-*) does not bear IC and thus there is no completive reading or single-occurrence focus interpretation. The final verbal construction of line c., *gaa-paashkijiishing*, is a singular past tense participle translated as 'the one that had blown' and differs from the clause-initial examples shown in bold that pertain to the completive aspect described above. As discussed earlier in 2.3.4 in regard to relative preverbs, the *gaa-izhi-* example shown above in (113a.) serves a discourse-sequencing function and gets translated as 'so then ...' or 'and then ...'

I have shown the three main functions of IC in SW Ojibwe as a focusing device: *wh*-questions, participles in relative clauses, and the just past/completive function. Importantly, I have provided criteria for distinguishing among them, relying on both morphological shape and syntactic position. I discuss each function at length in the syntactic analysis provided in chapter 4, positing a head movement explanation in checking off of syntactic features, reminiscent of *wh*-movement approaches for various languages of the world. In the next section I give a basic overview of Ojibwe constituent order and provide the structure necessary to account for the data.

2.7. WORD ORDER AND CLAUSE STRUCTURE

In this section I offer only the necessary information as background for the reader leading up to the subsequent chapters.[44] It has been long observed that the constituency order for Algonquian languages is "flexible"; some have even gone as far as describing the languages as having a "free" word order (Bloomfield 1957, 131; Dahlstrom 1991, 1995; Valentine 2001, 920; Guile 2001; Branigan and McKenzie 2002; Shields 2004; among many others). As discussed earlier in 1.4.1, due to the apparent "scattered" word order for Ojibwe and related Algonquian languages, the syntax of such languages is usually described in terms of nonconfigurationality (Hale 1983) while adhering to the pronominal argument hypothesis (PAH) developed by Jelinek (1984, 1989a, 1989b), which analyzes participant reference at the morphosyntactic level of the inflected verbs themselves or at the clause level concerning overt nominal constituents. While the former approach treats the affixes of inflected verb stems as arguments of the verb, "setting aside" nominal adjuncts that give the appearance of a "disorganized" clause structure (Brittain 2001, 29) (with the overt nominals being simply adjuncts that agree with the verb's morphology), studies taking the latter approach tend to argue for a verb-initial underlying basic constituency order with discourse-driven cases of movement of nominals to preverbal positions.

Despite the numerous attempts to characterize variability in language, the present discussion is not concerned with the internal structure of words, but rather the larger structure into which words enter. As mentioned above in 1.5.2.2, I follow Brittain (2001) in her C checks V^{CJ} hypothesis and adopt the split-CP hypothesis of Rizzi (1997) to account for both constituent arrangement and all syntactic environments of the conjunct. In 2.7.1 I define what constitutes an NP in Ojibwe. In 2.7.2 I provide an analysis of Ojibwe word order while positing VOS as the basic, most pragmatically neutral constituent order. This mirrors several claims that have been made for other Algonquian languages regarding postverbal position for NP arguments (Dahlstrom 1995; Mühlbauer 2003; Junker 2004; Johnson, Macaulay, and Rosen 2011; to name a few). Mühlbauer noticed that preverbal arguments were less common than postverbal arguments and bear "specific functions" (2003, 9). He determined Plains Cree to be a VSO language (15). For East Cree, Junker found that VOS is the "preferred unmarked word order" (2004, 349). Bruening (2001) identifies the basic order for Passamaquoddy as SVO, though noting the rare occurrence of all three overtly expressed. Textual counts for Bruening support the SVO order, and interpretation of sentences with two obviative arguments reinforce the case for the first argument associated with the subject.

Following the earlier contribution of Dahlstrom (1995), many word order studies of Algonquian languages have postulated TOPIC and FOCUS positions at the left periphery. Dahlstrom (1995) identifies a topic and focus structure for Fox, and Algonquian languages in general, that exists at the left periphery. I conclude this chapter with a brief discussion of the left periphery (2.7.3).

2.7.1. The Noun Phrase

Prior to providing my analysis of word order, I first define what constitutes an NP in Ojibwe, essentially what can be counted as an overt nominal constituent. Given above in (27) and (28) with examples, I follow Rhodes's (1996) NP template, repeated here in (114):

(114) Templatic ordering of optional elements (from Rhodes 1996, 1)
   (cat dem)-(cat Q)-(catN)-(cat rel cl)

By treating each element of the NP as "optional," Rhodes determines that any single element alone can make up the NP structure. I conclude that, in Ojibwe, an NP can be represented by any of the "optional" elements included above or simply by *pro* or a null constituent licensed by an agreement marker in the verbal morphology.

2.7.2. Basic Constituency Order

Given the polysynthetic character and nonconfigurational impression of Ojibwe, determining a basic word order is an arduous task. Native speakers generally accept multiple orders in elicitation translation tasks. In text-based counts, word order appears to be a free-for-all as almost every possible order can typically be found. For the purposes of determining a basic constituency order, I call attention to two previous studies on Ojibwe word order.

Tomlin and Rhodes (1979) determined the most pragmatically neutral constituent order for the Ojibwe dialect Odawa to be VOS. Their early contribution examined word order in textual materials from a century ago. While arriving at a VOS conclusion, they determined that deviations from the VOS order were a result of discourse-driven principles. Sullivan (2016) finds the same VOS preference while using a picture elicitation experiment.[45] Using random pictures as the sole prompt for eliciting spontaneous sentences, verb-initial renderings were overwhelmingly more common than any other orders with preverbal nominal arguments. The findings of Sullivan (2016) are provided in table 29.[46]

It should be stated that the sentences analyzed here represent the most discourse-neutral data of the study and include only the single-sentence data collected. Nevertheless, as the matrix clause totals clearly indicate,

Table 29. Findings from Sullivan (2016)

Order	Clause types	
ONE ARGUMENT	MATRIX CLAUSE (158 TOTAL)	DEPENDENT CLAUSE (45 TOTAL)
VS	80 (51%)	7 (16%)
SV	2 (1%)	19 (42%)[a]
VO	4 (3%)	0
OV	0	0
TWO ARGUMENTS	MATRIX CLAUSE	DEPENDENT CLAUSE
VOS	50 (32%)	2 (4%)
VSO	11 (7%)	0
SVO	2 (1%)	6 (13%)
TWO ARGUMENTS (CONT.)	MATRIX CLAUSE	DEPENDENT CLAUSE
OVS	3 (2%)	3 (7%)
OSV	0	0
SOV	0	8 (18%)
DITRANSITIVES	MATRIX CLAUSE	DEPENDENT CLAUSE
VSOO	2 (1%)	0
VOOS	4 (3%)	0
TOTALS	MATRIX CLAUSE	DEPENDENT CLAUSE
Verb-initial	151 (95%)	9 (20%)
Subject-initial	4 (3%)	33 (73%)
Object-initial	3 (2%)	3 (7%)

[a] The subject-initial dependent clause totals are misleading. In all nineteen examples recorded, the matrix clause consisted of a verb-initial ordering.

verb-initial orderings are greatly preferred to subject-initial constructions, in the ratio of 151:4. This provides a strong argument for Ojibwe being a verb-initial language. As a result and in agreement with Tomlin and Rhodes (1979) and Sullivan (2016), I conclude that the underlying, most basic constituent order for Ojibwe is VOS.

The issue of the scattered appearance of NPs in textual materials, that is, narratives, monologues, and so on still needs to be addressed. For the textual count I have opted to examine three narratives from Larry "Amik" Smallwood, the same speaker consulted in Sullivan (2016).[47] The stories

Table 30. Word order from narratives

Title	Total sentences	Constituent orderings		Total orderings (215)		
Gii-paashkijiisijigeyaan	43	VO	25	VO	81	37.67%
		OV	5	VS	56	26.05%
		VS	1	SV	46	21.39%
				OV	18	8.37%
Mayagi-manidoonsag	59	VS	20	SVO	6	2.79%
		SV	15	VOS	3	1.4%
		VO	11	VSO	1	.47%
		OV	2	OSV	1	.47%
		VOS	3	SOV	1	.47%
		SVO	3	OVS	1	.47%
		OSV	1	SVOO[a]	1	.47%
		SOV	1			
		SVOO	1			
Aadizookaanan	184	VO	45			
		VS	35			
		SV	31			
		OV	11			
		SVO	3			
		OVS	1			
		VSO	1			

[a] The only ditransitive occurrence in the texts examined consisted of a primary-secondary ordering.

examined are of varying length (from two to twelve pages) and substance (from two to multiple characters). The overall word order count is provided in table 30.

In the structures analyzed any "optional" element of NP shown in (121) above constitutes a counted argument.

Perhaps the most interesting aspect of the text analysis is the overall paucity of nominals in the text. This provides sufficient support and justification for picture elicitation experiments like those described in Sullivan (2016), where pictures show actions that prompt sentences rich in transitive verbs and overt nominal arguments. While 286 total sentences were included in the analysis, only 215 relevant analyzable structures occurred, due to the frequency of many sentences like the one shown below in (115):

(115) No overt NP constituent
azhigwa sa eni-maajiibizoyaan, bimibizoyaan,

azhigwa	sa	IC-ani-maajiibizo-yaan	bimibizo-yaan
now	EMPH	IC-go.along-motor.off-1s	driving.along-1s

gaa-izhi-baashkijiisijigeyaan
IC-gii-izhi-baashkijiisijige-yaan
IC-PST-rel.pv-blow.out-1s

'Then when I started off, I was driving along, and had a tire blow out'
(AS.Gii-paashkijiisijigeyaan)

This example, appearing in *Gii-paashkijiisijigeyaan*, an unpublished story collected by the author, the story with the smallest number of characters, consists of a temporal adverbial *azhigwa* 'now,' an emphatic particle, and three intransitive conjunct verbs.[48] The story is essentially about getting a flat tire and the process of changing it. There are no examples of all three constituents overtly expressed; in only one case was the subject overtly expressed, being that the narrator was the primary subject throughout the story.

The longest of the three narratives, *Aadizookaanan*, is the transcription of a video recording of a public storytelling performance. Therefore it has all of the transcription issues of spontaneous, nonstandard, informal speech, including much quotative language, fragments and numerous false starts, exclamations and interjectory expressions. As a result sentences were not always easy to parse in the transcription. Utterances not containing verbs were not counted as sentences:

(116) Example passage from *Aadizookaanan*

a. *Wa maajaad imaa, miish ingiw zhiishiibensag: "Wenabozho a'aw". "Wenabosh!"*

b. *Gaawiin ganage, bimosed: "Wenabozho!", ini zhiishiiban. Wenabozho, "Ha? Wenen?"*

c. *"O'omaa!" "Oo oo oo oo aaniin nichiimedog!*

d. *Nichiimedog! Aaniin ezhichigeyeg? "Oonh shaa omaa nibaa-agomomin."*

a. Wa he was going for it, then the little ducks (said), "That's Wenabozho." "Wenabosh!"

b. He ignored them as he was walking. "Wenabozho!" the duck (said). Wenabozho (said) "Huh? Who's there?"

c. "Over here!" "Oh, hello little brothers!

d. Little brothers! What are you doing?" "Oh we're just floating around."

For the relative root arguments including locative adjuncts, such prepositional elements pattern much like the typical core arguments and occur after the verb. Of twenty-four cases of a locative NP, only seven occurred preverbally.

With an underlying VOS word order established as a starting point for further inquiry, we can now attempt to account for the deviations prevalent in naturally occurring discourse. Essentially I argue for a movement analysis in which topicalized or focused NPs move out of their postverbal positions into positions at the left periphery, the subject of the next section.

2.7.3. The Left Periphery

It has long been observed in word order studies of Algonquian languages that the initial position serves for a "principle of emphasis" (Hockett 1939, 248). The claim made in this section follows the work of many studies in the Algonquian literature concerned with the preverbal positioning of NPs (Dahlstrom 1993, 1995, 2004; Mühlbauer 2003; Junker 2004; Johnson, Macaulay, and Rosen 2011; among others) in marked constructions. This study contributes to the investigation of this "cross-family tendency" of movement to the left periphery for discourse function purposes (Johnson, Macaulay, and Rosen 2011, 18).[49] Junker states that NPs at the left periphery in East Cree have focus interpretations and that the unmarked word order is always verb-initial (2004, 252).[50]

In accepting VOS as the basic underlying Ojibwe constituent order when all arguments of a verb appear, and VX (where X represents subject, object, or locative oblique) for cases when only one argument appears, then we must account for all cases that deviate from the basic order. By positing a left-periphery movement analysis we are able to account for every instance in which the basic order is violated. As table 31 illustrates, when taking into consideration topic maintenance (topic shifts, old topics, and

Table 31. Deviations

Title	Orderings	Top.	Foc.	Indef.	Quantifiers	Discontinuous NP
Gii-paashkijiisijigeyaan	OV (6)		6[a]		1	
	LV (4)		4			
	LVL (1)		1	1		1
Mayagi-manidoonsag	SV (15)	13	2	2		
	OV (2)		2		2	
	LV (1)	1				
	SVO (3)	3				
	VSO (3)	3[b]				
	SOV (1)	1				
	OSV (1)		1		1	
	LVS (1)	1				
Aadizookaanan	SV (31)	22	9 (1inv)	6		
	OV (11)	2	9	3		
	SVO (3)	1	2	2		1
	SOV (1)		1	1		
	OVS (1)		1	1		
	VSO (1)		1	1		1

[a] One of the five OV orderings was a ditransitive construction with only the secondary object overtly expressed.
[b] One of the three VSO renderings was of the inverse direction.

so on) and focus constructions (new information, restrictive, surprising content, indefinites, and quantifiers), all deviations can be accounted for.

As the table shows it is quite easy to adopt an analysis that accounts for every case of a marked word order. Following Dahlstrom (1995), indefinites and quantifiers are treated as a type of focus and all discontinuous NPs consist of either a floating quantifier or indefinite pronoun.

It is worth mentioning that while OV did not occur in Sullivan's (2016) picture elicitation experiment, it has appeared to a significant degree in narratives and is very common in sentence elicitation translation tasks, especially in the dialect survey to be discussed in chapter 3. SVO renderings are also extremely common in English translation tasks and often are the results of "being specific," according to native speaker consultants.[51]

When presented with the English prompt, "She sings the songs that I gave her," one speaker replied with the example shown in (117):

(117) *onagamonan iniwen nagamonan gaa-miinag*

o-nagamon-an   iniwen   nagamon-an   IC-gii-miiN-ag
3-sings-0p   DET   song-0p   IC-PST-give.h/-1>3

'She sings the song I gave her' (RD.14.06.11.E)

After reflecting on her response, she indicated that in order to be specific regarding the gender *she*, she then responded with the following sentence, with a preverbal NP 'that woman':

(118) "Being specific it's a SHE"

a'awe ikwe *onanagamonan iniwenan nagamonan gaa-miinag*

that woman sings those songs I gave her (RD.14.06.11.E)

Ultimately the data do not require nor suggest a subject-initial underlying order for Ojibwe. Grammatical mechanisms easily account for all orders that deviate from the (pragmatically) neutral underlying order.

Several word order studies of related Algonquian languages have provided similar accounts for the varied appearance of NPs with respect to the verb. Johnson, Macaulay, and Rosen identify preverbal arguments as being associated with either a topic or focus interpretation, while "postverbal arguments are in the default position" in Menominee (2011, 1). Before moving ahead I offer a brief discussion of focus and topic while providing relevant examples for both.

2.7.3.1. Focus

Focus is generally defined as a sentence-level construct that is pragmatically or semantically determined (Gundel and Fretheim 2004). This definition is rather straightforward though there have been proposals for subtypes of focus as well. Dahlstrom (1995) identifies what she refers to as "restrictive focus," providing the Fox (Meskwaki) example below in (119), where the function of focus is to restrict information:

(119) Restrictive focus (from Dahlstrom 1995, 11)

[FOC še·ški=meko kehkeše·wi]   [OBL i·nahi] ahte·wi
only = emph charcoal   there be.[there] 0/ind.ind
'only charcoal was there'

The example provided below in (120) shows a similar construction of restrictive focus from my data:

(120) Restrictive focus

mii	gemaa	eta	bezhig	ishkwaandem	ogii-atoon
thus	maybe	only	one	door	he.put.it

'He made only one doorway.' (AS.Aadizookaan)

As mentioned earlier Dahlstrom notes that indefinite pronouns and quantifiers "pattern with focus" in Fox (1995, 11–12).[52] This has also been pointed out for Menominee (Shields 2004, 373; Johnson, Macaulay, and Rosen 2011, 8) and for SW Ojibwe (Sullivan 2016). An example of a preverbal indefinite with a quantifier is provided in (121), with the indefinite and quantifier bolded:

(121) **akina**   **gegoo**   aanjisemagad
      every   **something**   it.changes
      '**Everything** is changing.' (Smallwood 2013b, 111)

Another example of an indefinite pronoun in focus position is provided below in (122). In this example it is the indefinite object that is fronted to the preverbal position. The focused object is shown in bold:

(122) Indefinite object focus

mii	**gaawiin**	**awiya**	ogii-waabamaasiin
thus	**no**	**someone**	he.didn't.see

'He didn't see **anybody**.' (AS.12.03.01.N)

Quantifiers are also commonly found in the preverbal focus position and often are the preverbal element of a discontinuous constituent. The example provided in (123) illustrates this with the quantifier and the nominal it modifies bolded:

(123) Discontinuous NP with preverbal quantifier
niibowa ge onishwanaaji'aan **iniw giigoonyan**
many also he.wastes.them **those fish**
'And he wastes **a lot of the fish**' (Smallwood 2013b, 112)

Johnson, Macaulay, and Rosen also mention focus containing "surprising content" (2011, 8). The unusual or atypical information substantiates the somewhat unusual and atypical word order. This is illustrated in the example from Sullivan (2016), shown here in (124) where the speaker offered the sentence after seeing a picture of a man biting his dog:

(124) Surprising content
Aw gaawanaadizid inini odakwamaan iniw odayan.
DET IC-crazy-3S man 3-bite-DIR-3' DET his.dog
'**The crazy man** is biting his dog.'

Since focus is defined as new information, the whole sentence in this "surprising" context is taken as focal. In the *Aadizookaanan* story, the helldiver is alarmed to realize that Wenabozho has tricked them and is killing the ducks one at a time:

(125) He he he! **Wenabozho** ginisigonaan omaa! Zaagijiba'iweg!
exclamation **PN** he.kills.us here run.out$_{IMP}$
'Hay hay hay! **Wenabozho** is killing us here! Run out!' (AS.Aadizookaan)

With the general definition and sub-types given for focus constructions, we turn to the discussion of topic in the next section.

2.7.3.2. Topic

Topic is usually defined in terms of *aboutness* (Gundel 1988; Reinhart 1982; Aissen 1992[53]; Dahlstrom 1995; Gundel and Fretheim 2004; among others). It is sometimes discussed in terms of old or given information (see Gundel and Fretheim 2004). Extremely common in the texts examined for this study, fronted topics are also used in topic maintenance strategies, whether a new topic is introduced or an old one returned to the foreground. This is illustrated nicely below in in (126), where in the second line (b.), the NP *ingiw gigiigoonyiminaanig* occurs preverbally as the result of a topic shift:

(126) Topic maintenance

a. *Niibowa imaa oziigwebinaan mayaanaadadinig.*
many there he.pours.it that.which.is.harmful

b. *Akina go ingoji miish **ingiw gigiigoonyiminaanig** zhigwa*
all EMPH somewhere thus **those our.fish** now

c. *ge **wiinawaa** azhigwa moozhitoowaad iw ezhi-nishwanaajichiged aw*
also **them** now they.feel.it that how.s/he.ruin.things that

Chi-mookomaan
Whiteman

A. 'He (the Whiteman) spills in many harmful things, B. and all over, **our fish now too**, C. **they** are feeling the effects of the Whiteman's ways of spoiling them' (Smallwood 2013b, 111)

The example above shows how the object has been moved out of its postverbal position and brought to the left periphery for TOPIC purposes. As table 31 above indicates, the overwhelming majority of subject-initial constructions are the result of topic maintenance strategies.

Proposing a flat structure, Dahlstrom identifies four positions "to the left of verb: Topic, Negative, Focus, and Oblique." All of these positions, with the exception of topic, are daughters of S, while topic is the sister of S (Dahlstrom 1995, 3).

(127) Word order template (Dahlstrom 1995, 3)

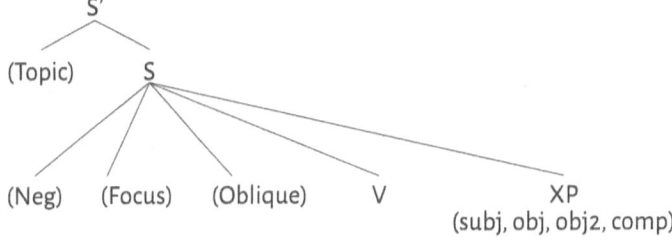

According to analyses for many other languages (for example, De Swart and De Hoop 1995 for Hungarian) and in line with the claims made here, these positions are generated empty, and the relevant material generated elsewhere in S can be moved there.

For Menominee, Johnson, Macaulay, and Rosen (2011) show evidence of the preverbal positions shown in (128), making the distinction between an external and internal topic position:

(128) External and internal topic (Johnson, Macaulay, and Rosen 2011)

[External topic] [Focus] [Internal topic]

This analysis falls in line with Aissen (1992), Dahlstrom (2004), and Mühlbauer (2003), who differentiate between two types of topics. Johnson, Macaulay, and Rosen (2011) state that an external topic in Menominee is generated "in situ, and may or may not correspond to an argument of the verb." The use of the inner topic position in Cree is related to topic maintenance for Mühlbauer, who states, "Inner topic is often used to introduce new discourse referents, who will be the subject of some span of discourse. Once this introductory topic-marking has been made, the nominals can be returned to a post-verbal position" (2003, 10).

An interesting similarity found between Menominee as discussed in Johnson, Macaulay, and Rosen (2011) and the Ojibwe presented here and in Fairbanks (2008) is focused restrictive NPs signaled by the particle *eneq* in Menominee and *mii* in Ojibwe. Fairbanks describes the many uses of *mii* in Ojibwe, including its use as a "deictic particle" providing "further focus" to an NP that is already in a focus position (2008, 176). An example of such usage is provided below in (129):

(129) *mii* as 'further focus'

Ataage aw bezhig ikwe meskwaanig ogoodaas.

ataage	aw	bezhig	ikwe	IC-miskwaa-ni-g	o-goodaas
gambles	DET	one	woman	IC-is.red-OBV-0$_{CONJ}$	3-dress

Mii imaa chi-ataagewigamigong *gaa-danaakizowaad.*

mii	imaa	chi-ataagewigamig-ong	IC-gii-danaakizo-waad
thus	there	big-casino-LOC	IC-PT-pictured.there-3p

'The woman in the red dress is gambling. **They are in a big casino** where the photo was taken.' (AS.12.08.15.P)

Johnson, Macaulay, and Rosen (2011) use *eneq* as a diagnostic for the type of NP, when the NP and *eneq* both occur before the verb. Preverbal NPs can appear on either side of *eneq*: "external topics precede *eneq* and internal topics follow it" (169). Their analysis distinguishes three preverbal positions in Menominee: external topic, focus, and internal topic. They show in the diagram in (130) that their analysis is in line with the articulated left periphery (Rizzi 1997).

(130) Menominee left periphery (Johnson, Macaulay, and Rosen 2011, 17)

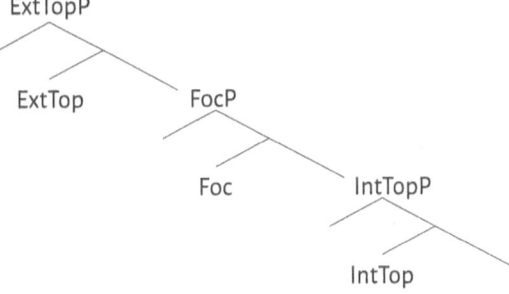

In their analysis topicalized and focused noun phrases sit in the specifier positions of ExtTopP, FocP, and IntTopP. Since *eneq* (and presumably *mii* for Ojibwe) mark focus, they sit in the head position of FocP.

Such arguments can be made for Ojibwe as well, though the word order facts are given a slightly different treatment in chapter 4. The example shown below in (131), from Sullivan (2016), suggests supporting an analysis like Johnson, Macaulay, and Rosen (2011) in regard to the arrangement of the preverbal positions. The preverbal elements are bolded:

(131) Preverbal positions (example from Sullivan 2016)

Biindigeshimowag omaa waabanda'iwe-niimi'iding ongow Anishinaabeg.

biindigeshimo-wag	omaa	waabanda'iwe-niimi'idi-ng	ongow	Anishinaabe-g
dances.in-3p	here	shows.people-dances-X	DET	Indian-3p

O'ow nitam miigwani-gikiwe'on   obiindigeshimotaadaan.
o'ow   nitam   miigwani-gikiwe'on   o-biindigeshimotaad-am
DET   first   feather-flag   3-dance.it.in-TI1

Miinawaa **ingiw aanind gikiwe'onan**   obi-dakonaanaawaa
miinawaa   ingiw   aanind   gikiwe'on-an   o-bi-dakon-am-naawaa
and   DET   some   flag-0p   3-here-hold.it-TI1-3p>0

ingiw zhimaaganishag.
ingiw   zhimaaganish-ag
DET   soldier-3p

'They are dancing in during grand entry. **First the eagle staff** is danced in. **And some** veterans are holding **flags**.'

With the necessary grammatical information established, we can now discuss variation found in what Valentine (1994) determined to be the language spoken in the SW Ojibwe territory.

THREE

Methodology

The study presented here is based on a corpus of data obtained by the author in a variety of settings. Data collected through primary fieldwork sessions with fluent native speakers serve as the basis for the majority of claims presented in this thesis. While concerned primarily with the geographical distribution and variation concerning the use of participles and the morphological shape of relative clauses, the claims put forth here may not represent the community norm nor the historical norm for each respective community. Some issues and innovations discussed in the following sections may very well merely represent individual stylistic variation as opposed to geographic dialect variation criteria. I have made the most earnest effort in seeking out native speaker consultants from other native speaker consultants and have chosen to present only the data from such individuals identified by other trusted individuals. My goal was to use what Bowern (2008, 131) refers to as "ideal consultants," that is, someone who "is a native speaker of the language under study, and an excellent second-language speaker of the contact language." Quite relevant for my purposes is what she describes as "semi-speakers" having "valuable knowledge" (137–38). A few of my consultants were individuals who hadn't used the language much recently (outside of ceremony and other public speaking roles) and who were observed increasing in fluency as our work progressed. There are very degrees of fluency among such "rusty speakers," as observed by Valentine (1994, 27), who remarks on the excitement of such speakers regaining a command of the language in a similar way to my experience here.

In light of the pace of language obsolescence in this area, I do not solely attribute certain innovations to such obsolescence. Many of the proposed innovations appear to be generations old, having occurred in communities where the language had thrived until recent years. Morphological leveling by analogy is common crosslinguistically and, with the vast number of possibilities in the verbal inflectional morphology, not unexpected for an Algonquian language. I do not assume a purist stance in this analysis but merely provide a snapshot of the language spoken by my elder consultants as compared to that spoken by earlier generations that I have had access to. I have been reminded on numerous occasions to avoid historical speculation since first documentation does not necessarily represent "the right way." Much of the early work was the result of missionaries and their mission to translate biblical literature into Ojibwe. Keeping that in mind as well as the "language learner perspective" of those early missionaries, as well as of myself, has been crucial in the collection of data analyzed in this study. Many of my contemporaries have approached the archival sources from another perspective. When stumbling upon old verb paradigms and documents showing difference compared to the language in use by our current speakers, there has been a tendency to assume that what we learn and teach today is somehow "wrong" or that we've "lost" certain features that the archival material suggests. The natural phenomenon of language change is often disregarded as if somehow current speakers speak a less "pure" or contaminated variety of Ojibwe.

I have made every effort to include as much data as possible, providing illustrative examples from as many communities as I was able to visit. Unfortunately, some communities had lost all of their living speakers prior to my embarking on this study. Students and educators from those communities should do their own research surrounding the history of their respective communities, as this study has shown that historical ties between various bands of Ojibwe are reflected in the varieties of language used in those communities. In this chapter and throughout the volume I make numerous references to speakers and varieties from "the north" and "the south." I apply these terms loosely to speakers and communities of SW Ojibwe only, arbitrarily including some Border Lakes communities in the northern classification. Given the widespread nature of Ojibwe in its various varieties, I do not use "northern" as a generalization that includes northern speakers of Ojibwe or northern communities north of this SW Ojibwe territory. Additionally the use of "Border Lakes" in this study applies specifically to

Nigigoonsiminikaaning (Red Gut) and Lac La Croix and the speakers consulted from those communities, as I have not surveyed or worked in those communities at all. I refer to any other speakers or varieties by their larger dialectal classifications (Odawa, Saulteaux, Severn, and so on), relying heavily on those groupings identified in Valentine (1994).

Before moving into the findings of this study, I feel inclined to provide the reader with a little background on the study of dialectology and how the standard method both differs and compares to the work carried out here. While it is perhaps too late in the game to do a full-scale dialect study in each SW Ojibwe community, I have opted to include as much as I have obtained over the course of my journey as a language warrior and more recently as a linguist. This research is by no means intended to serve as an exhaustive say in regard to dialect variation but, more precisely, as a description of how modern speakers speak Ojibwe in these communities. The intention is to not speak on behalf of each community in regard to how the language is used there, since, as Valentine is quick to point out, "pronunciation may vary considerably within the same community, so that a single speaker may not be representative, and indeed, *cannot* be, of the greater community" (1994, 174). As in Valentine's work, some of the findings presented here are based on work with a single individual and therefore may not be representative of the entire community. Similar to Valentine's findings, what are identified here as features of variation are not definitive since nearly every feature can be shown to vary, even within the same community and among the same *speakers*.

The method employed here is reminiscent of traditional dialect studies albeit on a much smaller scale. In my language learning experience, language variation has been an unavoidable reality; L2 speakers of Ojibwe can all attest to the variation described here. The findings of this chapter present the linguistic variables; linguistic variable is defined as "a linguistic unit with two or more variants involved in covariation with other social and/or linguistic variables" (Chambers and Trudgill 1998, 50). Isoglosses track the distribution of such variables, though, as in any dialect study, they are hardly ever definitive in any concrete sense. As will be seen, many of the features and lines indicating their distribution crisscross within communities, challenging the commonly held opinion that any given reservation has a clear-cut "dialect" that is uniquely its own. Also, the notion of a "relic" feature, as described by Chambers and Trudgill, is widely observed in Ojibwe, where one feature seems sensibly plotted as a northern or southern feature and then occurs on the other end of the spectrum, with no apparent lines connecting it to the communities where it is more widely attested (94).

While there are many types of features and isoglosses one might identify as being relevant for Ojibwe dialectology, the grading of such features is problematic. With the title and focus of this study being concerned chiefly with the morphosyntactic shape of relative clauses, it is obviously the main concern. One can pursue dialectology from a number of angles, including isoglosses pertaining to the lexicon, pronunciation, phonology, and what Chambers and Trudgill classify as "grammatical isoglosses" (98). These include both morphological isoglosses and syntactic isoglosses. While this study aims to provide a bit of each type, the focus is mainly on participles as what might be considered a morphosyntactic isogloss.

I have made every attempt in my fieldwork to obtain what Bowern describes as "naturalistic data." Such data can be collected in a number of speech genres including "conversations with or without you as a participant or observer ... semi-structured or structured interviews ... semi-monologic data ... written language such as diary entries, newspaper opinion columns and blog posts" (2008, 122). I have also had the privilege in this twenty-first century to engage in text messaging with native speakers, some of whom I've had a hand in teaching the modern double-vowel orthography. Many of the original speaker spellings are retained here, often providing hints regarding what constitutes a parsable word, and illustrating a key point regarding variation.

Keeping in mind Labov's "observer's paradox," I have strived to collect such naturalistic data; at the same time I am guilty of seeking the "pure" form of Ojibwe, similar to Wolfgang Viereck's study of English (cited in Chambers and Trudgill 1998, 46), while fully aware that there is likely no such thing as a variety that doesn't show signs of influence from other languages or varieties. This is precisely the nature of *endangered* language documentation and how it differs from dialect studies of more secure and healthy languages. Being fully aware that my work and the attention I paid to form put my speakers on their best linguistic behavior, I find it is necessary given the current situation regarding Ojibwe.

It is important to make the distinction between what Chambers and Trudgill identify as markers and indicators. Both involve linguistic variables though markers are "subject to stylistic variation as well as class, sex and/or age variation." Indicators, on the other hand, do not involve such stylistic variation and speakers seem less aware of indicators than markers. Any easy diagnostic in telling the two apart involves whether or not the variable is the subject of "overt stigmatism," which applies to regional identity and allegiance to a particular variety: "one obvious indication that a variable is a marker rather than an indicator is that it is the subject of unfavourable comment in the community." Another factor in identifying a marker is the fact that "the variable is involved in an ongoing linguistic change" (Chambers and Trudgill 1998, 72). This is relevant for the discussion of participles, of which speakers are well aware and attribute as being a marker of their linguistic identity.

An important reminder to readers engaged in community language work is the dangers behind the implications of the word *dialect*. The word is often used loosely to cover everything from a particular writing system to actual divisive linguistic phenomena. Valentine warns, "Modern perceptions of dialects often only represent linguistic epiphenomena, and there may be a substantial mismatch between what the linguistic forms suggest and the ways in which speakers choose to identify themselves" (1994, 43). Additionally, community and speaker understandings and claims about local dialect are not always accurate. On more than one occasion I have heard things like, "We don't say *boozhoo* here because it is actually from French," only to run into another speaker from the same community who greeted me with that very word.[1] Classroom environments are notorious for throwing around the word *dialect*, often involving claims that turn out not to have merit when the data from speakers in those communities are examined. Speakers themselves will argue about dialect while having a very difficult time articulating just what it is that makes their variety different from another. Essentially this study aims to identify what some of the features of variation are, so that differences between dialects can be embraced. As David Crystal suggests, communities should appreciate variables of linguistic diversity while they "strive to maximize them as symbols of local identity" (2000, 9).

In the next section I describe the survey that was carried out with speakers from the SW Ojibwe communities. Some of the individuals consulted I have known for much of my life; I have established considerable rapport in their communities as a member and active participant in both cultural and spiritual activities. Others I met for the first time the same day the survey was conducted and haven't seen since. I engaged in Ojibwe with all my consultants, to alleviate the reliance on English and establish some credibility as someone other than an alien from the university with a slew of recording equipment. I recorded our conversations and, quite often, managed to prompt them into telling me stories, from which many of the examples presented here were obtained. The data collected in such circumstances are presented as being from the speaker who provided the speech sample, not necessarily as the community or dialectal norm; at the same time I have assumed that where a speaker comes from is reflected in their speech. Many of the atypical forms and patterns therefore may only represent idiolectal innovations or free variation. However, perhaps even more interesting is the investigation into how speakers deal with differences themselves. Included following the findings is a discussion of mutual intelligibility between dialects, and the notion of innovation and age-graded variation.

3.1. SURVEY APPARATUS

With many of the parameters provided by Nichols (2011, 2012) as the point of departure, and piggybacking off of the work of Valentine (1994), I developed a survey questionnaire. The survey used in this study was determined largely in response to the variation observed during fieldwork for the Ojibwe People's Dictionary and in both Nichols's (2011) observations and (2012) report (to the National Science Foundation). In addition, many of the questions and tasks included in the survey questionnaire were based on my own L2 speaker observations while learning Ojibwe. While it is difficult to collect a full consistent paradigm of any particular verbal order or mode, the difficulty cannot solely be attributed to language obsolescence, as Nichols (1980) had related such difficulties among speakers in Mille Lacs in the 1970s. In many of the communities visited over the course of this study, few speakers remained, hardly constituting any surveyable speech community.

Interviews with speakers included a number of different tasks. The first task was to attempt to engage the participant in a conversation in Ojibwe where I asked about community ties and questions that might pertain to each individual's own language socialization experience. This allowed me to get familiar with the speech of the speaker, especially important for those with whom I wasn't previously acquainted. I then administered a number of translation tasks using English prompts, Ojibwe back-translations, and manipulations of data. The survey involved both "direct" and "indirect" questionnaires (Chambers and Trudgill 1998, 21); it required direct elicitation both ways but also featured open-ended questions and plenty of conversation between myself and the participants. For northern speakers, I would provide a sample sentence or form that illustrated certain features characteristic of the southern varieties. For southern speakers, I would present them with an example elicited from a northern speaker. This allowed me to test the range of intelligibility between the two varieties while simultaneously eliciting "correction" data that were representative of the participant's own variety. I would also get their opinions regarding grammaticality and "correction" preferences on a number of grammatical points. In many cases, regarding my own ideas and understanding of the language as well as certain aspects of the theory I was developing, I would create sentences and ask speakers to back-translate them and provide grammaticality judgments. Each question designed to elicit an example containing some aspect of variability was spaced out throughout the course of the interview so that no two questions targeting the same feature were asked consecutively.

When working out translations with each speaker, I would ask them to volunteer with their translation first. I would then render my own version to see what their preferences were. Speaker-preferred translations have been maintained here. In cases where such translations did not capture the literal meaning of a particular utterance, I have attempted to include speaker-approved literal glosses as well. As a trained field linguist and active user of the language, I am fully aware of the pitfalls of elicitation in all its forms. As any Algonquianist can attest, literal, word-for-word translation of the source language into the target language typically results in the target phrase or sentence being rendered in the exact same ordering of words and phrases of the metalanguage. In all cases where I have obtained relevant examples outside of direct elicitation, I have opted to use such examples to illustrate the points made throughout this study.

The reader is urged to keep in mind that the elicited examples merely represent each speaker's particular offering of the target phrase or sentence on that particular given occasion. It isn't much of a stretch to anticipate a different form when attention is given to any example. As observed by Valentine, forms collected under direct elicitation "may not be reliable" (1994, 199). The reason for the issue is often that there may be multiple ways to express what your prompt conveys in the target language. One such case is given below in (132). The purpose of the prompt was to determine whether or not the speakers showed initial change (IC) on /oo/. Both speakers shown here opted to use a personal demonstrative pronoun emphatic strategy (with one emphasizing the fact that the subject is a male), rather than the participial form I was after:

(132) Prompt: 'He is the one who is loading up the car.'
    a. wiin   boozitaaso
    PRN   s/he.loads.car (LW.14.07.16.E)
    Intended: *Mii (w)a'aw b**waa**zitaasod*
                mii   (w)a'aw   **IC**-boozitaaso-d
                thus   DET   **IC**-loads.vehicle-3$_{\text{CONJ}}$

    b. wiin   a'aw   inini   boozitaaso
    PRN   DET   man   s/he.loads.car (GH.14.07.16.E)
    Intended: *Mii (w)a'aw b**waa**zitaasod*
                mii   (w)a'aw   **IC**-boozitaaso-d
                thus   DET   **IC**-loads.vehicle-3$_{\text{CONJ}}$

The morphology of Ojibwe can also make it hard to determine through elicitation the animacy status of a noun referent. When attempting to determine whether or not 'bread' was considered animate or inanimate for a Border Lakes speaker, the following sentence was elicited:

(133) gii-izhaa   adaawewigamigong   ji-naaji**bakwezhigan**ed
     PST-go   store   to-fetch.**bread**
     'She went to the store to get bread' (GJ.14.01.09.E)

While it is a great sentence, the fact that the speaker chose to use a verb with an incorporated medial (*bakwezhigan* 'bread') does not provide a clue regarding the animacy status of the noun referent. A similar issue occurred with a speaker from the Leech Lake reservation when I was attempting to determine the animacy status of 'cars' in his community. When I asked him to translate 'I have two cars,' he responded with the following:

(134) *niniizhoodaabaane*
     ni-   niizho-   **daabaan**   -e
     1-   two-   **car**   -INCORP
     'I have two cars' (JB.13.07.17.E)

After trying multiple numbers of cars to no avail, I then showed him a picture of two boys washing a car, hoping to get an overt nominal for cars that I could use for determining animacy status. It was almost as if the speaker knew what I was after and was playing hard to get by providing the example shown here:

(135) *giziibiigidaabaanewag ingiw gwiiwizensag*
     giziibiig-i-**daabaan**-e-wag   ingiw   gwiiwizens-ag
     wash.with.water-EPEN-**car**-INCORP-3p   DET   boy-3p
     'those boys are washing a car' (JB.13.07.17.E)

While the mystery of the animacy status of cars in this community could not be solved based on these prompts alone (I eventually resorted to 'I touched the car,' to which he provided an example clarifying the animate status of cars in Onigum), the strategies he provided are very crucial to our understanding of Ojibwe and speakers' pride in being able to convey a great deal of information in the most economical manner.

In another instance with a different speaker, problems arose with properly identifying participants in focus of a particular argument of a participle. The source of the confusion can most likely be attributed to structural differences between the English prompt and the Ojibwe target, particularly the notion of voice as well as directionality in the Ojibwe verbal system and the multiple ways in which the intended sentence can be conveyed:

(136) Prompt: 'I know the man whom the woman hit'

ingikenimaa	a'aw	inini	**gaa-pakite'ogojin**	iniw	ikwewan
I.know.h/	DET	man	who$_{OBV}$.hit.h/$_{PROX}$	DET	woman$_{OBV}$

Lit. 'I know the man, who it was the woman he was hit by' (AS.13.07.16.E)

The Ojibwe sentence provided is perhaps better translated as 'I know the man, who it was the woman he was hit by,' triggering a passive structure when translated into English. To make sure I was accounting for the participant reference I had intended, I often resorted to drawing pictures and providing context for many examples in our sessions.

Aside from the formal survey described above, a number of different sources have been consulted over the course of this study. The data collected by Nichols for the Ojibwe People's Dictionary (OPD) shed light on many of the parameters discussed by Nichols (2011). Those parameters are included to some degree below and references are made to many of the examples provided by the OPD. Typically, OPD sentences are the result of a speaker being asked to "use it [the entry-word] in a sentence"; they are spontaneously created by the speaker without much context. Sentence examples appearing here from the OPD are cited according to the speaker who provided the example as well as the entry from the web page on which they appear.

Certain speakers may consider certain dialects as being more prestigious than others and may want to identify with those communities that they perceive to be prestigious (Valentine 1994, 82). Many speakers are multidialectal: they can produce forms atypical for their own variety for a range of reasons. One such instance occurred in one of my interviews, where a speaker produced examples that I had previously never heard her use when telling stories or conversing freely. The speaker was from a more northern community while the interview was held in a southern-speaking community. In a couple of different cases, speakers from the more northern communities produced classic southern participle forms and then after realizing what they had said, changed their mind and provided a different rendering, further evidence that participles are indeed a linguistic "marker" for geographical variation in the sense used by Chambers and Trudgill (1998).

In addition to the data collection techniques described above, I have relied heavily on archival material from a range of different locales and sources. These are discussed in the following section.

3.2. ARCHIVAL DATA

The terms *archival* and *archived* are used loosely here to mean any older record of the language I have been able to access, regardless of whether or not it exists in an official archive. Such data often come from published texts (such as Nichols 1988a, 1988b; Baraga 1850, 1878; Wilson 1870; Josselin de Jong 1913; to name a few); university archives, such as the Wisconsin Native Language Project (1970); old audio recordings; and handwritten documents. I am fully aware of the limitations imposed by working with such material, since much of the earlier documentation was done for translation purposes.[2] Much of the material cited also comes from documents created via dictation, posing yet another threat to the authenticity of the language presented.

In addition to documents I have managed to obtain a wealth of audio recordings from many communities dating as far back as the 1970s. Some of these were originally recorded on reel-to-reel and audiocassette tapes, later digitized (often by me) and transcribed and translated with the assistance of a local speaker. Other narratives cited appeared in handwritten stories by the speakers themselves, transliterated (by me) into the double-vowel orthography. These are extremely precious in that they provide clues regarding what constitutes a parsable word in the mind of an Ojibwe speaker.[3] Once I began my journey studying SW Ojibwe subdialects, individuals from the respective communities provided me with copies of their old tapes and documents. In the best-case scenarios, their recorders were left running while speakers (who have since passed on) provided monologues and engaged in conversations. Since I did not have access to these individuals personally (many of them had passed away even before I was born), I never had the opportunity to discuss the various forms they provided or their preference regarding translation. As a result all examples from such sources should be treated as tentative.

For present-day communities where the language is still spoken, the archival material from those communities allows for the study of linguistic change in "real time," that is, comparing the language in a community at one point in time to how it is spoken there some time (say, twenty years) later (Chambers and Trudgill 1998, 76). Since no speakers consulted for this study have children who speak the language, it is not possible to study the language in "apparent time," where the speech of older residents is compared to that of younger generations. Instead the older generation is accounted for in the archived material, while the remaining speakers of today serve as the younger generation, though they are from different time periods. It is important to note that all archival sources consulted consist only of the speech of elders of their given time. Consequently, all the records available for Ojibwe include only the speech of elders with no records of speech from younger speakers.

Regardless of which approach is taken to the investigation of change, archival material informs us that language changes, despite what we may think or hope. What we might often assume to be features characteristic of a particular locale turn out to be innovations that may or may not occur in other places. In essence, we assume for endangered languages that older speakers of the language are more fluent than younger ones. Valentine notes convergence and obsolescence as well as cultural shifts where earlier ways of life reflected more lexically rich areas of traditional culture. Also, the expressive power of the Ojibwe word is seen to decrease across generations:

> Younger speakers also appear to have less facility in certain highly valued forms of verbal art to kernalize [sic] conceptually complex notions into single, morphologically complex words, by exploiting the rich polysynthetic resources of the language. (Valentine 1994, 10)

Remarkably there still are strong speakers of Ojibwe in the southwestern communities, some of the best of whom contributed to this study.

Ultimately, as Brittain states, "dialects of a single language differ minimally" (2001, 5), while Rhodes and Todd determine that morphological differences are the "best criteria" for determining dialect variation in Ojibwe (1981, 56). Therefore the findings presented below are largely morphological differences, with discussions in 3.3.7 and 3.3.8 of, respectively, phonological and lexical variation.

3.3. FINDINGS

As we will see, data collected from older sources reveal that some parameters for variation appear to be rather recent innovations while others seem to be at least a couple of generations old. Age-graded variation is key in the assessment of internal dialect relationships for Valentine, who discusses variation in Algonquin (1994, 378), as well as for Rhodes and Todd, who mention the age-graded language variants in Naskapi (1981, 56). The findings of this study are presented rather arbitrarily here, with no particular parameter being more pronounced than another.

The reader is referred to the list of abbreviations for the complete key of speakers, communities, and the data code conventions used here. Examples are presented as anonymous in the glossing if they suggest obsolescence or if they could in any way be deterimental to the reputation of the speaker. Many comparisons are made to Valentine (1994) and Nichols (2011, 2012) as those studies outline some of the key aspects of the language that show variation. If anything, the examples contained in this study continue their discussions, providing elaboration and updates in a sense for many communities that had not received any attention in previous works. Sometimes the variation described is significant, with clear breaks in homogeneity in a convenient north-south axis. Other times the variation is more erratic, mentioned only for the sake of it being variable, even if that variation exists only with respect to speakers from the same community, or even the same speaker.

3.3.1. *ji-/da-* Complementizer, *jibwaa/dabwaa*

According to Rhodes, the *ji-* complementizer is derived historically from either **gici-* or **gaci-* through the lost loss of the first, unstressed syllable (1985, 548). Valentine (1994, 375) finds *giji-* still in use in Algonquin (Amos). The complementizer is a pv1 in the Nichols classification and "occurs as the unchanged representative of /ga-/, /da-/, and /daa-/ in the conjunct order" (1980, 135).[4] It is only used with conjunct inflection carrying a meaning similar to that of infinitival *to* in English, or 'in order to,' as illustrated in the example below:

(137) wa mii sa azhigwa **ji**-ando-wiisiniyaan

wa	mii	sa	azhigwa	**ji**-ando-wiisini-yaan
Excl	thus	EMPH	time	**to**-go-eats-1s$_{CONJ}$

'Well I guess its time for me **to** go eat' (NJ.11.12.13.N)

While *ji-* is the complementizer consistently observed in the speech of speakers of Red Lake, Leech Lake, and the Border Lakes, the complementizer appears to have been replaced by *da-* at some communities of the Mille Lacs reservation and throughout Wisconsin:

(138) *da-* complementizer

a. *Ishke dash gaawiin geyaabi ginoondanziimin **da**-gabe-bimaadizid*

ishke	dash	gaawiin	geyaabi	gi-noond-am-zii-min	**da**-gabe-bimaadizi-d
see	but	NEG	still	2-hear.it-TI1-NEG-21p	**to**-full.extent-lives-3$_{CONJ}$

a'aw Anishinaabe noongom

a'aw	Anishinaabe	noongom
DET	Indian	today

'Nowadays we no longer hear of Anishinaabe **living to be that old**.' (LS.AmbeSaNoo)

b. *Niiywogon wiineta **da**-gii'igoshimod*

niiyogon	wiineta	**da**-gii'igoshimo-d
four.days	just.h/	**to**-fasts-3$_{CONJ}$

'He was **to fast** for four days all alone' (CB.Opichi)

c. *weweni giga-ganawendaamin **da**-wiisiniyang **da**-ashamang*

weweni	gi-ga-ganawend-am-min	**da**-wiisini-yang	**da**-asham-ang
careful	2-FUT-take.care.of.it-TI1-21p	**to**-eats-21p	**to**-feed.h/-21p>3_{CONJ}

giniijaanisinaan
our.child

'We have to take care of it **to eat** and **to feed** our children' (Benton 2013, 163)

d. *aaniindi **da**-atooyaan*

aaniindi	**da**-at-oo-yaan
where	**to**-put.it-TI2-1_{CONJ}

'Where do I put it' (Bainbridge 1997, 54)

e. ***da**-ozhitoowaad ow, yo'ow madoodooswan*

da-ozhit-oo-waad	ow	yo'ow	madoodooswan
to-make.it-TI2-3p_{CONJ}	DET	DET	sweatlodge

'**to** build this sweat lodge' (Rogers 2013, 126)

f. *gaawiin dash owii-kashkitoosiinaawaa **da**-anishinaabemowaad*

gaawiin	dash	o-wii-gashkit-oo-sii-naawaa	**da**-anishinaabemo-waad
NEG	but	3-FUT-able-TI2-NEG-3p	**to**-speak.Indian-3p_{CONJ}

*gaye **da**-nisidotamowaad*

gaye	**da**-nisidotam-waad
also	**to**-understands-3p_{CONJ}

'But they won't be able **to speak** Indian **or (to) understand**' (JChosa.13.20.03.N)

Age-graded comparison of archived material with modern varieties shows the use of *da-* at Lac Courte Oreilles is at least one generation old (139). While the examples above all show the use of the complementizer translated as an infinitival, the *ji-/da-* complementizer is also translated with the complementizer 'that,' as in the first occurrence of *da-* below, though carrying the same infinitival meaning:

(139) Miish iwapii **da**-zhiibiniketawang manidoo, **da**-miigwechiwi'ang ow sa inendaagoziyang miinawaa wiidookawangwaa agiw gidewe'iganinaanig

'And that is the time **that** we extend our arms out to the manidoo **to** thank him for our being considered again to help out with those drums of ours' (PM.Dewe'igan)

This appears to be a more recent innovation in communities at St. Croix, where speakers a generation ago were still using *ji-*, as shown here in (140):[5]

(140) *ji-izhi-gaagiigidod*
'to speak in such a way' (Mosay 1996, 36)

Historical documentation from the mid-nineteenth century show the *ji-* complementizer was once used in the areas where it now appears to have been replaced completely by *da-*:

(141) *ji-* complementizer in Wisconsin (Nichols 1988a, 31)

iw dash wiikaa miinawaa **ji**-mamoosiweg

iw	dash	wiikaa	miinawaa	**ji**-mam-oo-siw-eg
DET	but	ever	again	**to**-take-TI2-NEG-2p$_{CONJ}$

'that you may not be able **to** take it again'

Additionally the related tense marker *jibwaa-* 'before,' consisting of the complementizer and the tense preverb *bwaa-*, shows the same pattern of variation: *jibwaa-* is used consistently in the north, but where the complementizer is *da-*, the tense preverb is *dabwaa-*:[6]

(142) *dabwaa-* tense preverb

a. ***dabwaa**-maajitaad **da**-gii'igoshimod*

da-bwaa-maajitaa-d   **da**-gii'igoshimo-d
to-lest-starts-3$_{CONJ}$ **to**-fasts-3$_{CONJ}$

'**Before** (a young man) goes out **to** fast' (LS.Makadeked)

b. ***dabwaa**-dagoshing aw wayaabishkiiwed.*

da-bwaa-dagoshin-g   aw   IC-waabishkiiwe-d
to-lest-arrives-3$_{CONJ}$ DET   IC-is.white-3$_{CONJ}$

'**before** the Whiteman arrived.' (Benton 2013, 162)

Some speakers from the districts of Mille Lacs (Aazhoomog) appear to use both interchangeably:

(143) *ji-/da-* in free variation

 a. *mii go **dabwaa**-biindigeyaan*
 '**before** I even got inside' (AS.Aamoog)

 b. *gii-nibenaazhikawaa **jibwaa**-wiisinid*
 'He was sent to bed **before** he ate' (AS.14.05.20.E)

With the frequent alternation between /d/ and /j/ in palatalization environments, the alternation here should not be too much of a surprise. The modal prefix *ji-/da-* differs from the tense preverb *da-*, discussed above in 2.3.4, used in third-person unprefixed future tense:

(144) *da-* tense preverb

 da-*minozowag*

da-	minozo	-wag
FUT-	is.well.cooked	-3p$_{IND}$

 'They'll cook well' (AS.Aadizookaan)

It also differs from the prefixed future tense marker *da-* of the independent order found in Wisconsin and eastern Minnesota, which takes a personal prefix:

(145) *da-* 1/2 tense preverb

 a. *Ishke dash gaawiin geyaabi memwech in**da**-mamoosiinan*

ishke	dash	gaawin	geyaabi	memwech	in-**da**-mam-oo-siin-an
see	but	NEG	still	necessary	1-**FUT**-take-TI2-NEG-0p

 inow mashkikiinsan

inow	mashkiki-iins-an
DET	medicine-DIM-0p

 'I no longer **have to** take (diabetes) medication' (LS.AmbeSaNoo)

b. *Akawe maa, in**da**-wiindamaage o'ow* . . .
akawe   maa   in-da-wiindamaage   o'ow
first   EMPH   1-FUT-tell.people   DET
'First of all, I'm going to tell about this . . .' (Rogers 2013, 126)

c. *ingiw Manidoog gi**da**-naadamaagowaag*
ingiw   manidoo-g   gi-da-naadamaw-igw-waa-g
DET   spirit-3p   2-FUT-help.h/-INV-2p-3p
'the manidoog will help you' (Staples and Gonzalez 2015, 28)

Such uses of *da-* appear to be a peculiarity of the southern communities. I have found no examples of this use of the prefixed future tense marker *da-*, or the complementizer *da-*, north of Mille Lacs.

3.3.2. Preterit Peripheral Suffixes

The vowel of the preterit peripheral suffixes varies between /ii/ [i] and /e/ [e]. Baraga (1850) reported the high front vowel /ii/ in his early work in northern Michigan. Nichols recorded /e/ in his fieldwork at Mille Lacs, contrary to most recorded Ojibwe dialects that show the connective /ii/ between the preterit suffix /-ban/ and a peripheral suffix (1980, 186). The /e/ variant is also reported for Western Algonquin, in western Quebec; in Ontario at Nipissing, Osnaburgh, and Whitefish Bay; and in Minnesota at Red Lake (Valentine 1994, 380). Speakers consulted from Lac Courte Oreilles in Wisconsin pattern with speakers at Mille Lacs, showing /e/:

(146) Preterit plural *-eg*

a. *nimishoomisiban**eg***
'my late grandfathers' (EB.Dewe'igan)

b. *akiwenziiyiban**eg***
'late old men' (PM.Dewe'igan2)

c. *mindimooyenyiban**eg***
'late old ladies' (AL.WNLP.2)

With the exception of the finding reported by Nichols (1980), the majority of speakers in Minnesota consulted in this study employ /ii/. It is perplexing at this point to determine if this variant constitutes any regional parameter for variation, especially when two speakers from the same area (Aazhoomog) each employ a different variant:

(147) Variation at Aazhoomog
    a. *mindimooyenyibaneg*
    'late old ladies' (Staples and Gonzalez 2015, 24)

    b. *nimishoomisibaniig*
    'my late grandfathers' (AS.13.07.16.E)

Additionally the suffix *-eg* is used by speakers from Red Lake, along with the other variant *-iig*:

(148) *ningii-noondaan ko iwe nimishoomisibaniig*
    'I used to hear *nimishomisibaniig*' (RD.14.06.11.E)

The same alternation occurs with obviative nouns in the preterit mode. Speakers who provide *-iig* for plural preterit animate nouns provide obviative forms with the same vowel:

(149) Preterit obviative *-en/-iin*
    a. *nizhishenh ozhishenyibaniin*
    'my uncle's uncle' (AS.12.10.30.N)

    b. *obaabaayibanen*
    'h/ late father' (Benton 2013, 161)

The variable appears to go unnoticed by most speakers. After eliciting *nimishoomisibaniig* from two elders from Leech Lake, I asked them if they had ever heard *nimishoomisibaneg*, to which one replied, "*Mii iwe gegwe-ikidoyaan!*" 'That's what I was trying to say!'

3.3.3. Neutralization of Inanimate Plural in Conjunct

One particular parameter that consistently shows a north/south distinction concerns inanimate plural agreement inflection in the conjunct order of inanimate intransitive (VII) verbs. Valentine describes this neutralization of number in the conjunct order for inanimates occurring in all southern dialects (1994, 388). This appears to be a significant parameter of geographical variation observed at least since Baraga (1850, 377) and the fieldwork of Nichols (1980), which occurred in the 1960s and 1970s. "Correction" data from northern speakers (Lac La Croix and Ponemah) yields interesting and consistent results. Speakers from the north insist on providing the plural suffix when presented with a southern construction lacking the inanimate plural conjunct suffix:

(150) Original prompt: *Mii wanising iniw Anishinaabe-izhinikaazowinan.*
'Indian names are being lost' (Clark 2001, 68)

a. *mii wanisingin anishinaabewinikaazowinan* (GJ.14.01.09.GJ-C)

mii	wanisin-g-**in**	Anishinaabe-izhinikaazowin-an
thus	is.lost-0$_{\text{CONJ}}$-**0p**$_{\text{CONJ}}$	Indian-name-0p

b. *mii ani-wanisingin iniwen izhinikaazowinan* (RD.14.06.11.GJ-C)

mii	ani-wanisin-g-**in**		iniwen	izhinikaazowin-an
thus	go.along-is.lost-0$_{\text{CONJ}}$-**0p**$_{\text{CONJ}}$		DET	name-0p

Two speakers from the Leech Lake community at Inger commented on the example being "fine" but preferred the construction without the plural morphology. Another speaker from Aazhoomog rejected *wanisingin* but accepted the participle form *wenisingin*, resulting in a relativized and topicalized interpretation:

(151) *mii **wenisingin** iniw Anishinaabe-izhinikaazowinan*

mii	**IC**-wanisin-g-**in**	iniw	Anishinaabe-izhinikaazowin-an
thus	**IC**-is.lost-0$_{\text{CONJ}}$-**PL**$_{\text{PRT}}$	DET	Indian-name-0p

'It is Indian names that are being lost '(AS.13.07.16.GJ-C)

Nichols (2011) determined that for speakers at Mille Lacs (and in the south in general), plural inanimate agreement morphology occurs only with participles in relative clauses (as in [151] above) where a core argument is head:

(152) *akina gegoo imaa gaa-ozhibii'igaadegin*

akina	gegoo	imaa	IC-gii-ozhibii'igaade-g-**in**
all	something	there	IC-PST-is.written-0$_{\text{CONJ}}$-**PL**$_{\text{PRT}}$

'all the things **that were written** there' (AS.Gii-nitaawigiyaan)

When consulting speakers from northern communities, the plural is indicated for all types of RCs, regardless of whether the head of the RC is a core argument or a relative root argument, as shown here in (153):

(153) *mii imaa nangona eteg**in** mazina'iganan*

mii	imaa	nangona	IC-ate-g-**in**	mazina'igan-an
thus	there	EMPH	IC-is.put-0_{CONJ}-**PL$_{PRT}$**	book-0p

'That's **where** the books are' (GJ.15.07.16.GJ-C)

Southern speakers don't employ the suffix outside of the core argument participles used in relatives, as the example below in (154) indicates, where the subject (*nagamonan* 'songs') is plural but the RR argument relativized is singular:

(154) *mii dash iwapii niiwin ishkwaaj aniw nagamonan **eyaabadak***

mii	dash	iwapii	niiwin	ishkwaaj	aniw	nagamon-an	IC-aabadad-g
thus	then	that. time	four	last	DET	song-0p	IC-is.used-0_{CONJ}

'And then that is **when** those four last songs that are used' (PM.Dewe'igan.2)

For all speakers consulted from northern communities, plural inanimate agreement morphology appears in the conjunct order (as in [150a.] and [150b.]), while for southern speakers, number in the conjunct order is neutralized (as seen in the original prompt for [150]). Interestingly, at Inger, the same speakers who accepted the omission of the plural suffix discussed in (150) above provided the examples shown below in (155), this time opting to use the plural marker:

(155) Inanimate conjunct plural number (northern)

a. *gego biizikangen ini makazinan onzaam michaag**in***

gego	biizik-am-ken	ini	makazin-an	onzaam	michaa-g-**in**
don't	wear.it-TI1-NEG	DET	shoe	-0p excess	is.big-0_{CONJ}-0p$_{CONJ}$

'If the shoes are big don't wear them' (LW.GH.14.07.16.E)

b. *giishpin wiinak**in** iniw badaka'iganan gidaa-giziibiiginaanan*

giishpin	wiinad-g-**in**	iniw	badaka'igan-an	gi-daa-giziibiigin-am-an
if	is.dirty-0_{CONJ}-$0p_{CONJ}$	DET	fork-0p	2-MOD-wash.it-TI1-0p

'If the forks are dirty wash them' (LW.GH.14.07.16.E)

Though no such examples of inanimate plural marking in the plain conjunct exist in my data from the south, RCs are easy to elicit with southern speakers, with the plural head always showing number agreement with the participle:

(156) VII number inflection (southern)

a. Singular

gii-maadaasin iw aniibiishibag gaa-pangising

gii-maadaasin	iw	aniibiishibag	IC-gii-bangisin-g
PST-blow.away	DET	leaf	IC-PST-falls-0_{CONJ}

'The **leaf that fell** blew away' (AS.14.07.15.E)

b. Plural

gii-maadaasinoon iniw aniibiishibagoon gaa-pangisingin

gii-maadaasin-oon	iniw	aniibiishibag-oon	IC-gii-bangisin-g-**in**
PST-blows.away-$0p_{IND}$	DET	leaf-0p	IC-PST-falls-0_{CONJ}-**PL**$_{PRT}$

'The **leaves that fell** blew away' (AS.14.07.15.E)

According to Valentine, Odawa, Nipissing, and "Michigan Chippewa" all pattern with "Minnesota Chippewa" in regard to inanimate number neutralization in the conjunct, though variation in "Minnesota Chippewa" is not mentioned (1994, 388). He lists Algonquin, Northwestern Ojibwe, Severn Ojibwe, and Saulteaux as dialects that employ a plural suffix.

Valentine also discusses the use of a plural suffix for inanimate objects of the VTI paradigm (1994, 352). He provides the following example from Algonquin where a plural suffix is used on both the first- and third-person forms of VTIs:

(157) Algonquin VTI conjunct plural (from Valentine 1994, 352)

Mii	gabe-giizhig	gegaad	ge-izhitaayaan	biinish	dash	niizhidana
so	all.day	almost	I.was.busy	until	then	20

giji-ozhitoowaan**in**	giji-ozhitoo**jin**	gewiin	nizhoomisim
I.made.them.**INAN.PL**	he.made.them.**INAN.PL**	h.too	my.old.man

'I was busy almost all day at it, until I had made 20 of them, and my husband too made them . . .'

All northern and southern speakers surveyed for the current study provided examples where inanimate object number was neutralized in the plain conjunct with transitive verbs:

(158) VTI inanimate number

a. *iishpin gikendang iniw nagamowinan da-zhaabowe.*

iishpin	gikend-am-**g**	iniw	nagamowin-an	da-zhaabowe
if	knows-TI1-0$_{CONJ}$	DET	song-0p	FUT-sings.accompaniment

'If she knows the songs she will sing along' (AS.13.07.16.E)

b. *giishpin agindang gakina mazina'iganan da-chi-gikendaaso*

giishpin	agind-am-**g**	gakina	mazina'igan-an	da-chi-gikendaaso
if	reads.it-TI1-0$_{CONJ}$	all	book-0p	FUT-great-is.wise

'If she reads all the books she will be smart' (EG.13.08.07.E)

However, with regard to participles and RCs, inflections for plural objects in transitive verbs occur in the southern communities, but are not found in the north:

(159) *niwii-ayaanan iniw aabajichiganan ayaabajitoojin a'aw inini*

ni-wii-ay-aa-an	iniw	aabajichigan-an	IC-aabajit-oo-**d-in**	a'aw	inini
1-FUT-have.it-TI4-0p	DET	tool-0p	IC-use.it-TI2-**3-PL**$_{PRT}$	DET	man

'I need the tools the man is using' (AS.13.07.16.E)

This is a variable discussed in 3.3.13.1 with regard to southern strategies for participle formation.

3.3.4. Number under Obviation

Another important variable in Ojibwe regional variation concerns the treatment of plural arguments under obviation. Valentine observes that the obviative plural occurs in some varieties but not others, noting its widespread existence in Berens, "occurring over most of western Ontario, south to the Minnesota border, and into all of Saulteaux" (1994, 421). For varieties with an obviative plural, the plural marking occurs on nouns and verbs in the independent order, but is neutralized in the conjunct. The example below illustrates all three cases in point:

(160) Obviative plural
[$_a$ owaabamaa'] [$_b$ migiziwa'] [$_c$ gizhiibaayaashinid]
o-waabam-aa-'   migizi-**wa'**   gizhibaayaashi-**nid**
3-see.h/-DIR-**OBV.PL** eagle-**OBV.PL** whirls.in.wind-**OBV**$_{CONJ}$
[$_a$ He sees them$_{OBV.PL}$] [$_b$ the eagles$_{OBV.PL}$] [gliding around in a cirlce$_{OBV}$]

'He sees the eagles gliding around in a circle' (Jones 2013a, 13)

The singular obviative form lacks the glottal stop, represented by /'/:

(161) Obviative singular
owii-mawadisaawaan Gaagaagiwan ji-aadizookamaagowaad
o-wii-mawadiS-aa-waa-**n**   Gaagaagi-**wan**
3-FUT-visit.h/-DIR-3p-**OBV**$_{SG}$ Raven$_{PN}$-**OBV**$_{SG}$

ji-aadizookamaagowaad
ji-aadizookamaw-go-waad
to-tell.legends.to.h/-INV-3p$_{CONJ}$

'They were going to visit **the Raven**$_{SG}$ so **he**$_{SG}$ could tell them stories' (Jones 2013b, 23)

All speakers consulted from the Border Lakes region have a number distinction for obviative arguments in the independent order verbal inflection as well as the obviative noun:

(162) *Makoons niibiwa ogii-agwaawebinaa' giigoonya'*
makoons   niibiwa   o-gii-agwaawebin-aa   -'   giigoonh-**a'**
PN   many   3-PST-throw.ashore-DIR   -**PL**$_{OBV}$ fish-**PL**$_{OBV}$
'Makoons threw **many of the fish** onto the shore' (Jones 2013a, 18)

The example below exemplifies the difference between the singular (163a.) and the plural obviatives (163b.):

(163) Obviative singular vs. plural
    a. ogii-ando-mawadisaa**n**   ogozis**an**
    she.goes.to.visit.h/$_{OBV.SG}$ h/.son$_{OBV.SG}$
    'She went to visit her son' (GJ.14.01.09.E)

    b. ogii-ando-mawadisaa'   ogozisa'
    she.goes.to.visit.them$_{OBV.PL}$ h/sons$_{OBV.PL}$
    'She went to visit her sons' (GJ.14.01.09.E)

For speakers of the southern communities, there is no obviative plural marking option. The following example illustrates this point; 'their spirits' is contextually plural, though not overtly marked morphologically:

(164) *Gindidawizi**wan** ojichaag**owaan** aano-go gii-chaagidenig*
    gindidawizi-**wan**   o-jichaag-**owaan**   aano-go   gii-chaagidenig
    is.whole-**OBV**   3-spirit-**POSS.3p>3'**   even.though   PST.burn.CONJ

    inow   owiiyawiwaan
    inow   owiiyaw-iwaan
    DEM   3.body-POSS.3p>0p

    'Their spirits are whole even though their bodies are burned' (Staples and Gonzalez 2014, 24)

The absence of an obviative plural marker in southern varieties results in structural ambiguity where the singular and plural forms are morphologically identical, as the examples below in (165) indicate:

(165) Structural ambiguity
    a. ogii-o-mawadisaan   iniw   oozhishenyan
    s/he.goes.visit.h/   DET$_{OBV}$ grandchild$_{OBV}$
    'she went to visit her **grandson**' (AS.13.07.16.E)

b. ogii-o-mawadisaan   iniw   oozhishenyan
s/he.goes.visit.h/   DET_OBV   grandchild(ren)_OBV
'she went to visit her **grandsons**' (AS.13.07.16.E)

Many speakers remark in surprise when this is called to their attention, appearing never to have realized this ambiguity prior to our sessions, suggesting it is not as much of a concern for speakers as it is for L2 learners.

Nichols (2011) states that the obviative plural inflection can be found only in Minnesota, at Bois Forte; no information from Grand Portage is available however. He provides the example shown below in (166):

(166) Bois Forte obviative plural (from Nichols 2011)
       Aaniish, a'aw idash akiwenzii-ma'iingan oganoonaa' i'iw oniijaanisa'.
       | well | that | and/but | old man wolf | he addresses them | those | his children |
       Now the old wolf (3) addressed his (3) children (3'p) (Midaasoganzh, retranscribed from Jones 1.162)

The example shows not only the obviative plural inflection on both the verb and the obviative noun, but also the demonstrative *i'iw*, identical in form to *i'iw* 'that,' an inanimate singular referent.

This example occurs in the William Jones collection of texts collected over a century ago; Nichols had no speakers from Bois Forte to consult concerning variation or to determine whether or not the obviative plural inflection is still used by speakers there. However, while speakers of the Lake Vermilion community near Tower, Minnesota, do show the plural obviative argument inflection, as illustrated in (167), speakers of the more northern community of Nett Lake do not, so the structural ambiguity shown in (165) is illustrated again in (168):

(167) Obviation at Lake Vermilion
       a. Singular
       ogii-awi-mawidisaan   ogozisan
       she.went.to.visit.h/   h/son_OBV-SG
       'she went to visit her son' (RB.13.08.06.E)

b. Plural
ogii-mawadisaa'   ogozisa'
she.visited.them$_{OBV-PL}$ h.sons$_{OBV-PL}$
'she visited her sons' (RB.13.08.06.E)

(168) Obviation at Nett Lake
a. Singular
ogii-mawadisaan   ogozisan
she.visited.h/$_{OBV}$ h/son$_{OBV}$
'she visited her son' (EG.13.08.07.E)

b. Plural
ogii-mawadisaan   ogozisan
she.visited.h/$_{OBV}$ h/son$_{OBV}$
'she visited her sons' (EG.13.08.07.E)

When attempting to back-translate examples collected from the Lake Vermilion community with the speaker from the Nett Lake community, the speaker observed, "That's another dialect." Such insight provides us with evidence that variation can occur on the same reservation, especially if speakers there have different histories and historical ties to different places. This is discussed briefly in 3.4.1.

3.3.5. Restructuring of Dependent Stems

Many dependent noun stems commonly show variation, though such variation does not appear to be determined by a north/south distinction. Dependent nouns, such as kinship terms and body parts, and some verb stems with relative roots show variation among modern speakers. Kinship terms, which are inherently possessed nouns, occur with the possessor built into the stem, rather than by the affixation of the possessor typical of noun possession:

(169) =*ookomis* 'grandmother'

nookomis   *gookomis*   *ookomisan*
'my grandmother'   'your grandmother'   'h/ grandmother$_{OBV}$'

Many younger speakers, especially in the south, appear to have reanalyzed the dependent stems based on the second-person form above, and affix the typical personal prefix for nondependent noun stem possession to the second-person form:

(170) =*gookomis* 'grandmother' reanalysis

*ni*gookomis   *gi*gookomis   *o*gookomisan
'my grandmother'   'your grandmother'   'h/ grandmother'

Valentine (1994) finds such variation at Red Lake, with the dependent form of *niibid* 'my tooth' given as *niwiibid*, in which the third-person form is reanalyzed as the stem. Nichols provides *niwiinizisan* and *niinizisan* for 'my hair (pl.)' and determines such variation to be age-graded, with younger speakers showing the reanalyzed independent form (1980, 45). Valentine observes similar restructuring to some degree for Odawa, Western Algonquin, and North Bay, which show the "reanalyzed stem from—gookom," for my grandmother, *nigookomis* (1994, 308).

In one narrative I collected from an anonymous speaker, three different variants occurred in his speech. The first (171a.) appears to be the typical restructuring mentioned by Valentine, where the first-person possessive marker is prefixed to the reanalyzed second-person possessive form. With regard to the second variant (171b.), the speaker appears to have overgeneralized the possession rule, prefixing the first-person possession marker on top of the already possessed dependent stem. The example shown in (171c.) shows the traditional pattern observed by Nichols (1980):

(171) Variants of 'my grandmother'
     a. **ni**gookomis
     b. **nin**ookomis
     c. **n**ookomis

Two speakers from the Ponemah community at Red Lake responded with the typical dependent stem forms shown in (172a.), while another from Ponemah provided a reanalyzed form, built on the first-person dependent stem (172b.):

(172) Variation at Ponemah
  a. *Binesi **ookomisan** ominwenimaan mishiiminan*
    'Binesi's grandma likes apples'
  b. *gwiiwizens gaa-pi-ombigii'igod iniw **onookomisan** nitaa-ojibwemo*
    'The boy that was raised by his grandma speaks good Ojibwe'

In addition to dependent noun stems, the lexical preverbs *niiji-* 'my fellow,' *giiji-* 'your fellow,' and *wiiji-* 'h/ fellow' appear to be undergoing the same change. Traditionally, and still among older speakers, stems of this sort are treated similarly to dependent stems:

(173) **niiji**-*gikinoo'amaaganag*   **giiji**-*gikinoo'amaaganag*   **wiiji**-*gikinoo'amaaganan*
       'my fellow students'   'your fellow students'   'h/ fellow student(s)$_{OBV}$'

Innovations such as those described above for dependent noun stems appear to be occurring here as well, where the third-person form is treated as the inflectable stem:

(174) Restructuring of lexical preverb
  a. **niwiiji**-*gikinoo'amaaganag*
    'my fellow students'
  b. **giwiiji**-*gikinoo'amaaganag*
    'your fellow students'
  c. **owiiji**-*gikinoo'amaaganan*
    'h/ fellow students$_{OBV}$'

Since each pattern can be found in both the north and the south, and even within the same community, the variable does not seem to reflect any geographic distribution criteria of regional dialect variation.

3.3.6. Core Demonstratives

Perhaps the most obvious feature of geographic dialect variation is concerned with what Nichols (2011) refers to as "core demonstratives." As discussed above in 2.3.2 demonstrative pronouns show considerable variation from community to community. Many plural animate demonstrative forms are pronounced by speakers outside of Mille Lacs and Leech Lake

Table 32. Demonstrative pronouns

Gender	Gloss	Mille Lacs	Ponemah and Border Lakes	Odawa	Wisconsin
ANIMATE	'this'	wa'aw	wa'awe	maaba	wa'aw
	'that'	a'aw	a'awe	aw, wa	ya'aw
	'these'	ongow	ogowe(g)	gonda	wogow
	'those'	ingiw	igiwe(g)	giw	agiw
INANIMATE	'this'	o'ow	o'owe	maanda	yo'ow
	'that'	i'iw	i'iwe	iw, wi	i'iw
	'these'	onow	onowe(n)	nonda	onow
	'those'	iniw	iniwe(n)	niw	aniw

without a nasal, for example, *ogo* versus *ongow, igi* versus *ingiw*. Valentine finds forms without the nasal at Kingfisher Lake, Ontario (1994, 129). Also in the communities of Lac du Flambeau and Lac Courte Oreilles, Wisconsin, as well as Ponemah, Minnesota, plural animate demonstratives occur without the nasal. The archived material found in Baraga (1850), Schoolcraft (1851), Josselin de Jong (1913), and Nichols (1988a) present demonstratives with no nasal, suggesting that what Nichols (1980) recorded at Mille Lacs is the exception for Ojibwe. Additionally, many speakers consulted from the St. Croix communities, especially at Round Lake, provide demonstrative pronouns that pattern with Mille Lacs and not the characteristic "Wisconsin" (nasal-less) forms provided here. The nasalized plural forms (*ingiw, ongow*) can also be found at Leech Lake, both in the northern community of Inger and the more southern communities of Onigum and Boy Lake. Nichols (2011) also gives full forms for Ponemah that are common at both Nett Lake and the Border Lakes communities.

Table 32 compares the demonstrative pronouns found by Nichols at Mille Lacs (1980) and at Ponemah (2011), along with the Wikwemikong Odawa forms provided in Valentine (1994, 425), as well as the Wisconsin forms I collected at Lac Courte Oreilles, Hertel, and Lac du Flambeau.[7]

Demonstratives are also commonly reduced in running speech, a feature of the language that has been that way for a while (see Nichols 1988a for numerous cases of *aw* versus *a'aw*). When sentences were elicited, as in (175a.), it was common for northern speakers to provide the full forms (*a'awe, ogoweg, iniwen,* and so on); however, when short phrases were elicited from the same speakers, such as 'this book,' 'that dog' (175b.), the shorter forms (*aw, a'aw, ogow, iniw*) were common:

(175) Sentential examples vs. phrase-level elicitation

a. Sentential

ningikenimaag	**igiweg**	ininiwag	gaa-miinaawaad	iniwen
I.know.them	**those**	men	who.gave.them	those$_{OBV}$

ikwewan	bebezhigoganzhiin	maagizhaa	gaye	mishtadim
women$_{OBV}$	horses$_{OBV}$	maybe	also	horse

indaa-ikid
I.should.say

'I know the men who gave the horses to the women, or maybe I should say *mishtadim*' (RD.14.06.11.E)

b. Phrase-level
igiw animoshag
those dogs
'those dogs' (RD.14.06.11.E)

The examples below in (176) show how the same speaker from Ponemah provided a long form for an inanimate plural demonstrative in (176a.), whereas the example shown in (176b.) shows the shorter form in the obviative context:

(176) Demonstrative variation

a. onagamonan	**iniwen**	nagamonan	gaa-miinag
he.sings.songs	**those**	songs	which.I.gave.him

'He sings the songs I gave him' (RD.14.06.11.E)

b. oga-gojimaamaan	**iniw**	opiniin
h/.will.smell.them	**those**	potatoes$_{OBV}$

'He will smell the potatoes' (RD.14.06.11.E)

Another interesting finding concerning pronouns involves the existence of what Nichols calls "disjunctive personal pronouns" (1980, 63). These are similar to the "affirmative pronouns" in Plains Cree (Wolfart 1973, 4.5) and express "surprise or affirmation." The modern forms collected near Aazhoomog differ slightly from those recorded by Nichols in regard to vowel quality and carry an accusative type of meaning:

(177) Disjunctive personal pronouns

Nichols 1980	Modern	Gloss
niinidog	*niinedog*	'that's me!'
giinidog	*giinedog*	'that's you!'
wiinidog	*wiinedog*	'that's h/!'

These were found only in the speech of one modern speaker who happens to be the nephew of Nichols's (1980) chief consultant, suggesting they are not in very widespread usage.

The "Wisconsin" demonstratives shown in table 32 are relevant to the discussion of vowel quality in 3.3.7.3.2, where /a/ is in place of /i/ and vice versa:

(178) *minawaa aniw onaabeman*
    'and her husband' (JChosa.13.20.03.C)

Vowel quality is treated below in 3.3.7.3 in the discussion of phonological variation, to which we now turn.

3.3.7. Phonological Variation

Though the main focus of this chapter is on morphological variation, I provide a few remarks on phonological variation observed over the course of this study. Valentine finds that stress rules vary from dialect to dialect though no investigation of stress is provided here (1994, 50). Most of the variation observed is very subtle and could very well be overlooked in a less thorough investigation. As we will see, much of the variation described here does not split along geographical lines; in a few cases, it represents mere relic features. Valentine observes that there are some "minor lexically-constrained phonological deletions" that occur in SW Ojibwe (1994, 447); only those most relevant to the current study are discussed here.

3.3.7.1. Nasal Behavior

As we will see in this section, the behavior of the nasal /n/ adds an interesting dimension to the picture of variation in SW Ojibwe. Certain aspects of the variation are more pronounced than others.

3.3.7.1.1. Initial /n/

Widely observed by students of Ojibwe is the variation in the use of the dubitative adverb *(n)amanj* 'I don't know; I wonder.' Nichols (1980) finds the form *amanj*, without the initial nasal, at Mille Lacs; it is the form preferred by many modern speakers there. In the easternmost Mille Lacs community, both *namanj* and *amanj* are attested by speakers of the same generation:

(179) *(n)amanj* at Aazhoomog

　a. *amanj*
　'I don't know' (LS.15.06.18.C)

　b. *namanj iidog ge gaa-kiziindame'owaanen*
　'I wonder if I even wiped' (AS.Aamoog)

Further east into Wisconsin, both forms are attested at Lac Courte Oreilles, even from the same speaker:

(180) **amanj** *iwapii*, **namanj** *minik*, **amanj** *iwapii gaa-wiindamowaagwen dabwaa-oo'iding*
　'I'm not sure, of when they would name the dates before coming together' (PM.Dewe'igan2)

At Lac du Flambeau, only the nasal-less form was recorded:

(181) **amanj** *izhinikaadeg iw that slingshot*
　'I don't know what that slingshot is called' (JChosa.13.20.03.C)

Aside from Lac Courte Oreilles and Aazhoomog, *namanj* only was found at Lake Vermilion, Onigum, and Ponemah, with speakers from Lac La Croix, Nett Lake, Inger, Boy Lake, and Ponemah preferring *amanj*. At Ponemah, both variants were found:

(182) Variation at Ponemah

a. ***namanj*** *igo waa-soogiponogwen*
'I wonder if it's going to snow.' (ES.12.03.28.E)

b. ***amanj*** *ezhinikaazogwen*
'I wonder what her name is' (RD.14.06.11.E)

Also, one Ponemah speaker used each variant during the same session:

(183) Same speaker same day

a. ***namanj*** *ezhichigegwen.*
'I don't know what the heck he is doing.' (12.04.03.RT.E)

b. ***amanj*** *iidog gaa-izhigwen.*
'I have no idea what she said to me.' (12.04.03.RT.E)

As the above examples indicate the dubitative pronoun does not seem to follow any consistent pattern in regard to geographic distribution.

Another instance of initial /n/ deletion does, however. Nichols (2011) tracks the distribution of initial /n/ in the preverb and root *(n)andaw-/(n)ando-*. He finds speakers at Red Lake (Ponemah), northern Leech Lake, and Bois Forte supplying the forms without the initial nasal (*anda-/ando-*), while speakers at Mille Lacs and southern Leech Lake provide examples with the initial /n/ (*nanda-/nando-*). He notes age-graded variation in regard to this variable: for older speakers, the /n/ comes back following a prefix, whereas for younger speakers, the root has been completely reanalyzed as lacking the nasal. Nichols also notes how the root is analyzed in reduplication strategies used by older speakers compared to younger ones. The example below in (184a.) shows the prefix without the nasal, whereas (184b.) shows how the /n/ comes back with the addition of a personal prefix:

(184) /n/ replacement

a. *nigikendaan ge-izhi-**ando**-wiisiniyaan*
'I know where I'll get my meal' (Jones 2013a, 12)

b. *gi**nanda**wenimigoo ji-wiikoongetaagoziyan*
'we would like you to say the blessing' (Jones 2013a, 21)

All speakers consulted from Mille Lacs, Aazhoomog, Lac Courte Oreilles, St. Croix, and Lac du Flambeau use the initial /n/ variant, while speakers from Leech Lake (both southern and northern), Red Lake, Bois Forte, and the Border Lakes show variation in regard to if and when the nasal returns. One speaker from a Border Lakes community provided examples of each variant, in the exact same environment, following a third-person prefix *o-*:

(185) Before third-person prefix *o-*

a. *ikwewag **onanda**-waabamaawaan odaabaanan*
ikwew-ag   o-nandawaabam-aa-waan   odaabaan-an
woman-3p   3-look.for.h/-DIR-3p   car-OBV
'the women are looking for a car' (Anonymous.E)

b. ***odandone'aan** ogozisan gaa-maajiiba'iwenid*
od-andone'-aa-n   o-gozis-an   IC-gii-maajiiba'iwe-nid
3-search.for.h/-DIR-OBV   3-son-OBV   IC-PST-flees-OBV
'she is looking for her son who ran away' (Anonymous.E)

The example shown above in (185b.) is striking since the root in this case appears to have been reanalyzed as *ando-*, to the degree where the speaker chose to provide the epenthetic /d/, which only occurs when personal prefixes are attached to verbs that begin with a vowel.

One Ponemah speaker (younger than Nichols's Ponemah consultant) treats the root without the initial nasal in all recorded uses and conjugations. By comparison to archived material from the area (Josselin de Jong 1913, 2), we can determine that such pronunciations are an innovation, occurring within the past few generations. However, archived material from Bois Forte in Jones (1919) shows the nasal-less *andaw-/ando-*, suggesting the variation in that region is quite old.

For Leech Lake, an area noted by Nichols (2011) as having a north-south division with treatment of the *(n)andaw-/(n)ando-* root, southern speakers show variation, contrary to Nichols's claims. One speaker from Onigum, the southernmost community of Leech Lake, appears to have reanalyzed the root, treating it without the initial /n/:

(186) odaabaanan obaa-**andaw**aabamaawaan ikwewag
'The women are looking for a car' (JB.1307.17.E)

Another from Boy Lake uses each variant, in exactly the same environment:

(187) Free variation (Whipple 2015, 70)
   a. *babaa-**n**andawaabamaawaad*
   'to go around looking for h/'

   b. *babaa-**a**ndawaabamaad*
   'to go around looking for h/'

With no examples collected of such variation south of Leech Lake, we can assume this is an innovation occurring in the north that has not yet occurred in the south.

A number of other lexical items show variation with respect to initial /n/ within SW Ojibwe and throughout the Ojibweyan family. Certain words with initial nasals are found in Baraga's (1850, 481) and Nichols's (1980, 134) data that seem to have dropped the nasals in more modern varieties, for example, *ningoji* 'somewhere' is *ingoji* more commonly today. Surprisingly, at least one speaker from a Border Lakes community still maintains the initial /n/ in her pronunciation:

(188) *gaawiin **ningoji** niwii-izhaasii noongom gaa-giizhigak*
   'I'm not going anywhere today' (NJ.OPD.ningoji)

Valentine records a variant of the degree adverbial *aapiji* with an initial /n/, *naapiji*, in Severn Ojibwe (1994, 185). He also provides discussion on the varying initial /n/ on *(n)ingod-* 'one' (447) and the first-person prefix *(n)in-*, *(n)im-* (448), as well as a stray "northern" variant worth mentioning, *asemaa* 'tobacco' as *nasemaa* (130). The reader is referred to that study for more discussion of the behavior of initial /n/.

3.3.7.1.2. Final Nasal in Negation Suffix -*sii(n)*

Another feature showing considerable variation in its distribution is what Valentine refers to as the "augment -n which occurs on negative animate intransitive verbs with first person inflection" (1994, 398). According to Nichols, it is a feature of Mille Lacs Ojibwe "shared with Severn Ojibwe, but not with the adjacent Western dialect or the Lake Superior dialect described by Baraga" (1980, 212). Valentine finds the "distribution of this feature erratic and not usable as a means of distinguishing dialects" (1994, 398). Where Valentine assumes it is only an augment occurring on VAIs with first-person inflection, it is much more widespread in the SW Ojibwe data. Nichols (1980) gives examples of a VAI with first-person inflection, VTA 1>3 (first-person participant acting on a third-person object) inflection, and VTA 2>1 inflection, all showing the final /n/. Where Baraga (1850, 105) recorded the negative VAIs without the /n/, he provided examples of the VTI paradigm showing the final /n/ (350), suggesting that the final /n/ represents an old pattern for the negative singular. Such uneven distribution and conflicting accounts suggest that the variable would be hard to track; what we find is that there are preferences for the /n/ generally held across the southern communities in most conjugations, while in the north it is less common. The following example illustrates this point, with only one speaker north of Mille Lacs (Ponemah) using the /n/:

(189) Final augment /n/ VAI 1s: 'I'm not hungry'
    a. *Gaawiin nibakadesii**n*** (Aazhoomog)
    b. *Gaawiin nibakadesii* (Onigum)
    c. *Gaawiin aapiji niwii-wiisinisii* (Lac La Croix)
    d. *Gaawiin imbakadesii* (Nett Lake)
    e. *Gaawiin niwii-wiisinisii* (Nett Lake)
    f. *Gaawiin niwii-wiisinisii* (Lac La Croix)
    g. *Gaawiin nibakadesii**n*** (Ponemah)
    h. *Gaawiin ninoonde-wiisinisii**n*** (Ponemah)
    i. *Gaawiin nibakadesii* (Inger)
    j. *Gaawiin imbakadesii* (Inger)

For negation with VAIs with third-person inflection a similar pattern emerges, though this time speakers at Inger and Nett Lake opt to use the augment /n/:

(190) Final augment /n/ VAI 3s: 'She doesn't speak Ojibwe'
   a. *Gaawiin ojibwemosiin* (Aazhoomog)
   b. *Gaawiin nitaa-ojibwemosii* (Onigum)
   c. *Gaawiin nitaa-anishinaabemosii* (Lake Vermilion)
   d. *Gaa nitaa-anishinaabemosii* (Lac La Croix)
   e. *Gaawiin anishinaabemosii* (Nett Lake)
   f. *Gaawiin ojibwemosii* (Lac La Croix)
   g. *Gaawiin nitaa-ojibwemosiin, gaawiin anishinaabemosiin* (Ponemah)
   h. *Gaawiin ojibwemosiin* (Inger)

Interestingly, one speaker from Mille Lacs provided the examples below for the VAI first-person negative, in one case using the final /n/ and in the other not:

(191) Free variation
   a. *gaawiin nimbakadesiin*
   'I'm not hungry' (Clark and Gresczyk 1991)

   b. *gaawiin nizagaswaasii*
   'I don't smoke' (Clark and Gresczyk 1991)

Archived material from Wisconsin shows both, with the final /n/ being employed only in all VTI conjugations; *-sii* is used elsewhere:

(192) Wisconsin archived data
   a. *gaawiin dash niwaabandanziin*
   'But I don't see it' (Nichols 1988a, 38) vti 1s>0

   b. *gaawiin dash nindaa-gashkitoosiin*
   'But I can't . . .' (Nichols 1988a, 83) vti 1s>0

   c. *gaawiin gego anishaa daa-ikidosii*
   'whatever he says would not be in vain' (Nichols 1988a, 43) vai 3s

   d. *gaawiin gii-izhichigesii*
   'he didn't do so' (Nichols 1988a, 90) vai 3s

e. *gaawiin dash niwii-aagonwetawaasii*
'I will not refuse him' (Nichols 1988a, 46) vta 1s>3s

f. *gaawiin ganabaj nindebenimigosii*
'Perhaps he does not tell me the truth' (Nichols 1988a, 62) vta 3s>1s

g. *gaawiin wiikaa nmaji-doodawaasii*
'I never do bad to him' (Nichols 1988a, 67) vta 1s>3s

h. *gaawiin dash ogii-naadisiin*
'But he didn't go after it' (Nichols 1988a, 69) vti 3s>0

i. *gaa wiikaa awiya odaa-gashkitoosiin*
'No one will be able to . . .' (Nichols 1988a, 78) vti 3s>0

When negated VTIs are elicited, the preference for the /n/ holds with one exception: both speakers from Lac La Croix provide examples (193d. and 193 f.) without the /n/:

(193) VTI 3s>0s negation: 'He didn't see it'
  a. *gaawiin ogii-waabandanziin* (Aazhoomog)
  b. *gaawiin ogii-waabandanziin* (Onigum)
  c. *gaawiin ogii-waabandanziin* (Ponemah)
  d. *gaawiin ogii-waabandanzii* (Lac La Croix)
  e. *gaawiin ogii-waabandanziin* (Nett Lake)
  f. *gaawiin ogii-waabandanzii* (Lac La Croix)
  g. *gaawiin owaabandanziin* (Ponemah)
  h. *gaawiin ogii-waabandanziin* (Ponemah)
  i. *gaawiin ogii-waabandanziin* (Inger)

For the first-person conjugations, similar examples are provided, with speakers from Lac La Croix showing *-sii*, as demonstrated below in (194):

(194) VTI 1s>0s negation: 'I didn't eat it'
  a. *gaawiin ngii-miijisiin* (Aazhoomog)
  b. *gaawiin ingii-miijisiin* (Lake Vermilion)

c. *gaawiin niin ingii-miijisii* (Lac La Croix)
d. *gaawiin nimiijisiin* (Nett Lake)
e. *gaawiin niin ingii-miijisii* (Lac La Croix)
f. *gaawiin ingii-miijisiin* (Ponemah)
g. *gaawiin ingii-miijisiin* (Inger)

Interestingly, the same speaker from Nett Lake who provided the final /n/ in both (194e.) and (194d.) above gave the example in (195) omitting the final /n/ during a conversation, which we might consider more "naturalistic" in the fieldwork sense:

(195) *Gaawiin niin ingikendanzii, gaawiin wiikaa nizhawenimigosii*
'I don't know, nobody ever loved me'

When VTAs are elicited, the /n/ is less common, only occurring at Aazhoomog and with one speaker from Lac La Croix:

(196) VTA 1s>3s negation: 'I don't know her'
a. *gaawiin ingikenimaasiin* (Aazhoomog)
b. *gaawiin ingikenimaasii* (Onigum)
c. *gaawiin ingikenimaasiin* (Lake Vermillion)
d. *gaawiin ingikenimaasii* (Lac la Croix)
e. *gaawiin ingikenimaasii ikwe* (Nett Lake)
f. *gaawiin ingikenimaasii* (Lac la Croix)
g. *gaawiin ningikenimaasii* (Ponemah)
h. *gaawiin ingikenimaasii* (Inger)

For VTA 3>3', all speakers and sources consulted show the final /n/, suggesting it has more of object- or theme-related function marking obviation.

Today the final nasal is a feature assumed to be prevalent in the south, with the nasal-less counterpart *-sii* more common in the north. As far as the data consulted for this study show, speakers in the north use *-sii* more consistently, though even for the same speaker variation can occur. In all the examples collected from eastern Minnesota and Wisconsin, no cases of *-sii* without the nasal occurred:

(197) Wisconsin *-siin*

    a. *gaawiin awiya ingii-kikinoo'amaagosiin*
    'Nobody taught me' (JChosa.13.20.03.C)

    b. *gaawiin giwaabamigoosiin*
    'You are not seen' (EB.Dewe'igan)

    c. *gaawiin ogii-waabamaasiin*
    'He didn't see her' (EB.Dewe'igan)

    d. *mii gaawiin ogii-waabamigosiin*
    'They didn't see her' (EB.Dewe'igan)

    e. *gaawiin wiin ogii-nisidawinawaasiin*
    'She didn't recognize him' (EB.Dewe'igan)

    f. *gaawiin gegoo bakaan indaawisiin*
    'I am nothing else' (Benton 2013, 161)

    g. *gaawiin anishaa ndizhichigesiin*
    'I'm not doing this for no reason' (Benton 2013, 163)

    h. *gaawiin chi-mookomaan mashkikiiwinini ingii-waabamaasiin*
    'I didn't see a white doctor' (Benton 2013, 161)

    i. *gaawiin ingii-noondawaasiin awiya zhaaganaashiimod*
    'I didn't hear anyone speak English' (Benton 2013, 161)

    j. *gaawiin naa gikinoo'amaadiiwigamigong ingii-izhaasiin*
    'I didn't go to school' (Benton 2013, 161)

    k. *gaawiin-sh da-baapinojigeyaan indoonji-izhichigesiin*
    'I'm not making a mockery by doing this' (PM.Dewe'igan1)

Ponemah speakers appear to use either variant interchangeably. The example below shows one speaker using the /n/ and the other not:

180   *Methodology*

(198)   Ponemah negation: 'I haven't eaten all day long'
   a. *Mii go gabe-giizhig gaawiin nindoonji-wiisinisii* (12.03.28.ES.E)
   b. *Gaawiin ingii-wiisinisiin gabe-giizhig* (12.04.03.RT.E)

With regard to the variation and inconsistency observed at Leech Lake, certain speakers from the more southern communities will pattern with the trends of using /n/ in all independent forms of negation (as observed in Whipple [2015]), while other speakers from southern Leech Lake show a more uneven distribution with sporadic use of the variable. At this point, in terms of regional variation, it is safe to say that speakers in the south favor using the /n/ in all cases of negation in the independent order for first, second, and third persons for VAI, VTI, and VTA, while variation is more widely observed in the north.

3.3.7.1.3. Final Nasal /n/ Behavior

Another related phenomenon involves the behavior of /n/ word-finally in a number of contexts. Valentine (1994, 130) discusses nasals lost at the end of VII stems, shown in table 33. Valentine attributes the loss of the final nasals as being "probably due to back-formation," since all of the conjunct forms lose the /n/ and take the conjunct suffix /g/, for example, *zoogipog, minookamig, dagwaagig, onaagoshig* (131). For SW Ojibwe variation is especially frequently observed when eliciting VIIs that end in *-amon* 'a road' and *-aagamin* 'a liquid.' In the examples provided below, both by speakers from Ponemah, the final nasal is observed in their pronunciation:

(199)   *-amon* 'road' verbs (Ponemah)
   a. *gii-inamon iko imaa.*
   'There used to be a road there.' (12.03.28.ES.E)

   b. *miikana iko gii-pi-inamon.*
   'There used to be a road that led here.' (12.04.03.RT.E)

The examples elicited from a speaker from Aazhoomog show the 'road' words without the nasal:

Table 33. Nasal-less VIIs in Odawa (from Valentine 1994, 131)

English gloss	Other dialects	Odawa
it snows	zoogipon	zoogipo
it is spring	minookamin	nimookami
it is fall	dagwaagin	dagwaagi
it is evening	onaagoshin	onaagoshi

(200) *-amo* 'road' verbs (Aazhoomog)

    a. *babigwadamo*

    'it is a bumpy road' (AS.15.08.12.TM)

    b. *wawaashkadamo*

    'it is a curvy road' (AS.15.08.12.TM)

Other instances of the loss of final nasals in Valentine (1994) apply to inflectional processes found in Odawa, provided in table 34. Though the examples from table 34 above do not apply to SW Ojibwe, another aspect of the loss of final /n/ is relevant in the discussion of verb inflection. For some more conservative Ojibwe speakers, a number distinction exists regarding the object of VTIs with a third-person plural subject. For a singular object no nasal occurs at the end of the verb (201a.). For a plural object number agreement is expressed via a final /n/, as shown in (201b.):

(201) Number agreement in VTI 3p>0

    a. *ogikendaanaawaa*

o-gikend-	-am	-naawaa	
3-know.it-	-TI1	-3p>0s	

    'they know it$_{INAN.SG}$' (NJ.15.06.08.E)

    b. *ogikendaanaawaan*

o-gikend-	-am	-naawaa	**-n**
3-know.it-	-TI1	-3p	**-0p**

    'they know **them**$_{INAN.PL}$' (NJ.15.06.08.E)

182   Methodology

Table 34. Loss of final nasal in verb inflection

Gloss	Other dialects	Odawa
'We (13) are leaving' First-person plural suffix Independent order	nimbiizhaamin	mbiizhaami
'our pail'	nindakikonaan	ndakkonaa
'our pails' First-person plural suffix noun possessor	nindakikonaanig	ndakkonaanig

The same number distinction shown above in (201) also holds for inanimate noun possession (3p>0s-*iwaa*, 3p>0p-*iwaan*). For some speakers in the south, the final /n/ expressing plural agreement has been leveled off or is used for both the singular and the plural, resulting in no overt morphology indexing object number. The example shown below illustrates this point, with the object agreement in the participle (morpheme bolded), but not in the possessed noun:

(202) Number agreement 3p>0p

*ingii-naniibikimaag ingiw gwiiwizensag gaa-wanendamowag***in**

in-gii-naniibikim-aa-g   ingiw   gwiiwizens-ag   IC-gii-wanendamaw-ag-**in**

1-PST-scold.h/-DIR-3p   DET   boy-3p   IC-PST-forget.h/$_{\text{rel}}$-1>3-**PL**$_{\text{PRT}}$

*odizhinikaazowin***iwaa**.

od-izhinikaazowin-**iwaa**

3-name-**3p>0**

'I scolded the boy**s** whose name**s** I have forgotten' (Anonymous.E)

One final feature of variation concerning final nasals involves the plurals of nouns with nasalized vowel finals. The standard in the double-vowel orthography is to represent the nasalized vowel in the singular form with -*nh* following the vowel to signal nasalization. For plurals, the nasalized quality of the vowel typically selects a specialized plural suffix, where the nasalization (-*nh* of the singular) is represented only as /n/ in the plural form. Nichols (2011) notes the variation observed where the vowel is not always nasalized in the singular. The following example provides the standard SW Ojibwe singular and plural of one such case:

(203) SW Ojibwe final nasalized vowel

Singular	Plural	Gloss
asabikensh**iinh**	asabikeshi**inyag**	spider; spiders

The variation observed by Nichols at Ponemah is provided below in (204), compared to the forms he previously collected at Mille Lacs:

(204) Variation of final nasalized vowels at Ponemah (from Nichols 2011)

Ponemah	Mille Lacs	Gloss
giingoo; giingoonh	giigoonh	'fish'
abinoonjii; abinoonjiinh	abinoojiinh	'child'
waawaabiganoonjii; waawaabiganoonjiinh	waawaabiganoojiinh	'mouse'

When testing plurals with my consultants, I found that more frequently occurring nouns with nasalized vowel finals maintain the old pattern of plurals observed by Nichols at Mille Lacs (such as *abinoojiinh* 'child'; *abinoojiinyag* 'children'), whereas perhaps less frequently occurring nouns are subject to variation, as seen in the examples below, (205a.) coming from a southern speaker and (205b.) coming from a northern speaker:

(205) Nasalized vowel final noun plurals

a. *waawaabiganoojiinh; waawaabiganoojiig*
'mouse; mice' (Southern)

b. *waawaabiganoojii waawaabiganoojiig*
'mouse; mice' (Northern)

While the data doesn't suggest any pattern of geographical variation, variation does exist. For more discussion on the loss of final /n/, the reader is referred to Valentine (1994, 425–26).

The example above in (204) showing variation in regard to nasals at Ponemah also shows the phenomenon of what Nichols (2011) calls "nasal spreading." This is treated in the next section.

3.3.7.1.4. Nasal Spreading

Nasal spreading or nasal harmony, as described by Nichols (2011), consists of seven different phenomena observed at Ponemah. The first involves the spreading of a nasal from a nasalized final vowel, as shown above in (204) and illustrated here in (206), where the original nasal element is underlined and the nasals as the result of spreading are in bold:

(206) Final nasal vowel

Gloss	Ponemah	Mille Lacs
fish	gii**n**goo; gii**n**goo**nh**	giigoo**nh**
child	abi**n**oo**n**jii; abi**n**oo**n**jii**nh**	abi**n**oojii**nh**
mouse	waawaabiga**n**oo**n**jii; waawaabiga**n**oo**n**jii**nh**	waawaabiga**n**oojii**nh**

The second involves a nasal cluster, where the nasal appears to metathesize onto the preceding stop:

(207) Nasal cluster

Gloss	Ponemah	Mille Lacs
chipmunk	a**n**go**n**gos	ago**n**gos
count it	a**n**gidan; a**n**gi**n**dan	agi**n**dan
s/he reads	a**n**gidaaso	agi**n**daaso

Where the examples above all involve nasal spreading within the initial element, the third type of nasal spreading observed by Nichols (2011) involves spreading from a nasal cluster in the final or medial, as shown in (208):

(208) Nasal cluster in final or medial

Gloss	Ponemah	Mille Lacs
s/he snores	ma**n**dwe**n**gwaami	madwe**n**gwaam
s/he wets the bed	zhi**n**gi**n**gwaami	zhigi**n**gwaam
s/he has a nightmare	ze**n**gigwashi	zegi**n**gwashi
set it down off back	ba**n**gindoondan	bagidoo**n**dan
s/he chews noisily	ma**n**dwe**n**jige	madwe**n**jige
h/ head is cold	giika**n**ji**n**dibewaji	giikaji**n**dibewaji

In the fourth type of nasal spreading observed at Ponemah, the nasal appears to spread to the third-person prefix from the root of the verb. A more restricted case of spreading, Nichols provides for the standard *odoombinaan* 's/he lifts it' *ondoombinaan* and *ondoobinaan*, with the original labialized nasal /m/ no longer pronounced in the root.

For the fifth type, he provides one example where the nasal appears to have spread from the prohibitive suffix to the verb stem: *gego bawaandangen* from *gego bawaadangen* 'don't dream of it.' For the sixth type, he questions whether bilabial stop /b/ can block the spreading, as in the case of *giikiibingwashi* 's/he is sleepy,' with no examples of **giikiinbingwashi* attested. However, he does provide *wiindabindiwaad* for *wiidabindiwaad* 'if they sit with each other' and *owääbadaan* from *owaabandaan* 's/he sees it.' For the final type, he proposes the spread of the nasal in the other direction, as in *diindiinsi* from *diindiisi* 'blue jay' and in both directions, as in *obiindaandawaandaan* for *obiidaandawaadaan* 's/he climbs here on it.'

While I have only one case in my data that involves spreading of the first type, it occurred in the speech of only one of my Ponemah consultants. Fiero (pers. comm.) noticed an example of this metathesis in McBride (1987a):

(209) *gii-baataangazhiishimonogwen*

    gii-   baataa-   -ganzh-   -shimono   -gwen
    PST-   stuck-   -claw-   -fall   -DUB
    'fall with talons stuck in s.t.' (McBride 1987a)

This suggests more work is needed in that area to determine if this is a matter of geographic variation or an innovation on a more restricted scale.

3.3.7.2. Initial /g/

Another initial segment subject to frequent deletion in Ojibwe is initial /g/. Valentine provides evidence that "/g/ is weaker than other obstruents," by showing how it deletes word-initially in some dialects (1994, 128). Valentine notes that some dialects "show sporadic loss of /g/ initially . . . [the] same words with and without /g/ are attested" (1996, 300). He provides the example *gakina* 'all,' reduced to *akina* without the initial /g/. Archived data indicates that initial /g/ deletion is much more common among southern speakers, with /g/ deletion having taken place quite some time ago for certain southern communities. In the south, it is not uncommon not only to hear *akina*, but also *kina*, with the initial vowel deleted.[8] The following reduced form occurs in a handwritten story from Lac Courte Oreilles:

(210) **kina** *ingwaji ogii-nandawaabamaan*
 'he looked everywhere for him' (CB.Manoomin&Opichi)

When speakers from northern communities were surveyed, only one speaker (from Lake Vermilion) provided *akina* for 'all'; the majority provided *gakina*. At Inger and all points south of Inger, *akina* was the main form provided, with the exception of one speaker at Aazhoomog, who preferred *gakina* and another at Lac Courte Oreilles using both forms interchangeably.

Another common case of initial /g/ deletion concerns locative adverbial *gakeyaa* 'in a certain direction; way.' Common in the south is *akeyaa*, and similar to the vowel deletion mentioned above for *(a)kina*, perhaps even more common in fast speech is *keyaa*. A text message from a native speaker is shown below, spelled as it appeared in his original message:

(211) *Mii iw keyaa*
 'That's the way' (AS.12.02.27.TM)

The majority of speakers from northern communities consulted for this study pronounce the word with the /g/, with one even using a longer, older variant *inagakeyaa*:

(212) *Aaniindi giin* **inagakeyaa** *gaa-pi-izhaayan omaa gii-pi-dagoshinan?*
 'Which **way** did you take to get here?' (ES.12.03.28.E)

The long form is common in the north and has become somewhat characteristic of the Border Lakes region. Ironically, what has become regarded as a northern feature is also found in historical documents in Wisconsin:

(213) **inakakeyaa** *iwidi wenji-mooka'ang*
 'To the east' (Nichols 1988, 32–33)

Baraga (1850, 482) recorded *nagakeyaa* 'toward,' without the initial vowel. As trends in historical linguistics go, lexical items tend to get shorter over time. This appears to be the case for *inagakeyaa*, which can be summarized as occurring in the following stages:

(214) *inagakeyaa* →   *nagakeyaa* →   *gakeyaa* →   *akeyaa* →   *keyaa*

Another observation made over the course of this study involves initial /g/ deletion with the grammatical adverbial *giishpin* 'if,' resulting in *iishpin*. Text messages from a native speaker show spellings without /g/:

(215) *Giga ozhaashkikoshin **iishpin** ozhaashikwaamagak waabang*
       'You're going to slide if it's slippery tomorrow.' (AS.12.02.27.TM)

What I had originally assumed to be a pronunciation preference of one of my consultants in the south occurred with a speaker from Ponemah:

(216) *giga-bakinaage **iishpin** wiidookook*
       'If she helps you, you will win' (RD.14.06.11.E)

While this coincidence is interesting, it does not necessarily result in any observable trend regarding variation.

3.3.7.3. Vowel and Glide Quality

There are a few pronunciation variables concerning vowels and glides that require some discussion regarding their distribution. Some involve labialization of velar stops /g/ and /k/, resulting in a lower vowel than the non-labial variant. Other variables involve vowel quality and, specifically, vowel height in regard to numerous words across several grammatical categories. Another varying feature concerns glides and particular inflections that show variation. These are discussed in the following sections.

3.3.7.3.1. Labialization and Rounding

The labialized stops appear to have been observed since the mid-nineteenth century in SW Ojibwe, with Baraga spelling general Ojibwe *dagoshin* 's/he arrives' as *dagwishin*, with a /w/ following the velar stop /g/ (1850, 180). This is also a common pronunciation in Wisconsin and as far west as Mille Lacs. Valentine finds the following in Algonquin, compared here to their "general" SW Ojibwe counterparts (1994, 139):

(217) | Algonquin | General Ojibwe | Wisconsin |
|---|---|---|
| *dagwishin* 's/he arrives' | *dagoshin* | *dagwashin* |
| *onaagwishin* 'it is evening' | *onaagoshin* | *onaagwashin* |
| *ningwizis* 'my son' | *ningozis* | *ningwizis* |

Handwritten stories from Wisconsin verify the tendency, as the example from Lac Courte Oreilles reveals (repeated from [210] above) where the General Ojibwe degree adverbial *ingoji* 'somewhere; anywhere' is spelled here as *ingwaji*:

(218) kina   ingwaji   ogii-nandawaabamaan
     all   somewhere   he/.looked.for.h/
     'He looked everywhere for him' (CB.Manoomin&Opichi)

The unvoiced velar stop is also spelled as labialized here in regard to General Ojibwe *iskode* 'fire':

(219) *ishkwade*
     'fire' (RCarley.Opichi)

Additionally, old documents from Wisconsin spell General Ojibwe *gii-bitaakosing* 'hitting against' as *gii-bitaakwising* (Nichols 1988, 33) with the labialization of the unvoiced stop, suggesting that such pronunciations are not an innovation.

Similar to the Wisconsin pronunciations above in (217), Nichols provides *ba-dagwashinan* 'when you arrive here' (1988, 38). No such cases of labialization were recorded north of Mille Lacs, with the exception of Ponemah, where the particle *godino(o)* is pronounced as *gwadinoo* by at least one speaker:

(220) *Gaawiin na gwadinoo biindigeyaan?*
     'Can I go in?' (12.03.28.ES.E)

A different speaker from Ponemah provided an additional example, shown in (221b.) below compared with a different speaker from the Border Lakes (221a.):

(221) Labialization
    a. Border Lakes
    *ogii-ozhaawash**ko**baganaamaan ikwewan inini*
    'The man gave the woman a black eye. (GJ.14.01.09.E)

    b. Ponemah
    *ogii-ozhaawash**kwa**baganaamaan a'awe ikwe iniw ininiwan*
    'The woman gave the man a black eye' (RD.14.06.11.E)

Valentine characterizes the phenomenon as /wi-/ occurring instead of /o/ only "after g" and not as a matter of labialization or rounding per se (1994, 138). His later paper gives *ningodwaaswi* 'six' as a related variable for *ningodwaaso* (1996, 297).⁹ In none of my data outside of Wisconsin, Mille Lacs, and Ponemah does this variable occur.

3.3.7.3.2. Vowel Height /i/ versus /a/

Another pronunciation variable concerning vowel quality involves the alternation of back mid-open vowel /a/ ([ʌ]) and the higher front mid-close vowel /i/ [ɪ]. Both are often articulated as schwa in fast speech and can be difficult to properly account for in transcriptions. As seen in table 33 above showing core demonstrative pronouns, the forms collected in Wisconsin differ from their Minnesota counterparts in respect to the initial vowel /a/ instead of /i/, for example, *agiw* 'those$_{ANIM}$,' and *aniw* 'those$_{INAN}$; that/those$_{OBV}$.' The data from Lac Courte Oreilles, Round Lake, and Lac du Flambeau show the forms with the lower vowel /a/.

In the speech of Angeline Williams (Bloomfield and Nichols 1991), such pronunciations are pervasive. There is even variation between the vowels in the other direction.[10] The variation in articulation of the vowels is illustrated in table 35, compared to the corresponding versions of Baraga (1878). Valentine mentions that this is a significant feature for Odawa and notes widespread variation in Severn, describing the phenomenon as being "lexically constrained" (1994, 429).

Table 35. Angeline Williams's variation (from Valentine 1994, 429)

Baraga (c. 1878)	Williams (c. 1941)	English gloss
igiw, agiw	*agiw*	those (anim.pl. DEM)
ikwe, akwe	*akwe*	woman
ikwezens	*akwezens*	girl
ininaatig	*aninaatig*	hard maple tree
inini, anini	*anini*	man
iniw, aniw	*aniw*	that, those (obv.anim DEM)
ishkode	*ashkode*	fire
ishkonan 'spare it'	*ashkonanaad*	spare s.o. from killing
ishkwaa-	*ashkwaa-*	after
ishkwaach	*ashkwaach*	last (time), at the end
ishkwaandem	*ashkwaandem*	door
ishpadinaa	*ashpadinaag*	be high land, be a ridge
iwedi	*awedi*	that over there
bikwaakwad	*bakwaakwad*	ball
bingwi, bangwi 'ashes'	*bangwaaboo*	lye
gigizheb	*gagizheb*	in the morning
mikan	*making*	find s.t.
mikaw	*makawaad*	find s.o.
mikigaade	*makigaadeg*	be found (VII)
mikwendan (VTI)	*makwenimaad*	think of s.o., remember s.o.
mazinahigan	*mizinahigan*	book
ningwa'akaan	*nangwa'akaan*	cemetery
wazhashkwedoo	*azhashkwedoo*	cork, mushroom; n.b., *ozhashkwedoo* in many dialects
mazinahigan	*mizinahigan*	book, paper
mazinaakide	*mizinaakide*	be printed (VII)

A recording of two ladies at Lac Courte Oreilles included a discussion of whether they should spell *inwewin* 'language' with an /a/ or an /i/ suggesting the variable is at least somewhat salient to speakers from such dialects with respect to literacy. Documents from Wisconsin show *apine* 'always' for the more standard *apane*, showing the variable is not recent (Nichols 1988, 80). One case in my data from Aazhoomog is *akwe* 'woman,' but the speaker is not consistent in this pronunciation.

Another more restricted variable involves the pronunciation of *niibowa* 'many; much; a lot.' Both vowels /ii/ and /o/ show variation in articulation as seen in (222), with the variants shown collected in their respective locations:

(222) *niibowa* variation

Ponemah	B.L.	Leech Lake	Aazhoomog	LCO
niibowa	niibiwa	nebowa/niibowa	nebowa/niibowa	nebowa

Another case of variation in regard to vowel quality is the lexical item *okikaandag* 'jack pine,' pronounced with the lower initial vowel *akikaandag*. *Okikaandag* is attested at Leech Lake, the Border Lakes, and Ponemah, with *akikaandag* at Mille Lacs and Lac Courte Oreilles.

On a wider scale the variation is also observed in certain aspects of the morphology, where many speakers pronounce the second-person conjunct suffix *-yan* as *-yin* and the first-person plural inclusive conjunct prefix *-yang* as *-ying*; these are common variables for speakers from more northern communities:

(223) 21p conjunct -yang/-ying; 'It's time to eat!'
    a. *Mii i' ji-wiisiniyang* (Ponemah)
    b. *Mii iw ji-wiisiniying* (Border Lakes)

Some speakers from Ponemah pronounce the suffix with the higher vowel, a characteristically modern northern pronunciation:

(224) *Mii zhigwa gegaa naawakweg ji-nawajiiying*
    'It's almost noon so we'll eat' (ES.OPD.zhigwa)

One case in particular arose during a session with a speaker from the Border Lakes region who not only used a higher vowel in the suffix, but also the labial glide:

(225) *Aaniin ezhinikaazowin?*
    'What's your name?' (LB.13.08.06.C)

This is another characteristic feature of the northern communities and is discussed in the next section.

192 Methodology

3.3.7.3.3. Articulation of Glides /y/ and /w/

As mentioned above in the discussion of (225), many speakers from northern communities supply a labial glide /w/ [w] where the more standard /y/ [j] occurs. This appears to be restricted in this case to suffixes following verb stems ending in /o/, as illustrated in the examples given below in (226):

(226) Labialized glide distribution

    a. *gaagiigido**waan***
    'when I speak' (LB.13.08.06.C)

    b. *gaa-ikido**waan***
    'what I said' (NJ.15.06.08.N)

    c. *Aaniin ezhinikaazo**win**?*
    'What's your name?' (LB.13.08.06.C)

    d. *babaamibatoo**waang***
    'running around there' (McBride 1987b.)

This feature doesn't appear to have completely replaced the palatal glide, but is restricted to /o/-final verb stems, as examples can easily be found from the same speakers without the /w/ in place of /y/:

(227) *mii imaa iwidi iidog ge-izhi-wiisiniyaambaan*
    'There is where I can eat!' (NJ.Zhishagagowe-Bakwezhigan)

What appears to be a feature of more northern varieties seems to be spreading south, as the following examples come from the southern communities at Leech Lake:

(228) Leech Lake /w/ in place of /y/

    a. *gaawiin ominjimendanzii gaa-ikido**waan***
    'He doesn't remember what I said' (JB.13.07.17.C)

    b. *ji-pajiishka'ogoo**waang***
    'to get shot' (Whipple 2015, 42)

c. *gii-adaawaamigoowaan*
'they borrow from me' (Whipple 2015, 70)

Also at Leech Lake, the variation is not completely definitive as examples can easily be found where the /y/ surfaces in the same environment:

(229) *Mii gaye niinawind gii-pajiishka'ogooyaang abinoojiinyiwiyaang*
'We all got shots too when we were kids.' (Whipple 2015, 42)

Valentine identifies another point of glide variation where the labial glide /w/ "coalesces with a following a to o in many dialects, especially in the south." He provides examples of such occurrences word-initially, such as *wanishkaa* 'he gets up from sleeping,' pronounced *onishkaa* in the south, and *wadikwan* 'branch' pronounced as *odikwaan*; there are also word-final examples, such as *makwa* 'bear' pronounced as *mako*, and interconsonantal example, such as *amikwag* 'beavers' pronounced as *amikog* (1994, 141). He states that there is "too much variation within regions for this to be of too much diagnostic value" but notes regional trends and recent developments for southern dialects (142).

Of all the examples Valentine provides as being northern variables, surprisingly, *wanishkaa* is attested in the south at Lac Courte Oreilles. Also, with respect to lexical items with an initial w- (wa-) coalescing to /o/ in the south, variation can be found for a number of words with *wagaji-* 'on top.' Valentine (1994, 450) mentions that while many dialects show the initial glide /w/ and low vowel /a/, SW Ojibwe "often" lacks it. The glide-initial forms are widely attested in Wisconsin, at both Lac Courte Oreilles and Lac du Flambeau. Note that in the example below, the forms collected at Lac du Flambeau lack the initial glide, though the vowel is the lower, nonround vowel /a/, not /o/. The more common southern forms are provided in parentheses:

(230) *wagid=* in Wisconsin

a. **wagid**akamig (**ogid**akamig)
'on top of the ground' (PM.Wagidakamig)[11]

b. **agi**jayi'ii (**ogi**jayi'ii)
'on top of it' (JChosa.13.20.03.C)

c. **agid**aakii (**ogid**aakii)
'on top of the hill' (JChosa.13.20.03.C)

The Ojibwe People's Dictionary provides many cases of *agid=* classified as a feature of Mille Lacs, with *ogid=* forms provided by a speaker from Ponemah. A few examples list *wagid=*, though no indication is made regarding their distribution. In a story from White Earth, the following example occurs, with the *wagid-* root:

(231) Bezhig aw inini **wagij**idaabaan ayaa
'The one man was on top of the wagon' (AB.Naytawaush)

Another example of this variation is seen in the preverb *niiyo-* 'four,' alternating with *niiwo-*. The Ojibwe People's Dictionary provides several examples of audio from Leech Lake and Ponemah with *niiyo-* pronunciations, listing *niiwo-* examples with no indication of their distribution. The following examples occur in data from Lac Courte Oreilles:

(232) *niiwo-* 'four'
   a. *nii**y**wogon*[12]
   'four days' (CB.Manoomin&Opichi)

   b. *nii**w**ogon*
   'four days' (EB.Dewe'igan)

   c. *gii-nii**w**o-giizhigadinig gii-pi-azhegiiwe a'aw Manoomin*
   'On the fourth day Manoomin came back' (RCarley.Opichi)

   d. *gii-nii**w**ogonagak*
   'on the fourth day' (RCarley.Opichi)

Another seemingly related phenomenon involves the pronunciation of *giiyose* 's/he is hunting.' The OPD notes that *giiyose* is attested by speakers from Ponemah, with one of those same speakers also providing *giiwose*. The pronunciation also occurs in a story from Redby, another community at Red Lake:

(233) *babaa-gii**wo**sed*
   'going around hunting' (McBride 1987)

It is also common at Mille Lacs and in Wisconsin:

(234) *mbaa-gii**wo**se*
   'I go around hunting' (JChosa.13.20.03.C)

Valentine observes the deletion of glides /w/ and /y/ "intervocalically as a common casual speech phenomenon" (1994, 140). The rounded quality of the following vowel appears to determine the articulation of the preceding glide (labial) for speakers who show this variation.

Another relevant variable concerning glides involves the intensifying preverb *(w)enda-* 'really; completely; just so' (preverb 42 in the Nichols [1980, 265] classification). The preverb is often also translated as 'especially' (Staples, pers. comm.). For Maude Kegg, the /w/ only surfaced intervocalically, when a preceding prefix occurred, resulting in *enda-* in the unprefixed forms:

(235) *(w)enda-* (from Kegg 1991, 48)
   a. *enda-nishkaadizi*
   'she was just mad'

   b. *ni**w**enda-ondendam*
   'I was determined'

Interestingly, at least one speaker from Leech Lake pronounces the preverb without the glide, even in prefixed forms:

(236) *ni-**enda**-minwendam*
   'I'm glad' (Whipple 2015, 76)

Another variant *waanda-* occurs for some speakers at Aazhoomog and Ponemah, with the glide and higher front vowel /aa/:

(237) *waanda-* variant
   a. ***waanda**-jiikinaagozi gaye*
   'she was real cute too' (AS.Waabooyaanish)

b. ni**waanda**-debisinii naa
'I'm very full' (RT.OPD.debisinii)

Such variation does not seem to be too widespread but is worth mentioning regarding the discussion of *(w)enda-*.

3.3.7.4. Other Points of Variation

The following subsections treat remaining points of variation. The variation observed is more restricted than some of the previous variables discussed above. They are grouped here for convenience.

3.3.7.4.1. Women's Names -k(we)

One feature that does show variation in regard to a north-south geographic distribution is women's names. Many women's names in the north resemble vocative forms of the south:

(238) Women's names

Southern	Northern
Ningaabii'anookwe 'Woman of the West'	Ningaabii'anook
Giizhigookwe 'Sky Woman'	Giizhigook

Many kinship terms and personal names have corresponding truncated vocative expressions used when calling out to someone. The examples shown here in (239) illustrate such truncation in the vocative:

(239) Ojibwe vocative
    a. Kinship terms
    (i.) *nookoo!*
    'grandma!'   short for *nookomis* 'my grandmother' (NJ.15.06.08.E)
    (ii.) *omaa bi-izhaan* **gwis**
    'come here son'   short for *ningwizis* 'my son' (AS.14.07.19.C)
    (iii.) *maam!*
    'mom'   short for *nimaamaa* 'my mother' (AS.JoeShibiash)

b. Personal names

(i.) *Aaniin Migiz!*
'Hello Migizi!'   short for *Migizi* PN (JN.15.07.18.C)

(ii.) *Naawakamigook*
'Naawakamigookwe!'   short for *Naawakamigookwe* (Kegg 1991, 6)

(iii.) *Wenabosh!*
'Wenabozho!'   short for *Wenabozho* PN (AS.Aadizookaan)

Nichols provides a number of vocative forms all resulting in "subtraction from the stem" (1980, 60). In a number of instances with speakers from Mille Lacs and Aazhoomog, I have heard truncated forms of VAIs used as a sort of vocative expression in greetings, typically with playful teasing and demeaning connotations, some of which are included below:

(240) VAI vocative expressions

a. *Aaniin bagonez!*
'Hey you with the hole' from *bagonezi* VAI 's/he has a hole' (AS.AaniinBagonez)

b. *Aaniin wiinendaagoz!*
'Whats up dirtball' from *wiinendaagozi* VAI 's/he is considered dirty' (AS.12.10.TM)

c. *Aaniin chi-wiisin!*
'Hello big eater' from *chi-wiisini* VAI 's/he eats a lot' (LS.pc)

According to Nichols (2011), the northern forms resembling southern vocative expressions do not have distinct vocative forms. In one example from Leech Lake, the name (shown in bold) takes the obviative marker *-an*, where one might expect the *-we* to return suffixing *-yan* or *-wan* in the case of obviation:

(241) *Ogii-kagwejimaan* **Ningaabii'anookan**
'She asked Ningaabii'anook' (GH.LW.14.07.16.E)
Not **Ningaabii'anook****weyan***

When I solicited opinions on the matter, Eugene Stillday (Ponemah) remarked on how women's names with *-kwe* are perceived as doubly marked for their female specification since, for him, the final /k/ indexes the name as a woman's, with the *-we* (*-kwe*) forms being redundant. Because it is an important cultural value to maintain the use of traditional Ojibwe names in the exact manner in which they were received, many consultants prefer to use the full form of names where more regular truncation processes in the vocative might be expected. When asked about the women's names *Giiwedinook* and *Giiwedinookwe* (Woman of the North), one speaker from Aazhoomog indicated that *Giiwedinook* would be used in the case of "calling to them," suggesting the vocative truncation for women's names is still productive for his variety. Another lady from Ponemah indicated her opinion that *Giiwedinookwe* "is better" when presented with the option of how to call out to her, suggesting the vocative is less productive in her variety. To the best of my knowledge I know of no traditional women's names given south of Leech Lake in what we might consider the *southern* vocative form, suggesting a regional variable.

3.3.7.4.2. /t/ Epenthesis

Common across the Algonquian family is the consonant epenthesis strategy widely known in the literature as /t/ epenthesis. For Ojibwe, and most other languages, it involves an epenthetic /t/ surfacing after the vowel of the personal prefixes (pronominal clitics) *ni*, *gi*, and *o-* when attaching to a verb-initial stem (either noun or verb). An example of /t/ epenthesis in SW Ojibwe is given here:[13]

(242) /t/ epenthesis

a. 1st person *ni-*[14]

(n)in*d*oondamendaan

nin-	d-	ondamend-	-am
1	/t/$_{EPEN}$-	be.preoccupied.with.it-	-TI1

'I am preoccupied with it; worried about it'

b. 2nd person *gi-*

gi*d*oondamendaan

gi-	d-	ondamend-	-am
2	/t/$_{EPEN}$-	be.preoccupied.with.it-	-TI1

'You are preoccupied with it; worried about it'

c. 3rd person *o-*

odoondamendaan

o-	**d-**	ondamend-		-am
3	/t/_{EPEN}-	be.preoccupied.with.it-		-TI1

'S/he is preoccupied with it; worried about it'

Most speakers agree in their use of /t/ epenthesis, though Nichols (2011) reports variation in Ponemah with respect to personal prefixes and /aa/-initial stems, an example of which is given here in (243):

(243) Glide epenthesis: *aabajitoon* VTI2 'use it' (from Nichols 2011)

Gloss	Ponemah	Elsewhere
'I use it'	**ni**y*aabajitoon*	**nid***aabajitoon* (nind-, ind-, nd-)
'You use it'	**gi**y*aabajitoon*	**gid***aabajitoon*
'S/he uses it'	**o**w*aabajitoon,* **o**y*aabajitoon*	**od***aabajitoon*

When eliciting paradigms on /aa/-initial stems with another speaker from Ponemah, no glide epenthesis occurred; instead, the speaker made use of the typical /t/ epenthesis strategy:

(244) Ponemah /t/ epenthesis (Anonymous.E)

*in**d**aabajitoon* 'I use it'

*gi**d**aabajitoon* 'You use it'

*o**d**aabajitoon* 'S/he uses it'

However, similar variation is attested in the casual speech of one speaker at Aazhoomog though when attention was called to it in transcribing, the speaker preferred to replace the epenthetic /d/. No other such cases of glide epenthesis occur in my data.

Another aspect of what may be treated as a type of /t/ epenthesis was reported by Nichols among some Mille Lacs speakers, where epenthesis occurred after the future prefix *ga-* (see discussion of pv1 in 2.3.4), which he described as "a characteristic treatment of Wisconsin dialects" (1980, 134). However, Rhodes proposes that the *ga-* preverb in both Ojibwe and Cree descend from PA **kataw-*, "an intentive future" (1985, 548). The presumed epenthesis only occurs with vowel-initial verb stems, as seen in a handwritten story from Lac Courte Oreilles:

(245) apane besho omaa nigad-ayaa
'I will always be close by' (RCarley.Opichi)

The appearance of the stop before vowel-initial stems resembles /t/ epenthesis after *ga-* and is pervasive in the old documents from Wisconsin, occurring after all three personal prefixes (246), as well as after the initial change (IC) form *ge-* (247):

(246) /t/ epenthesis after *ga-* (Nichols 1988)

a. *ningadawi-wiindamawaa*

nin-	ga-	**d-**	awi-	wiindamaw	-aa
1-	FUT-	/t/$_{EPEN}$-	go-	tell.h/-	-DIR

'I shall report to him' (35)

b. *gigadishkonaanaawaa*

gi-	ga-	**d-**	ishkon-	-am	-aawaa
2-	FUT-	/t/$_{EPEN}$-	reserve.it-	-TI1	-2p>0

'you will reserve it' (74)

c. *ogadayaan*

o-	ga-	**d-**	ay-	-aa
3-	FUT-	/t/$_{EPEN}$-	have.it-	-TI4

'he will have it' (75)

(247) Following *ge-* (Nichols 1988)

a. *gedako-minoga'igeyan*

ge-	**d-**	ako-	minoga'ige-yan
IC-FUT-	/t/$_{EPEN}$-	as.long-	cut.well-2s$_{CONJ}$

'as far as you will cut well' (44)

b. *gedapiichikawadwaa*

ge-	**d-**	apiichikaw	-adwaa
IC-FUT-	/t/$_{EPEN}$-	work.on.h/.so.long	-2s>3p$_{CONJ}$

'as long as you will work on them' (45)

With the exception of the example from Lac Courte Oreilles, no other cases of this type occur in my data. Ningwance (1993) suggests similar epenthetic strategies in Manitoba, where some speakers epenthesize /d/ before /w/ initial stems (cited in Valentine 1996, 304), though this is likely the result of a treatment of /wa/ as a vowel that is unique to Saulteaux (Nichols, pers. comm.).

3.3.7.4.3. Syncope

Another important parameter in the discussion of Ojibwe dialect variation is vowel syncopation. Where the previous section dealt with the addition of material, specifically the epenthesis of a dental or alveolar stop [d] in between vowels, syncope involves the deletion of material, in this case mainly vowels in weak stress positions. According to Valentine, "syncopation-like processes have evidently been active at some level in nearly all Ojibwe dialects for quite some time" (1994, 162). Although the process is not anywhere nearly as prolific as syncope in Odawa, SW Ojibwe does show some evidence of vowel and initial syllable deletion.

Valentine (1994, 163) observes, in regard to data obtained at Mille Lacs by Nichols, that it is common in the southern communities to delete the first syllable of the intensifying lexical preverb (see the discussion in 2.3.4 of pv4) *gichi-* to *chi-*, as in common expressions *chi-mookomaan* 'Whiteman' (literally 'big knife') and *chi-bikwaakwad* 'basketball,' *chi-oodenaang* 'in the big city; Twin Cities,' and *chi-aya'aa* 'elder.' In some cases for some speakers, the initial syllable *gi-* comes back when following a prefix:

(248) *gaa-izhi-**gichi**-basikawaanag*

      IC-gii-   izhi-   **gichi-**   basikawaazh   -ag

      IC-PST- pv3$_{REL}$- **greatly-** kick.h/   -1>3$_{CONJ}$

      'So I kicked it **real good**' (AS.Gii-nitaawigiyaan)

No examples are attested for *chi-* with IC; instead, the *gi-* comes back in IC environments, including participles:

(249) *Chi aya aag nitum mii dash api **ge chi** mindidojig*

     chi-aya'aa-g   nitam   mii   dash   apii   **IC-gichi**   mindido-d-ig
     elder-3p   first   thus   then   when   **IC-great**   is.big-3$_{\text{CONJ}}$-PL$_{\text{PRT}}$

     'Elders first then the **real big** ones.' (AS.12.03.05.TM)

In other cases, among the same speakers, the initial syllable does not resurface:

(250) *ingii-**chi**-nibaa*

     in-   gii-   **chi-**   nibaa
     1-   PST-   **greatly-**   sleeps

     'I slept **hard**' (AS.13.08.16.TM)

The variable is in free variation for some, optionally occurring within a single environment:

(251) Free variation

     a. *ni**chi**-anishinaabemag*

     ni-   **chi-**   Anishinaabe   -m   -ag
     1-   **great-**   Indian   -POSS -3p

     'my elders' (Whipple 2015, 6)

     b. *in**gichi**-anishinaabemag*

     ni-   **gichi-**   Anishinaabe   -m   -ag
     1-   **great-**   Indian   -POSS -3p

     'my elders' (Whipple 2015, 36)

Valentine also notices deletion of *gi-* in verbs such as *gikendam* 's/he knows,' reduced to *kendam*, and the previously mentioned variable *(g)akina*; as Valentine points out, these deletions involve a metrically weak position and also occur before a fortis consonant, making them susceptible to deletion (1994, 163). I have also heard *gaawiin goji* 'nowhere' by speakers in fast speech (from *ingoji* 'somewhere').

In addition to the observations made by Valentine, several other words and inflections shows patterns of syncopation, specifically those with /a/

in initial position. This process is illustrated below in (252) with an ad hoc list of attested vocabulary items involving syncope:

(252) Frequently reduced SW Ojibwe lexical items

General Ojibwe	SW Ojibwe	Gloss
apane	(a)pane	'always'
akawe	(a)kawe	'first of all'
asemaa	(a)semaa	'tobacco'
agwajiing	(a)gwajiing	'outside'
ani-	(a)ni-	'going away'

Some older speakers, especially from northern communities, have expressed their disapproval of such deletions. Speakers in the north especially have a tendency to associate such pronunciations with the southern communities. Many speakers in the south, however, are proud of such pronunciations, suggesting they are a marker of linguistic identity. It should be noted that although many express their disapproval of and even disgust at such syncopated forms, one such speaker provided the example shown below in (253), realizing his initial utterance (253a.) then providing the second (253b.):

(253) [$_a$. Wa. **Chi**-mewinzha naa gii-waabaminaambaan] [$_b$. Wa. **Gichi**-mewinzha naa gii-waabaminaambaan]
 'Long time no see' (Anonymous.E)

Personal prefixes are also notoriously reduced or deleted completely. It isn't uncommon in just about every community to hear *ga-waabamin* as a 'I'll see you' salutation lacking the expected *gi-* second-person prefix. Utterances like the one below are typical colloquial Ojibwe, though hardly ever reflected in the written form, as speakers and editors often insist on replacing the missing prefix:

(254) zhoomiingwetaagonaanig ganabaj
 O-zhoomiingwetaw-igw-naan-ig   ganabaj
 2-smile.at.h/-INV-21p-3p   perhaps
 'They're smiling at us I think.' (ES.12.03.28.C)

Such deletion is not new, as this occurrence in a story from Redby in 1987 shows:

(255) *ga-debibinigowaa manidoog i'imaa*
    O-ga-debibiN-igw-waa   manidoo-g   i'imaa
    2-FUT-grab.h/-INV-2p   spirit-3p   there
    'some spriit(s) will get you there' (McBride 1987b.)

Another commonly omitted syllable is found with *gikinoo'amaadiiwigamig* 'school' and the *gikinoo*= root in general, especially in the south with pronunciations *kinoo-maadiiwigamig* 'school,' *kinoomaagozi* 's/he is a student; goes to school,' and one case of *akinoo'amaagewin* 'a teaching' in Wisconsin with a folk etymology (*aki* 'Earth,' *iNinoo'amaage* 'points for people') pertaining to 'pointing on the earth.'

Many variants of the conjunctive adverbial *miinawaa* 'and; again' are also recorded throughout the region. Common at Mille Lacs and Aazhoomog is *naa* and forms with variable vowel quality, for example, *minowa*, attested in Wisconsin, and *mina* at Redby. Syncope was not a targeted parameter on the survey used here, so a more thorough investigation, especially in the north, is necessary before anything conclusive can be said in regard to deletions in that region.

3.3.8. Lexical Variation

Though not anywhere nearly as profound as the variation observed by Valentine (1994) regarding lexical items, variation does exist and warrants a brief discussion here. Valentine states, "Chippewa shows its closest affinity with Border Lakes" (1994, 464); while lexical variation was not an intentional point of exploration in the survey used here, the subsequent discovery of variation is worth noting. Table 36 illustrates some of the variation observed. As the table indicates, some variants occur within the same community. Regarding the last example, 'already,' I have a number of examples from Ponemah using *(a)zhigwa* as such. Many of my consultants from the south associate *azhigwa* to mean 'now' and reject its use as 'already.' At Lac Courte Oreilles, two variants of the seemingly related and "archaic" *zhayiigwa* have been recorded (Nichols and Nyholm 1995), including *ayiigwa*, as seen in the example below:

Table 36. Lexical variation in SW Ojibwe[a]

Gloss	Variant-1	Community	Variant-2	Community
'help h/'	wiidookaw	LCO, LL, ML, SC, LDF, LLC, NL, RL	wiiji'	RG, LLC, LV, NL
'table'	adoopowin	LCO, LL, ML, SC, LDF, RL	adoopowinaak	RL, LLC, LV, RG
'horse'	bebezhigoganzhii	LCO, SC, LDF, ML, LL, RL	mishtadim	RL, RG
's/he is hungry'	bakade	LCO, SC, LDF, ML, RL, LL, NL	noondeskade	LLC, RG, LV, RL, ML
'already'	(a)zhigwa	RL	aazha	RG, LLC, LV

[a] Community codes are as follows: ML Mille Lacs, SC St. Croix, LCO Lac Courte Oreilles, LDF Lac du Flambeau, LL Leech Lake, RL Red Lake, NL Nett Lake (Sugarbush), LV Lake Vermilion, LLC Lac La Croix, RG Red Gut

(256) **ayiigwa** dash iwidi ani-bangishimog mii imaa da-anwebiyan
already then there the.sun.goes.down thus there you.will.rest
'Over there [to the west] the sun is already going down, there you will rest' (EB.Dewe'igan)

Other aspects of variation involve the structure of the verb stem, discussed in the following sections.

3.3.8.1. Body-Part-Incorporating Suffix -e

With regard to lexical variation across Ojibwe dialects, an important observation made by Valentine (2002, 115) involves body-part-incorporating final -e for VAIs. For 'mouth' verbs, Valentine finds three distinct finals: /-i/, /-e/, or a zero morpheme. Nichols (2011) finds that in regard to certain body-part medials, including /-zid-/ 'foot,' speakers in all communities give forms that take the incorporating final -e both postmedially, as in *bookozideshin* 's/he falls and breaks foot' as well as a final, as in *bookozide* 's/he has a broken foot.' However, he cites variation regarding the medial /-doon-/ 'mouth' as well as "others" he doesn't list. For /-doon-/, verbs are attested at Mille Lacs taking the postmedial -e, as in *gaasiidoone'o* 's/he wipes h/ (own) mouth,' but not as a final, as in *biimidoon* 's/he has a twisted mouth.' This differs from the forms attested at Ponemah, northern Leech Lake, and Bois

Forte, which show the final *-e* as in *biimidoone* 's/he has a twisted mouth.' The following example shows some inflected forms elicited from a speaker from Aazhoomog illustrating the lack of the final *-e*:

(257) *onzaamidoon* VAI 's/he talks too much': *onzaam-* 'excess' *-doon* 'mouth' (AS.13.07.16.E)

a. Independent 3s
onzaamidoon

b. Conjunct 3s
onzaamidoong

c. Conjunct 1s
onzaamidoonaan

d. Conjunct 2s
onzaamidoonan

When eliciting such /-doon-/ verbs, all speakers surveyed from Ponemah, Bois Forte, and the Border Lakes communities provide forms with the final *-e*, while speakers from Leech Lake (both northern and southern LL) and all points south give examples with the zero morpheme.[15]

In addition to the /-doon-/ 'mouth' verbs described above, a number of other body-part medials appear to not take the final *-e* but rather the zero morpheme, in the south. Valentine (2002, 86) finds similar patterns in southern Ojibwe dialects and points out that this appears to be specific to body-part medials that end in /n/. For instance, the medial /-aakigan-/ 'chest' appears to be one such case, with the verb *ozaawaakigan* 's/he has a yellow chest' occurring twice in a story at Lac Courte Oreilles, once in the independent third-person form *ozaawaakigan* and again as a participle in the example given below in (258):

(258) *a'aw bineshiinh mekadewindibed miinawaa* **wezaawaakigang**

a'aw bineshiinh IC-makadewindibe-d miinawaa IC-**ozaawaakigan**-g
that bird IC-has.black.head-3 and IC-**has.yellow.chest**-3

'that bird with the black head and yellow chest' (RC.Opichi)

Another speaker provides *dewaakigan* for 's/he has chest pain; chest aches' (GH.OPD.dewaakigan). It should be stated that locative adverbials resemble the VAIs lacking the *-e*, such as *naawaakigan* 'in the middle of the chest,' attested by speakers in the north as well as the south.

Another body-part medial that doesn't show the final *-e* for speakers from the south is /-aawigan-/ 'back':

(259) *indewaawigan*
 'I have a backache' (Clark and Gresczyk 1991)

Variation appears to occur at Leech Lake, with different speakers from Inger providing examples without the *-e* in (260a.), and with the *-e*, as seen in (260b.):

(260) Variation at Leech Lake /-aawigan(e)-/
 a. *dewaawigan*
 's/he has a backache' (LW.OPD.dewaawigan)

 b. *bookwaawigane*
 's/he has a broken back' (GH.OPD.bookaawigane)

The data collected for this study shows no final *-e* for /-doon-/ 'mouth,' /-aakigan-/ 'chest,' or /-aawigan-/ 'back' south of Leech Lake, but at all points north the final *-e* is observed, with variation at northern Leech Lake.

3.3.8.2. -ngwaam(i) Verbs

Another type of lexical variation involves the VAI final *-ngwaam(i/o)* in verbs pertaining to 'sleep,' such as *madwengwaam* 's/he snores.' Similar to the *-doon* 'mouth' verbs discussed above in 3.3.8.1, Valentine (2002, 116) finds the same three variants across Ojibwe: /-i/ attested in Severn Ojibwe and Northern Ojibwe; /-o/ found at Curve Lake, Ontario, and in Northern Algonquin; and the zero form in SW Ojibwe and some Odawa dialects (such as Walpole Island, according to Rhodes 1985). Nichols (2011) treats variation observed at Ponemah where the final includes /i/, such as *madwengwaami*. Speakers consulted from Leech Lake and all points south provide forms identical to those noted by Nichols from Mille Lacs, given below in (261):

(261) *boogidingwaam* VAI 's/he farts in their sleep': *boogidi* 'farts' -*ngwaam* 'sleeps' (AS.13.07.16.E)

a. Conjunct 3s
boogidingwaang

b. Conjunct 1s
boogidingwaamaan

c. Conjunct 2s
boogidingwaaman

d. Independent negative 3s
gaawiin boogidingwaanziin

e. Participle 3p
bwaagidingwaangig

Speakers from Leech Lake give the southern forms provided above, while speakers from Ponemah provide examples with the final /i/, *boogidingwaami* (RD.14.06.11.E). Interestingly, not noted by Nichols (2011) but represented in the OPD is the variation observed in examples provided by speakers from the Border Lakes communities who treat such verbs with a final /o/, as in *boogidingwaamo* 's/he farts in his/her sleep,' and *boogidingwaamowag* 'they fart in their sleep' (GJ.14.01.09.E).

3.3.8.3. -aadage/-aadagaa *Verbs*

One last observation regarding lexical variation involves the final -*aadagaa* 'swim,' as in *bimaadagaa* 's/he swims along.' Nichols (2011) reports having observed the final -*aadage* at Ponemah, though his entries in the OPD show examples from one Ponemah speaker providing -*aadagaa* (see OPD entry *bimaadagaa*). The other variant, -*aadage*, is attested by Border Lakes speakers: for example, *babaamaadage* 's/he swims around' (GJ.14.01.09.E). No other cases of the -*aadage* variant occur in my data outside of the examples provided by Border Lakes speakers.

3.3.9. Animacy Status

The animacy gender status of certain items is a relevant parameter for variation, often in a north-south polarity. Perhaps most notably, while cars are typically animate in the south, they are inanimate for many northern speakers. The bolded components in the examples below in (262) and (263) exemplify the animacy status of 'cars,' encoded via agreement throughout the sentence by means of the verb type used, the demonstrative pronoun, and the plural marker on the noun itself. When presenting a southern speaker the example shown in (262), he offered the example provided in (263) with the animate status of 'cars' characteristic of the southern varieties:

(262) Northern example of inanimate 'car' (Ponemah)

*gagiizhibaa**bidewan** **iniwen** odaabaan**an***
gagiizhibaa**bide-wan**   **iniwen**   odaabaan-**an**
it.goes.around(and around)-**0p**   DET$_{INAN}$ car-**0p**

*gegwejikanidii**magakin***
IC-gagwejikanidii-**magad-in**
IC-race.eachother-**AUG**$_{INAN}$-**PL**$_{CONJ}$

'The race cars are going around and around' (ES.OPD.odaabaan)

(263) Southern "correction"

*gagiizhibaa**bizowag** **ingiw** odaabaan**ag***
gagiizhibaa**bizo-wag**   **ingiw**   odaabaan-**ag**
s/he.goes.around(and around)-**3p**   DET$_{AN}$ car-**3p**

gegwejikazhiwejig
IC-**gagwejikazhiwe-d-ig**
IC-**races-3**$_{AN.CONJ}$-**PL**$_{PRT}$

'The race cars are going around and around' (AS.14.07.22.GJ-C)

A pattern holds where 'cars' are treated as animate by all speakers consulted from Leech Lake and all points south; as inanimate for all speakers

210 *Methodology*

consulted from Ponemah; as variable with speakers from the Border Lakes; and as animate for speakers at both Lake Vermilion and Nett Lake on the Bois Forte reservation.

The animacy status of 'airplane' is also variable. All collected forms consist of a participle construction, though the shape of the participle varies in regard to IC and verb choice, as the examples below in (264) indicate, with only one speaker from Lac du Flambeau treating 'airplane' as animate (shown in bold). All examples shown appeared in sentential examples verifying their status in regard to animacy:

(264) 'airplane' variation

    a. *bemisemagak*
    IC-bimise   -magad
    IC-it.flies   -AUG$_{0.CONJ}$ (inanimate: AS.13.07.16.E)

    b. *bemibideg*
    IC-bimibide   -g
    IC-it.motors.along   -0$_{CONJ}$ (inanimate: JB.13.07.17.E)

    c. *gaa-bimisemagak*
    IC$_{REL}$-   bimise   -magad
    IC-   it.flies   -AUG$_{0.CONJ}$ (inanimate: LB.13.08.06.E)

    d. *gaa-bimisemagak*
    IC$_{REL}$- bimise   -magad
    IC- it.flies   -AUG$_{0.CONJ}$ (inanimate: EG.13.08.07.E)

    e. *bemisemagak*
    IC-bimise   -magad
    IC-it.flies   -AUG$_{0.CONJ}$ (inanimate: GJ.14.01.09.E)

    f. *gaa-bimisemagak*
    IC$_{REL}$-   bimise   -magad
    IC-   it.flies   -AUG$_{0.CONJ}$ (inanimate: RD.14.06.11.E)

g. *bebaamaasing*
IC-babaamaasin -g
IC-it.is.blown.about -0_CONJ (inanimate: GH.LW.14.07.16.E)

h. *gaa-bimibideg*
IC_REL- bimibide -g
IC- it.motors.along -0_CONJ (inanimate: NJ.15.06.08.E)

i. *ishpiming **bemised***
ishpiming IC-**bimise** **-d**
up.above IC-s/he.flies -3_CONJ (**animate**: JChosa.13.20.03.E)

While the distinction concerning 'airplane' doesn't seem to be geographically based, there exists variation in its treatment.

Certain foods and items of clothing also vary in their animacy status. 'Potatoes' are animate according to examples collected at Ponemah, Leech Lake, and throughout the south, but inanimate for some northern speakers of the Border Lakes region. At Bois Forte, speakers of the more southern Lake Vermilion community treat potatoes as inanimate (265a.), while a speaker at the more northern community of Nett Lake (Sugarbush) provided the example shown in (265b.), exemplifying its animate status in his variety:

(265) Animacy status: *opin* 'potato' na/ni

a. *ingii-**miijinan** niizh opin**iin***
in-gii-**miij-in-an** niizh opin-**iin**
1-PST-**eat.it-TI3-0p** two potato-**0p**
'I ate two potatoes' (RB.13.08.06.E)

b. *niizh opin**iig** nind**amwaag***
niizh opin-**iig** nind-**amo-aa-g**
two potato-**3p** 1-**eat.h/-DIR-3p**
'I'm eating two potatoes' (EG.13.08.07.E)

Another food item that shows variation with respect to its animacy status is 'carrots.' They are unanimously verified south of Leech Lake as inanimate, but treated as animate by certain speakers at Ponemah. For the Border Lakes speakers, I have recorded examples showing varying forms:

(266) Animacy status: *okaadaak* 'carrot' na/ni

    a. *giishpin **miijiyaan** okaadaak**oon** weweni inga-inaab*

giishpin	**miij-in**-yaan	okaadaak-**oon**	weweni	in-ga-inaabi
if	eat.it-TI3-1$_{CONJ}$	carrot-0p	properly	1-FUT-see

    'If I eat carrots I will see good' (LB.13.08.06.E)

    b. *giishpin **amwagwaa** okaadaak**oog** inga-na'aab*

giishpin	**amo**-agwaa	okaadaak-**oog**	in-ga-na'aabi
if	eat.h/$_{VTA}$-1>3p	carrot-3p	1-FUT-see.well

    'If I eat carrots I will see good' (GJ.14.01.09.E)

Certain items of clothing also show similar variation. 'Pants' and 'underwear,' which are commonly considered animate in the more southern communities, are inanimate in the north:

(267) Inanimate 'pants'

    *gaawiin o**minwendan**ziin giboodiyegwaazon **biizikang***

gaawiin	o-**minwendan**-ziin	giboodiyegwaazon	**biizikan**-g
NEG	3-like.it$_{VTI}$-NEG	pants	wear.it$_{VTI}$-3>0$_{CONJ}$

    'She doesn't like wearing pants' (GH.14.07.16.E)

All speakers at Leech Lake and all points north treat 'pants' as inanimate, while all speakers consulted from the south treat them as animate.[16]

'Underwear,' however, previously determined to be inanimate at Mille Lacs (Nichols and Nyholm 1995, 276), is animate among certain speakers from Aazhoomog and Lac Courte Oreilles. After verifying the inanimate status of 'pants' with a Leech Lake speaker from Inger, the following exchange took place:

(268) Inanimate status of 'underwear' at Leech Lake

MS:	*Gibiitooshkigan*	*dash?*	*Gibiizikaan*	*ina?*	*Gemaa*	*gibiizikawaa*
	your.underwear	but	you.wear.it$_{VTI}$	QP	or	you.wear.h/$_{VTA}$

    'What about your underwear? Do you wear it? Or you wear h/'

LW:	*Gaawiin*	*niin*	*nibiizikanziin*
	NEG	1s	I.wear.it$_{\text{VTI-NEG}}$

'I don't wear it/them'

Though her response stimulated a great deal of laughter by all present, and embarrassment on my end, it exemplified the inanimate status of 'underwear' for her in that she indirectly answered my question using a transitive inanimate (VTI) verb.

3.3.10. TA -*aw* Stem Contraction

Another parameter showing considerable variation has been observed concerning contraction of inflected forms of VTA -*aw* stems.[17] Nichols notes the contraction with following /i/ to /aa/ (1980, 155–56), as in the inverse (3>2/1) forms illustrated below:

(269) VTA -*aw* stem contraction: 3>1/2

a. *ingii-wiidookaag*

in-	gii-	wiidookaw	-ig
1-	PST-	help.h/	**-INV**

'she helped me' (AS.13.07.16.E)

b. *gigii-wiindamaag*

gi-	gii-	wiindamaw	-ig
2-	PST-	tell.h/	**-INV**

'she told you' (RD.14.06.11.E)

All speakers consulted for this study provided the contracted forms for the inverse (3>2/1) forms shown above in (269). An inflection showing variation involves the 1>2 participant arrangement, which Valentine states "show[s] coalescence variably across dialects" (1996, 296), with speakers providing pronunciations such as those given below in (270). Nichols describes such contraction as "/aw/ contracts to oo before /-N/" (1980, 268). The example shown in (270a.) is an uncontracted, signature northern form, while the example (270b.) shows the contraction characteristic of southern speakers:

(270) VTA -*aw* stem contraction: 1>2

    a. *ginoond**awi**n*

gi-	noondaw	-in
2-	hear.h/	-1>2

    'I hear you'

    b. *ginoond**oo**n*

gi-	noondaw	-in
2-	hear.h/	-1>2

    'I hear you'

The variation in regard to this inflection is interesting. While all speakers consulted from Leech Lake and all points further south provide the contraction shown above in (270b.), instability surfaces for some when the negatives are elicited:

(271) VTA -*aw* stem no contraction: 1>2 Ind. NEG

    *gaawiin giwii-wiidook**awi**sinoon*

    'I won't help you' (Anonymous.E)

Another speaker from the same community provided the example shown in (272) with the contraction, showing variation exists in that community:

(272) VTA -*aw* stem contraction: 1>2 Ind. NEG

    *gaawiin gidaa-wiidook**oo**sinoon*

    'I won't help you' (Anonymous.E)

For all speakers consulted from Ponemah and all points south of Leech Lake, examples provided show the contraction of -*aw* stems in both the positive and negative independent forms of the 1>2 conjugations. At Bois Forte, one speaker from Lake Vermilion provided the positive form that does not show the contraction, shown in (273a.), whereas the negative form in (273b.) does:

(273) VTA -*aw* stem contraction: 1>2

    a. *giga-wiindam**awi**n*

    'I will tell you' (RB.13.08.06.E)

b. *gaawiin gidaa-wiindamoosinoon*
'I won't tell you' (RB.13.08.06.E)

Another speaker from Nett Lake (Sugarbush) provided elicited examples that did not show contraction in either polarity for this inflection. The majority of speakers consulted from the Border Lakes region provided examples showing no contraction in either the positive or negative conjugations, while one (NJ) provided one example in the independent positive with no contraction and another in the independent negative with the contraction (as in [273b.] above).

For the conjunct inflections, a similar pattern emerges. Speakers at Ponemah, Leech Lake, and all points south provided contracted forms in the conjunct 1>2 (*-oonaan*) and for the conjunct 3>2 (*-ook*), as shown here in (274a.), compared to (274b.) from a more northern speaker of the Border Lakes region:

(274) VTA -*aw* stem contraction: 3>2 conjunct

a. Leech Lake (Inger)

*giishpin wiidook**ook** ga-niiwezhiwe*

giishpin	wiidookaw-iN-g	ga-niiwezhiwe
if	help.h/-INV-3>2$_{CONJ}$	FUT-wins

'If she helps you, you will win' (GH.LW.14.07.16.E)

b. Border Lakes (Lac La Croix)

*giishpin wiidookaw**ik** giga-mamige*

giishpin	wiidookaw-iN-g	gi-ga-mamige
if	help.h/-INV-3>2$_{CONJ}$	2-FUT-take.pot

'If she helps you, you will win' (GJ.14.01.09.E)

Dialects showing the contraction appear to have maintained the feature (as opposed to having innovated it), as it occurs as well in archived material from the south:

(275) VTA -*aw* stem contraction from Wisconsin (Nichols 1988a)

a. *mii apii begidinam**oo**naan*

'is what I sell you' (44)

b. *gaawiin wiin owidi ojiibikaawid gibagidinam**oo**sinoon*
'I reserve the root of the tree' lit. 'I do not offer you the root' (44)

c. *gedanokiit**oo**neg*
'who will work for you' (80)

d. *giwaawiindam**oo**ninim*
'I promise it to you' (80)

Another interesting observation made in sessions with speakers from the Border Lakes area in regard to VTA inflections is the variation found in 2>1p conjugations.[18] Whereas the classic southern inflection is *gi*-VTA-***imin***, one speaker from Nigigoonsiminikaaning (Red Gut) has a different inflection, shown below in (276):

(276) *gigii-wiiji'**inaam***

gi-	gii-	wiiji'	**-inaam**
2-	PST-	help.h/	**-1p**

'you helped us' (NJ.15.06.08.E)

Valentine (1994, 331) describes the feature as characteristic of "Northern Ojibwe" and shows variation between *-inaam* and *-inaan*, with the latter also observed in Cree. No other cases of this variation occur in my data.

3.3.11. Initial Vowel Change

Initial Change (IC) is one particular parameter that is central to the subsequent discussion of participles and ultimately to that on relative clauses. As discussed in 2.6 IC involves an ablaut process affecting the first vowel of a verbal complex. The "traditional" pattern for IC, observed as early as Baraga (1850) and verified at Mille Lacs by Nichols (1980), is given again in (277):

(277) SW Ojibwe Initial Change (IC)

Unchanged vowel	*Changed vowel*
a	e-
i	e-

o	we-
aa	ayaa-
e	aye-
ii	aa-
oo	waa-

As I briefly mentioned in 2.6, the pattern shown above in (277) for IC does not hold among all speakers of SW Ojibwe.[19]

Nichols (2011) discusses this variation and identifies three patterns. The first targets all vowels, which undergo their typical change as indicated in (277) above. This is the pattern he observed at Mille Lacs, southern Leech Lake, and in one speaker from northern Leech Lake. For the second pattern, he lists cases that do not show IC on /aa/ and /e/ from two speakers at northern Leech Lake and two from Ponemah. The third pattern shows no IC at Red Lake or Bois Forte for long vowels /aa/, /e/, and /oo/.

With regard to /aa/, no cases of IC are found in my data from Ponemah. In one session with a Ponemah speaker, after eliciting *Awenen aakozid* 'Who is sick?' with no IC, I asked if she had ever heard *Awenen ayaakozid* (showing IC), to which she replied, "That sounds like *old* Ojibwe." For northern Leech Lake speakers (Inger), IC on /aa/ is variable: one consultant provided examples with the usual IC pattern, but another showed no IC. For southern Leech Lake, I have data from one speaker at Onigum with no IC and some from Boy Lake with IC, suggesting that Leech Lake is a transitional zone between the south, where all vowels are attested with IC, and the north, where no speakers north of Inger provide examples of IC on /aa/. At Bois Forte, neither speakers at Nett Lake (Sugarbush) nor those at Lake Vermilion provided examples of IC with /aa/. The same is true of all Border Lakes speakers consulted for this study.[20] Instead speakers at these locations gave unchanged conjunct verbs in their responses, that is, *awenen aakozid*, or supplied the relativizing complementizer *gaa-*, that is, *awenen gaa-aakozid*.

For IC on /e/, a similar pattern emerges. No speakers at Ponemah provided examples of IC on /e/; for northern Leech Lake, the same speaker with IC on /aa/ also shows IC on /e/ with the other consultant shows IC on neither vowel. For southern Leech Lake, one speaker from Onigum did not make the change on /e/. All speakers from Bois Forte and the majority from the Border Lakes communities provided examples showing no IC on /e/; instead they provided plain conjuncts or made use of the relative complementizer *gaa-*, as discussed above for /aa/.

Interestingly, while the characterization of patterns provided in Nichols (2011) implies that all speakers make the change on /ii/, at least one case to the contrary occurs in my data. One speaker from a Border Lakes community did not make the change, instead providing examples with the *gaa-* relativizing complementizer in every instance of elicitation.

In regard to IC on /oo/, Nichols's (2011) patterns hold again with respect to Ponemah and Bois Forte, with no examples occurring in my data. For northern Leech Lake, the process appears to be variable, as seen below in (278), with (278a.) showing no IC and (278b.) showing IC:

(278) IC on /oo/ at Inger

a. *awenen b**oo**zitaasod*
'who is loading up the car' (LW.GH.14.07.16.E)

b. *awenen b**waa**gidingwaang*
'who farts in their sleep' (LW.GH.14.07.16.E)

For the Border Lakes speakers, I have only one token of IC on /oo/ (*awenen bwaakojaaned* 'who has a broken nose'); all other speakers provided plain conjunct forms of the relativizing complementizer *gaa-* in place of IC.

Overall the generalizations made in Nichols (2011) hold here, though this variation, especially concerning Border Lakes, is in need of more detailed exploration. Additionally, IC on /o/ occurs in all varieties, changing to /we/, yet evidence to the contrary is found at Nett Lake, with one speaker failing to provide IC forms on /o/. The observable trend found among the communities north of Leech Lake is the increasingly more common use of the *gaa-* relativizing complementizer.

As mentioned briefly in 2.6, for speakers who have both a *gii'-* past tense marker and *gii-* potential preverb, the relative complementizer *gaa-* is nearly homophonous with the past tense prefix *gii'-* under IC [*gaa-*]. Evidence against a past tense analysis involves three differences between the two. First, the *gaa-* relativizer can co-occur with a tense marker, either future or past, as seen below in (279):

(279) *gaa-* relativizer with tense markers

    a. Future

    *oga-biijimaandaanan opiniin **gaa-wii**-miijid*

o-ga-biijimaand-an-an	opiniin	**gaa-wii'**-miijin-d
3-FUT-smell.it-TI1-0p	potatoes	**REL-FUT**-eat.it-3

    'Then he will smell the potatoes **that he will eat**' (NJ.15.06.08.E)

    b. Past

    *ominwendaan babagiwaan **gaa-gii'**-miinag*

o-minwend-an	babagiwaan	**gaa-gii'**-miizh-ag
3-like.it-TI1	shirt	**REL-PST**-give.h/-1>3

    'He likes the shirt **that I gave him**' (NJ.15.06.08.E)

The second argument against a past tense analysis is the fact that the relative complementizer does not condition the strengthening of stops and fricatives found with the past tense marker (discussed in 2.2.2). Compare the examples below in (280), where (280a.) shows an example of the past tense tensing of the following stop (b → p), whereas (280b.) shows the relativizer that does not condition such an alternation:

(280) *gaa-*$_{\text{IC.PST}}$ versus *gaa-*$_{\text{REL}}$

    a. *awenen **gaa-p**oogidid*

awenen	**IC-gii-b**oogidi-d
who	**IC-PST**-s/he.farts-3

    'Who far**t**ed?' (RD.14.06.11.E)

    b. *awenen apane **gaa-b**oogidid*

awenen	apane	**gaa-b**oogidi-d
who	always	**REL**-s/he.farts-3

    'Who keeps far**t**ing?' (RD.14.06.11.E)

A third piece of evidence against a past tense analysis, and likely origin of the *gaa-* relativizer, is the distinction made by some speakers between tense preverbs *gii-* and *gii-*$_2$. Mentioned briefly in 2.3.4, the "potential" *gii-*$_2$ prefix is distinct from the past tense *gii-* in that it does not condition the tensing of a following consonant, as indicated above in (280a.). The past tense *gii'-* appears to have a glottal stop at its coda, though the articulation of the stop is very subtle in fast speech and data from only one speaker shows the distinction, illustrated below in (281), where (281a.) involves the "potential" *gii-₂* under IC, ultimately resulting in *gaa-*$_{REL}$, and (281b.) shows the glottalized "past" marker, conditioning the loss of the feature [voice]:

(281) 'Potential *gii-₂*' vs. 'past *gii-*'[21]

    a. *awenen **gaa-b**iinitood*

    awenen   **IC-gii-₂**-biinit-oo-d

    who   **IC-POT**-clean.it-TI2-3$_{CONJ}$

    'Who **is** cleaning it?' (NJ.15.06.08.E)

    b. *awenen **gaa'-p**iinitood*

    awenen   **IC-gii'-**biinit-oo-d

    who   **IC-PST**-clean.it-TI2-3$_{CONJ}$

    'Who cleaned it?' (NJ.15.06.08.E)

Regardless of the origin of the *gaa-* relativizing complementizer, its existence substantiates a significant variable in regard to geographical variation within SW Ojibwe. Not only having significant implications for the discussion on the form and extent of IC in the region, it also is quite relevant for the discussion of the iterative, to which we now turn.

3.3.12. Iterative Suffix

Valentine mentions an "iterative suffix" /-in/, "which is used with changed conjuncts to express periodic or habitual actions" (1994, 315). The meaning carried by the iterative focuses on the temporal properties of a repeated event or action as a sort of pluralizing morpheme. Iterative verbs get translated as 'whenever X' or 'the times that X.' Compare (282a.) with (282b.) below:

(282) Changed conjunct vs. iterative

    a. *gaa-minikweyaan*

    IC-gii-   minikwe   -yaan

    IC-PST-   drinks   -1$_{CONJ}$

    'when I drank; after I drank'

b. *gaa-minikweyaanin*
IC-gii-	minikwe	-yaan	**-in**
IC-PST-	drinks	-1$_{CONJ}$	**-ITER**

'**the times** that I drank' (LS.13.05.15.N)

This iterative suffix is seemingly related to the suffix employed in participles with subject and object relatives, triggering the /t/ palatalization mentioned in 2.3.3.1, where the third-person conjunct marker /d/ [d] palatalizes to /j/ [dʒ]:

(283) *dasing ebijin iwidi minikwe*

dasing	IC-abi-**d-in**	iwidi	minikwe
every.time	IC-be.there-3$_{CONJ}$-ITER	over.there	drinks

'**every time he is there** he drinks' (Baraga 1850, 136)

Valentine (1994, 315) provides *ekidojin* for 'whenever he said something' and one southern speaker exemplified the focus of "multiple times" by using it with a proper name for 'Friday':

(284) *nayaano-giizhigakin gida-abwezo-inanjigemin*

IC-naanogiizhigad-**in**	gi-da-abwezo-inanjige-min
IC-Friday-**ITER**	2-FUT-sweats-eats.certain.way-21p

'We'll go eat Thai food **on Fridays**' (LS.14.11.23.C)

When back-translating examples, the majority of speakers, both northern and southern, seldom recognize it; only two speakers consulted from the southern communities could translate them with any reliability. Aside from the fact that the iterative seems to have become obsolete in the majority of SW Ojibwe varieties and only one verified living speaker still produces it, there is not much else to say about it other than it provides clues to an even more complex system of Ojibwe verbal inflection in the past.

3.3.13. Participles

Previously mentioned in the introduction to the study and 2.6.2, a primary diagnostic for dialect identification involves the morphological shape of participles. I define participles as the form of a verb used in relative clauses

Table 37. Sample conjunct order verbs (from Nichols 2011)

	Conjunct	Changed conjunct	Participle	
A typical use	'if'	'when'	'who'	
anokii 'works'				
A	anokiiwaad	enokiiwaad	enokiijig	ML, sLL
B, C	anokiiwaad	enokiiwaad		nLL, BF, RL
D	anokiiwaad	enokiiwaad	gaa-anokiiwaad	BF, RL
aakozi 'is sick'				
A	aakoziwaad	ayaakoziwaad	ayaakozijig	ML, sLL
B	aakoziwaad	ayaakoziwaad		nLL-1
C		aakoziwaad		nLL-2, BF, RL
D	aakoziwaad		gaa-aakoziwaad	BF, RL
boozi 'embarks'				
A	booziwaad	bwaaziwaad	bwaazijig	ML, sLL
B	booziwaad	bwaaziwaad		nLL
C		booziwaad		BF, RL
D	booziwaad		gaa-booziwaad	BF, RL

(RCs). The pattern observed in the south is an old one, appearing in the old records (Baraga 1850; Nichols 1988a; Schoolcraft 1851; to name a few), where a verb having undergone IC will take specialized suffixes indicating plural or obviative status when a third-person subject or object undergoes relativization. Singular participles, where the head of an RC is singular, are essentially identical to their changed conjunct counterparts. Though the tendency by a number of Algonquianists has been to treat participles as "nominalized verbs," strong arguments against such an analysis exist (see 1.4.4 above).

Nichols (2011) observes the variation found in SW Ojibwe and provides the information summarized in table 37, illustrating the variation. As table 37 shows, variation is observed in the changed conjunct, with considerable overlap found at northern Leech Lake, Bois Forte, and Red Lake (rows C and D for *aakozi* and rows C and D for *boozi*). The second point of variation involves participles, with the characteristic participial markings attested only at Mille Lacs and southern Leech Lake. As will be discussed in 3.3.13.2, several speakers from northern communities have strategies where participles have the exact morphological form of changed conjunct verbs, or where they employ the *gaa*-relativizing prefix with plain conjunct inflection.

A well-known point of variation is the characteristic southern *-jig* forms, shown above in table 37 for pattern A and also mentioned in chapter 1 and 2.6.2, where the third-person suffix /-d/ undergoes palatalization to /j/ as the result of the participial suffix (either *-ig* for animate plurals or *-in* for obviative or inanimate plurals):

(285) Southern participle

*waa-ondaadizi**jig***

IC-wii-	ondaadizi	-d	-ig
IC-FUT-	s/he.is.born	-3$_{CONJ}$	-PL$_{PRT}$

'the unborn' (Benton 2013, 163) lit. 'those who will be born'

Important for the topic of relativization, participle forms are used in relative clauses (RCs), delimiting a noun referent, as seen below in (286), where the participle is used as an RC in the *wh*-question:

(286) Southern relative clause

aaniin ezhinikaazowaad anishinaabewinikaazowaad iw

aaniin	IC-izhinikaazo-waad	anishinaabewinikaazo-waad	iw
what	IC-are.called-3p	indian.names-3p	DET

gaa-ayaajig imaa?

IC-gii-ayaa-d-ig	imaa
IC-PST-be-3$_{CONJ}$-PL$_{PRT}$	there

'What are their names, their Indian names [$_{RC}$ **of the ones who were there**?']
(GO.WNLP.3)

The examples given below in (287) illustrate the variation observed in SW Ojibwe. The example shown in (287a.) involves a southern obviative participle, bearing the obviative participial inflection *-in* targeting the obviative conjunct suffix *-nid* (*-ni +-d*), resulting in the doubly marked obviative participial inflectional complex -nijin, showing the palatalization of the /d/ to /j/. The example in (287b.) contains no such participial suffix -in, resulting in the plain conjunct obviative suffix -nid. Note that gaa- co-occurs with the past tense marker gii-$_2$ in (287b.):

(287) Southern vs. northern participle strategies
    a. Southern
    *onandawaabamaan iniw ogwisan gaa-kinjiba'iwe**nijin***

o-nandawaabam-aa-n	iniw	o-gwis-an	IC-gii-ginjiba'iwe-**nid-in**
3-look.for.h/-DIR-OBV	DET$_{OBV}$	3-son-OBV	IC-PST-runs.away-**OBV-OBV**$_{PRT}$

    'She is looking for her son **who ran away**' (AS.13.07.16.E)

    b. Northern
    *obaa-andowaabamaan ogozisan **gaa-gii**-maajiiba'iwe**nid***

o-baa-andowaabam-aa-n	o-gozis-an	**IC-gii**-maajiiba'iwe-nid
3-around-look.for.h/-DIR-OBV	3-son-OBV	**IC-PST**-runs.off-OBV

    'She is looking for her son **who ran away**' (RB.13.08.06.E)

This variation is discussed at length in the sections that follow. First, the participle formation strategies of southern speakers are given in 3.3.13.1. A brief discussion of innovations is provided in 3.3.13.2 and *gaa-* participle strategies are treated in 3.3.13.3.

3.3.13.1. Southern Strategies

Participles in the south can be formed on all verb types, in both polarities (negative and positive), and are pervasive in texts from southern speakers. Southern participles always consist of IC and, for plural and obviative cases, the specialized plural and obviative markers. VII participles, such as the one given in the example below, can be found in both the north and the south:

(288) VII Op participle
    *zwaangang**in** mazina'iganan*

IC-zoongan-g-**in**	mazina'igan-an
IC.it.is.strong-O$_{CONJ}$-**PL**$_{PRT}$	paper-Op

    'patents' (Nichols 1988b, 82) lit. 'papers that are strong'

The difference in plural marking is exemplified in this example, where the participle *zwaangangin* 'those that are strong' contains the plural marker *-in*, employed as a participial plural only in the south (but also as the conjunct inanimate plural of the north; see the discussion of inanimate number in 3.3.3), while the plural *-an* of *mazina'iganan* is the normal plural marker for inanimate nouns (following Nichols's noun class 1 classification).

However, the plural and obviative participles of all other verb types show a distinct form in the south that is not found in the north.[22] For animate intransitive verbs (VAI), participial forms exist in the south for both plural (289a.) and obviative (289b.) that do not occur in the north:

(289) VAI southern participles

a. Plural

weshki-ojibwemojig

IC-oshki-	ojibwemo	-d	-ig
IC-new-	s/he.speaks.Ojibwe	-3$_{CONJ}$	-PL$_{PRT}$

'Ojibwe second-language speakers' lit. 'those who are new speakers of Ojibwe' (AS.12.09.18.C)

b. Obviative

weshki-ojibwemonijin

IC-oshki-	ojibwemo	-ni	-d	-in
IC-new-	s/he.speaks.Ojibwe	**-OBV**	-3$_{CONJ}$	**-OBV**$_{PRT}$

'Ojibwe second-language speakers$_{OBV}$' lit. 'those$_{OBV}$ who are new speakers of Ojibwe' (AS.12.09.18.C)

The example provided below by a speaker from southern Leech Lake shows how the participles (shown in bold) delimit the referent of a noun, qualifying them for the relative clause definition provided in chapter 1:

(290)

niibowa	ogikenimaan	igo	iniw	Anishinaaben	**medewinijin**
many	she.knows.them	EMPH	DEM	Indians$_{OBV}$	**who.are.mide**

miinawaa	iniw	**nenaandawi'iwenijin**
and	DEM	**who.are.traditional.healers**

'She knows a lot of people, **Midewi people, medicine people**.' (Whipple 2015, 86)

Table 38. VTI third-person participles

	Singular subject	Gloss	Plural subject	Gloss
SINGULAR PARTICIPLE	a. *ayaabajitood* **3s>0s** or **3>0s**	's/he who uses it' or 'what$_{SG}$ s/he uses'	b. *ayaabajitoowaad* **3p>0s**	'what$_{SG}$ they use'
PLURAL PARTICIPLE: OBJ. RELATIVE	c. *ayaabajitoojin* **3s>0p**	'what$_{PL}$ s/he uses'	d. *ayaabajitoowaajin* **3p>0p**	'what$_{PL}$ they use'
PLURAL PARTICIPLE: SUBJ. RELATIVE			e. *ayaabajitoojig* **3p>0**	'they who use it/them'

For transitive inanimate verbs (VTI), the head of the RC can be the subject or the object, as illustrated in table 38, which outlines the number and foci of the participles. As example (a.) in table 38 indicates, for participles used in RCs where the relativized argument, either subject or object, is the head of the RC and singular, there is overlap in the form of the participle. Contrasting (a.) with (c.) and (b.) with (d.), we see the specialized plural inflection (-*in*) indicating that the relativized object is plural. In (e.), object number is neutralized in cases where the plural subject has been relativized. The example given below illustrates nicely how number is neutralized in the plain conjunct for inanimate objects, but is indexed on the verb in the form of the participle where the inanimate plural object is the head of the RC:

(291) Inanimate number: plain conjunct vs. participle

mii dash da-waabandang iniw miinan

mii	dash	da-waaband-am-g	iniw	miin-an
thus	then	FUT-see.it-TI1-3$_{CONJ}$	DET	berry-0p

ge-miijijin
ge-miij-in-d-**in**
IC-FUT-eat.it-TI3-3$_{CONJ}$-**PL**$_{PRT}$

'Then he will see the berries that he will eat' (AS.13.07.16.E)

Nichols provides the example shown below in (292) with the same VTI *waabandan* 'see it' used in (291) above, but this time occurring as a participle with a plural object head, in this case in a *wh*-question:

(292) *wegonenan gaa-waabandangin*

      wegonen-an   IC-gii-waaband-am-g-**in**

      what-0p   IC-PST-see.it-TI1-3$_{CONJ}$-**PL**$_{PRT}$

      'What (pl.) did he see?' (Nichols 1980, 149)

In another example from an archived source in Wisconsin, the inanimate object of a third-person plural subject undergoes relativization, resulting in the inflection seen previously from table 38 example (d.) above:

(293) *akawe miinawaa o'ow ga-wiindamooninim aniw*

      akawe   miinawaa   o'ow   ga-wiindamaw-ininim   aniw

      first   and   DET   FUT-tell.h/-1s>2p   DET

      *wiigiwaaman sa **gaa-abiitamowaajin** anishinaabeg*

      wiigiwaam-an   sa   IC-gii-abiit-am-waad-**in**   Anishinaabe-g

      lodge-0p   EMPH   IC-PST-inhabit.it-TI1-3p-**PL**$_{PRT}$ Indian-3p

      'I'm first going to tell you about the lodges **that the Anishinaabe people lived in**' (AM.WNLP.5)

The same inflection occurs with one speaker's way of saying 'sanitary napkins,' which has the literal meaning of 'what$_{PL}$ women use':

(294) *ikwewag ayaabajitoowaajin*

      ikwe-wag   IC-aabajit-oo-waad-**in**

      woman-3p   IC-use.it-TI2-3p-**PL**$_{PRT}$

      'sanitary napkins' (Clark and Gresczyk 1991)

In the example shown below in (295), the plural object 'their names' undergoes relativization resulting in the participial suffix *-in* with a first-person subject:

(295) VTI participle: 1s>Op

ingii-naniibikimaag ingiw gwiiwizensag

in-gii-naniibikim-aa-g   ingiw   gwiiwizens-ag
1-PST-scold.h/-DIR-3p   those   boy-3p

gaa-wanendamaanin odizhinikaazowiniwaa.

IC-gii-wanend-am-aan-**in**   od-izhinikaazowin-iwaa-n
IC-PST-forget.it-TI1-1$_{CONJ}$-**PL**$_{PRT}$ 3-name-3p$_{POSS}$-Op

'I scolded the boys whose names I have forgotten' (Anonymous.E)

For cases of obviation in the southern varieties, number is neutralized for obviative arguments, providing a compounded ambiguity, as illustrated below in (296):

(296) VTI 3' participles   Gloss   Code

ayaabajitoonid   'what$_{SG}$ s/he/they$_{OBV}$ uses'   3'>**Os**

ayaabajitoonijin   a. 'what$_{PL}$ s/he/they use'   3'>**Op**

                                b. 's/he/they who use it/them'   **3'>O**

For transitive animate verbs (VTA) a number of possibilities for participle inflection exist. In a simplified case, either the third-person subject or object of a VTA can undergo relativization, requiring a participle:

(297) VTA participles

a. Plural subject relativized

ingiw Manidoog gaa-pi-miinaajig iniw Anishinaaben

ingiw   manidoo-g   IC-gii-miiN-**aad-ig**   iniw   Anishinaabe-n
DET   spirit-3p   IC-PST-give.h/-**3>3'-PL**$_{PRT}$ DET$_{OBV}$ Indian-OBV

'the Manidoog **who gave it** to the Anishinaabe' (Staples 2015, 4)

b. Obviative object relativized

enawemaawaajin

IC-inawem-aa-**waa-d-in**
IC-be.related.to.h/-DIR-**3p-3**$_{CONJ}$-**OBV**$_{PRT}$

'the **one(s) who they are related** to' (Staples and Gonzalez 2015, 58)

Distinct participles are also formed when the third-person plural object of a first-person subject is relativized (298), or when the third-person subject is relativized (299):

(298) VTA participle: 1s>3p
*wenjida gaa-saagi'ag**ig***
wenjida   IC-gii-zaagi'-ag-**ig**
especially   IC-PST-love.h/-1>3-**PL**$_{PRT}$
'the **ones** I was especially close to' (Staples and Gonzalez 2015, 2)

(299) VTA participle: 3p>1s
*ongow gaa-nitaawigi'i**jig***
ongow   IC-gii-nitaawigi'-id-**ig**
DET   IC-PST-raise.h/-3>1-**PL**$_{PRT}$
'these **ones** that raised me' (AS.Gii-nitaawigiyaan)

The same holds for combinations involving the second person with respect to a third-person plural head:

(300) VTA participle: 2s>3p
*enawema**jig***
IC-inawem   -**ad**   -**ig**
IC-be.related   -**2>3**   -**PL**$_{PRT}$
'your close relatives' lit. 'the ones you are related to'
(Staples and Gonzalez 2015, 36)

(301) VTA participle: 3p>2s
*gaa-miini**kig***
IC-gii-   miiN   -**ik**   -**ig**
IC-PST-   give.h/   -**3>2**   -**PL**$_{PRT}$
'they who gave it to you' (AS.12.09.18.E)

Furthermore, relativized obviative arguments interacting with a first or second person show a specialized participial form, observed also by Baraga:

(302) Obviative marking on **3'>1** (Baraga 1850, 513)
*debenjiged ogii-inaan debenim**ijin**...*
IC-dibenjige-d	o-gii-iN-aa-n	IC-dibenim-**id-in**
IC-own.things-3	3-PST-says-DIR-OBV	IC-own.h/-**3>1-OBV**$_{PRT}$

'the lord said to **my lord**'

In a field session with a southern speaker, I collected the examples in (303) and (304), showing such markings are still employed today:

(303) *ogii-wiidigemaan iniw ikwewan menwenim**ijin***
o-gii-wiidigem-aan	iniw	ikwe-wan	IC.minwenim-**id-in**
3-PST-marry-3>3'	DET	woman-OBV	IC-like.h/-**3>1-OBV**$_{PRT}$

'He$_{PROX}$ married the woman$_{OBV}$ **who likes me**.' (AS.12.09.18.E)

(304) *ogii-wiidigemaan iniw ikwewan menwenim**agin***
o-gii-wiidigem-aa-n	iniw	ikwe-wan	IC.minwenim-**ag-in**
3-PST-marry.h/-DIR-3'	DET	woman-OBV	IC-like.h/-**1>3-OBV**$_{PRT}$

'He$_{PROX}$ married the woman$_{OBV}$ **that I like**.' (AS12.09.18.E)

In essence there is a distinct participial form for any possible VTA conjugation involving either a relativized plural third-person or obviative argument. The example in (305) shows the form for the third-person argument object of the first-person plural:

(305) VTA participle: **1p>3p**
*mii ingiw gaa-wiiji'**angijig** apane, chi-mookomaanag*
mii	ingiw	IC-gii-wiiji'-**angid-ig**	apane	Chimookomaan-ag
thus	DET	IC-PST-play.w/-**1p>3-PL**$_{PRT}$	always	white.men-3p

abinoojiinyag
abinoojiinh-ag
child-3p

'We played with those farmer kids, white kids.' (Whipple 2015, 62)

In addition to the arguments of intransitive and monotransitive verbs, participial morphology is also possible with ditransitives. Previously shown above in 2.3.3 and widely observed throughout the literature on Algonquian languages is the fact that secondary objects are not indexed in the morphology of ditransitive verbs in either the independent or conjunct orders of inflection, though they can be indexed on the participle if the secondary object (either plural or animate) is head of an RC, as examples (306) and (307) below reveal. Note the inflections are identical to the obviative participles above in (303) and (304):

(306) Secondary object relatives

    a. *onagamon**an** iniw nagamon**an** gaa-miin**agin***

    o-nagamon-**an**   iniw   nagamon-**an**   IC-gii-miiN-**ag-in**

    3-sings-**Op**   DET   song-**Op**   IC-PST-give.h/-**1>3-PL**$_{PRT}$

    'He sings the songs I gave him'(AS.13.07.16.E)

    b. *ingikendaan**an** iniw ikidowin**an** gaa-miizh**ijin***

    in-gikend-am-**an**   iniw   ikidowin-**an**   IC-gii-miiN-**id-in**

    1-know.it-TI1-**Op**   DET   word-**Op**   IC-PST-give.h/-**3>1-PL**$_{PRT}$

    'I know the words he gave me'(AS.13.07.16.E)

    c. *ogii-wanendaan**an** iniw dibaajimowin**an** gaa-miin**aajin***

    o-gii-wanend-am-**an**   iniw   dibaajimowin-**an**   IC-gii-miiN-**aad-in**

    3-PST-forget.it-TI1-**Op**   DET   story-**Op**   IC-PST-give.h/-**3s>3'-PL**$_{PRT}$

    'She forgot the stories she gave him' (AS.13.07.16.E)

    d. *ogii-wanendaan**an** iniw dibaajimowin**an** gaa-miin**igojin***

    o-gii-wanend-am-**an**   iniw   dibaajimowin-**an**   IC-gii-miiN-**igod-in**

    3-PST-forget.it-TI1-**Op**   DET   story-**Op**   IC-PST-give.h/-**3'>3s-PL**$_{PRT}$

    'She forgot the stories he gave her' (AS.13.07.16.E)

Historical documents from Wisconsin also include participles where the secondary object is relativized. In (308) the relativized argument is an obviative secondary object 'pine timber':

(307) *ninga-bagidinamawaa onow isa gegwejimijin*
 nin-ga-bagidinamaw-aa onow isa IC-gagwejim-**id-in**
 1-FUT-offer.it.to.h/-DIR DEM$_{OBV}$ EMPH IC-ask.h/-**3>1-PL**$_{PRT}$

 zhingwaakwan
 zhingwaak-an
 white.pine-OBV

'I will sell him the pine timber as he requests me to' (Nichols 1988a, 44)

The suffix used in the participle shown in (306c.) is essentially structurally indistinguishable from the forms provided below, but in this case, none involve a ditransitive verb and the relative argument is the obviate primary object rather than the plural inanimate secondary object:

(308) VTA participles: 3s>3'
 a. *ogii-piibaagimaan iniw ininiwan*
 o-gii-biibaagim-aa-n   iniw   inini-wan
 3-PST-holler.at.h/-DIR-OBV DEM   man-OBV

 gaa-pasiingweganaamaajin
 IC-gii-basiingweganaam-aad-in
 IC-PST-slap.h/.face-3s>3'-OBV$_{PRT}$

'She hollered at the man that she slapped' (AS.13.07.16.E)

 b. *miinawaa ayi'iin iniw akikoon iniw*
 miinawaa ayi'ii-n   iniw akik-oon   iniw
 and   PN-OBV   DET   pail-OBV   DET

 gaa-aabaji'aajin
 IC-gii-aabaji'-aad-in
 IC-PST-use.h/-3s>3'-OBV$_{PRT}$

'These pails they used . . .' (Whipple 2015, 26)

c. *aniw ikwewan **gaa-wiijiiwaajin***

aniw	ikwe-wan	**IC-gii-wiijiiw-aad-in**
DEM	woman-OBV	**IC-PST-go.with.h/-3s>3'-OBV**$_{PRT}$

'his woman he was with' (Benton 2013, 161)

Similarly, participles in the inverse (shown above in [306d.]) bear the inflection forcing palatalization in those environments, as shown again here in (309):

(309) VTA inverse participle: **3'>3s**

megwaa bimosed, bineshiinsan gii-makadewindibewan miinawaa

megwaa	bimose-d	bineshiins-an	gii-makadewindibe-wan	miinawaa
while	walks-3	little.bird-OBV	PST-has.black.head-OBV	and

*ozaawaakigan aniw bineshiinsan **gaa-noopinanigojin***

ozaawaakigan	aniw	bineshiins-an	**IC-gii-noopinazh-igo-d-in**
has.yellow.chest	DEM$_{OBV}$	little.bird-OBV	**IC-PST-follow.h/-INV-3-OBV**$_{PRT}$

'While he was walking along, a bird that had a black head and brown chest, that was the little bird **that was following him**' (RC.Opichi)

Participle marking also occurs with the indefinite actor (X) morphology (mentioned in 2.5) if the relativized argument is either third-person (310a.) or obviative (310b.):

(310) Participles: indefinite actor

a. *meta **begidininjig** imaa ji-manoominikewaad*

mii	eta	**IC-bagidin-ind-ig**	imaa	ji-manoominike-waad
thus	only	**IC-allow.h/-X>3-PL**$_{PRT}$	there	COMP-harvests.rice-3p

'only **the ones who were allowed** to rice would be ricing there' (Whipple 2015, 66)

b. *gaawiin ingii-waabanda'igoosiimin a'aw gookooko'oo*

gaawiin	in-gii-waabanda'-igoo-sii-min	a'aw	gookooko'oo
NEG	1-PST-show.h/-X>1-NEG-1p	DET	owl

gaa-nisinjin
IC-gii-nishi-ind-in
IC-PST-kill.h/-X>3-OBV$_{PRT}$

'They didn't show us the owl **that was killed**.' (Whipple 2015, 58)[23]

The example given in (311) below from Nichols (1980, 120) at Mille Lacs shows that inflections for participles with indefinite actor morphology were used during that time period as well:

(311) VTA participle: indefinite actor X>3p

*mii giiwenh ingiw **gwesinjig** bakadewaad*

mii	giiwenh	ingiw	**IC-goshi-ind-ig**	bakade-waad
thus	supposedly	DET	**IC-fear.h/-X>3-PL$_{PRT}$**	hungry-3p

'**Those who are feared** (windigos) are hungry' (Nichols 1980, 120)

Old documents from Wisconsin include cases where the participial morphology shows up on verbs with ditransitives, when the secondary object is relativized, as in (307) above. In (312) we see the plural object suffix on a verb with indefinite actor morphology, X>1s (312a.) and X>3s (312b.):

(312) VTA participle: indefinite actor

a. *ba-waawiindamaagooyaanin*

IC-bi-	waawiindamaw	-igoo	-yaan	-in
IC-here-	promise.h/	**-X>1**	**-1$_{CONJ}$**	**-PL$_{PRT}$**

'which$_{PL}$ I am promised here' (Nichols 1988a, 46)

b. *ba-waawiindamaw**injin***

IC-bi-	waawiindamaw	-ind	-in
IC-here-	promise.h/	**-X>3$_{CONJ}$**	**-PL$_{PRT}$**

'what$_{PL}$ he is promised here' (Nichols 1988a, 64)

A recording from a more modern Mille Lacs speaker includes the example provided below in (313), where the participial plural marker occurs on a VAI with indefinite actor morphology:

(313) wenji-boodaajige**ngin**

    IC-onji-   boodaajige   **-ng**   **-in**

    IC-from-   blow.on.things   -X$_{CONJ}$ -PL$_{PRT}$

    'tire valves' lit. 'where things are blown from' (Clark and Gresczyk 1991)

The example below, appearing in an old document from Wisconsin, illustrates how participle morphology is possible in the negative with indefinite actor morphology as well:

(314) VTA negative participle: X>3p

    gaa-miinaasiwinjig

    IC-gii-   miiN   -aa   **-si**   -wind   -ig

    IC-PST-   give.h/   -DIR   **-NEG**   -X>3$_{CONJ}$ -PL$_{PRT}$

    '**who were not** given it' (Nichols 1988a, 89, 90)

VTA participles also occur with inanimate actors in the inverse, as seen below in (315) with the inanimate actor and a second-person singular:

(315) VTA participles: **0p>2**

    ge-maajiishkaa'igoyanin

    IC-da-   maajiishkaa'   **-igo**   -yan   -in

    IC-FUT-   start.h/   **-INV**   -2s$_{CONJ}$ -PL$_{PRT}$

    '**those things** that get you started' (Clark and Gresczyk 1991)

As the discussion in this section has shown, participles in the southern communities consist of a range of possible combinations and inflections. Ultimately they involve an additional layer of inflection on top of an already complicated morphological system. With regard to their geographical distribution, VII plural participles are attested in the speech of all speakers consulted for this study, though the fact that the plain conjunct in the north also bears the plural morphology complicates this generalization. VAI, VTI, and VTA plural and obviative participial forms are attested at southern Leech Lake and all points south, with no such distinct participial forms attested at northern Leech Lake and all points north. However, many of the forms collected from modern southern speakers show variation when compared to those found in older sources from those communities. This is discussed in the following section.

3.3.13.2. Innovations

When analyzing data obtained from different time periods in the same communities, one can expect to notice changes that have occurred over time. Such changes may occur on all levels of linguistic structure. The specific aspect of language change discussed here concerns morphology—more precisely, how the morphology for a language like Ojibwe is realized, as determined by syntactic operations. Such changes in the morphology are often referred to as innovations. Innovations discussed here apply to those changes observed in regard to the form of certain participles.

The first innovation in participle shape involves how the participial plural marker surfaces following agreement suffixes with final *gW-* (*-ang* 21p>3, *-inang* 3>21p, *-eg* 2p>3, and *-ineg* 3>2p): it formerly occurred as /-og/ but now appears to have been replaced by analogy with /-ig/, the default shape for the plural marker of relativized third-person plural arguments. This is illustrated in table 39. The generalized "Old Ojibwe" column contains participles obtained from older records of the language (Baraga 1850; Schoolcraft 1851; Wilson 1870; Nichols 1980, 1988a;[24] and audio recordings from Lac Courte Oreilles c. 1982). The "Modern Ojibwe" column consists of forms collected by the author from speakers from Aazhoomog, Mille Lacs, East Lake, Onigum, Lac Courte Oreilles, St. Croix, and Lac du Flambeau. When doing back-translations, speakers reject the older variants and quickly produce "corrected" forms. Many of the "Modern Ojibwe" forms from table 39 represent those corrected forms, though many speakers in aforementioned southern communities provided plain conjunct endings when they weren't sure of the participle.

A related innovation regarding participles involves their form under negation. The conjunct negative suffix is /-siW/, which selects *-g* as its third-person marker "since it follows /-w/ rather than a vowel" (Nichols 1980, 215). In Nichols's terms, /-g/ "metathesizes with the /-w/":

> The metathesized /w/ is lost word-finally, vocalized to o before /-pan/ and contracted with the initial vowel of a peripheral suffix in the participles to o:

Table 39. Participle innovations: gW-

Gloss	Old Ojibwe	Modern Ojibwe
'the ones who we know' 21p>**3p**	*gekenimang**og***	*gekenimang**ig***
'the ones who know us' **3p**>21p	*gekeniminang**og***	*gekeniminang**ig***
'the ones who you (pl.) know' 2p>**3p**	*gekenimeg**og***	*gekenenimeg**ig***
'the ones who know you (pl.)' **3p**>2p	*gekenimineg**og***	*gekenimineg**ig***

nibaasig 'that he isn't sleeping'
nibaasigoban 'had he not been sleeping'[25]
nebaasigog 'they who are not sleeping'
(Nichols 1980, 215)

Essentially this process conditions the same environment for plural participles as the *gW-* forms provided in table 39. The example *nebaasigog* 'they who are not sleeping' now occurs as *nebaasijig* for all southern speakers consulted who have a distinct negative participial form. Ultimately the negative suffix provides a theme marker to which prototypically positive suffixes can then be adjoined. This innovation can again be explained by analogy: this time the third-person suffix *-g* is replaced by the default third-person conjunct suffix *-d*. As a result the default participle plural *-ig* surfaces, forcing $d \to j$ palatalization.

Examples showing this innovation (*-sijig*) appear in sources from 1982 in Wisconsin:

(316) *-sijig* innovation

 *waa-minikwe**sijig***

IC-wii-	minikwe	-si	-d	-ig
IC-FUT-	drinks	**-NEG**	**-3**$_{CONJ}$	**-PL**$_{PRT}$

 'the ones who don't want to drink' (PT.LCONewYearsPW.1982)

The analogy explanation accounts for the innovations above, but the example given below in (317) shows how one southern speaker provides the

238 *Methodology*

typical conjunct third-person suffix *-g*, though not with the trailing /-w/ that conditions the rounding of the following vowel:

(317) *ingikendaanan iniw nagamonan ingiw niimi'iwe-ininiwag*

in-gikend-am-an   iniw   nagamon-an   ingiw   niimi'iwe-inini-wag
1-know.it-TI1-PL   DET   song-0p   DET   singer-3p

gekendanzigig a'aw gaa-ozhitood

IC-gikend-am-**ziW-g-ig**   a'aw   IC-gii-ozhit-oo-d
IC-know.it-TI1-**NEG-3**$_{CONJ}$-**PL**$_{PRT}$ DET   IC-PST-make.it-TI2-3$_{CONJ}$

a'aw inini

DET   inini
that   man

'I know the songs that **the singers don't know** who made' (Anonymous.E)

The same type of innovation has occurred under negation with respect to obviative participles. In all of the older sources consulted for this study, the negative obviative participle suffix complex is *-sinigon*. Compare the "Old Ojibwe" example in (318a.) to (318b.i.) and (318b.ii.), both "Modern Ojibwe" forms collected by the author:

(318) Negative obviative participle innovation: 's/he$_{OBV}$ who doesn't go'

a. Old Ojibwe
*ezhaasinig**on***

IC-izhaa   -si-   -ni-   -g   **-on**
IC-goes   -NEG-   -OBV-   -3$_{CONJ}$ **-OBV**$_{PRT}$

b. Modern Ojibwe
i. *ezhaasinij**in***

IC-izhaa   -si-   -ni-   -d   **-in**
IC-goes   -NEG-   -OBV-   -3$_{CONJ}$ **-OBV**$_{PRT}$

ii. *ezhaasinig*

IC-izhaa   -si-   -ni-   -g
IC-goes   -NEG-   -OBV-   -3$_{CONJ}$

The form given in (318b.i.) can be explained by the same analogy used to account for the innovation above for the negative proximate plural participle complex -sijig, where the third-person suffix -d is selected over -g resulting in the palatalization triggered by the obviative participle suffix -in. The form given in (318b.ii.), however, is identical to the plain conjunct negative obviative form with no overt participial obviative marking.

One final comment on participle innovations in the south involves a few limited cases where speakers provided participles both in naturalistic speech settings and elicitation that did not show IC. The example shown below in (319), obtained from a southern Leech Lake community, shows one such case:

(319) No IC
niimijig

niimi	-d	-ig
dances	-3$_{CONJ}$	-PL$_{PRT}$

'dancers' (Anonymous.C)

It should be stated that this speaker did show IC on /ii/ when eliciting *wh*-questions, suggesting that cases like this may either be attributed to simple mistakes made in speech (as opposed to systematic errors) or that, for such speakers, participles are not treated as a form that requires IC.

Another major point of variation observed in SW Ojibwe involves another strategy for forming participles, specifically the use of *gaa-* participles in the northern communities.

3.3.13.3. gaa- Participles

As mentioned briefly in 1.3.3 and 2.6.2, speakers from northern communities in the SW Ojibwe region use a different strategy from the one described above in 3.3.13.1, where instead of using IC and the specialized participle inflections, they employ the use of a relativizing complementizer *gaa-* with plain conjunct verbal morphology. This is a common pattern observed widely across the Algonquian family and, as previously mentioned, I treat the *gaa*-complementizer as a type of IC, most likely derived from IC on the "potential" *gii-*$_2$ preverb in Nichols's (1980) classification. For the northern speakers consulted in this study, the environments in which they use the *gaa-* complementizer are identical to the environments in which southern speakers use IC. Furthermore, for northern speakers who use the *gaa-* prefix as well as IC, the two never co-occur. Speakers who use both use IC only with the short vowels, otherwise opting for the *gaa-* complementizer strategy. An example of a singular *gaa-* participle is shown below in (320a.), a plural example in (320b.), and an obviative example in (320c.):

(320) Northern *gaa-* participles

a. Singular

*mii awe **gaa**-zhawenimid*

mii	awe	**gaa**-zhawenim-id
thus	DET	IC-love.h/-3>1$_{\text{CONJ}}$

'that's **the one that** likes me' (RB.13.08.06.E)

b. Plural

*mii igiweg **gaa**-zhawenimiwaad*

mii	igiweg	**gaa**-zhawenim-iwaad
thus	DET	IC-love.h/-3p>1$_{\text{CONJ}}$

'those are **the ones who** like me' (RB.13.08.06.E)

c. Obviative

*ogozisan **gaa**-nitaa-anishinaabemonid*

o-gozis-an	**gaa**-nitaa-anishinaabemo-nid
3-son-OBV	IC-skilled-speaks.Ojibwe-OBV$_{\text{CONJ}}$

'her son is **the one that** speaks Ojibwe' (RB.13.08.06.E)

As the examples suggest the participles shown above for the northern communities are identical in shape to the past tense changed conjuncts mentioned in 2.4. Aside from the *gaa-* relativizer, they include no specialized morphology realized in cases of relativization, showing only the conjunct morphology. As shown throughout this study, the *gaa-* complementizer is not past tense and differs from the IC form of past tense marker *gii-*, which I claim is likely to have derived historically from the "situation" or "potential" *gii-*$_2$ preverb.

Another possible explanation is to posit the extension of the *gaa-* prefix that occurs in naming conventions. As discussed briefly in 2.6, there are a number of place-names throughout the SW Ojibwe region that consist of *gaa-* 'place of . . .' and some conjunct verb, for example, *gaa-miskwaawaakokaag* 'Cass Lake' or, literally, 'place of many red cedars.' Seemingly related is the *gaa-* used in personal names, some of which are very old, including *Gaa-biboonike(d)*, 'the winter maker' or, literally, 'the one that makes the winter.'[26] The connection made between proper name *gaa-* 'the one who' and the use of *gaa-* in participles is easy to make and plausible. Regardless of its historical etymology, I assume that *gaa-* is a relativizing complementizer and treat it as one morphological realization of IC being distinct from the IC form for *gii-* 'past,' *gaa-*.

Regarding their geographic distribution, *gaa-* participles are attested at Ponemah, Bois Forte, Red Gut, and Lac La Croix, and even as far south as Onigum on the Leech Lake reservation:

(321) *gaa-* participle: Onigum

gaa-zegiziwaad

gaa-	zegizi	-waad
IC-	is.scared	-3p$_{CONJ}$

'the scared ones' (JB.1307.17.E)

Interestingly, *gaa-* participles are rare among speakers consulted from Inger, the more northern Leech Lake community.[27] Speakers there provide IC forms with plain conjunct suffixes, as seen below:

(322) IC participle: Inger

mii a'aw ikwezens Memengwaa ezhinikaazod

mii	a'aw	ikwezens	Memengwaa	**IC-**izhinikaazo-d
thus	DET	girl	PN	**IC-**is.called-3$_{CONJ}$

'That's the little girl named Memengwaa' (GH.LW. 14.07.16.BT)

When back-translating, they reject the *gaa-* participle, stating explicitly, "it can't be *gaa-*, not if it's still her name," obviously associating *gaa-* with the IC form of *gii-*. It should be stated that not all speakers from the areas listed above provided *gaa-* participles all of the time. Very often, when 'who' questions were elicited, speakers provided plain conjunct verbs, showing no IC or *gaa-* relativizer.

Essentially we arrive at a three-way typology of participle formation for speakers of SW Ojibwe. These are given below in (323), where (323a.) shows the main strategy employed in the south, with IC and participial morphology indexing the relativized argument; (323b.) the IC forms with plain conjunct morphology; and (323c.), *gaa-* participles:

(323) Variation in participles: 'I know the kid **whose mom works here**'

a. IC with participial morphology
ingikenimaa a'aw gwiiwizens omaa

in-gikenim-aa	a'aw	gwiiwizens	omaa
1-know.h/-DIR	DET	boy	here

*omaamaayan **enokiinijin***

o-maamaa-yan	**IC-anokii-ni-d-in**
3-mom-OBV	**IC-works-OBV-3$_{CONJ}$-OBV$_{PRT}$** (AS.13.07.16.E)

b. IC with conjunct inflection
ingikenimaa abinoojiinh omaamaayan omaa

in-gikenim-aa	abinoojiinh	o-maamaa-yan	omaa
1-know.h/-DIR	child	3-mom-OBV	here

enokiinid
IC-anokii-ni-d
IC-works-OBV-3$_{CONJ}$ (GH.LW. 14.07.16.E)

c. *gaa-* participle
*ingikenimaa abinoojii omaamaayan **gaa-anokiinid** omaa*

in-gikenim-aa	abinoojii	o-maamaa-yan	**gaa-anokii-ni-d**	omaa
1-know.h/-DIR	child	3-mom-OBV	**IC-works-OBV-3$_{CONJ}$**	here (GJ.14.01.09.E)

In the next section I discuss the variation presented in this chapter, mutual intelligibility, and age-graded variation.

3.4. DISCUSSION

Perhaps more important than the differences observed and described in the sections above are the similarities found among varieties, a study of which would far exceed the one provided here. Valentine remarks how the "uniformity of the system across dialects" suggests a relatively recent divergence (1994, 213). It might also be surprising and somewhat counterintuitive that in communities where the language has fared better and been more vital, morphological leveling of certain paradigms has occurred sooner than in those communities where the language hasn't been used as much. If we were to draw maps and plot the isoglosses in the traditional manner of dialectology, we would see a rather messy graphic where no clear dividing line is drawn for any one feature of variation. Instead, with the exception of a few features, we'd see a number of crisscrossing features without much apparent patterning.

3.4.1. Geographic Variation

When attempting to analyze variation observed across a geographic span, it is important to consider both variation arising as the result of migration patterns and that arising from diffusion, or contact with speakers of other varieties or languages. When considering the Ojibwe spoken at Red Lake, Bois Forte, and the Border Lakes, we gradually see patterns that are often linked to Saulteaux (obviative plural, demonstratives, *gaa-* participles, etc.). Valentine notes northern features found in Saulteaux and suggests borrowing from Cree (1994, 358). With the creation of reservations in the mid-nineteenth century, it is assumed that speakers became more isolated from those in other places and more restricted in their collective locales, ultimately having an effect on language variety. Sadly the lack of linguistic records in the majority of communities prevents us from verifying this assumption.

One exception to this observation involves the Ojibwe of Mille Lacs, Minnesota. Facing pressure to relocate in the mid- and late nineteenth century, many Mille Lacs Ojibwe fled to the White Earth reservation to claim allotments. More importantly, many Mille Lacs members did not go to White Earth, with some going as far as Leech Lake, or heading east to settle at St. Croix and Lac Courte Oreilles. Many of the speakers consulted for this study can trace at least one line of their lineage to Mille Lacs, often having a parent or grandparent from there.

Undeniable in this study are the speakers' connections to places and how those places are revealed in their language. A good case in point involves the Bois Forte reservation. Drastic differences were observed at Bois Forte between the speech recorded by speakers at Nett Lake (Sugarbush) compared to that provided by speakers from Lake Vermilion. The two speakers from Lake Vermilion who provided examples with the obviative plural both have extensive ties to their sister community Lac La Croix, which is just north of the US-Canadian border. One of the Lake Vermilion speakers indicated that she was raised primarily at Lac La Croix though she had spent a great deal of time at Lake Vermilion in her youth. Her uncle, another Lake Vermilion speaker consulted, stated that he was raised in Lake Vermilion by his mother, who was from Lac La Croix. A Lac La Croix speaker participating in this study also expressed his connection to Bois Forte, having spent a considerable amount of time there as a youth. When we consider the history of these individuals and their families, it is less surprising to find linguistic variables (such as the obviative plural discussed in 3.3.4) occurring in their community but not others.

Essentially what we find in SW Ojibwe in regard to variation is similar to the findings of Valentine's (1994) study. There appears to be a northern constituency, which might be defined as those communities where we find the variants discussed in this chapter that do not occur in the south. However, what constitutes a "northern" variety is much more difficult to articulate than for a southern one. For example, Ponemah, a community where the language shows strong alignment with Border Lakes and Saulteaux in regard to some features (participles, IC, demonstratives, and lexical items), patterns with the south in regard to others (number under obviation and the phonological points discussed above).

Though all of the variables discussed in this chapter are interesting and worthy of analysis in their own right, the focus of this study is on participles: the variation shown in regard to their morphological shape and, more specifically, their role in relative clauses. The environments and strategies for participle formation for verbs used in RCs are given in table 40. The left-hand column lists the environment along with the verb type and a token verb of that type. The middle column is dissected into a northern column (giving examples with IC and the *gaa-* relativizer) and a southern column for strategies for plural participle formation. Translations of the participles are given in the southern column. The right-hand column is dissected in the same north-versus-south fashion that, aside from the overt morphological expression of plural number shown in VIIs, is mainly collapsible into one cell due to the identical shape of their plain conjunct morphology. Syllables with IC (including *gaa-*) and relevant participial suffixes are bolded and underlined. Person codes shown in boldface indicate which argument is head of the participle. Note the overlap concerning the suffixes of the northern participle forms and the plain conjunct forms:

3.4.1.1. Leech Lake as a Transitional Area

As one might expect, based on the discussion of variation in SW Ojibwe, speakers on the Leech Lake reservation provide data that are characteristic of both the north and south, with some degree of intermediate patterning. Valentine attributes the variation observed to changes in progress, even within a single speaker's own usage (1994, 11). Chambers and Trudgill use the analogy of a stone thrown in the water: the variable spreads like the waves created by the stone. This analogy is quite relevant to our understanding of Ojibwe at Leech Lake:

> Innovations diffuse discontinuously from one centre of influence to the other centres (the successive points where the stone hits) and from each of those into the intervening regions (in waves that sometimes overlap). (Chambers and Trudgill 1998, 166)

As mentioned time and time again throughout the above sections on variation, speakers from the more northern Leech Lake community Inger often pattern with speakers from the more northern Red Lake community Ponemah, while speakers from the more southern Leech Lake communities Boy Lake and Onigum pattern with speakers from the southern communities such as Mille Lacs and those in Wisconsin. In one session with speakers

Table 40. SW Ojibwe participle variation

Environment	Participial morphology (plural /-ig/ or /-in/)		Plural plain conjunct morphology	
	NORTH	SOUTH	NORTH	SOUTH
VII conjunct **0p** me*chaa* 'it is big'	me*chaa***in** or **gaa-**michaa**in**	me*chaa***in** 'those which are big'	michaa**in** 'if they are big'	michaag 'if it/they are big'
			NORTH AND SOUTH	
VAI conjunct **3p** *nagamo* 's/he is singing'	ne*gamo***waad** or **gaa-**nagamo**waad**	ne*gamo***jig** 'they who are singing'	nagamowaad 'if they sing'	
VAI conjunct **3'** *nagamo* 's/he is singing'	ne*gamo***nid** or **gaa-**nagamo**nid**	ne*gamo***nijin** 'the one(s) who is singing'	nagamonid 'if s/he$_{OBV}$ sings'	
VTI **3p>0** *ozhitoon* 'make it'	we*zhitoo***waad** or **gaa-**ozhitoo**waad**	we*zhitoo***jig** 'they who make it/them'		
VTI **3>0p** *ozhitoon* 'make it'	we*zhitoo***waad** or **gaa-**ozhitoo**waad**	we*zhitoo***waajin** 'the things they make'	ozhitoowaad 'if they make it/them'	
VTI **3'>0** *ozhitoon* 'make it'	we*zhitoo***nid** or **gaa-**ozhitoo**nid**	we*zhitoo***nijin** 'the one(s)$_{OBV}$ who makes it'	ozhitoonid 'if s/he/them$_{OBV}$ makes it/them'	
VTA **3s>3'** *ganawenim* 'take care of h/'	ge*nawenim***aad** or **gaa-**ganawenim**aad**	ge*nawenim***aad** 'the one$_{PROX}$ who takes care of h/them$_{OBV}$'		
VTA **3s>3'** *ganawenim* 'take care of h/'	ge*nawenim***aad** or **gaa-**ganawenim**aad**	ge*nawenim***aajin** 'the one$_{OBV}$ s/he$_{PROX}$ takes care of'	ganawenimaad 'if s/he$_{PROX}$ takes care of h/them$_{OBV}$'	
VTA **3'>3s** *ganawenim* 'take care of h/'	ge*nawenim***igod** or **gaa-**ganawenim**igod**	ge*nawenim***igojin** 'the one$_{OBV}$ that takes care of h/$_{PROX}$'		
VTA **3'>3s** *ganawenim* 'take care of h/'	ge*nawenim***igod** or **gaa-**ganawenim**igod**	ge*nawenim***igod** 'the one$_{PROX}$ who is taken care of by / them$_{OBV}$'	ganawenimigod 'if s/he/they$_{OBV}$ takes care of h/$_{PROX}$'	
VTA **1s>3p** *ganawenim* 'take care of h/'	ge*nawenim***agwaa** or **gaa-**ganawenim**agwaa**	ge*nawenim***agig** 'the ones who I take care of'	ganawenimagwaa 'if I take care of them'	

Table 40. Continued

Environment	Participial morphology (plural /-ig/ or /-in/)		Plural plain conjunct morphology
	NORTH	**SOUTH**	**NORTH AND SOUTH**
VTA **3p**>1s *ganawenim* 'take care of h/'	*genawenimiwaad* or *gaa-ganawenimiwaad*	*genawenimijig* 'the ones who take care of me'	*ganawenimiwaad* 'if they take care of me'
VTA **2s**>**3p** *ganawenim* 'take care of h/'	*genawenimadwaa* or *gaa-ganawenimadwaa*	*genawenimajig* 'the ones you take care of'	*ganawenimadwaa* 'if you take care of them'
VTA **3p**>2s *ganawenim* 'take care of h/'	*genawenimikwaa* or *gaa-ganawenimikwaa*	*genawenimikig* 'the ones that take care of you'	*ganawenimikwaa* 'if they take care of you'
VTA **1p**>**3p** *ganawenim* 'take care of h/'	*genawenimangidwaa* or *gaa-ganawenimangidwaa*	*genawenimangijig* 'the ones that we (excl.) take care of'	*ganawenimangidwaa* 'if we (excl.) take care of them'
VTA **3p**>1p *ganawenim* 'take care of h/'	*genawenimiyangidwaa* or *gaa-ganawenimiyangidwaa*	*genawenimiyangijig* 'the ones that take care of us (excl.)'	*ganawenimiyangidwaa* 'if they take care of us (excl.)'
VTA 21p>**3p** *ganawenim* 'take care of h/'	*genawenimangwaa* or *gaa-ganawenimangwaa*	*genawenimangig* 'the ones we (incl.) take care of'	*ganawenimangwaa* 'if we (incl.) take care of them'
VTA **2p**>**3p** *ganawenim* 'take care of h/'	*genawenimegwaa* of *gaa-ganawenimegwaa*	*genawenimegig* 'the ones you (pl.) take care of'	*ganawenimegwaa* 'if you (pl.) take care of them'
VTA **3p**>2p *ganawenim* 'take care of h/'	*genawenimiinegwaa* or *gaa-ganawenimiinegwaa*	*genawenimiinegig* 'the ones that take care of you (pl.)'	*ganawenimiinegwaa* 'if they take care of you (pl.)'
VTA **3p**>3' *ganawenim* 'take care of h/'	*genawenimaawaad* or *gaa-ganawenimaawaad*	*genawenimaajig* 'the ones$_{PROX}$ that take care of h/them$_{OBV}$'	*ganawenimaawaad* 'if they$_{PROX}$ take care of h/them$_{OBV}$'
VTA 3'>**3p** *ganawenim* 'take care of h/'	*genawenimigowaad* or *gaa-ganawenimigowaad*	*genawenimigojig* 'the ones$_{PROX}$ that h/they$_{OBV}$ take care of'	*ganawenimigowaad* 'if h/they$_{OBV}$ take care of them$_{PROX}$'
VTA **3'**>3p *ganawenim* 'take care of h/'	*genawenimigowaad* or *gaa-ganawenimigowaad*	*genawenimigowaajin* 'the one(s)$_{OBV}$ that takes care of them$_{PROX}$'	*ganawenimigowaad* 'if h/they$_{OBV}$ take care of them$_{PROX}$'

from Inger, I provided the prompt, "Binesi married the lady who I like"; one participant responded with the example given below in (324):

(324) *Binesi ogii-wiidigemaan ini ikwewan*

    Binesi   o-gii-wiidigem-aa-n   ini   ikwe-wan
    PN   3-PST-marry.h/-DIR-OBV   DEM$_{OBV}$ woman-OBV

    *gaa-minwenimag**in***
    IC-gii-minwenim-ag-**in**
    IC-PST-like.h/-1>3-**OBV**$_{PRT}$

'Binesi married the lady who I like' (LW.14.07.16.E)

After I read her example back to her, she exclaimed, "Not that one," and then repeated her example shown in (324), this time providing *gaa-minwenimag*, without the characteristic southern obviative participle marker *-in* used in the original offering shown above. We can only speculate on what triggered her to provide the original example, but the fact that it occurred, whether intentionally or not, is interesting to our purposes in accounting for variation.[28]

It is also interesting to note that speakers from this area fluctuate regarding their use of the plural for inanimates in the conjunct order (see 3.3.3), suggesting either that the morphology is not completely productive or a transition is in effect. The same can be said regarding core demonstratives (3.3.6) among speakers at Inger and Onigum, where classic southern demonstratives—*a'aw, wa'aw, i'iw, o'ow*, and so on—are attested, as are the longer forms characteristic of the more northern speakers—*(a)'awe, (i)'iwe, (o)'owe*, and so on. Initial vowel change (IC) is especially interesting at northern Leech Lake, as speakers from the same generation from the same community show differences with respect to IC (3.3.11).

Many features can be found in free variation within the speech of a single speaker (such as *nanda-* versus *anda-*, in 3.3.7.1.1, or the behavior of glides, in 3.3.7.3.3) with no apparent pattern to the variation. One speaker at Onigum even provided northern *gaa-* participles for some forms and southern participles for others:

(325) Participle variation at Onigum

    a. *gaa-* participles

    gaa-*zegizi*waad

    'the scared ones' (JB.1307.17.E)

    b. Southern participles

    w*aadookaagojin*

    'the one who is helping him' (JB.1307.17.E)

When taking into account the rich history of the Leech Lake reservation, we become aware of the three major groups that were settled there, specifically the Mississippi Band, the Pillager Band, and the Lake Superior Band. It is likely and expected that variation occurred at Leech Lake prior to the reservation's formal inception.

3.4.1.2. Intelligibility

Also interesting and informative is the degree of mutual intelligibility across speakers presented with linguistic forms that are not of their own variety. Throughout this study I have relied heavily upon back-translation and grammaticality judgments from speakers presented with examples from other communities, a strategy that essentially serves two purposes. The first involves their ability to comprehend and interpret the utterance, while the second consists of analyzing the "corrections" and opinions they provide regarding the utterance. This is one of the "main motivations" of generative dialectology, "providing an explanation or characterization of how speakers of different but related dialects are able to communicate" (Chambers and Trudgill 1998, 41). As will be shown, how mobile speakers have been and how much exposure to another variety they have had will determine how bi- or multidialectal they may be.

When back-translating the sentence shown in (326) below, all northern speakers consulted were able to accurately translate it, though none claimed to use the participial *-ig* in this manner, indexing the relativized secondary object of the ditransitive verb *miizh* 'give h/ it':[29]

(326) *geyaabi go indayaawaag ingiw mishiiminag **gaa-miizhiyanig***

geyaabi	go	ind-ayaaw-aa-g	ingiw	mishiimin-ag	**IC-gii-miiN-iyan-ig**
still	EMPH	1-have.h/-DIR-3p	DET	apple-3p	**IC-PST-give.h/-2>1-PL$_{PRT}$**

'I still have the apples that you gave me'

All "correction" data given were essentially the same, with the omission of the participial plural, even for southern speakers. Another example containing participial plural marking on a ditransitive verb *ataw* 'put it there for h/' was presented for back-translation and grammaticality judgments:

(327) *gimiigwechiwi'igoom onow okosijiganan **gaa-pi-atawiyegin***

gi-miigwechiwi'-igoo-m	onow	okosijigan-an	**IC-gii-bi-ataw-iyeg-in**
2-thank.h/-1p>2-2p	DET	gift-0p	**IC-PST-here-put.for.h/-2p>1-PL$_{PRT}$**

'We thank you for the **gifts you've put here for me**' (JN.13.12.15.N)

All of the speakers consulted provided translations suggesting they comprehended the form of the verb, though some articulated the plural number of 'the gifts' better than others. One speaker from Ponemah, however, simply replied, "I don't know what that means."[30]

It is also worth noting that intelligibility could be determined without translation in a number of cases. After I had presented each example from a different variety for intended back-translations, instead of translating a prompt, many participants provided "correction" data, offering a form of their specific preference but that carried the same meaning as the original. This is the case below for (328), presented to a speaker from Ponemah:

(328) *mii ingiw akiwenziiyag gaa-kikinoo'ama**wijig***

mii	ingiw	akiwenzii-yag	**IC-gii-gikinoo'amaw-id-ig**
thus	DET	old.man-3p	**IC-PST-teach.h/-3>1-PL$_{PRT}$**

'Those are the old men **who taught me**' (AS.13.01.30.E)

Rather than translate the example, the speaker provided the example in her own terms, lacking the southern participial form, to express the same meaning as the original structure:

(329) *mii ingiw akiwenziiyag gaa-kikinoo'ama**wiwaad***
    mii   ingiw   akiwenzii-yag   IC-gii-gikinoo'amaw-**iwaad**
    thus   DET   old.man-3p   IC-PST-teach.h/-**3p>1s**
    'Those are the old men **who taught me**' (RD.14.06.11.BT-C)

In another case, when presented with the participle shown below in (330) and asked to translate it, one speaker from a Border Lakes community admitted, "I'm not familiar with that":

(330) *gaa-kikinoo'am**oonangig***
    IC-gii-   gikinoo'amaw   **-inang**   **-ig**
    IC-PST-   teach.h/   **-3>21p**   **-PL**$_{PRT}$
    'the **ones who** taught us' (AS.13.01.30.E)

The example may have been perceived as strange by the Border Lakes speaker in that it not only contains the innovated form of the participial plural (3.3.13.2), but also contains the VTA -*aw* stem contraction not observed in some communities in the north (3.3.10), as well as the innovated participle marker after gW-/-ig/ in place of /-og/ (3.3.13.2). Speakers from Leech Lake and Ponemah, however, were able to accurately translate the form, though all provided "corrections" involving changing the participial plural suffix -*ig* to the plain conjunct pluralizer -*waa*, for example, *gaa-kikinoo'amoonangwaa*.

Regarding the case below, shown in (331), all speakers were able to provide accurate translations, though many also included comments on the form:

(331) *gaa-kikinoo'amawiyangij**ig***
    IC-gii-   gikinoo'amaw   -iyangid   **-ig**
    IC-PST-   teach.h/   -3>1p   **-PL**$_{PRT}$
    '**the ones** who taught us' (AS.13.01.30.E)

All speakers consulted from Ponemah, Inger, Bois Forte, and the Border Lakes supplied "corrections" with the plain conjunct morphology in place of the participial inflection. One speaker from Ponemah asked, "Why do you say it like that?" Another from Inger told me, "*Gaawiin-jig **niinawind** in-*

dikidosiimin" (**We** don't say *-jig*). One speaker at Lake Vermilion claimed to have never heard *-jig* used at all, even when checking more high-frequency southern participles such as *negamojig* 'singers,' *naamijig* 'dancers,' *wayaabishkiiwejig* 'white people,' and *gekinoo'amaagejig* 'teachers.'

When I attempted to back-translate examples of the obviative plural with a speaker at Nett Lake, he explicitly stated that they were from another dialect and didn't care to translate them for me. Ironically, the examples I provided him were collected less than thirty miles to the south on the same reservation.

In the other direction, back-translating northern *gaa-* participles with southern speakers yields interesting and often entertaining discussion. The examples provided below contain *gaa-* participles where the *gaa-* relativizer co-occurs with a tense preverb. The example in (332a.) consists of *gaa-* co-occurring with future tense marker *wii-*, whereas in (332b.) the *gaa-* relativizer occurs with the past tense marker *gii-*:

(332) *gaa-* participles[31]

    a. *ingikenimaa a'awe inini* **gaa-wii**-*nagamod*

        in-gikenim-aa   a'awe   inini   **gaa-wii**-nagamo-d

        1-know.h/-DIR   DET   man   **IC-FUT**-sings-3

        'I know the man who will sing'

    b. *ingikenimaa a'awe inini* **gaa-gii**-*nagamod*

        in-gikenim-aa   a'awe   inini   **gaa-gii**-nagamo-d

        1-know.h/-DIR   DET   man   **IC-PST**-sings-3

        'I know the man who sang'

One speaker from Mille Lacs translated (332a.) as 'I know the man who wanted to sing,' interpreting the structure as involving the past tense marker *gii-* stacked on top of the future prospective *wii-*, with *gii-* undergoing IC with the relativization of the subject. For the example given in (332b.), he directed me to "take out the *gii-*" in an attempt to "correct" the form. Leech Lake speakers consulted from Inger also dislike *gaa-* participles, especially when they are intended to convey the present tense. The example in (333) provoked lively discussion in a session with speakers from Inger:

(333) *gaa-* participle: present tense

*ingikenimaa awe inini **gaa**-ginoozid*

in-gikenim-aa	awe	inini	**gaa**-ginoozi-d
1-know.h/-DIR	DET	man	**IC**-is.tall-3

'I know the tall man'

The speakers at Inger would not accept a present tense reading as given in the translation of (333) above. They asked me if I would say *gaa-* and one implied that, with *gaa-*, "it means he isn't tall anymore," associating the *gaa-* relativizer with the IC form of the past tense marker *gii-*.

3.4.2. Age-Graded Variation

Age-graded variation is usually analyzed in one of two ways. The first, done in "apparent time," involves comparing the speech of older speakers to that of younger ones in the same speech community. This is not possible in SW Ojibwe given the endangered state of the language. All speakers consulted for this study were elderly, though some were older than others. The second approach, done in "real time," consists of analyzing the speech in a community over different time periods. This particular approach is possible for many of the communities that have archived language material and living speakers. Unfortunately, the data available for this study were very limited for many of the more northern communities discussed in this chapter. The unavoidable consequence of the limited data (both past and present) is the fact that anything that exists in documented form from both the past and the present is treated as the norm for that community.

The aim of studying linguistic changes in a particular community is to identify what represents retentions (features retained in the language that were observable in the speech of previous generations), and what represents innovations (features that have been changed compared to the speech of previous generations). Once innovations are identified, then hypotheses can be developed to account for them. Many innovations have already been discussed through the various sections of this chapter. In the discussion that follows, I present very isolated cases of linguistic change in "real time," a sort of study on age-graded variation albeit modern Ojibwe as spoken presently is compared to archived material from up to more than a hundred years ago.

Discussed above in 3.6, core demonstratives show considerable variation, even within the same community. For Ponemah, both the short, characteristic southern forms—*(a')aw* 'that,' *(o')ow* 'this,' and *(i')iw* 'that'—are attested in fast speech along with the longer, more characteristic northern forms—*(a')awe* 'that,' *(o')owe* 'this,' *(i')iwe* 'that,' and so on). In the archived material recorded by Josselin de Jong (1913), the short forms are pervasive, suggesting a later shift. Textual materials from Redby c. 1987 show both long and short forms occurring, as do narratives in DeBungie and Tainter (2014) and Stillday (2013a, 2013b, 2014):

(334) Demonstratives at Ponemah 1911 vs. 2014

a. *iwe* (DeBungie and Tainter 2014, 23)
*mii dash **iwe** gaa-izhi-miigwechiwi'aad*
'and then he thanked them'

b. *iw* (Josselin de Jong 1913, 3)
*Mii sa **iw** gaa-igod iniw gaa-kanoonigojin*
'So he was told by the one who spoke to him'

The example shown in (334b.) also illustrates another important feature in the obviative participle that occurs in *gaa-kanoonigojin* 'the one$_{OBV}$ who spoke to him$_{PROX}$.' As described in detail above, Ponemah speakers consulted for this study do not productively use the participial inflection characteristic of the south.[32] The examples below show participles from modern speakers at Ponemah, compared to participles occurring in the speech of Ponemah speakers consulted by Josselin de Jong (1913):

(335) Participles at Ponemah 1911 vs. 2013

a. *aniishnaa **gaa-ayaawaad** aya'aa . . .*
'Well, **the ones who were there** were . . .' (RT.12.04.12.N)

b. *bebaamaadiziwaad*
'**travelers; tourists**' (Stillday 2013a, 63)

c. *ogaawan **gaa-tebibinaawaad***
'the walleye **they had caught**' (Tainter 2013b, 74)

d. *gakina da-zaagijiba'idiwag imaa **eyaajig***
'All **who are inside (there)** will run out' (Josselin de Jong 1913, 4)

e. *ge-gizhiiba'idijig*
'**those who can** run fast' (Josselin de Jong 1913, 4)

f. *mii iniw **gaa-nisigojin** a'aw bizhiw*
'That's **the one by whom the lynx has been killed**' (Josselin de Jong 1913, 2)

Discussed above in 3.3.10, VTA *-aw* stem contraction occurs in the speech of modern speakers at Ponemah and also in the archived data, suggesting retention in that regard:

(336) VTA *-aw* stem contaction: Ponemah 1911 vs. 2013

a. *geget sa giwenda-gagiibaadiz onjida go gaa-gaazitawiyan gaa-izhi-gikinoo'am**oonaan***
'You are foolish indeed to neglect [lit. because you neglect] doing as I taught you.' (Josselin de Jong 1913, 4)

b. *Miinawaa dash minoch giwii-kikinoo'am**oon** ge-izhichigeyan*
'[Now] I am willing to teach you again how you must [lit. shall] do.' (Josselin de Jong 1913, 4)

c. *Bizindawishin gaa-wiindam**oonaan***
'Listen to what I told you' (Tainter 2013a, 45)

d. *giga-wiidook**oon***
'I will help you' (Tainter 2013a, 48)

Interestingly, when comparing the material in Josselin de Jong (1913) to the documentation from Wisconsin (Nichols 1988a, c. 1864) and Ontario (Jones 1917), we notice striking similarities among the three. Discussed above in 3.3.7.4.2, the /t/ epenthesis observed at Mille Lacs and at Lac Courte Oreilles was previously regarded as "a characteristic treatment of

Wisconsin dialects" (Nichols 1980, 134), yet it is also observed in the old documents from Red Lake, pointing to another relic relationship between the two places:

(337) /t/ epenthesis at Ponemah c. 1911

    a. *"Aaniindi dash ezhaayeg" gigadinaag*
    '"Where are you going?" You shall say to them' (Josselin de Jong 1913, 4)

    b. *mii iw gedinikwaa*
    'That's what they will say (to you)' (Josselin de Jong 1913, 4)

In other cases where /t/ epenthesis would be expected, it doesn't occur, suggesting the usage was variable even then:

(338) *owidi nindizhaamin giga-igoog nindawi-nishibaabinodaamin wiisaande asabiin iniw ezhi-wiinaawaad*

    'We are going yonder, they will say to you, we are going to play with the evergreen with dead bowels[33] [sic]-as they call nets' (Josselin de Jong 1913, 4)

Patterns of IC observed by Baraga (1850), Schoolcraft (1851), Nichols (1988a), Wilson (1870), Jones (1919), and Josselin de Jong (1913) were identical to the pattern still in use in most SW Ojibwe communities, a remarkable retention in light of the shift in the paradigm seen in northern communities and across the Algonquian family in general.

3.4.3. Free Variation

The last matter of discussion treated in this chapter deals with free variation. Free variation is commonly perceived as the occurrence of multiple variants in the speech of a subject or subjects with no apparent change in meaning. It is usually the last resort in accounting for variation—a submission of sorts for the field-worker. According to Chambers and Trudgill free variation is "not free at all, but is constrained by social and/or linguistic factors" (1998, 50). In this section I discuss cases of free variation and their implications for this study.

Many times, what we treat in the classroom and language-learning environment as geographical variation (*-sii* in the north; *-siin* in the south) doesn't hold when even one speaker is consulted. A commonly held view in the north is to teach independent negative VAI and VTIs with the final negative suffix *-sii*, as that is perceived to be a dialect feature of the north. As we saw in 3.3.7.1.2 the boundary and context for *-sii* versus *-siin* does not appear to be very clean-cut, suggesting that forms are in free variation. Take the following example below (repeated from [198] above) consisting of two renderings from two different speakers at Ponemah:

(339) Ponemah negation: 'I haven't eaten all day long'
    a. *mii go gabe-giizhik gaawiin nindoonji-wiisini***sii** (12.03.28.ES.E)
    b. *gaawiin ingii-wiisini***siin** *gabe-giizhik* (12.04.03.RT.E)

Similar cases of free variation can be found in most aspects of variation discussed in this study and in dialectology studies in general.

Another case worth noting is the inconsistency observed in the use of participles, of which numerous examples can easily be found. Based on the definitions of participles and RCs in this study, plenty of cases exist where participial inflections are not used where expected. One explanation comes from Bowern, who reminds us that "not all morphology is productive" (2008, 95). This has been quite clear in many sessions attempting to elicit plural object participles for third-person VTI1, for example, *mazina'iganan gaa-agindang***in** 'the books that s/he has read' (3s>op). Where expected, speakers consistently produce participles for VTI2 (*aabajichiganan gaa-aabajitoo***jin** 'the tools s/he used' [3s>op]), but refuse to produce or accept the same inflection for VTI1, insisting on the form where the object is unmarked for number (*gaa-agindang*). This may possibly be due to the fact that the TI1 verbs are essentially a VAI+O structure, explaining the lack of the typical TI inflectional pattern.

One particular speaker from Onigum provided both *gaa-pimosejig* 'the ones who walked,' showing third-person participle inflection, and *gaa-pimosewaad* for the same prompt, explicitly indicating that he says it "either way." Speakers ultimately show preferences for one form or another, especially in cases where more than one choice is available (Bowern 2008, 99). Valentine notes similar difficulty in identifying the inflectional pattern for participles, stating, "Sometimes speakers do not use full participial inflection in relative clause constructions" (2001, 589).[34] The examples below in (340) illustrate one such case. In (340a.), the speaker opts not to use a participle, though the relative-like translation suggests it should be expected. In (340b.) she uses a participle on the same verb, though the translation does not imply the expected context for one:

(340) Free variation
    a. No plural participle

Mii	miinawaa	nooshkaachigewaad	mii	iniw
thus	and	when.they.winnow.rice	thus	those

gaa-aabajitoowaad	iniw	nooshkaachinaaganan
what.they.used	those	birch.bark.baskets

'That's **what they use** (as a fan), birch bark baskets.' (Whipple 2015, 20)

    b. Plural participle

Ayi'iin	ge	wiigwaasi-makakoon	iniw
PN.pausal	also	birch.bark.boxes	those

gaa-aabajitoowaajin	gii-iskigamizigewaad
what$_{PL}$.they.used	when.they.made.syrup

'**They used to use** these birch bark boxes when they were sugaring.' (Whipple 2015, 26)

What we may consider "free variation" may very well be attributed to the notion that not all morphology is productive or the fact that speakers have multiple options to choose from. Perhaps more importantly and even more likely, the "variation" we observe is the result of shortcomings in our understanding of the language or the form in question.

With the variation observed detailed in the sections above, we now turn to the discussion of the structure necessary for accounting for the Ojibwe data.

FOUR

Relativization in Ojibwe

In this chapter I discuss the phenomenon of relativization in Ojibwe, making comparisons where appropriate to other languages both within the Algonquian family and outside. In 4.1 I present the data showing the distribution of participial morphology in RCs. I show the evidence for variation found in the morphological shape of participial formation and highlight the key distinctions between relativization of core arguments and oblique arguments with relative roots. In 4.2 I describe the relevant theoretical aspects of the minimalist program (Chomsky 1993) as employed in this analysis, providing a review of and departure from earlier works on related Algonquian languages. Section 4.3 proposes a feature-checking analysis of relative clause formation in Ojibwe. I account for the geographical variation discussed previously in 3.3.11 regarding IC, showing that the *gaa-* relativizer occurs in complementary distribution with overt IC. Following Rizzi (1997), I then posit a split-CP hypothesis, providing a unified analysis for all types of RCs in Ojibwe.

4.1. OJIBWE RELATIVE CLAUSES

There do not appear to be any restrictions on what can be relativized in Ojibwe. However there are limitations on which relativized arguments are overtly represented in the verbal morphology. As described in 3.3.13, when the head of the relative clause is either first or second person, or third-person singular (including inanimates), the form of the participle is morphologically identical to the changed conjunct form:

(341) Ambiguity in relative and changed conjunct
    a. *gaa-aabajitood*
    IC-gii-   aabajit-   -oo   -d
    IC-PST-   use.it-   -TI2   -3$_{CONJ}$
    'what s/he used; s/he who used it; after s/he used it'

b. *gaa-aabjitoowaad*

IC-gii-	aabajit-	-oo	-waad
IC-PST-	use.it-	-TI2	-3p$_{CONJ}$

'what (sg.) they used; after they used it'

In contrast to the constructions shown above in (341), when the head of the RC is third-person plural (including inanimates), the signature plural participial inflections occur, disambiguating the structure:

(342) Distinct plurals

a. *gaa-aabajitoojin*

IC-gii-	aabajit-	oo	-d	**-in**
IC-PST-	use.it-	TI2	-3	**-PL**$_{PRT}$

'the things s/he used'
*'after s/he used them'

b. *gaa-aabajitoojig*

IC-gii-	aabajit-	oo	-d	**-ig**
IC-PST-	use.it-	TI2	-3	**-PL**$_{PRT}$

'**they who** used it/them'
*'after they used it/them'

c. *gaa-aabajitoowaajin*

IC-gii-	aabajit-	oo	-waad	**-in**
IC-PST-	use.it-	TI2	-3p	**-PL**$_{PRT}$

'the things they use'
*'after they used them'

Note that in example (342b.) above, the number of the non-relativized object is neutralized, resulting in an ambiguous reading. In 4.3.2 I suggest this is a result of restrictions of focus in the syntax.

In the examples below I provide cases of pronominal RCs with an overt *wh*-pronoun (also called "indirect questions") in (343), followed by the complementizer type, the so-called *that* relative in (344) with no overt *wh*-pronoun:

(343) Pronominal RC

*o-nandawaabamaad **awenen**an idi gaa-ayininamaagojin*

o-nandawaabam-aad	**awenen**-an	idi	IC-gii-ayininamaw	-igod-in
go-look.for.h/-3>3'	**who**-OBV	there	IC-PST-wave.at.h/	-3'>3-OBV$_{PRT}$

'going to look for the person **who** was waving at him' (AS.aadizookaan)

(344) Complementizer type RC

*wiinawaa akawe agiw nitam **ge**-odaapinigejig*

wiinawaa	akawe	agiw	nitam	**IC-da**-odaapinige-d-ig
them	first.of.all	DET	first	**IC-FUT**-accepts.things-3$_{CONJ}$-PL$_{PRT}$

'it is these ones **that** are first to accept it' (PM.Dewe'igan)

Complementizer type RCs in Ojibwe are not derived solely from the attachment of a complementizer, as the tense marker *ge-* of (344) above, which has undergone IC, might suggest. Rather, as I will show, movement of the verb to CP in cases of relativization first involves merging of the verb with a null complementizer, then further movement to obtain IC. It should be stated that, unlike in English, ordinary complementizers (*ji-*, *da-*, or null) without IC cannot be used in RCs:

(345) Ungrammatical complementizer RCs

    a. *ji-* complementizer

*ji-nagamod

ji-	Nagamo	-d
COMP-	sings	-3$_{CONJ}$

*'the one who sings'

    b. *da-* complementizer

*da-baninang

da-	banin-	an	-g
COMP-	drop.from.hand-	TI1	-3$_{CONJ}$

*'the one who drops it'

c. null complementizer

*minwenimag

0-	minwenim	-ag
COMP-	like.h/	-1>3$_{CONJ}$

*'the one I like'

This differs from the use of the English complementizer *that* but is parallel to RCs in Romanian (Bențea 2010, 174).

As mentioned earlier, in Ojibwe an RC can be both prenominal to the NP it modifies, postnominal, or headless. Valentine (2001, 541) points out that RCs may be used to provide further specification of indefinite arguments. He also notes that RCs may consist of additional RCs and provides the following example:

(346) Multiple RCs (from Valentine 2001, 582)

Ngoding megwaa wshkinwewyaan, gii-dgoshin **bebaa-naanaad waa-gkinoohmaagzin'jin** widi gaa-bi-wnjibaad Carlisle Indian School.

'At one time when I was a young boy, there arrive (a man) *who went about fetching those who were to go to school* at the place from which he came, the Carlisle Indian School.'

A similar example occurs in my data, though unlike in (346), where the RCs modify two different entities, both RCs shown in (347) have the same referent, 'a motorcycle,' literally, 'two-legged motor vehicle':

(347) Multiple RCs

*obimibizoni'aan [iniw **naazhoogaadenijin***

o-bimibizoni'-aa-n	iniw	IC-niizhoogaade-ni-d-in
3-ride.h/-DIR-OBV	DET	IC-is.two.legged-OBV-3-OBV$_{PRT}$

***medwebizonijin**] wa'aw gechi-mindidod.*

IC-madwebizo-ni-d-in		wa'aw	IC-gichi-mindido-d
IC-heard.motoring-OBV-3-OBV$_{PRT}$		DET	IC-great-is.big-3

'This big person is riding a **motorcycle**.' (AS.12.09.25.P)
Lit. 'He is riding h/ [the$_{OBV}$ two.legged$_{OBV}$ motorized.vehicle$_{OBV}$] this big.person'

The example in (347) also contains the participle *gechi-mindidod* 's/he who is very big,' which is yet another RC and subject of the sentence.

As will be argued for in 4.3.3 prenominal RCs are internally headed, while postnominal RCs and headless relatives are externally headed. The Ojibwe ordering of RCs is D-NP-RC or D-RC-NP. The latter involves an internal RC while the former is the more typical externally headed RC, as in the diagram in (348).

(348) External RC (most common and typical)

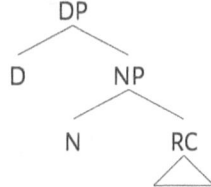

(349) Internal RC

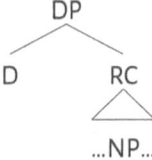

RCs in Ojibwe can be classified based on the status of the arguments undergoing relativization. Though their structure is essentially the same, they differ in regard to their morphological representation of the feature [plural]. The typology is discussed in the next section.

4.1.1. Findings: Core Argument versus Relative Root Arguments

So far I have demonstrated a division between relative clause strategies in the northern and southern regions of SW Ojibwe. Mentioned briefly in 1.2.2 and 2.3.4, relative roots (RRs) play a critical role in the shape of RCs. While core arguments (subjects and either primary or secondary objects) easily undergo relativization with the relevant IC and participial morphology, RRs—the other type of RC in Ojibwe—involve the relativization of a relative root argument. As described in detail in 2.3.4 RRs can be attached via prefixation or, in some cases, they can occupy the initial slot (per the classification given in 2.3). These have been referred to as "inherently" relative in Algonquian (Bruening 2001, 163) and comprise various types of adjuncts, including locative phrases and adverbials pertaining to manner or degree. The consensus in the Algonquian linguistic tradition is that these RRs serve to introduce oblique arguments (Bloomfield 1925; Voorhis 1974; Goddard 1987; Rhodes 1996; LeSourd 2001; Bruening 2001; among others). Goddard makes the observation that these oblique arguments are always inanimate and "almost always singular" (1987, 111), though exceptions can be found for both animacy status and number.

For RCs depicting manner, or adverbial information on how a particular action is carried out, the relative root preverb *izhi-* attaches to the verb. These verbs are often translated as 'in a certain way' or 'to a certain place':

(350) *Bebakaan gigii-**izhi**-miinigoomin, da-**izhi**twaayang*
 bebakaan gi-gii-miiN-igoomin da-**izhi**twaa-yang
 all.different 2-PST-give.h/-X>21p to-has.**certain**.way-21p
 'We were given various things, various ways to practice our spiritualties.' (AS.Gii-nitaawigiyaan)

Some verbs contain the root *iN-* built into the verb:

(351) *Anooj igo **in**akamigizi*
 anooj igo **in**akamigizi
 various EMPH does.**certain**.thing
 'He's doing it any old way.' (ES.OPD.inakamigizi)

The manner root serves a dual purpose, functioning as described above in (350) and (351), but also as a goal adjunct, with propositional, locative connotations as exemplified by the examples below:[1]

(352) *Zhaawanong gii-**izhi**dooneni*
 zhaawanong gii-**izhi**dooneni
 to.south PST-points.**certain**.way.with.lips
 'He motioned to the south with his lips.' (ES.OPD.izhidooneni)

The allomorph of the root surfaces with a lower vowel when adjoined to a bilabial stop at the onset of the final:

(353) Allomorph relative *iN-*

a. *Adaawewigamigong **a**patoo*
adaawewigamig-ong   apatoo
store-LOC   runs.to.**certain**.place
'She's running to the store.' (ES.OPD.apatoo)

b. *Noongom bakaan **a**pagizowag*
noongom   bakaan   **a**pagizo-wag
today   different   dance.**certain**.way-3p
'Today they dance different.' (AS.14.03.03)

For degree phrases (or measure phrases), one of two relative roots is used. For distance in both spatial and temporal phrases, the relative root *ako-* is employed. The examples given below are repeated from 2.3.4:

(354) *ako* relative root

a. *Aaniin **eko**onagak jiimaan?*
aaniin   IC-**ako**onagad-k   jiimaan
how   IC-is.**so.long**-0_CONJ   boat
'How **long** is the boat?' (NJ.OPD.akoonagad)

b. *Mii ishkwaaj gii-minikwed gaa-**ako**-ayaawaad abinoojiiyan*
mii   ishkwaaj   gii-minikwe-d   IC-gii-**ako**-ayaaw-aad   abinoojii-yan
thus   last   PST-drinks-3_CONJ   IC-PST-**REL**-have.h/-3>3'   child-OBV
'She doesn't drink **since** she's had kids.' (ES.12.03.28E)

Outside of relativization, the relative root verbs get translated as 'so long; a certain length; for so long':

(355) **akw**aakozi
's/he is a certain length' (as in a tree)

For degree phrases concerned with intensity or extent of a verbal event, the relative root *apiit-* is used:

(356) mii **epiichi**-nitaa-odaabii'iweyaan
      mii   **IC-apiichi**-nitaa-odaabii'iwe-yaan
      thus   **IC-REL**-skilled-drives-1_{CONJ}
      'That's **how good** I can drive.' (AS.12.12.09.C)

Outside of relativization, the verbs bearing this relative root carry similar meaning and are translated as 'for a certain extent; for so long':

(357) *"Waasa go **apiichaa**" gidinendam.*
      waasa   go   **apiichaa**   gid-inendam
      far   EMPH   is.**certain**.distance   2-thinks
      'You think it is far from here.' (ES.OPD.apiichaa)

In addition to the relative roots described above concerning manner and degree, locative RCs are formed with the relative root *ond-*. These include locative phrases in the pure sense, as shown in (358a.); source, as in (358b.); and cause or reason, as in (358c.):

(358) *ond-* relative root
      a. Locative phrase
      *Jaachaabaaning **onj**ibaa awe inini*
      jaachaabaaning   **onj**ibaa   awe   inini
      Inger   comes.**from**   DET   man
      'That man comes **from** Inger' (ES.OPD.onjibaa)

      b. Source
      *waabanda'ishin **wendin**aman onow nibwaakaaminensan*
      waabanda'-ishin   **IC-ond**in-am-an   onow   nibwaakaamin-ens-an
      show.h/-$2>1_{\text{IMP}}$ **IC**-get.**from**-TI1-$2s_{\text{CONJ}}$ DET   smart.berry-DIM-0p
      'show me **where you get** these smart berries.' (Oakgrove 1997, 32)

      c. Cause/reason
      *Mii iw gaa-**onji**-gikinoo'amaagoowiziyang . . .*
      mii   iw   IC-gii-**onji**-gikinoo'amaagoowizi-yang
      thus   DET   IC-PST-**REL**-is.taught-21p
      'That is **why** we were taught . . .' (Staples and Gonzalez 2015, 34)

For locative adjuncts the relative root *daN-* is used. The example below in (359) shows that this root has an irregular pattern in regard to IC:

(359) *daN-* relative root

a. No IC on root

*miish imaa gaa-izhaad imaa bangii imaa awas gaa-o-**dan**ashkadizod*

miish	imaa	IC-gii-izhaa-d	imaa	bangii	imaa	Awas	IC-gii-o-**dan**ashkidizo-d
thus	there	IC-PST-goes-3	there	little	there	other. side	IC-PST-go-crap.**there**-3

'So he went a little further out of the way there to **where he took his crap**.' (AS.Gii-shizhookang)

b. With IC

*Aaniindi **en**danoong?*

Where   **IC**-danoon-ng

Where   **IC**-keep.in.certain.place-IA$_{CONJ}$

'Where is it kept?' (AS.14.05.29.C)

As mentioned in 2.6.1 locative *wh*-questions without a relative root are not always subject to initial change:[2]

(360) *Aaniindi **gii**-waabamad?*

aaniindi   gii-waabam-ad

where   PST-see.h/-2>3$_{CONJ}$

'Where did you see h/?'

As will be discussed below such RCs suggest that without the relative root, the verb does not move to the head of the FocP where IC occurs.

In addition to the RCs consisting of a relative root, manner RCs may also be licensed by a locative adverbial *akeyaa* 'in a particular direction; way,' as shown below without IC:

(361) *mii iwidi **akeyaa** gii-anokiid*

mii   iwidi   **akeyaa**   gii-anokii-d

thus   there   **that.way** PST-works-3$_{CONJ}$

'that is what she did for work' (AS.Gii-nitaawigiyaan)

Temporal RCs may also be licensed by a temporal adverb *apii* 'when' or *azhigwa* 'now' with IC:

(362) Temporal RCs with *apii/azhigwa*

a. *Mii iw **apii** gaa-paashkaapid aw indedeyiban*

mii	iw	**apii**	IC-gii-baashkaapi-d	aw	in-dedey-iban
thus	DET	**when**	IC-PST-burts.out.laughing-3_{CONJ}	DET	1-dad-PRET

'That is **when** my old man busted out laughing' (AS.Gii-shizhookang)

b. ***azhigwa** eni-dagoshimoonod*

azhigwa	IC-ani-dagoshimoono-d
now	IC-go.along-arrives-3_{CONJ}

'**when** he arrives over there' (Staples and Gonzalez 2015, 56)

Temporal RCs may also consist of inflections of the "iterative" mode, mentioned in 2.3.4 and more widely attested in older records of the language. Though these are extremely rare, I feel inclined to include them here in my description as they serve as evidence to the full range of possibility within the language:[3]

(363) Iterative mode

a. *nayaano-giizhigak**in** gida-abwezo-inanjigemin*

IC-naanogiizhigad-**in**	gi-da-abwezo-inanjige-min
IC-Friday-**PL**	2-FUT-sweats-eats.certain.way-21p

'We'll go eat Thai food **on Fridays**' (LS.14.11.23.C)

b. *baandigeyan**in** omaa endaayaan apane nimoojigendam*

IC-biindige-yan-**in**	omaa	IC-daa-yaan	apane	ni-moojigendam
IC-enter-2s-**PL**	here	IC-dwell-1s	always	1-glad

'**Whenever** you come into my house I am always glad' (Clark and Gresczyk 1991)

Also, perhaps related, is the plural inflection seen in (364) below, where the plural morphology indexes the various homes of the plural subjects on an intransitive verb:

(364) *endaawaajin*

IC-	daa	-waad	-in
IC-	dwell	-3p	-PL$_{PRT}$

'their homes' lit. 'the places where they live' (Schoolcraft 1851, 376)

As the data indicate, other than the presence of the RRs themselves, there is no participial morphological signature of the plural third person–headed subject and object relatives. They are basically identical to their corresponding changed conjunct forms, long observed in Algonquian (Bloomfield 1925). As a result, for the communities of the north that do not employ the plural participial suffixes, there is twofold overlap—of the singular forms, as in the north, and in the form of core argument RCs and relative root constructions. In the next section I provide the theoretical framework for the subsequent syntactic analysis accounting for this phenomenon.

4.1.2. Variation in Relativization Strategies

The data collected and examined over the course of this study reveal the differences in the formation of RCs. While the southern communities show a dichotomy in the morphological shape of the conjunct verb and that of the RC, speakers in the northern communities do not show the contrast between such clause types. As discussed in 3.3.11 IC does not appear to be the same in the north as in the south. While most southern speakers show the full range of IC on all seven vowels, northern speakers make use of what appears to be a special morpheme, which I call the *gaa-* relativizer. The examples below in (365) illustrate this distinction between the south and the north:

(365) Participle strategies

a. Southern participle RC

ingikenimaa a'aw gwiiwizens omaa omaamaayan

in-gikenim-aa	a'aw	gwiiwizens	omaa	o-maamaa-yan
1-know.h/-DIR	DET	boy	here	3-mom-OBV

enokiinijin

IC-anokii-ni-d-**in**

IC-works-OBV-3$_{CONJ}$-**OBV**$_{PRT}$

'I know the kid whose mom works here.' (AS.13.07.16.E)

b. Northern participle RC

*ingikenimaa abinoojii omaamaayan **gaa**-anokii**nid** omaa*

in-gikenim-aa	abinoojii	o-maamaa-yan	**gaa**-anokii-**ni-d**	omaa
1-know.h/-DIR	child	3-mom-OBV	IC-works-OBV-3$_{CONJ}$	here

'I know the kid whose mom works here.' (GJ.14.01.09.E)

As the data suggest the *gaa-* prefix is itself a relativizing morpheme, appearing to have replaced, or to be in the process of replacing, the productive process of IC. Similar processes have occurred in other Algonquian languages, as mentioned earlier in 2.6. As a result both the core argument RCs and relative root constructions are morphologically ambiguous. This is discussed in the following section.

4.2. THEORETICAL FRAMEWORK

As mentioned in chapter 1 I propose a feature-checking analysis to account for the variation found in Ojibwe relativization. In 1.5.2.1 I provided the basic tenets for the derivation of the independent order with a feature-checking analysis reminiscent of those provided by Brittain (2001) and Bruening (2001). Following the work of several Algonquianists (Brittain 2001; Johansson 2013; among others), I offer a head-movement analysis to account for the derivation of the various orders of verbal inflection. The preliminaries of my analysis are sketched out here, providing the details necessary for the analysis provided in 4.3.

4.2.1. Plain Conjunct Morphosyntax

It has long been observed in Algonquian linguistic studies that the conjunct order appears to be associated with the complementizer position (Valentine 1994; Campana 1996; Brittain 2001; to name a few). Such is the approach taken in the current study; where a conjunct verb appears, we account for it with a CP layer. As described in 2.4 plain conjunct verbs are employed as verbal complements, as shown in (366a.), conditionals (366b.), and as other dependent clauses (366c.). For the examples below, I posit a null complementizer:

(366) Conjunct and the complementizer position

a. Verb complements

*azhigwa gii-moonenimind a'aw gwiiwizens ani-oshki-ininiiwi**d***

azhigwa	gii-moonenim-ind	a'aw	gwiiwizens	ani-oshkiininiwi-**d**
now	PST-realize.h/-X>3	that	boy	progess-be.a.young.man-3$_{CONJ}$

'as soon as they realized **that** a boy was becoming a young man'
(LS.Gii'igoshimowin)

b. Conditionals

*giga-bakinaage iishpin wiidook**ook***

gi-ga-bakinaage	iishpin	wiidookaw-**ik**
2-FUT-wins	if	help.h/-**3>1**$_{CONJ}$

'You will win **if** she helps you' (RD.14.06.11.E)

c. Dependent clauses

*miish iidog gaa-izhi-ikidowaad **wii-maajaawaad** gaye wiinawaa*

miish	iidog	IC-gii-izhi-ikido-waad	**wii-maajaa-waad**	gaye	wiinawaa
then	PN$_{DUB}$	IC-PST-REL-says-3p$_{CONJ}$	**FUT-leaves-3p**$_{CONJ}$	also	them

'So then they said **that they wanted to leave** too' (Mitchell 1997, 39)

As seen in the second clause above in (366c.) and (367) below, in infinitival-like clauses, complementizers *ji-* or *da-* attach to the left of the verb:[4]

(367) Infinitival environments

a. *gii-izhaa adaawewigamigong **ji**-naajibakwezhigane**d***

gii-izhaa	adaawewigamigong	**ji**-naajibakwezhigane-**d**
PST-go	to.the.store	**to**-fetches.bread-3$_{CONJ}$

'She went to the store **to** get bread.' (GJ.14.01.09.E)

b. ***da**-gawajisig*

da-gawaji-si-g
COMP-freeze.to.death-NEG-3$_{CONJ}$
'so not **to** freeze to death' (AS.Gizhaagamide)

It is also common to treat IC as a form of complementizer (Brittain 2001), as illustrated below with past tense completive aspectual properties:

(368) **gaa**-ombaakwa'wag

IC-gii-	ombaakwa'w	-ag
IC-PST-	raise.h/	-1>3$_{CONJ}$

'**After** I had jacked it (anim.) up . . .' (AS.Gii-passhkijiisijiged)

As mentioned in 3.3.3 conjunct morphology concerning number for inanimates is a parameter for geographic variation. For southern varieties, there is no plural marking on plain conjuncts (369a.), whereas northern varieties show the plural (369b.):

(369) Inanimate plural in conjunct

   a. **Southern, no plural shown**

   iishpin michaamagak iniw makizinan gego biizikangen

iishpin	michaamagad-**k**	iniw	makazin-an	gego	biizik-am-gen
if	is.big-**0**	DET	shoes-0p	don't	wear.it-TI1-NEG

   'If the shoes are big, don't wear them' (AS.13.07.16.E)

   b. **Northern, plural shown**

   *giishpin michaag**in** gego biizikangen*

giishpin	michaa-g-**in**	gego	biizik-am-gen
if	is.big-0$_{CONJ}$-**0p**	don't	wear.it-TI1-NEG

   'If they (the shoes) are big, don't wear them' (RB.13.08.06.E)

For participles in RCs where the head is plural, speakers from both northern and southern varieties employ the plural inflections:

(370) Inanimate plural participle

   a. Southern

   *akina gegoo imaa gaa-ozhibii'igaade**gin***

akina	gegoo	imaa	IC-gii-ozhibii'igaade-**g-in**
all	thing	there	IC-PST-is.written-0$_{CONJ}$-**PL**$_{PRT}$

   'the thing**s** that were written (above)' (AS.Gii-nitaawigiyaan)

b. Northern

niizh gegoo niwaabandaanan wezhaawashkwaagin

niizh	gegoo	ni-waaband-am-an	IC-ozhaawashkwaa-**g-in**
two	thing	1-see.it-TI1-0p	IC-is.yellow-0$_{CONJ}$-**PL**$_{PRT}$

'I see two things **that** are blue' (NJ.12.08.25.N)

Interestingly, although plural number is explicitly represented in the conjunct morphology of VIIs, northern speakers do not use the plural markings with TI verbs when the head of the RC is an inanimate plural, while southern speakers typically do:

(371) Plural VTI participles

a. Southern

ingii-adaawenan iniw naabishebizonan gaa-ozhitoojin Binesi

in-gii-adaawe-n-an	iniw	naabishebizon-an	IC-gii-ozhit-oo-d-**in**	Binesi
1-PST-buys-0-0p	DET	earring-0p	IC-PST-make.it-TI2-3-**PL**$_{PRT}$	PN

'I bought the earrings that Binesi made.' (AS.13.07.16.E)

b. Northern

ingii-adaamaa naabishebizonan Binesi gaa-gii-ozhitood

in-gii-adaam-aa	naabishebizon-an	Binesi	gaa-gii-ozhit-oo-d
1-PST-buy.from.h/-DIR	earring-0p	PN	IC-PST-make.it-TI2-3

'I bought the earrings that Binesi made.' (GJ.14.01.09.E)

The examples given above in this section illustrate the relationship in Ojibwe between the conjunct and the complementizer position. When a conjunct verb is used, it is a morphological realization of the complementizer position. I propose then, following Brittain (2001), that verbs specified with the feature [conjunct] raise to the head position of CP in the familiar T to C movement manner. I assume that, prior to this movement, phi-features are checked and case is assigned within *v*P and TP respectively, necessary for the selection and realization of the verb's theme. Before continuing, I provide a review of the relevant literature on which the current analysis is based.

4.2.1.1. Brittain (2001)

Brittain (2001) provides an account of the distribution of the Algonquian conjunct verb from the theoretical perspective of the minimalist program (Chomsky 1993, 1995, 1998), dealing with Western Naskapi of the Cree-Montagnais-Naskapi (CMN) language complex but extending her analysis to "members of the Algonquian language family in general" (3).

Brittain reanalyzes the person hierarchy in terms compatible with the minimalist framework. In her terms she has reanalyzed theme signs as object agreement (6). Rather than appealing to the hierarchy, which poses questions from a learnability standpoint (45), she claims that speech-act participant (SAP) arguments (*pro*) bear the feature [person] while animate non-SAPs (*pro or wh-phrase*) do not but rather bear the feature [+animate]:

> The formal split evidenced in the agreement morphology of the Algonquian verbal system, distinguishing local and non-local forms, is taken to be the morphological realization of this fundamental difference between SAP and nonSAP arguments. (37–38)

Another piece of her analysis, mentioned above and relevant for the current analysis, is that the four TA agreement theme signs are in fact object agreement morphology. I assume the same for Ojibwe and follow Brittain's approach for the assignment of argument structure and case marking occurring with the raising of the verb to T realized by the selection of the theme sign.

At this point it can be determined that CP is the host for the conjunct morphology in Algonquian. As described in chapter 1, the independent inflectional order, used in main clause contexts, can be accounted for within a TP structure. In this approach any embedded (conjunct) clause requires the projection of a CP layer. Brittain observes the crosslinguistic association between a CP projection and a subordinate clause (as described in Bresnan 1972) and also with clauses containing a *wh*-phrase, citing Petesky (1982). Essentially she defines a conjunct verb as a verb carrying the feature [conjunct] [CJ]. She claims that C is the checking position and a CP projection is independently motivated with a verb bearing the feature [CJ] needed to satisfy the featural requirement of C (Brittain 2001, 4). Similar to my analysis provided in 1.5.2.2, she arrives at an analysis for verbs of the independent order being checked, in her terms, within IP:

> For both Conjunct and Independent verbs, movement through IP is motivated by the requirement to check *phi*-features and Case. Movement to C is dependent on the presence of the feature [CJ], distinguishing Conjunct verbs from Independent verbs. (73)

The data drive the need to posit different structures for inflectional orders; application of the theory yields desirable and structurally sound results. In example 372 I provide diagrams for the independent (372a.) and conjunct (372b.) orders.

(372)

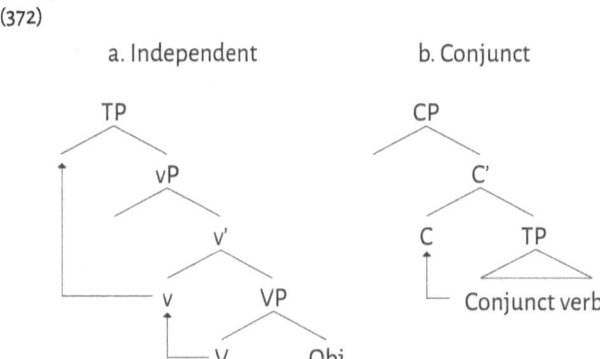

    a. Independent   b. Conjunct

We have now established the structural distinction between the two main orders of verbal inflection for Ojibwe. In order to further differentiate between IC forms and participles used in RCs, we'll need another mechanism for making that distinction. Since *wh*-phrases and subordinate clauses, along with syntactic accounts of more discourse-driven phenomena such as focalization and topicalization, usually require a CP-level structure, the highly inflectional forms of Ojibwe verbs beg for a more fine-grained CP structure. In the next section I provide the background for the theoretical framework adopted to account for the structural distinction between clause types and relativization in Ojibwe.

4.2.2. Split-CP Hypothesis (Rizzi 1997)

As evidenced by the details provided above, the CP area appears to be a crowded phrase, responsible for hosting dislocated nominal arguments under topicalization and focalization, conjunct verbs that move to C to satisfy the feature [conjunct] of C, and *wh*-operators of the interrogative mode. One might wonder where in such a structure could relativization occur? Similar observations were made earlier in Rizzi's remarks on the traditional X-bar schema as being "too simplistic" (1997, 281). So was born the cartographic approach to the fine-grained articulation of the clause architecture. Just as earlier attempts sought to decompose the TP into various heads to account for phenomena such as tense, aspect, and mode, so did the case for CP and the various discourse-driven factors of syntax such as Topic, Focus, relativization, and *wh*-questions. The left periphery as described by Rizzi (1997) includes the ForceP, determining the clause type;[5] FocP, where focalized elements are moved; TopP, where topicalized elements move; and FinP, where the finiteness of a clause is determined. The split-CP hypothesis provides loci for syntactic structural and movement operations accommodating peculiarities found among languages concerning relativization, interrogatives, and various clefting and fronting phenomena. In Rizzi's model, TopP can be expressed over or under FocP.

(373) Rizzi (1997) split CP

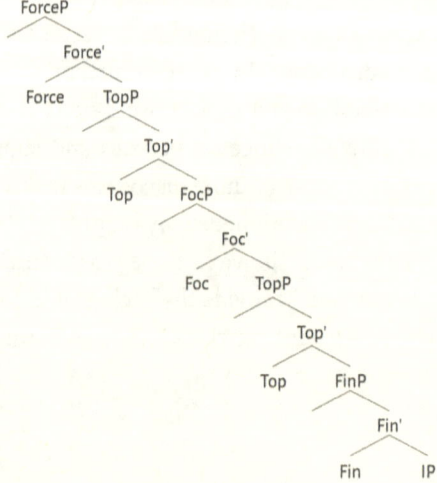

It should be noted that not all clauses necessitate the full projections of the split CP. The various projections of the split-CP framework arise only as required by the derivation for purposes of checking features that often also entail providing a locus for movement to the left periphery. Following the raising hypothesis of Brittain (2001), I assume that plain conjuncts project a single CP layer and do not require a split-CP analysis. However, for changed conjuncts and participles, clause types that can only occur with conjunct verbs, Ojibwe shows evidence of successive cyclic movement. The first position to which verbs move to in the split CP in such structures is determined to be in the Finite Phrase (FinP) and is discussed in the following section.

4.2.2.1. FinP as Host to Conjunct

The notion of finiteness is considered to be a valid linguistic distinction though languages vary on how such information is realized in a verb's morphology. Rizzi points out that various languages "tend to split verbal paradigms into two classes of forms" (1997, 284), a very important observation for our purposes in analyzing Ojibwe independent and conjunct clause types. In this traditional sense finite verbs are considered to be fully inflected, or more so than their nonfinite counterparts. The example provided below illustrates how such a distinction is made in English:

(374) She took off [following the trail].

The bracketed clause in (374) above represents a nonfinite clause while the matrix clause is finite. As part of the inflectional system, tense also factors into some analyses of finiteness; it is often the definitive criterion. Part of the "fully inflected" nature of the nonbracketed clause includes the past tense inflection of the verb 'take.' Note that tense is not specified in the bracketed nonfinite clause in (374).

Similarly, as observed for various Algonquian languages, the tense interpretation of an embedded clause is often determined by the tense of a higher clause. Such is the case for Ojibwe, as shown below in (375):

(375) o*gii*-waabandaan chi-waabashkikii [imaa **ayaamagadinig**]
o-**gii**-waaband-am chi-waabashkikii imaa **ayaamagad-ini-g**
3-**PST**-see.it-TI1 great-swamp there **it.is-OBV-0**$_{CONJ}$
'He **saw** a big swamp that **was** there' (AS.Aadizooked)

The bracketed clause above in (375) is in the conjunct order and occurs without tense. The past tense interpretation is dependent on the tense of the independent verb of the nonbracketed clause. However, plenty of examples can be found where tense is in fact represented overtly on conjunct verbs, as shown below in the bracketed clause in (376):

(376) *gii*-tajisewag noozhishenyag [**gii**-pi-mawadish**iwaad**]
gii-dajise-wag noozhishenh-yag **gii**-bi-mawadish-**iwaad**
PST-late-3p my.grandchild-3p **PST**-come-visit.h/-**3p>1s**$_{CONJ}$
'My grandchildren **were** late when they **came** and **visited** me.' (RT.12.04.03.E)

Radford describes FinP as serving the function of marking a clause finite or nonfinite, specifically by marking a clause as infinitival (2004, 333). He also assumes that movement to higher projections must first move to FinP, in observance of the head movement constraint of Travis (1984; cited in Radford 2004, 334). When this analysis is extended to Ojibwe, this approach is in line with the null complementizer argued for above in 4.2.1 and shown in the above examples. FinP is also host to the infinitival complementizers *ji*-and *da*-. In light of Rogers's (1978) determination that Ojibwe has no infinitives, I argue in 4.3.1 that the evidence for a finite distinction is seen in the complementizer morphology. Whether null or the infinitival *ji*-/*da*-, complementizers merge only with conjunct verbs. The choice of complementizer depends on the feature [finite], where a conjunct verb carrying the feature [+finite] merges with the null complementizer, while a conjunct verb with a [-finite] feature merges with *ji*-/*da*-. With the dichotomy of inflectional orders observed in Ojibwe, Rizzi's (1997) FinP is ideal for checking the formal feature conjunct [CJ]; it also checks [finite] for verbs bearing the null complementizer and [-finite] for the infinitival complementizers *ji*-/*da*-. These features are valued by moving to the head position of FinP from T, reminiscent of T → C raising for other languages. More on the feature bundles of the various clause types is given in 4.3.1.

Since conjunct verbs are the only type of Ojibwe verbs able to undergo IC, a major distinction in clause types, we can posit a head position above FinP. As Rizzi's split-CP template illustrates, FinP is structurally lower than the Focus Phrase, the locus for what has here been described as initial change, to which we now turn.

4.2.2.2. FocP Host to IC

In this section I argue that initial change is the morphological realization of the movement of the conjunct verb from FinP to FocP. This can account for everything that has been referred to as changed conjuncts, relative root arguments in RCs, and *wh*-questions. Essentially I treat all of these constructions as involving head movement to FocP. Rizzi's system allows for overt NPs to occupy canonical specifier positions, making space within the CP level a nonissue. This analytical approach is driven by the data: IC can only occur on conjunct verbs. The association of initial change with focus comes as no surprise, given the numerous references to IC serving some sort of focus function in the Algonquian literature (Rogers 1978; Nichols 1980; Blain 1999; Lochbihler and Mathieu 2013; Brittain 2001; Bruening 2001; among others). Rizzi's (1997) template provides the structure for this association to be applied to a phrasal projection in the syntax. The relationship between focalization, *wh*-questions, and RCs is widely observed crosslinguistically though, given the Ojibwe data shown concerning each and their differences in morphological shape, the FocP projection in Rizzi's system can make the right predictions concerning their derivation. I first give a brief review of *wh*-questions in Ojibwe and how they are accounted for in the FocP layer. I then discuss changed conjuncts as the morphology's response to the verb's movement to FocP.

Ojibwe is a *wh*-fronting language with a number of interrogative pronouns (A-pronouns). The pronouns are given in table 41, along with an example of their usage, repeated from 2.6.1.

Wh-agreement in Ojibwe is realized morphologically by IC. All A-pronouns in Ojibwe trigger IC on conjunct verbs with the feature [wh] as well as NP arguments undergoing focalization. This comes as no surprise, as many comparisons have been drawn in syntactic analyses of focus and *wh*-questions (Chomsky 1977; Rochment 1978, 1986; Motapan-

Table 41. A-pronouns and *wh*-questions

A-pronoun	Varying form(s)	Gloss	Example	Gloss
aaniin	aaniish; aansh	'how; what (abstract)'	Aaniin ezhichigeyan?	'What are you doing?'
aaniin apii	aaniin wapii; aaniin wapiish; ampiish; aaniish apii; aansh apii	'when; what time'	Aaniin apii gaa-pi-dagoshinan?	'When did you get here?'
aaniin dash	aaniish; aansh	'why; what for'	Aaniish wendiyan?	'What is the matter with you?'
aaniindi	aandi; aandish	'where'	Aaniindi wenjibaayan?	'Where are you from?'
awegonen	awegonesh; wegonen; wegonesh	'what (concrete)'	Awegonen waa-miijiyan?	'What do you want to eat?'
awenen	awenesh; wenen; wenesh	'who'	Awenen gaa-piidood?	'Who brought it?'

yane 1998; Brittain 2001; to name a few). In Brittain's (2001) terms, both include NP being fronted to the CP level, specifically SpecCP. Others have argued against such a movement analysis (see Bruening 2001 and Lochbihler and Mathieu 2013), due to the lack of a higher projection to accommodate other elements with CP (topicalized adverbials, determiners, and so on). By adopting a Rizzian approach, we can account for a *wh*-operator (A-pronoun) in the specifier position of FocP while the inflected verb moves up the structure carrying the *wh*-feature, satisfying the *wh*-criterion at Foc (Rizzi 1997, 299).

(377) *wh*-movement to FocP: *awenen gaa-kinjiba'iwed?* 'Who ran away?

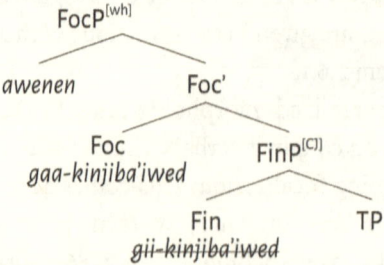

Further movement of the A-pronoun to the specifier position of TopP is permitted in cases of an intervening topicalized element, or to Spec, ForceP in cases of relativization (to be treated in the next section).

Given the relationship between *wh*-constructions and focalized elements, it is no surprise that verbs whose arguments undergo focalization also bear IC. The analysis put forth here accounts for changed conjuncts: those with temporal properties focusing on an event "just past" in the Baraga (1850) sense; "a single occurrence," as described by Nichols (1980); and those with "completive aspectual properties" per Fairbanks (2012).[6] All are claimed to bear the feature [wh] resulting in IC. Further evidence for IC occurring at the FocP level comes from the fact that changed conjuncts always appear at the left edge of a clause, as shown in the examples below with the changed conjunct appearing at the edge of the first clause in (378), and at the left edge of a complement clause in (379):

(378) a. *Mii miinawaa bezhig ayaazhoosing biiwaabik gii-aabajitooyaan gii-keshawa'amaan gii-keshawa'amaan iniw biimiskoniganan.*

b. **Gaa-keshawa'amaan**, *mii kina gaa-izhi-ombaakwa'wag weweni.*

a. 'And then again I used the 4-way tire iron to loosen up those lug nuts.

b. **After loosening them up**, I then carefully jacked the car up all the way.' (AS.Gii-paashkijiisijigeyaan)

(379) *ingii-ni-maajaamin **gaa**-ishkwaa-wiisiniyaang*
'We headed out **when** we were done eating' (AS.15.07.22.C)

The split-CP structure allows for intervening temporal adverbials and both focalized and topicalized NPs, given the available specifier positions and the recursive nature of the TopP:

(380) [$_{Matrix}$*Mii imaa asemaa naa wiisiniwin achigaadeg*] *azhigwa awiya*

mii	imaa	asemaa	naa	wiisiniwin	achigaade-g	azhigwa	awiya
thus	there	tobacco	and	food	is.placed-0$_{CONJ}$	when	someone

gaa-ishkwaa-ayaad

IC-gii-	ishkwaa-	ayaa	-d
IC-PST-	quit-	being	-3$_{CONJ}$

'This is the feast that is held at dusk **immediately after someone** has passed' (Staples and Gonzalez 2015, 30)

The structure of the split CP easily accounts for the various clause types described thus far. The analysis has been extended to other languages of the world, providing evidence for the argument for some sort of universal (see Henderson 2006 for an extension of the split CP to Bantu languages). Essentially the various projections in Rizzi's (1997) model are optional and only arise when needed. The argument made in this section is that IC is the morphological realization of *wh*-agreement on conjunct verbs, which occurs at the FocP level, coincidentally, a projection higher than FinP where conjunct morphology is realized. Given the related nature of *wh*-questions and RCs, we need a higher projection to distinguish *wh*-questions from RCs, especially from those with an overt relative pronoun (A-pronoun). Rizzi (1997) shows that both Top and Foc are compatible with a relative operator, but, based on data from Italian, he shows that relative operators can occur before topicalized and focalized elements and determines that the specifier position of ForceP, the highest projection in the CP structure, is the locus for relative pronouns.

Following Rizzi (1997), I conclude that RCs in Ojibwe are housed in ForceP, the highest functional syntactic projection and the subject of the next section.

4.2.2.3. ForceP and RCs

Prior to Rizzi's split-CP proposal, Chomsky (1995) described the nature of Force as sometimes being expressed overtly via morphological marking on the head itself, specific to clause type, such as declaratives, interrogatives, and relatives as well as serving as a host to an operator of the given type. ForceP then is responsible for the determination of clause type and serves as the ultimate probe in the feature-checking configuration. This is not too much of a stretch away from previous analyses of Algonquian languages where the clause type (independent, conjunct, subjunctive, and imperative) is determined in C and thus is reflected in verbal inflection (Ritter and Wiltschko 2009).

As with the previous sections concerning a structural host for the various Ojibwe clause types in the CP structure, RCs in Ojibwe also beg for a split-CP structure. As discussed over the course of this thesis, IC can only occur on conjunct verbs, and verbs in RCs can only involve conjunct verbs with IC. It is then not at all surprising that the Rizzian approach predicts the exact structure for the derivation of Ojibwe RCs. In order for a verb to be in an RC, it must first obtain conjunct inflection via movement to FinP (discussed above in 4.2.2.1), then to FocP to acquire IC in a *wh*-agreement configuration. To eliminate any potential for ambiguity between a *wh*-question and an RC, the strong [REL] feature on verbs in RCs is checked by movement to the head position of ForceP, whose specifier serves as a host to overt *wh*-pronouns (A-pronouns) or, more commonly in Ojibwe, a null relative operator.

In Rizzi's terms, "relative operators occupy the specifier of Force, the one position which cannot be proceeded by topics, while question operators occupy a lower position" (1997, 298). Cartographers to follow, including Bențea (2010), posit the discourse features adopted here, such as [+relative], [+declarative], [+wh], and so on for the various heads of the CP. However, their articulation of the specifics of movement differ from that of the current study.[7]

Contrary to previous approaches arguing for phrasal movement, I propose a head movement account where the verb moves up the structure, checking off feature requirements of the higher heads. This approach allows for the intervening elements such as overt *wh*-pronouns and personal pronouns as well as various adverbials that sometimes occur in RCs and *wh*-questions. This explains the cyclic nature of Ojibwe participles employed in RCs that first must acquire conjunct inflection prior to obtaining IC. Only conjunct verbs with IC can be participles, evidence for the justification of the structure provided in (381).

(381) The Ojibwe split CP

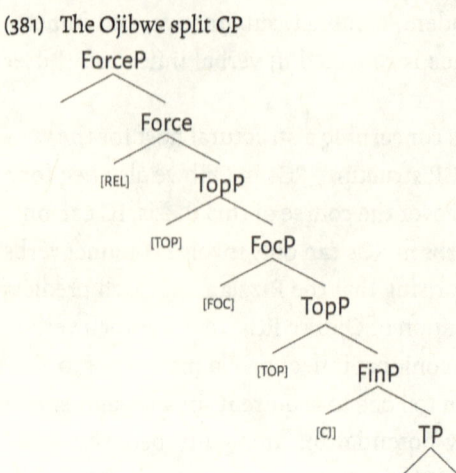

As the structure illustrates, the featural composition of the heads will determine how far up the verb is to raise. We can account for plain conjuncts via FinP, which allows for either the infinitive or null complementizer to occupy the specifier position. Movement of a verb to FinP is realized morphologically as a conjunct suffix. In cases of IC for changed conjuncts, it is clear that IC can only occur on conjunct verbs; the relationship between IC and a focus interpretation is quite clear. Upon checking the featural requirements of FinP and acquiring the conjunct morphology, the verb raises again to FocP to satisfy [FOC], the *wh*-feature requirement of FocP. The specifier position of FocP houses *wh*-elements (A-pronouns) in canonical *wh*-questions. The [FOC] feature is realized morphologically as IC. As the diagram shows, challenges provided by the surface word order for languages like Ojibwe are less of an issue in this regard given the recursive nature of TopP, allowing topics to follow or precede focalized elements. Finally, in the case of Ojibwe RCs, which by the definition provided here can only involve the conjunct verbs bearing IC with specialized morphology (in the case of subject and object relatives), the verb raises again to ForceP, the highest projection in a clause. Realization of relative morphology that triggers palatalization on an already conjunct suffix gives evidence for a cyclic movement analysis. This is discussed in the next section.

4.2.3. Cyclicity and Phases (Bruening 2001)

In Chomsky's (2000, 2001) "phase theory," syntactic derivations are sent to the other interfaces (conceptual intentional and perceptual-articulatory) in stages. Each stage of the derivation is termed a phase. The syntactic phases are CP and vP. According to the theory a phase and its contents are no longer accessible to the syntactic derivation upon being sent to the interfaces as it has "essentially been changed from a syntactic representation into representations that are interpretable at the two interfaces" (Bruening 2001, 15).

Bruening (2001) articulates a cyclic movement analysis for Passamaquoddy, where only items at the left edge of a phase are available for further movement and other operations. I propose the same for Ojibwe. Chomsky's phase impenetrability condition, given below in (382), spells out such restrictions:

(382) Phase impenetrability condition (Chomsky 1999, 2000)
In phase α with head H, the domain of H is not accessible to operations outside α, but only H and its edge.

At the vP level, where the arguments of the verb have been introduced, only those that occur at the left edge of the clause are available for further syntactic operations. This includes the head of the highest projection of the phase as well as its specifier(s) (Bruening 2001, 15). Ultimately, in order for a constituent to move to a higher position for feature-checking purposes, it has to first move to the edge of its phase. This explains the successive cyclic nature of movement.

For RCs in Ojibwe, the current analysis assumes a cyclic head movement explanation where a verb carrying the feature [REL] raises first to TP, for purposes of case assignment (in the realization of the theme sign and checking of features) and tense, and then to FinP, where the conjunct morphology is realized.

286 *Relativization in Ojibwe*

(383) Movement to FinP

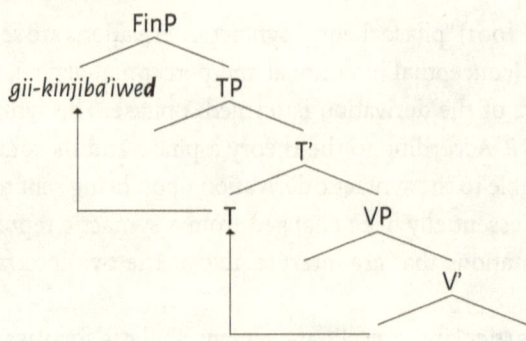

Further movement to FocP then accounts for IC in a *wh*-agreement fashion. For dialects where the *gaa-* relativizer or the aorist preverb *e-* is preferred, these are essentially the morphological realizations of IC.

(384) Movement to FocP

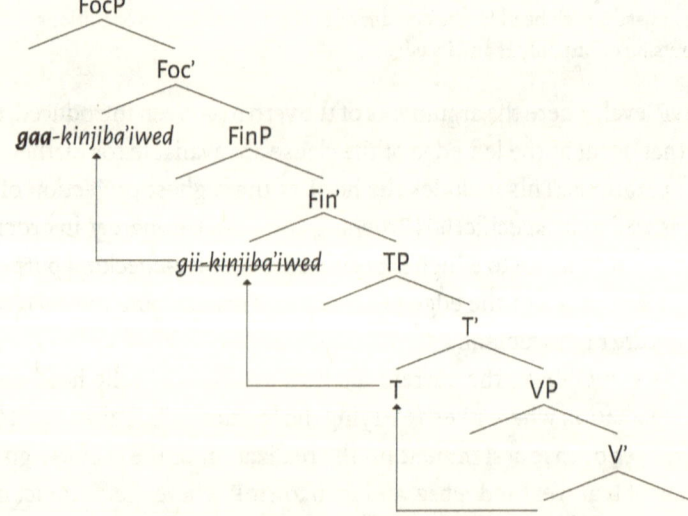

Finally, for RCs, a final movement operation takes place to ForceP. Here the signature participle marking of subject and object RCs (third-person plural head) is realized, forcing palatalization of the third-person suffix /d/. The reader is reminded that only conjunct verbs are subject to IC and only conjunct verbs with IC are compatible with the participial endings. This is evidence for the cyclic movement analysis through the split CP that is employed in (385).

(385) Movement to ForceP

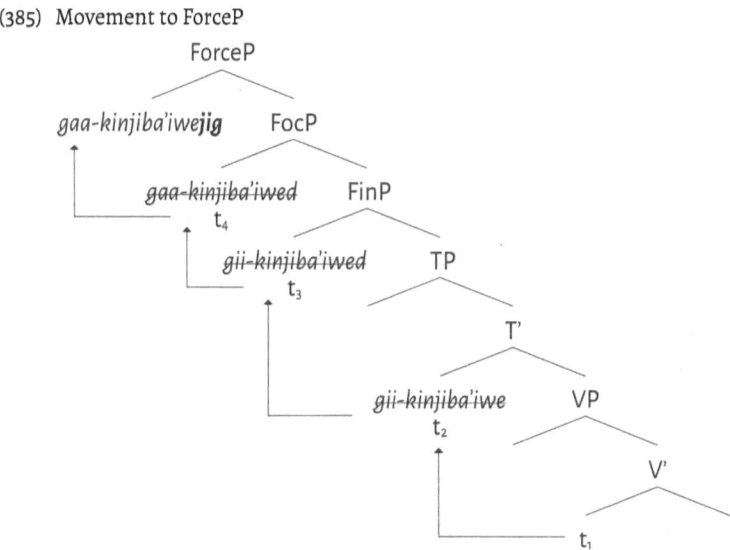

As the diagrams suggest, the clause types conjunct, changed conjunct, and relative can be accounted for via movement operations to a higher head. The movement proposed is required due to uninterpretable features of the relevant heads. The specifics of the feature bundles of each head are discussed in the next section.

4.3. REFINING THE ANALYSIS

Given the complex verbal morphology and the asymmetry found in the inflectional orders of verbs, it seems then that the head movement analysis postulated above through a split CP is ideal in accounting for the empirical Ojibwe data. This is similar to cartographic approaches for English (Kayne 1994; Bianchi 1999, 2000; De Vries 2002), Bantu languages (Henderson 2006), and Romanian (Bențea 2010), where an articulated left periphery in the spirit of Rizzi (1997) is necessary to capture the various forms and the observed variation. For RCs, each distinct head enters the derivation with uninterpretable features, forcing movement of the relative verb to the respective heads. The specifics of the feature bundles are discussed below.

4.3.1. Feature Bundles

The standard assumption concerning a split-CP analysis is that the articulated CP structure only appears when required by the derivation. More specifically the heads are only present when they make a semantic (featural) contributon. For instance when an NP constituent is either topicalized or focalized (or one of each occurs), the CP will split into a Finite Phrase, a Topic/Focus Phrase, and a Force Phrase. Feature bundles of the relevant heads determine if there is any movement involved and what the morphological realizations are to the various projections. In cases of a CP with no topicalization, focalization, relativization, or *wh*-interrogatives, the features of both the ForceP and FinP are "syncretized," collapsing together on a single C head, reminiscent of traditional analyses of the complementizer position (Radford 2004, 335). C (or any of its internal projections in the split sense) acts as a probe, searching its c-command domain for a relevant goal with the compatible featural composition. In the case of the Ojibwe split CP, such features are strong and trigger movement to the higher C position for feature satisfaction purposes.

Ojibwe, then, offers an ideal system for the argument supporting a split-CP structure. Each clause type can be differentiated based on its morphological shape. Appealing to the "mirror principle" (Baker 1985), each morphological realization is a reflection of the syntactic structure. The symmetry observed between Ojibwe clause types and the split-CP model of Rizzi (1997) is a striking correlation and provides significant support for the split-CP model. As mentioned above, each head in the split-CP system carries features that determine the variation found across clause types. These are discussed in turn below.

For the plain conjunct, movement to C is required to satisfy the strong features of C. This entails that the features of ForceP, namely [DEC] for declarative, [CJ] for conjunct, and [FIN] for finite are collapsed onto a single head, call it C, of a simplex CP structure. To differentiate between finite verbs and the aforementioned infinitival (taking the prefix *ji-/da-*), the feature [FIN] can be satisfied in either polarity: for infinitives, the feature is [-FIN], for plain conjuncts, the feature is [+FIN]. For the infinitives, the features [-FIN] and [CJ] require movement to the head position of CP, where it is merged with the infinitival prefix *ji-/da-*. For plain conjuncts the combination of the strong features [+FIN] and [+CONJ] triggers head movement to CP, where it is merged with the null complementizer described above in 4.2.1. Both instances of movement to CP give rise to the morphological realization of the obligatory conjunct suffix. This is essentially the C checks V[CJ] hypothesis of Brittain (2001) discussed above in 4.2.1.1. The specifier position of CP hosts the possibility of an overt adverbial such as *giishpin* 'if'.

(386) Plain conjunct CP *giishpin ikidod* 'if s/he says'

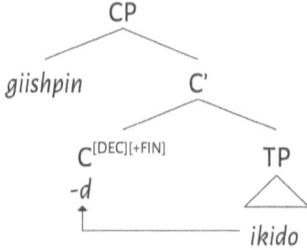

As (386) indicates, the verb moves from the head position of TP to the head position of CP. This is similar to the usual T to C movement put forth to explain auxiliary inversion for languages such as English. Since Ojibwe verbs inflect for person, tense, and number, it should come as no surprise that the entire verb complex undergoes T to C movement in the conjunct order.

It should now be clear that the processes for the various conjunct clause type derivations follow that of the split-CP structure of Rizzi (1997). This also holds for changed conjuncts, essentially, conjunct verbs that bear IC. To reiterate, only verbs inflected for the conjunct order (verbs that have undergone T to C movement) are subject to IC. Determined above in 4.2.2.2, IC has been analyzed as an instance of focalization, where the conjunct verb moves to the head position of FocP. The similarities described in 4.2.2.2 between focalized verbs and *wh*-movement in interrogatives are striking. Both require IC, which is determined here to be a process of [FOC] agreement. FocP bears the strong features [FOC] and [WH]. Since both can apply only to a conjunct verb, movement to FinP is required before the subsequent movement to FocP takes place. The derivation of such a structure requires the CP to split into the relevant projections. The specifier position of FocP hosts adverbials, focalized NPs, or overt *wh*-pronouns (A-pronouns).

(387) Changed conjunct split CP: *ajina gaa-kaagiigidod* 'after speaking for a little while'

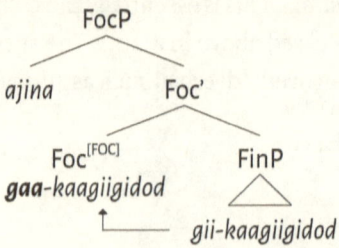

For varieties of Ojibwe where IC is realized via a prefixing strategy (*gaa-* or *e-*), the same movement operations occur, though the prefix, rather than the ablaut process discussed in detail in 2.6, shows the realization of the movement in the morphology.

The featural composition of ForceP determines whether a NP is in focus or *wh-*. For instances of Focus, the Force head bears the feature [DEC] while the interrogatives are determined by the feature [wh-]. The distinction is illustrated in (388), where (388a.) shows focalization and (388b.) shows an interrogative.

(388)

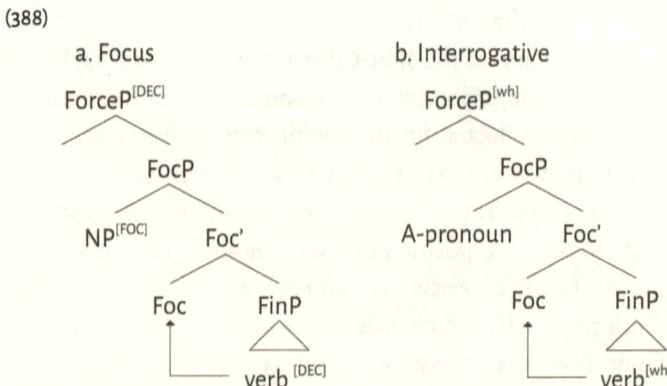

Table 42. Palatalization in ForceP

	3p -ig	3' -in
Conjunct (FinP)	maajaa**d** maajaa-**d** leaves-3$_{CONJ}$'s/he leaves'	maajaani**d** maajaa-ni-**d** leaves-**OBV**-3$_{CONJ}$'s/he$_{OBV}$ leaves'
Changed conjunct (FocP)	*mayaajaad* IC-maajaa-**d** IC-leaves-3$_{CONJ}$ 'upon leaving'	*mayaajaanid* IC-maajaa-ni-**d** IC-leaves-OBV-3$_{CONJ}$ 'upon leaving$_{OBV}$'
Relative clause ("participle") (ForceP)	*mayaajaajig* IC-maajaa-**d**-**ig** IC-leaves-3$_{CONJ}$-**PL**$_{PRT}$ 'they who are leaving'	*mayaajaanijin* IC-maajaa-ni-**d**-**in** IC-leaves-OBV-3$_{CONJ}$-**OBV**$_{PRT}$'s/he/they$_{OBV}$ who are leaving'

With ForceP responsible for determining the force of the clause (declarative versus interrogative), the similarities in *wh*-question and relativized structures are disambiguated. While the verbs of each occupy the head position of FocP, the specifier of FocP hosts the obligatory *wh*-pronoun in interrogatives. One might then wonder about the occurrence of overt pronominal *wh*-pronouns in RCs.

Aside from differentiating between *wh*-interrogatives and focalization, ForceP also makes the distinction between *wh*-interrogatives and RCs. As shown in 4.1 Ojibwe RCs may have an overt pronominal relative operator. Following Rizzi (1997, 298), relative operators occupy the specifier position of ForceP. Given the function of Force, it is obvious that the potential ambiguity of a *wh*-interrogative and an RC can be disambiguated by the featural composition of the Force head. For RCs, ForceP bears the feature [REL]. Given our successive-cyclic movement approach, only conjunct verbs can bear IC, and only changed conjuncts can bear the feature [REL]. The morphological realization of movement from FocP to ForceP is evidenced in the plural or obviative marking of the participles, or core argument RCs with a third-person plural or obviative head. Rather than the typical conjunct plural marker *-waa(d)* (for plurals) and *-nid* for obviatives, a specialized suffix occurs for each, triggering the palatalization discussed in 2.3.3.1. The key morphological distinction between changed conjuncts and RCs is best observed when the head of the clause is either third-person plural (3p) or obviative (3'), as illustrated in table 42.

The claim made in this section involves the featural composition of relevant heads in the split-CP structure. Where a plain conjunct is used, features of ForceP [DEC] and FinP [FIN] are collapsed onto a single head, reminiscent of C in traditional approaches. For changed conjuncts, verbs move from the head position of FinP to that of FocP. This movement is realized by IC, be it ablaut of the leftmost vowel of the verb complex or by the *gaa-* or *e-* prefixes of the northern and eastern varieties. Featural composition of the ForceP determines whether or not the derivation requires a *wh*-pronoun (for interrogatives) or not (for focalization). For Ojibwe RCs, determined by the feature [REL] of ForceP, only those elements in the domain of the split CP are susceptible to further movement operations. As the data indicate, only conjunct verbs with IC can take the participial markings of the core argument (subject and object) RCs. Now that we have established a system that can account for the surface contrast of the morphological form of verbs in the inflectional sets conjunct, changed conjunct, and participle, we can now account for the various intervening elements that may arise.

4.3.2. The Structure of the Ojibwe CP

The split complementizer system of Ojibwe argued for here provides the framework for the analysis of surface word order within a clause. Clearly articulated by Rizzi (1997), the left periphery is the host to fronted NPs undergoing topicalization or focalization. Though these are definitely discourse-driven phenomena, their syntactic loci is worthy of attention if we are to devise a structure than can account for the various clause types found in the world's languages. While the argument made thus far provides the framework for differentiating clause types, it seems necessary to test the framework with the empirical patterns found in Ojibwe.

An important characteristic of the Rizzian template is the specifier position for each projection. As Kayne (1994) points out, a movement analysis like that provided here adheres to the linear correspondence axiom (LCA), which restricts each maximal projection to one specifier, one complement, and one adjunction. The specifier position of each projection hosts movement of NPs out of their canonical positions in a typical clause structure.

In a sense, languages vary regarding to what degree this system is exploited for discourse purposes. The argument made here involves the split CP of Ojibwe as the ideal structural template for accounting for not only the clause type but also the surface word order.

For complementizers, either the infinitive *ji-/da-* or the null complementizer, movement to FinP must occur to satisfy the strong features of FinP. The specifier position of FinP hosts the overt adverbials that often occur and are said to trigger conjunct inflection.

Rizzi's (1997) model shows that TopP can occur before or after FocP, where FocP is sandwiched in between. This is an important point when adapting his theory to suit Ojibwe. Discussed at length in 2.7, Ojibwe word order is best described as preferring verb-initial renderings. In what can be analyzed as an issue of V to T raising, overt nominal expressions occur most frequently after the verb. When taking into account discourse-driven notions such as Topic and Focus, we see instances of the arrangement of constituents in a number of possible surface orders. While Rizzi's template may be best suited for dealing with word order phenomena of the independent inflectional order, its architecture may also be exploited for embedded clause types, that is, conjunct, changed conjunct, and participle. In example (389) below, I give the morphological glossing for a complex sentence that occurred in a text in my data. In the subsequent examples (390) and (391), I zero in on the embedded structures, making use of the Rizzian split CP:

(389) *onaanaagadawaabamaan iniw odoodaabaanan*

o-naanaagadawaabam-aa-n   iniw   od-odaabaan-an
3-examine.h/-DIR-OBV   DET   3-car-OBV

gaa-ishkwaabizonijin a'aw ikwe
IC-gii-ishkwaabizo-ni-d-in   a'aw   ikwe
IC-PST-stalls-OBV-3$_{CONJ}$-OBV$_{PRT}$ DET   woman

'The woman is checking out her car that has stalled out' (AS.12.09.25.P)

The sentence provided in (389) is presented in the tree diagram shown in (390). Since the sentence is declarative in force and is not a relative construction, the CP layers ForceP and FinP have been collapsed onto a single C head.

(390)

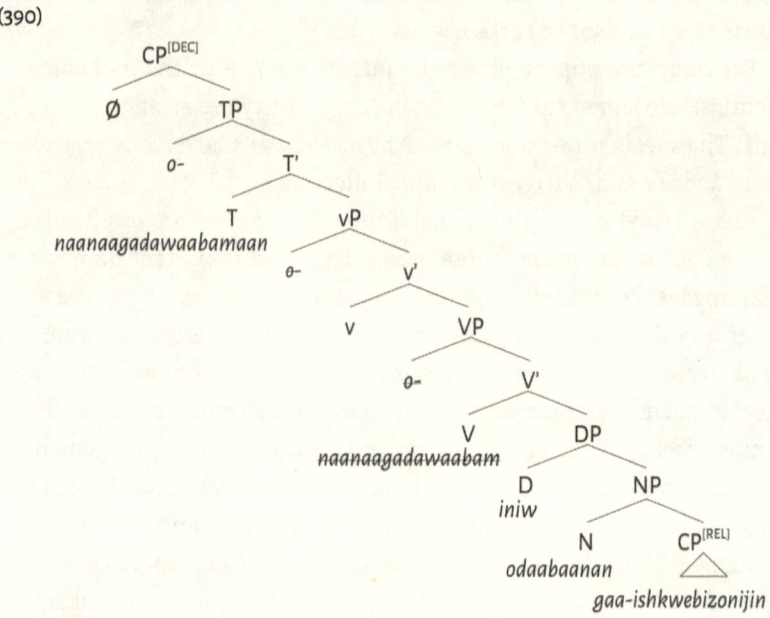

The example in (391) is an inset of CP[REL] from (390).

(391)

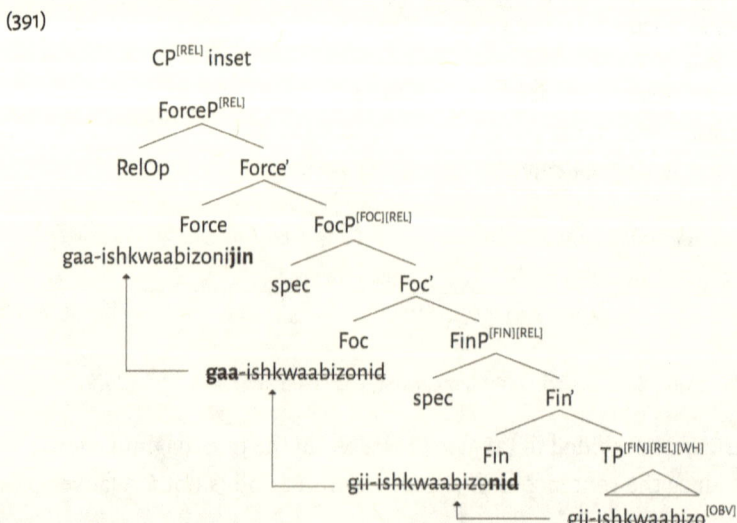

The diagram in (391) shows a successive cyclic movement analysis positioning Ojibwe RCs in the familiar analysis of *wh*-movement of more well-known languages. Discussed in detail in 2.7, Rizzi's template allows for topicalized and focalized NPs to occupy the specifier positions of those phrases. With the recursive nature of CP, we can now easily account for the word order phenomena that exist in a language like Ojibwe.

Before moving on, we still need to determine what factors play a role in the secondary object inflection and relative root (RR) constructions, specifically RCs targeting an adjunct. Compare the examples below: (392) involves an instance of merger, where the argument has been relativized and the verb bears the morphology specific to subjects and objects, while (393) consists of singular secondary object that, while being an RC, does not include the signature RC morphology of subjects and objects:

(392) *mii ingiw gekinoo'amawag**ig***

mii	ingiw	IC-gikinoo'amaw-ag-**ig**
thus	DET	IC-teach.h/-1>3-**PL**$_{PRT}$

'Those are **the ones** who I teach' (AS.13.07.16.E)

(393) *mii iw gekinoo'amawag**waa***

mii	iw	IC-gikinoo'amaw-ag-**waa**
thus	DET	IC-teach.h/-1>3-**3p**$_{CONJ}$

'That is **what** I teach them' (AS.13.07.16.E)

For the example in (392), the RC involves a plural third-person object. The head of the RC is third person. Therefore, during the derivation, the object carries a feature [plural]. In the independent order, this feature is spelled out as /g/ and follows the direct theme sign /aa/:

(394) Independent object plural

nigikinoo'amawaag

ni-	gikinoo'amaw	-aa	-g
1-	teach.h/	-DIR	-3p

'I teach **them**'

In the conjunct, this plural feature is spelled out as *-waa* and follows the 1s>3 agreement marker:

(395) Conjunct object plural
*gikinoo'amawag**waa***
gikinoo'amaw	-ag	-waa
teach.h/	-1s>3	-3p

'that I teach **them**'

For the form shown in (392) above, however, the plural feature after relativization is spelled out as *-ig*:

(396) *gekinoo'amawag**ig***
IC-gikinoo'amaw	-ag	-**ig**
IC-teach.h/	-1s>3	-PL$_{PRT}$

'**they who** I teach'

Contrasting (397) with (396) above, the content of what is being taught is inherently singular:

(397) *mii iw gekinoo'amaw**ag**waa*
Mii	iw	IC-gikinoo'amaw-**ag-waa**
thus	DET	IC-teach.h/-**1**>3-3p$_{CONJ}$

'That is **what** I teach them'

This explains the lack of participial morphology of the subject and object relatives in the adjunct RCs. The same holds for adjunct locative RCs: where the head of the RC is a place, it is inherently singular. Discussed in detail in 4.1.1, the participial inflections signature of the subject and object relatives are not shown where the head of the RC is an adjunct. The explanation put forth here has to do with the structural differences in number assignment between the core arguments and relative root constructions.

(398) *mii imaa wenjibaa**waad***
mii	imaa	IC-onjibaa-**waad**
thus	there	IC-come.from-3p$_{CONJ}$

'That is **where** they are from'

The same relative root is used in the example below, but this time the head of the RC is the subject, a core argument:

(399) *mii ingiw wenjibaajig imaa*

mii	ingiw	IC-onjibaa-**d-ig**	imaa
thus	DET	IC-come.from-**3**$_{\text{CONJ}}$-**PL**$_{\text{PRT}}$	there

'They are **the ones who** come from there'

In the older varieties of the language such as that described by Schoolcraft (1851, 376), the locative properties described here could be plural, resulting in the example below, where the participle inflection is employed, carrying the meaning of 'more than one particular locale' (repeated from [364] above):

(400) *endaawaaj**in***

IC-daa	-waad	**-in**
IC-dwells	-3p$_{\text{CONJ}}$	**-PL**

'their homes' (Schoolcraft 1851, 376)

The productivity of this inflection is exemplified in table 43, where the original spellings have been maintained (shown in italics). Similarly, temporal RCs work in the same fashion, where the temporal focus of the RC is inherently singular. These often occur with the temporal adverbs *apii* 'when' or *azhigwa* 'now; at the time.' This is the focus on a particular occurrence, 'just past' and completive aspect:

(401) *mii iw **apii** Anishinaabeg memoo**waad** i'iw mashkiki*

mii	iw	**apii**	Anishinaabe-g	IC-mam-oo-**waad**	i'iw	mashkiki
thus	DET	**time**	Indian-3p	IC-take.it-TI2-**3p**	DET	medicine

miinawaa iw wiigwaas.

miinawaa	iw	wiigwaas
and	DET	birch.bark

'That's **the time** the Indians get the medicine and the birch bark' (Whipple 2015, 18)

Table 43. 'Homes' (from Schoolcraft 1851, 376)[a]

Singular		Plural	
Aindau-yaun endaayaan	'My home'	Aindau-yaun-in endaayaan**in**	'My home**s**'
Aindau-yun endaayan	'Thy home'	Aindau-yun-in endaayan**in**	'Thy home**s**'
Aindau-d endaad	'His home'	Aindau-jin endaa**jin**	'His home**s**'
Aindau-yaung endaayaang	'Our home (ex.)'	Aindau-yaung-in endaayaang**in**	'Our home**s** (ex.)'
Aindau-yung endaayang	'Our home (in.)'	Aindau-yung-in endaayang**in**	'Our home**s** (in.)'
Aindau-yaig endaayeg	'Your home'	Aindau-yaig-in endaayeg**in**	'Your home**s**'
Aindau-waud endaawaad	'Their home'	Aindau-waujin endaawaa**jin**	'Their home**s**'

[a] John Nichols (pers. comm.) points out that the forms given here seem odd given the fact that Schoolcraft provides the -*gW* inflections in participles (shown above in 3.3.13.2), where we would expect *endaayangon* given the same environment. We can only speculate on whether or not Schoolcraft regularized the pattern or if these were the historical forms, and whether the previously mentioned "innovated" forms follow that pattern or this is a pattern of the iterative.

Similar to the locative RCs discussed above in (400), older varieties of the language suggest that plural number can be expressed in temporal oblique RCs as well. This is essentially the iterative mode discussed in 2.3.4 and, under the current analysis, involves the movement of the verb into ForceP, triggering palatalization (where applicable) and resulting in the signature participial suffixes. The example below in (402) (repeated from [363b.] above) shows how the iterative suffix is also permitted with second-person morphology, pluralizing the temporal qualities rather than the argument:

(402) *baandigeyan**in** omaa endaayaan apane nimoojigendam*
    IC-biindige-yan-**in**   omaa   IC-daa-yaan   apane   ni-moojigendam
    IC-enter-2s-**PL**   here   IC-dwell-1s   always   1-glad
    '**Whenever** you come into my house I am always glad.'
    (Clark and Gresczyk 1991)

Manner RCs behave the same way in regard to number assignment. Manner appears to be an inherently singular property as well. Manner RR verbs often occur with the locative adverbial *akeyaa* 'in that direction; in that way.' The example below in (403) shows a manner RC, with a third-person subject and no participial morphology:

(403) *ambe daga waabanda'ishin akeyaa gaa-apagizowaad*
　　　ambe　　　daga　　　waabanda'-ishin　　　akeyaa　　　IC-gii-apagizo-waad
　　　come.on　please　show.h/-2s>1s.$_{IMP}$　how　　IC-PST-dance.certain.way-3p
　　　'Show me how they were dancing' (AS.13.01.31.N)

No examples occur in the data where a plural head triggers the participial morphology for a manner RR, though it would not come as much of a surprise if examples were found indicating the *various ways* in which an action is carried out.

In addition to the RCs described here, there are occurrences of what might appear to be exceptional cases of relativization. These apply to adjuncts without a relative root. Discussed earlier in 2.6.1, verbs used in locative constructions in Ojibwe without an RR typically do not exhibit IC. The example below shows one such case:

(404) *mii imaa gii-pawaajiged aw akiwenzii*
　　　mii　　imaa　　gii-bawaajige-d　　aw　　akiwenzii
　　　thus　there　PST-dream-3$_{CONJ}$　that　old.man
　　　'That is where the old man had the dream' (AS.13.01.31.N)

Note that the past tense marker *gii-* does not undergo IC to *gaa-*. From a syntactic point of view, this is a case where *wh*-agreement does not apply, which disqualifies such constructions as RCs in the current analysis. Though the English translation makes use of an English RC, the Ojibwe is perhaps more accurately translated as 'The old man had his dream THERE,' where *mii* operates as a specifier in FocP with a null operator in the head Foc position. The VP *gii-pawaajiged* lies in the head position of FinP, accounting for the lack of IC. Similarly, cases with no IC can be found in temporals with *apii* and *azhigwa*, as shown below in (405):

(405) *mii dash imaa wapii gegoo wawaaniziyaang*

mii	dash	imaa	wapii	gegoo	wawaanizi-yaang
thus	then	there	time	something	is.stumped-1p$_{CONJ}$

'and that's when, if we need to know something' (Benjamin 2006)

The lack of IC suggests that this is not an RC by the definition provided here. Rather than focusing on a "single occurrence" in the sense indicated in Baraga (1850), this is a generalized 'when'; such cases do not require movement out of FinP to obtain IC in FocP.

Given the structure of the split CP advocated for here in this chapter, a locus for the particle *mii* needs to be provided.[8] Following Fairbanks (2008), *mii* has a variety of functions: a deictic particle (406a.), an aspectual marker (406b.), and a veridical marker (406c.):[9]

(406) About *mii*

a. *mii* as deictic particle

mii a'aw manidoo *gaa-pi-wiindamaaged wii-naadamawaad*

mii	**a'aw**	**manidoo**	IC-gii-bi-wiindamaage-d	wii-naadamaw-aad
Dpart	**DET**	**spirit**	IC-PST-here tells-3	FUT-help.h/-3>3'

inow Anishinaaben

inow	Anishinaabe-n
DET	Indian-OBV

'**She is the manidoo** that came and told that she will help the Anishinaabe' (Staples 2015, 44)

b. *mii* as aspectual marker

***mii gii-nisaad** iniw waawaabiganoojiin aw gaazhagens*

mii	**gii-niS-aad**	iniw	waawaabiganoojii-n	aw	gaazhagens
AM	**PST-kill.h/-3>3'**	DET	mouse-OBV	DET	cat

'The cat **has killed** a mouse' (AS.12.09.25.P)

c. *mii* as a veridical marker

*Aaniishnaa wiin gaawiin gegoo gii-izhichigesiin **mii** aw*

aaniishnaa	wiin	gaawiin	gegoo	gii-izhichige-siin	**mii**	aw
after.all	3$_{DEM}$	NEG	something	PST-does-NEG	**V.M.**	DET

indedeyiban gaa-kagiibaadizid akina gego gaa-izhichiged

in-dede-iban	IC-gii-gagiibaadizi-d	akina	gego	IC-gii-izhichige-d
1-dad-PRET	IC-PST-is.foolish-3	all	thing	IC-PST-does-3

'After all, she didn't do anything; it was **[truly]** my father that was the foolish one that did everything' (AS.Gii-nitaawigiyaan)

The use shown in (406a.) involves a case of relativization. The spec-Force position hosts the relativized NP, while the head position of Force hosts the verb of the RC. As discussed by Fairbanks (2008), *mii* serves a specifier to what is analyzed here as a DP. The aspectual *mii*, shown in (406b.) above, can be argued to reside in spec-FinP, with aspectual features carried over from TP. For the veridical usage, it could be argued that *mii* exists as a strengthener that can further delimit the referent of an NP (as in [406c.]), or that it occurs with the independent order in a DegreeP, as seen here in (407):

(407) *mii gaawiin ingikendanziin*
     'I don't know'

As Fairbanks (2009, 229) suggests, we may be dealing with a number of different *mii*s, as the various functions are seemingly unrelated.

Another issue worthy of attention is the use of participles in *awenenag* 'who-PL' and *awegonenan* 'what-PL' *wh*-questions. In (408) below, the question is given, followed by the tree diagram in (409) illustrating its internal structure.

(408) *Awenenag ingiw ininiwag gaa-nagamojig?*

awenen-ag	ingiw	inini-wag	IC-gii-nagamo-d-ig
who-3p	DET	man-3p	IC-PST-sings-3-PL$_{PRT}$

     'Who are those men that sang?'

302 *Relativization in Ojibwe*

(409)
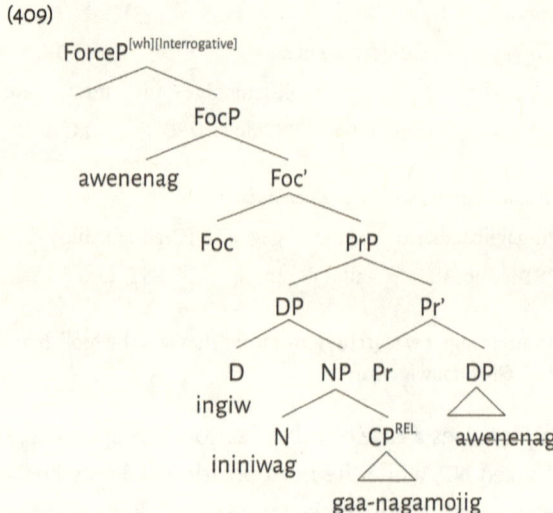

As the diagram indicates, 'who' questions result in a copular structure where the participle *gaa-nagamojig* is generated as a postnominal RC (CP^{REL}). The RC has its own CP where the verb has undergone movement to ForceP, spelled out morphologically as a plural participle. A similar structure can be provided to account for *awegonenan* 'what-PL' questions, as shown below in (410):

(410) *Awegonenan iniw aabajichiganan gaa-aabajitoowaajin?*
      awegonen-an   iniw   aabajichigan-an   IC-gii-aabajit-oo-waad-in
      what-0p   DET   tool-0p   IC-PST-use.it-TI2-3p-PL$_{PRT}$
      'What tools did they use?' (AS.15.08.04.BT)

Given the framework provided by the split CP, all issues pertaining to possible surface word order complications are easily handled by the structure. Perhaps more importantly, all issues pertaining to word order demand such a structure.

Given the restriction imposed by the LCA, that each projection of the split CP can have only one specifier, one adjunction, and one complement, the structure given above in (409) holds in accounting for the interrogative pronoun as well as the DP, both preceding the RC. Given the structure of

RCs thus far, this would suggest that "bare" or "headless" relatives are internally headed. This is the subject of the following section.

4.3.3. Internally versus Externally Headed RCs

Languages differ regarding where the head of an RC originates. In the Algonquian family, RCs can be internally headed (Goddard 1987, for Fox), or internally or externally headed (Bruening 2001, for Passamaquoddy). The diagram in (411) shows the structure of an externally headed RC, where by definition the noun whose referent is delimited by the RC falls outside of the CP.

(411) External RC

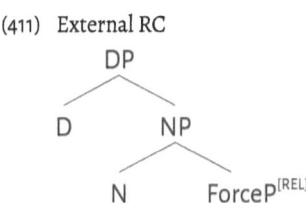

As the diagram suggests, the head noun occurs before the CP[REL] and is external to the RC. Given the split-CP structure advocated for here in this study, this structure accounts for all postnominal RCs in Ojibwe, such as the one given in (412).

(412) [$_{DP}$[$_{NP}$ akiwenziiyibaneg] [$_{RC}$ gaa-kaagiigidojig]]
    'the old men that did the speaking' (PM.Dewe'igan2)

The externally headed analysis holds for the postnominal occurrence of RCs, though the much rarer reverse order requires a different approach. Valentine (2001, 580) also finds the occasional case of the RC preceding the noun it modifies with no particular difference in meaning. This is the "light term RC" in the Rhodes (1996) classification. In internally headed RCs, the head noun originates within the relative CP and is moved into spec-FocP. Head movement of the relative verb from Foc to Force strands the head noun at spec-FocP, resulting in the prenominal ordering of the RC. An example of an internally headed RC is given in (413), along with the generic structure of an internal RC in (414):

(413) [$_{DP}$ ingiw [$_{REL}$ bebiiwizhiiwijig [$_{NP}$ abinoojiinyag]]]
'young children' lit. 'those who are tiny, children'
(Staples and Gonzalez 2015, 118)

(414) Internal RC

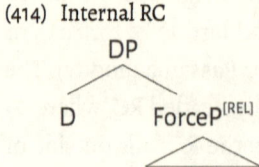

The internal structure of the ForceP of the internally headed RC shown in (414) is given in (415).

(415)

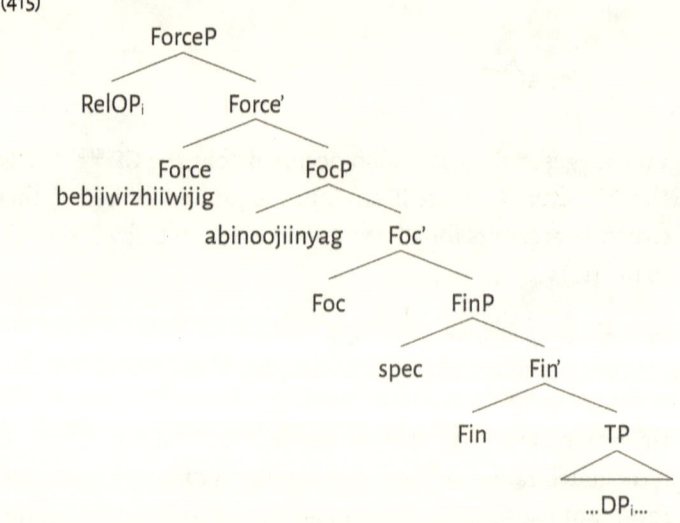

The advantage for adopting the structure posited in (415) for prenominal RCs is twofold. First, the word order of the various RCs in Ojibwe suggests such a structure to account for prenominal RCs. Second, from a theoretical perspective, such a structure does not force any movement operation of the RC outside of the CP level. When accounting for the variation found in the two orderings, a pattern begins to emerge. While postnominal externally headed RCs serve a function in adverbial clauses delimiting the referent of an NP, prenominal internally headed RCs work more like compounds in English. Below in (416) are several examples where this pattern holds:

(416) Prenominal internally headed RCs

a. *obapakite'aan   aw   gagwedaganewinini   [gezhiibidenig   chi-mashkimod]*
s/he.hits.it   DET   boxer   [that.which.   big-bag]
                                  goes.fast
'The boxer is hitting the **speed bag**' (AS.12.09.25.P)

b. *niminopwaag   [gaakanaamoozojig   giigoonyag]*
I.like.taste.of.them   [those.which.are.fried   fish]
'I like the taste of **fried fish**' (JC.TWO)

c. *begonezid   biitooshkigaans*
that.with.a.hole   underwear
'**crotchless panties**' (AS.15.06.11.TM)

d. *gaawanaadizid   inini*
he.who.is.crazy   man
'**crazy man**' (AS.12.09.25.P)

e. *mekadewindibed   ikwe*
she.with.dark.hair   woman
'**brunette**' (AS.12.09.25.P)

f. *bebiiwaabaminaagozijig   awesiinyag*
those.which.appear.to.be.tiny   animals
'**little animals**' (Staples and Gonzalez 2015, 14)

g. *mendidojig   awesiinyag*
those.who.are.big   animals
'**big animals**' (Staples 2015, 14)

h. *dekaagamig   nibi*
cold.liquid   water
'**cold water**' (AS.Flicking)

As the examples indicate, in all of the above cases where the RC appears in a prenominal position, the head noun plays a semantic role inside the RC. For the externally headed postnominal RCs, the RC serves more of a parenthetic function, by providing additional information that delimits the noun referent.

4.3.4. Concluding Remarks

In this chapter I have argued for a split-CP approach to account for Ojibwe relativization. The majority of the data on which the analysis is based comes from the southernmost speakers of SW Ojibwe. The distinction between core argument participles and RR constructions has been maintained for the most part in those communities, though I assume the same structure for more northern varieties. The only difference between the two is how the morphology responds to the syntax.

In the south, morphological realization of syntactic movement operations can be observed in the morphology in cases of conjunct inflection, initial change, and participial suffixes; in the north, the extent of IC has shifted, relying more heavily on the *gaa-* relativizer. I provided evidence for *gaa-* being analyzed as a version of IC by being in complementary distribution with traditional IC strategies, suggesting that they are both alternative realizations of the same functional head. Though the heads in the CP domain are fixed, similarities and differences are found crosslinguistically concerning how the morphology is realized by the heads (Henderson 2006, 77).

Since both varieties examined in this study have a conjunct order of inflection, there is no exception to account for, though realizations of certain conjunct inflections can differ between speakers, as seen in 3.3.10. While it is accepted in the PAH framework that independent verbs raise from the base-generated position and move upward, acquiring their relevant affixes, such an approach can be extended to the conjunct, as seen in Brittain (2001) for Naskapi. The range of functions the conjunct serves patterns with what is typically found in a complementizer position. The recursive nature of language and the Ojibwe data described demand a structure like that posited here; Mühlbauer's (2003) claim that each verb requires its own embedded structure in the syntax bears fruit when considering the data and the alternative approaches for its analysis.

The split-CP hypothesis of Rizzi (1997) provides a syntactic framework for handling the data from a language like Ojibwe. Head movement through the projections of the split CP accounts for the empirical distinctions found between the various clause types. With C providing the landing site for *wh*-movement, conjunct verbs, and topicalized and focalized material, the C position begins to get rather crowded. The split-CP framework not only accommodates the word order phenomena found in Ojibwe by providing the structural positions for movement to the left periphery, but the data demand such a structure. In accounting for the variation of participial morphology that is seen in core argument RCs in the south, where the head is either third person, inanimate plural, or obviative third person—a pattern that does not exist among the northern speakers consulted for this study—I assume the formal features are the same but that they no longer involve the morphological or surface morphological features.

FIVE

Conclusions

Regardless of which theoretical approach is taken in analyzing the Ojibwe data presented in this thesis, our understanding of Ojibwe grammar and the variation observed has been enhanced by the current undertaking. Comparing fresh data from the remaining native speakers in the SW area with archived material from previous generations, we can begin to account for linguistic change and how such processes occur in endangered and often marginalized indigenous languages.

In this chapter I provide a review in 5.1 of the previous chapters and conclusions drawn. In 5.1.1 I highlight specific trends in related Algonquian languages and some of the tendencies observed over time. Section 5.2 focuses on the limitations of this study, treating language obsolescence in 5.2.1, access to speakers in 5.2.2, and my own L2 understanding and perhaps unavoidable interference in 5.2.3. In 5.3 I make comparisons to related phenomena occurring in several other Algonquian languages, beginning with the most closely related languages, Odawa and Potawatomi. In 5.3.1 I discuss initial change (IC) and the trends observed across the Algonquian family. The discussion of participles and their various forms is provided in 5.3.2, with connections made to Proto-Algonquian (PA) in 5.3.2.1. Section 5.4 provides directions for future research.

5.1. REVIEW

In chapter 1 I provided the basic introduction to the study. By defining relative clauses, I introduced the reader to the variation observed in SW Ojibwe concerning participles and their role in RCs. In section 1.2.2 I gave the background information on Ojibwe grammar for the introductory understanding of participles and RCs in Ojibwe, making explicit the difference between core arguments and relative root arguments. The relevant literature concerning dialectology and variation in Ojibwe is provided in 1.3, using the current study to fill a massive void in the Algonquian literature. Section 1.4 reviews some the literature on the syntax of RCs in Ojibwe and other related Algonquian languages. The theoretical preliminaries are treated in 1.5, providing the theoretical underpinnings on which the current analysis is built. Section 1.6 concludes the chapter.

Chapter 2 provides a sketch of the most relevant aspects of Ojibwe morphosyntax necessary for the thorough discussion of RCs. This is mainly done in the traditional, descriptive Algonquian linguistic tradition. I provide the basics on Ojibwe lexical and morphosyntactic derivation, giving the reader an understanding of how typical syntactic phenomena of more widely explored languages are manifested in the morphology of a polysynthetic language like Ojibwe. All of the previously treated aspects of the grammar introduced in chapter 1 are given a more lengthy and detailed description in chapter 2. In 2.7 I discuss word order and account for the deviating orders via the split-CP structure of Rizzi (1997).

An in-depth account of the methodology employed in this study is given in chapter 3 along with the types of data obtained over the course of the study. The findings of the survey are provided in 3.3, with each variable discussed in turn, along with its distribution. Participles and the varying forms are discussed at length in 3.3.13, along with the innovations observed. The discussion in 3.4 treats geographic variation, age-graded variation, intelligibility among speakers, and free variation.

The theoretical components of the analysis are provided in chapter 4. After reviewing in depth RCs and core arguments versus relative root arguments, I make an association between the observed varying strategies, noting that IC and the *gaa-* relativizer are in complementary distribution, essentially, morphological realizations of *wh*-movement. In 4.2, borrowing heavily from the work of Brittain (2001), I articulate the structural and featural differences between verbs inflected for the independent order and the conjunct. The split CP of Rizzi (1997) provides the various heads necessary for accounting for the Ojibwe data. Each projection posited by Rizzi provides the host for head movement, with each successive movement operation showing a morphological realization. Differences in the feature bundles determine how and where the head must move, with each subsequent movement showing evidence in the morphological shape of the moved verb. Word order facts alone can account for the distinction between internally headed RCs and externally headed RCs.

Essentially I have provided the theoretical mechanism necessitated by the Ojibwe data, some of which may be relevant to other Algonquian languages. By providing the data and positing the current analysis, I open the door to the theoretical exploration of Ojibwe by future researchers, grounded in the tradition of quality fieldwork with emphasis placed on accounting for both naturalistic and current data. This is essentially the door that I found closed when embarking on my study of Ojibwe syntax.

5.1.1. Implications of the Findings

Valentine remarks on how southern dialects have undergone recent "varying degrees of attrition, making the language stronger at points in the north, which lends it to a measure of prestige" (1994, 82). Ironically the southern dialects reviewed in this study are the very dialects that have managed to retain the participial inflections not observed in the north. Commonly, among North American indigenous languages that have north-south constituencies, vitality is found more often in the north. This has been observed for Cayuga, where the northern (Ontario) variety appears to have been more vital, at least until recently, whereas speakers of the southern (Oklahoma) variety struggle with even the simplest body part elicitation (Mithun 1989, 248). The reverse can be seen in Potawatomi, where the southern group in Kansas is often viewed as having retained more of the language compared to constituencies in the north (Wisconsin, Michigan, and Ontario).

It is also important to consider that language change cannot always be attributed to language death, as Campbell and Muntzel observe for Nahua, for which "completely parallel changes have taken place in other completely viable Nahua dialects," making it difficult to distinguish "normal contact-induced changes from changes due to the language death situation" (1989, 195). This is precisely the irony in the retention of participles in the south—it is an almost frozen feature in an otherwise rapidly obsolescing language.

Relative clauses, interestingly, are notable in relation to language loss;

as Hill points out, the "reduction in the frequency of relative clauses in the usage of speakers in late stages of language death has been identified in languages of diverse genetic and typological affiliations" (1989, 149). As observed in the earlier works of Dressler (1972) and Dorian (1973), structures that are more morphologically and phonologically marked are typically unstable constructions found among dying languages (Hill 1989, 152).

Also important to take into account is language contact situations and what implications they may have for a particular endangered language. In considering the more northern varieties examined in this study, such as those spoken by the communities in northern Minnesota and along the Border Lakes region of Ontario, to the immediate north we find Saulteaux-, Cree-, and Oji-Cree-speaking groups. Investigation into the morphology of those languages can lend a clue to the similarities found within Ojibwe dialects. This is precisely the kind of "counterexample" that Hoenigswald (1989, 353) seeks in the investigation of obsolescence. Such examples are taken into consideration in 5.3, after the following brief discussion of the limitations of this study.

5.2. LIMITATIONS

Over twenty years ago Rand Valentine remarked on the rapid decline of Ojibwe south of the U.S.-Canadian border:

> In the United States nearly all Ojibwe speakers are bilingual, and many children are only learning the language as a cultural symbol in educational programs, rather than in the home as an integral part of their lives. (Valentine 1994, 87)

Since then the language has continued to decline in most SW Ojibwe communities, many of which have no remaining native speakers. However, for some communities, the language has been maintained by speakers who are now elderly, the majority of whom are the last speakers in their families and communities. Gradually, but steadily, more and more young Anishinaabe people are working toward learning their language and bringing the language back to their communities and homes. The data presented here and the conclusions drawn are just that, a snapshot of SW Ojibwe as used in the final stages of language death or, for the more hopeful, in the early stages of revival.

One cannot produce an adequate and just study of SW Ojibwe without addressing the obvious head on: the language has undergone a tremendous amount of obsolescence in the past few generations. It is extremely late in the day for a full-scale report on Ojibwe dialects in the area. Though I have done my best at providing such a resource, I am guilty of many of the same touch-and-go types of field sessions as the researchers before me. Ultimately I assume that the lack of participial inflections in the north is the result of morphological leveling, though not necessarily the result of language decline. The language has fared much better in those communities where the leveling has occurred than in the south.

5.2.1. Obsolescence

Language obsolescence occurs when a language or the use of a language becomes somehow obsolete. Common especially in more morphologically synthetic languages is the notion of morphological reduction, specifically the reduction of allomorphy and the leveling of paradigms (Campbell and Muntzel 1989, 191). Contemplating how this occurs for Ojibwe, one can assume that one possible explanation for the lack of participial inflection may derive from the common Ojibwe convention of speaking in the collective singular, especially in traditional-type narratives.

Morphological reduction or simplification often occur in a manner that is often characterized as being "easily segmentable, less diversified allomorphically ('leveled') and hence, more 'transparent' semantically" (Hoenigswald 1989, 350). With the increasingly unstable nature of IC and the more complex morphophonological processes of participial inflection, the innovations that have occurred in the north should be expected among the "putative characteristics of dying languages" (349). In the south, where the inflections have been maintained, almost counterintuitively, speakers have maintained the productive use of the inflections in spite of the rapidly declining domains in which the language is used.

Ojibwe is exceptional in that it appears to involve both types of language death, radical and gradual, put forth by Campbell and Muntzel (1989). "Radical death" is described in their terms as occurring when "speakers shift by the masses out of self defense from oppression" (183). Insofar as Ojibwe speakers began the shift to English with the typical process of colonization, this would fit the pattern of a radical death. However, this shift has also been quite gradual. "Gradual death" is described by Campbell and Muntzel here:

> such situations have an intermediate stage of bilingualism in which the dominant language comes to be employed by an ever increasing number of individuals in a growing number of contexts where the subordinate language was formerly used. This situation is characterized by a proficiency continuum determined principally by age (but also by attitude and other factors). Younger generations have greater proficiency in the dominant language and learn the obsolescing language imperfectly, if at all. (185)

Remarkably, in light of the experience of the Ojibwe people, the language is still spoken. With the conscious effort in some communities to reverse language shift, the language will continue to be spoken. This is possible with the assistance of many of the great speakers who contributed to this study.

5.2.2. Access

Another limitation of the study is the access to speakers that I had. Though I had no trouble finding consultants in areas where the language is used, many areas had already lost their remaining speakers prior to my arrival. In many cases the remaining speakers were hospitalized, too sick for me to visit, or they had become deaf.

It is also important to note that I did not consult every single speaker available in each community. As described at the beginning of chapter 3 I made every effort to seek out individuals revered in their respective communities as strong speakers. In places such as Mille Lacs or Ponemah, there remain hundreds of speakers that I have not had an opportunity to work with. Therefore the claims made in this study about variation cannot be taken as absolute.

5.2.3. L2 Interference

I also take responsibility for my own second-language understanding of Ojibwe, which may skew my ability to examine the language objectively.

Linguistic competence for researchers like me is based on previous research rather than natural acquisition. Therefore, discussions regarding innovation ultimately take for granted that the old documentation represents the norm for a generalized SW region. This is most likely relevant concerning the complex morphological shape of participles. Though no variation was reported in the early documentation of participles, variation is likely to have existed even then. Baraga supports this assumption, reporting that the *-jig* participles described in his study are in fact a corruption due to the palatalization of the third-person conjunct marker /-d/. He states that the participles should end in /-dig/ but that the corruption is established. He reports that speakers of Grand Portage, Fort William, and other areas of the north shore of Lake Superior "have conserved this genuine pronunciation" though he provides no examples (1850, 26).

5.3. COMPARISONS WITHIN THE ALGONQUIAN FAMILY

In determining what might be regarded as an innovation or retention, we compare data of related languages and make predictions about what the protolanguage was like. This is precisely how Valentine describes the work of Algonquian comparative linguistics: "We are essentially faced with a collection of linguistic varieties reflecting varying retentions or innovations with respect to Proto-Algonquian" (1994, 43). Building off the work of Algonquianists before us and the claims made regarding PA, we can determine whether a particular feature is a retention or innovation. In 1946 Bloomfield's reconstruction of PA determined that Ojibwe was the only language having negative inflection for the conjunct order, suggesting an innovation for Ojibwe in that regard. Bloomfield's primary source for Ojibwe was Odawa; thus he assumed a generalization of conjunct negation occurring in the south (Valentine 1994, 66).

Also, like some of the Border Lakes and Saulteaux varieties of Ojibwe reported in 3.3.4, Fox (Meskwaki) contains a plural obviative form (Goddard 1987, 105). The obviative plural also exists in Passamaquoddy (Bruening 2001, 40)[1] but is lacking in Potawatomi (Hockett 1966, 65) and Odawa (Valentine 2001). Most relevant to the current study is the cross-family variation regarding the shape of IC and participles and their comparison

Table 44. IC patterns for Algonquian languages (from Costa 1996, 57)[a]

PA	Cree	Ojib	Potaw	Fox-K	Mi-Ill	Shawn	Menom	AGV	PEA
*a	e·	e·	e·	e·	e·	(e·)	e·	$V_·$	e·
*e/C_	e·	e·	e·	e·	e·	(e·)	e·	$V_·$	e·
*e/#_	e·	e·	e·	ye·	i·	ye·	e·	$V_·$	e·
*we/o	we·	we·	e·	we·	we·	we·	we·/o·	$V_·$	we·
*a·	ay-	ay-	—	—	—	—	ay-	V_n	—
*e·	ay-	ay-	—	—	—	—	ay-	V_n	—
*i·	a·	a·	a	—	e·	(a·)	ay-	V_n	—
*o·	ay-/wa·	wa·	a	—	—	—	ay-	V_n	—

[a] The IC patterns given above are misleading in that *ay-* prefixes to the existing vowel and is not the realization of that vowel under IC.

to the proposed protolanguage. Each is discussed in turn in the sections below.

5.3.1. IC

An integral aspect of the grammar for the current study involves the morphological shape of initial change and the syntactic function that it provides. With the variation described in 3.3.11, the productive ablaut process of IC is unstable; speakers have devised strategies and alternatives to the regular process. Interestingly, this is a very common tendency found among languages of the Algonquian family. Pointing to the insufficient account provided by Bloomfield (1946), Costa (1996) reconstructs IC in PA, relying on data from all of the attested daughter languages.[2] Costa provides the same pattern for IC in Potawatomi as in Ojibwe, with two exceptions. The vowels /a/ and /e/ do not change in Potawatomi, similar to the second pattern of Nichols (2011), discussed above in 3.3.11. As with Nichols's (2011) third pattern, Costa (1996, 43) reports no IC on the vowels /a/, /e/, and /o/ for Miami-Illinois,[3] while the Eastern Algonquian grouping shows no IC on all long vowels. Table 44 illustrates the distribution of IC from Costa (1996), with the PA vowels in the leftmost column and the corresponding IC realizations for the daughter languages in the other columns. Compare the patterns of IC in table 44 with Costa's (1996) reconstruction of IC in PA in table

Table 45. IC in Pre-PA (Costa 1996, 62)

Plain		Changed
**a	→	**eˑ
**e	→	**eˑ
**i	→	**yeˑ
**we	→	**weˑ
**aˑ	→	**ayaˑ-
**eˑ	→	**ayeˑ-
**iˑ	→	**aˑ
**oˑ	→	**ayoˑ

45. As the tables reveal, Ojibwe has been rather conservative in its retention of IC on all seven existing vowels. For languages that have innovated in regard to IC, a couple of different innovations have occurred throughout the family. Treated in chapter 4 as realizations of *wh*-agreement and alternatives to the actual ablaut pattern, the *gaa-* relativizing preverb is used by speakers of Ojibwe and an initial *e-* preverb, known in the literature as the aorist, by some, more eastern speakers (Odawa). Costa reposts a number of Algonquian languages with the *e-* prefix, including "Fox-Kickapoo, Ojibwa, Potawatomi, and Cree" (1996, 53).[4] Other languages, such as Cheyenne or Shawnee, show a special preverb or change affecting only a subset of the vowel inventory, specifically in not targeting long vowels (those that require "breaking" in the sense given in Nichols 2012), as seen in table 44.

In relation to language change, the patterns observed with prefixed strategies make the use of IC much more regular and with a "straightforward" motivation in that it "greatly reduces the number of variant forms of the verb stem that one uses" (Costa 1996, 42). Widespread among many Algonquian languages is the *gaa-* preverb, discussed at length throughout this study. Brittain (2001) reports both the *e-* prefix, which she calls the "[a]-complementizer," and the two different *gaa-* preverbs for Naskapi, one she treats as monomorphemic and the other as bimorphemic.[5] The bimorphemic *gaa-* is similar to the Ojibwe past tense marker *gii-* under IC. She treats this productive ablaut IC as consisting of "[a]-comp infixation" (2001, 82). She determines the monomorphemic *gaa-* prefix to be an innovation and calls it "reanalyzed *kâ*," essentially [a]-complementizer reanalyzed (Brittain 2001, 96).

Interestingly the distinction made between the two is based on their distribution in different syntactic environments, essentially the same as found in the northern communities surveyed for the present study. Monomorphemic (reanalyzed) *kâ* "at the head of relative clauses and focus constructions . . . functions as a complementizer and does not denote past temporal reference." In many Cree-Montagnais-Naskapi dialects, bimorphemic *kâ* at the head of complement clauses denotes past tense (Brittain 2001, 96). The following example in (417) shows the syntactic environments for each:

(417) Syntactic environments for *kâ-* (Brittain 2001, 97)

   a. Bimorphemic *kâ-*: complement clauses, some main clauses containing *wh*-phrase

   b. Reanalyzed *kâ-*: (present tense) relative clauses, focus constructions

Brittain also notes that, similar to the more northern varieties of Ojibwe treated in this study, the reanalyzed *kâ-* can also co-occur with tense markers (2001, 100–101). She notes that, in the Cree-Montagnais literature, the preverbs are treated as distinct (Starks 1992) or as one and the same (James 1991). Wolfart (1973) proposes that the reanalyzed version arose historically from the IC form of the past tense preverb.

Also like Ojibwe, *kâ-* reanalysis has not occurred in every dialect of Cree-Montagnais; both Brittain (2001) and Wolfart (1973) note how the reanalysis is seen as a shift, more frequently used among younger speakers. Based on the similarities found in related Algonquian languages, the innovations observed in SW Ojibwe are not unusual and are perhaps to be expected. As for the morphological shape of participles, similar patterns emerge. This is discussed below.

5.3.2. Algonquian Participles

This study, following Valentine's (1994) analysis, suggests that the additional markings found in the southern varieties of Southwestern Ojibwe are not an innovation but in fact a remnant of the older form of the language. Evidence for this claim is that in very closely related languages, mainly Odawa and Potawatomi, similar additional participial markings are found. Furthermore, Valentine indicates that the obviative participle marker *-nijin* is retained in Algonquin, an eastern Ojibweyan language of eastern Ontario and Quebec (1994, 338):

> But northern Algonquin has not only lost the formal distinction between participles and simple conjunct forms of verbs, it has also evidently generalized the participial forms to all cases involving an animate obviative third person ... in Algonquin, all verb forms inflected for obviative arguments in all four classes appear to be derived from historical participial forms. (339–40)

Algonquin then, a language that has lost participial inflections, has replaced the normal obviative conjunct mark *-nid* with the obviative participle marker *-nijin* (51). Similarly, in Cree, Wolfart (1973) gives the third-person conjunct suffix *-cik*, essentially his orthographical rendering of *-jig*. Valentine attributes this to an historical form having an animate plural attached (1994, 315). Interestingly, when examining the data of the northernmost varieties (Severn), participles do occur "sometimes"; on the southern edge of Severn, a distinction is made between singular and plural obviative participles (343–44). Also found in Valentine's "northern" grouping is the VAI third-person conjunct order suffix /-j/ instead of the typical southern marker /-d/ (315). Such deviation suggests that these Northern Ojibwe forms show evidence of palatalization, which could easily be attributed to historical participial forms.

Similar to the analysis presented here, Goddard (1987) states that RCs in Fox (Meskwaki) are composed of participles, which he describes as follows:

> Participles are formed on verb stems and combine features of verbal and nominal inflection. The nominal inflection on the participle marks the head of the participial phrase, provided the head is third person. (Participles with first and second person heads, which do not have nominal suffixes, will not be considered in this paper.) The head may bear any number of different grammatical relations to the verb or to other words in the sentence. (105)

Like the SW Ojibwe participles described here, Fox participles do not employ the typical conjunct third-person suffix *-waa*. A few differences can be found in Fox participles as compared to Ojibwe, the first being a third-person singular participial form in Fox:

(418) Singular **3s**>1 participle (from Goddard 1987, 109)
    ke-teminawita
    IC-keteminaw   -it   **-a**
    IC-bless   -3>1   **-ANsg**
    'the one that blessed me'

The corresponding Ojibwe form does not include this additional singular marking:

(419) Singular **3s**>1 participle
    zhewenimid
    IC-zhawenim   -id
    IC-bless.h/   -3>1
    'the one that bless(ed) me'

Specialized third-person and obviative third-person participles are also found in Passamaquoddy (Bruening 2001), but have been either lost or blended in Cree and Menominee (Hockett 1950, 280). In the next section I discuss participles in PA.

5.3.2.1. PA Participles

When determining whether a language has innovated or retained a particular feature, comparative data from closely related languages are used in the postulation of a proto- form, essentially a parent language from which the modern languages descend. This is precisely the work done by Bloomfield (1925, 1946) and furthered by Michelson (1935), Hockett (1950, 1966) and the many works of Goddard, Pentland, and Proulx. As discussed above in 5.3.1 southern dialects of Ojibwe show retention of the actual ablaut process of IC, while some of the northern varieties treated here have innovated, much in the same way as related Algonquian languages have done.

320 *Conclusions*

Based on the conclusions reached in the comparative studies, the same can be said of participles.

For Proto-Central-Algonquian, including Ojibwe, Cree, Potawatomi, and Menominee, Hockett (1950, 282) provides *-a·t* and *-a·čik*, (essentially *-aad* and *-aajig* in the modern orthography) for the participial forms of **3s**>3' and **3p**>3' respectively. The forms survive today in Ojibwe and Potawatomi while in Cree and Menominee they have been "lost or blended with the simple conjunct" (280). Proulx's "Lake Eastern" grouping includes "Cheyenne, Fox, Illinois, Kickapoo, Miami, Ojibwa, Potawatomi, Shawnee, and the eastern languages." This grouping, according to Proulx, "shares the most innovations" (1980, 4). Proulx notices that the participle forms have replaced the independent order forms in Micmac though he provides no examples. He does not determine whether the participial forms for the Lake Eastern grouping are a shared innovation or retention but cites Bloomfield's (1946) reconstruction for PA.

Bloomfield (1946, 457–58) reconstructs participles for PA providing the ending *-a* for the animate singular and *-i* for the inanimate singular. The animate singular *-a* has been retained in Fox (shown above in [418]). It is essentially the Fox forms that Bloomfield's participle reconstruction is based upon, providing the examples shown below in (420):

(420) Singular PA participles (Bloomfield 1946)

a. *peemaatesita*
IC-bemaatesi   -t   -a
IC-lives -3_{CONJ} $-AN_{SG}$
'one who lives'

b. *neesaata*
IC-neS   -aa-   -t   -a
IC-kill.h/   -DIR- -3_{CONJ} $-AN_{SG}$
'he who killed the other'

c. *miinaki*[6]
miiN   -ak   -i
give.h/ $-1>3_{CONJ}$ $-IN_{SG}$
'that which I gave to him'

Bloomfield remarks on how the plural forms are "not made with the usual conjunct endings but are derived from the singulars," pointing to the nominal plurals (458). He provides the plural forms *-iki* for animates and *-ili* for inanimates, shown here in (421):

(421) Plural PA participles (Bloomfield 1946)

a. *peemaatesičiki*

IC-pemaatesi	-t	-iki
IC-lives	-3$_{CONJ}$	-PL$_{PRT.AN}$

'they who live'

b. *miinakini*

miiN	-ak	-ili
give.h/	-1>3$_{CONJ}$	-PL$_{PRT.INAN}$

'those which I gave him'

In addition to the proto- forms of participles given above, Bloomfield also makes a number distinction concerning the obviative, with a singular participle form *-ili* and a plural participle *-ihi*. Bloomfield's examples are shown here in (422):

(422) PA obviative participles (Bloomfield 1946)

a. *peemaatesiničini*

IC-pemaatesi	-ni	-t	-ili
IC-lives	-OBV$_{CONJ}$	-3$_{CONJ}$	-SG$_{PRT.OBV}$

'the other who lives'

b. *peemaatesiničihi*

IC-pemaatesi	-ni	-t	-ihi
IC-lives	-OBV$_{CONJ}$	-3$_{CONJ}$	-PL$_{PRT.OBV}$

'those others who live'

Despite the fact that the obviative plural inflection is absent in the majority of the SW Ojibwe communities, the retention of participial inflections is just that, a retention of a feature of the protolanguage and not an innovation, at least for the Proto-Central-Algonquian grouping. Regarding the singular participle shown above in (420) for PA and (418) for Fox, in Ojibwe we can attribute the lack of the vowel in the singular forms to an extension of the "final lax vowel deletion" rule of Kaye and Piggott (1973, 346).

For the more northern communities treated in this study lacking the inflections and innovations regarding IC, it may be plausible to consider that they descend from a more western constituency that had not "innovated" in the sense of Proulx's (1980) Lake Eastern grouping. However, this would be all too unlikely given the existence of participles in northern regions (Severn) and evidence of their historical existence to the northwest (Cree).

As shown in this study archival data from generations past shed light on our understanding of variation and language change in real time, so long as there are current data to compare it to. As more tapes and records of the language surface and tribes make an effort to make those records available, our understanding of variation, language change, and each of the issues addressed over the course of this study will be furthered.

5.4. DIRECTIONS FOR FUTURE RESEARCH

By and large there is a great amount of work to do for the study of Ojibwe syntax and, perhaps most importantly, variation in the language. I have striven to provide a starting point for researchers interested in Ojibwe, taking the classic Algonquian traditional descriptive approach and recasting the data in a way that is not only transparent by current traditions in syntax but also analyzed in the most minimal, usual way. Rather than positing ad hoc rules or stipulative explanations, I have accounted for the data in a manner that is driven by the data, making use of the various theories and structures provided by those before me.

As others have arrived at different, often contradictory conclusions to those made here, they are sure to question, challenge, and disprove any of the claims made in this thesis. Such criticisms are welcomed and encouraged in the spirit of advancing our understanding of Ojibwe and all of the beautiful expressive ability contained within it and the variation found throughout it. I encourage all researchers embarking on Ojibwe or any other endangered language to be as meticulous and thoughtful about the data as possible, basing all theories or claims on sound understanding of the language and to avoid direct translation elicitation at all costs. We have all too often seen the results of such work.

In regard to Ojibwe and Algonquian syntax in general, the starting point is the pronominal argument hypothesis (PAH) and which particular approach to endorse, if any. From there, the inflectional subsystems should be explored and their contrasting form and distribution accounted for, typically resulting in a raising analysis as seen here but argued against elsewhere (Bruening 2001; Richards 2004; Lochbihler and Mathieu 2013). Regardless of the syntactic tradition followed or the specific interests of the researcher, these languages are a gold mine for linguistic research.

With the extreme divergence observed among the languages of the Algonquian family and the disappearance of invaluable speakers of these languages, it becomes increasingly more difficult to make claims about the language, especially as new areas of interest and inquiry emerge. The research investigating L1 acquisition for those Algonquian languages still vital enough to have in-home L1 acquisition occurring (see Chisasibi Child Language Acquisition Study) is perhaps most valuable and intriguing as more and more young people are dedicating their work to revitalization. Immersion schools and L2 programs provide an endless supply of research topics including acquisition, lexical innovation, extension, and, ultimately, language change on a much different level.

APPENDIX

VTA Paradigms

The following table shows the morphological complexity of the transitive animate verb. The verbs used in the paradigms are the consonant stem *zhawenim* 'have compassion for h/' and, where applicable for cases of VTA stem contraction (3.3.10), *bizindaw* 'listen to h/' is used. All relevant VTA stem contractions are given on the second line.

Persons		Positive		Negative	
s	o	INDEPENDENT	CONJUNCT	INDEPENDENT	CONJUNCT
1s	2s	gizhawenimin gibizindoon	zhawenimiinaan bizindoonaan	gizhawenimisinoon gibizindoosinoon	zhawenimisinowaan bizindoosinaan
	2p	gizhawenimininim gibizindooninim	zhawenimiinagog bizindoonagog	gizhawenimisinooninim gibizindoosinooninim	zhawenimisinowagog bizindoosinagog
	3s	nizhawenimaa	zhawenimag	nizhawenimaasiin	zhawenimaasiwag
	3p	nizhawenimaag	zhawenimagwaa	nizhawenimaasiig	zhawenimaasiwagwaa
	3'	nizhawenimimaan	zhawenimimag	nizhawenimimaasiin	zhawenimimaasiwag
2s	1s	gizhawenim	zhawenimiyan	gizhawenimisiin	zhawenimisiwan
	1p	gizhawenimimin	zhawenimiyaang	gizhawenimisiimin	zhawenimisiwaang
	3s	gizhawenimaa	zhawenimad	gizhawenimaasiin	zhawenimaasiwad
	3p	gizhawenimaag	zhawenimadwaa	gizhawenimaasiig	zhawenimaasiwadwaa
	3'	gizhawenimimaan	zhawenimimad	gizhawenimimaasiin	zhawenimimaasiwad
3s	1s	nizhawenimig nibizindaag	zhawenimid	nizhawenimigosiin nibizindaagosiin	zhawenimisig
	1p	nizhawenimigonaan nibizindaagonaan	zhawenimiyangid	nizhawenimigosiinaan nibizindaagosiinaan	zhawenimisiwangid
	2s	gizhawenimig gibizindaag	zhawenimik bizindook	gizhawenimigosiin gibizindaagosiin	zhawenimisinok bizindoosinok
	2p	gizhawenimigowaa gibizindaagowaa	zhawenimineg bizindoomeg	gizhawenimigosiiwaa gibizindaagosiiwaa	zhawenimisinoweg bizindoosinoweg
	21p	gizhawenimigonaan gibizindaagonaan	zhawenimiinang bizindoonang	gizhawenimigosiinaan gibizindaagosiinaan	zhawenimisinowang bizindoosinowang

3'	ozhawenimaan	zhawenimaad	ozhawenimaasiin	zhawenimaasig
3s	ozhawenimigoom obizindaagoon	zhawenimigod bizindaagod	ozhawenimigosiin obizindaagosiin	zhawenimigosig bizindaagosig
3p	ozhawenimigowaan obizindaagowaan	zhawenimigowaad bizindaagowaad	ozhawenimigosiiwaan obizindaagosiiwaan	zhawenimigosigwaa bizindaagosigwaa
1p	gizhawenimigoo gibizindaagoo	zhawenimigooyan bizindaagooyan	gizhawenimigoosiin gibizindaagoosiin	zhawenimigoosiwan bizindaagoosiwan
2s				
2p	gizhawenimigoom gibizindaagoom	zhawenimigooyeg bizindaagooyeg	gizhawenimigoosiim gibizindaagoosiim	zhawenimigoosiweg bizindaagoosiweg
3s	nizhawenimaanaan	zhawenimangid	nizhawenimaasiwaanaan	zhawenimaasiwangid
3p	nizhawenimaanaanig	zhawenimangidwaa	nizhawenimaasiwaanaanig	zhawenimaasiwangidwaa
3'	nizhawenimimaanaan	zhawenimimangid	nizhawenimimaasiwaanaan	zhawenimimaasiwangid
21p	gizhawenimaanaan	zhawenimang	gizhawenimaasiwaanaan	zhawenimaasiwang
3s	gizhawenimaanaanig	zhawenimangwaa	gizhawenimaasiwaanaanig	zhawenimaasiwangwaa
3p	gizhawenimimaanaan	zhawenimimang	gizhawenimimaasiwaanaan	zhawenimimaasiwang
3'	gizhawenimim	zhawenimiyeg	gizhawenimisiim	zhawenimisiweg
2p	gizhawenimimin	zhawenimiyaang	gizhawenimisiimin	zhawenimisiwaang
1s	gizhawenimaawaa	zhawenimeg	gizhawenimaasiwaawaa	zhawenimaasiweg
1p	gizhawenimaawaag	zhawenimegwaa	gizhawenimaasiwaawaag	zhawenimaasiwegwaa
3s	gizhawenimimaawaa	zhawenimimeg	gizhawenimimaasiwaawaa	zhawenimimaasiweg
3p	nizhawenimigoog nibizindaagoog	zhawenimiwaad	nizhawenimigosiig nibizindaagosiig	zhawenimisigwaa
3'				
1s	nizhawenimigonaanig nibizindaagonaanig	zhawenimiyangidwaa	nizhawenimigosiinaanig nibizindaagosiinaanig	zhawenimisiwangidwaa
1p				

328 Appendix

Persons		Positive		Negative	
S	O	INDEPENDENT	CONJUNCT	INDEPENDENT	CONJUNCT
	2s	gizhawenimigoog / gibizindaagoog	zhawenimikwaa / bizindookwaa	gizhawenimigosiig / gibizindaagosiig	zhawenimisinokwaa / bizindoosinookwaa
	2p	gizhawenimigowaag / gibizindaagowaag	zhawenimineg / bizindooneg	gizhawenimigosiiwaag / gibizindaagosiiwaag	zhawenimisinowegwaa / bizindoosinowegwaa
	21p	gizhawenimigonaanig / gibizindaagonaanig	zhawenimimnangwaa / bizindoomangwaa	gizhawenimigosiinaanig / gibizindaagosiinaanig	zhawenimisinowangwaa / bizindoosinowangwaa
	3'	ozhawenimaawaan	zhawenimaawaad	ozhawenimaasiwaawaan	zhawenimaasigwaa
X	1s	nizhawenimigoo / nibizindaagoo	zhawenimigooyaan / bizindaagooyaan	nizhawenimigoosiin / nibizindaagoosiin	zhawenimigoosiwaan / bizindaagoosiwaan
	1p	nizhawenimigoomin / nibizindaagoomin	zhawenimigooyaang / bizindaagooyaang	nizhawenimigoosiimin / nibizindaagoosiimin	zhawenimigoosiwaang / bizindaagoosiwaang
	2s	gizhawenimigoo / gibizindaagoo	zhawenimigooyan / bizindaagooyan	gizhawenimigoosiin / gibizindaagoosiin	zhawenimigoosiwan / bizindaagoosiwan
	2p	gizhawenimigoom / gibizindaagoom	zhawenimigooyeg / bizindaagooyeg	gizhawenimigoosiin / gibizindaagoosiin	zhawenimigoosiweg / bizindaagoosiweg
	21p	gizhawenimigoomin / gibizindaagoomin	zhawenimigooyang / bizindaagooyang	gizhawenimigoosiimin / gibizindaagoosiimin	zhawenimigoosiwang / bizindaagoosiwang
	3s	zhawenimaa	zhawenimind	zhawenimaasiin	zhawenimaasiwind
	3p	zhawenimaawag	zhawenimindwaa	zhawenimaasiiwag	zhawenimaasiwindwaa
	3'	zhawenimaawan?	zhawenimimind	zhawenimaasiiwan?	zhawenimaasiwind

NOTES

1. Basic Introduction to the Study

1. In using the term *strategy* here I do not imply that such choice is optional, as common uses of the term may suggest. In contrast I use the term in regard to the different surface forms of the clause type that are found to occur.
2. See McNally (2009) for a contrary case at White Earth regarding the use of Ojibwe in Christian prayer service and hymn singing.
3. I recently had the opportunity to sit down and visit with Joe Chosa, a ninety-four-year-old veteran of World War II and the last known native speaker of Ojibwe at Lac du Flambeau, Wisconsin. Joe passed away May 23, 2016.
4. A more detailed account of Ojibwe morphosyntax is given in chapter 2.
5. English *that* is not specific to RCs but is also used to introduce complement clauses as well as *so-that* resultatives (Andrews 2007, 231).
6. I follow Valentine's (1994) approach to classifying variation in Ojibwe as compared to "general" Ojibwe, which represents the commonalities most found across dialects.
7. In the examples that follow I have opted to gloss the participle morpheme and plural or obviative marker as one unit, PL_{PRT} and OBV_{PRT} respectively.
8. All examples cited as Benton (2013), Rogers (2013), and Smallwood (2013) come from the original recordings and do not necessarily match the representation in print. I served as an editor for the project, though the final edited versions were erroneously not used in the publication.
9. The verb *onjibaa* in (22) above contains the initial *ond=*, which undergoes palatalization to *onj=* in this case. More on palatalization is given in 2.3.3.1.
10. As discussed in 2.6 and 3.3.11, some northern dialects no longer show a productive ablaut process of IC on certain vowels.
11. The full VTA paradigm for the neutral mode is given in the appendix.
12. Greenberg (1960) attempted to group all North American Indian languages into three families. His groupings were the subject of much scrutiny; it is generally agreed that the genetics of languages in Native North America is much more diverse and complex than Greenberg had concluded.
13. Sapir (1913) is credited as being the first to suggest that the Californian languages Yurok and Wiyot are related to the Algonquian languages further east. It was concluded that these languages were not descended from PA but rather from Proto-Algic, an even older ancestor (Valentine 1994, 89).
14. One such example is the form of the modern Odawa demonstratives *maanda* and *maaba*. Rhodes (2012) points out that Baraga's (1850) grammar of South-

western Ojibwe includes these, suggesting the quite likely possibilities that the languages were either not as distinct or in close contact. Also, these forms appear in the transcriptions of post-treaty petitions of the mid-nineteenth century in Wisconsin, providing further support (Nichols 1988a). Valentine (1994, 445) cites personal communication with Nichols suggesting that Baraga's works "have Ottawa in them" and continues, "it seems reasonable that communication between these two dialects was probably quite common, and that 'pure' dialects have not existed for a long time on the eastern range of Southwestern."

15. Cree has completely replaced the Ojibwe once spoken at Rocky Boy, which retains its original designation as a Chippewa Cree reservation (Vern Gardipee Sr., pers. comm.), while Cree and Michif, a mixture of Cree, French, and Ojibwe, are the only indigenous languages spoken to any degree at Turtle Mountain (Alex Decoteau, pers. comm.).
16. See Schoolcraft (1851, vol. 6) for a discussion of the history of the treaties, with specific prices negotiated and territory ceded.
17. For a brief but concise overview of the Ojibwe reservation period and boarding school experience, see Treuer (2010).
18. Valentine (1996, 304) also mentions the issue of *anda-* vs. *nanda-* as a common phonological parameter for variation.
19. Certain forms recorded from Border Lakes speakers show a final /o/ *-ngwaamo*. This is discussed in 3.3.8.2.
20. TI1 and TI2 represent verb subclasses of the transitive inanimate type where TI1 stems end in /d/ whereas TI2 stems end in /t/.
21. Rhodes also shows "partitive constructions" consisting of the ordering Q-det-N (1996, 2).
22. Lee Staples (LS), an Aazhoomog speaker and prominent spiritual leader among the SW Ojibwe, sometimes gives a traditional Anishinaabe name *e-niizhoowewidang*, 'the one who is heard in twos.' This is one of the few examples I have discovered in all of my work and exposure to SW speakers.
23. Relative roots in Rhodes's terms are essentially the same as the relative prefixes or roots mentioned above in 1.2.2 and in further detail in 2.3.4.
24. Johns makes no mention of "participles" per se, though her "WH-forms" in relative clauses are essentially the same in function as "participles" in other traditions.
25. Johansson (2013, 222) mentions one consultant's acceptance of a possessed RC and suggests that deverbal nouns in Blackfoot "begin their lives as relative clauses" and that the form accepted is "in transition." Similar transitions occur in Ojibwe and will be discussed in 2.6.2 in the discussion of "de-participlized nouns."
26. See Brittain (2003) for a distributed morphology (DM) account.

27. A full listing of possible theme signs is given in 2.5.
28. The second-person form for (42) and (43) is identical to the first-person form with the exception of the personal prefix *gi-* rather than the first person marker *ni-*.
29. See Henderson (2006) for an account of Bantu languages.

2. Ojibwe Morphosyntax

1. John Nichols (pers. comm.) suggests that the work of Baraga (1850) is better representative of "General Ojibwe" and cautions against the use of the first variety available in print as the standard.
2. The convention among Algonquianists working on Odawa (Valentine, Rhodes) is to represent the glottal stop with /h/. In the standard SW Ojibwe orthography, /h/ is reserved solely for what Valentine (1996, 301) refers to as "paralinguistic/exclamatory forms" such *hay* 'darn'; *howa* 'great!'; *ahaw* 'okay' and /n/ combination with /-h/ to represent word-final nasalization. This is restricted to certain singular nouns such as *abinoojiinh* 'child' and in a few discourse particles such as *giiwenh* 'supposedly.'
3. Pronunciations from modern speakers show inconsistencies regarding the "tensing" mentioned here.
4. The first known "Ojibweyan" text was published in 1644 in France in the "Jesuit Relations." Recorded there are orthographic /r/ and /l/, assumed to be liquids not found in any variety of SW Ojibwe. However, Valentine finds /l/ in place of /n/ in the Algonquin community at Rapid Lake, Quebec (1996, 301).
5. Both the medial and final morphemes in this example are themselves multimorphemic. The medial can be parsed as follows =*gidigw*= 'knee' =*e* incorporating suffix. The final =*shin* can be parsed =*shi*= and =*n*.
6. Morpheme gloss of =*shin* courtesy of the Ojibwe People's Dictionary.
7. There has been an attempt of late by Algonquianists to reclassify particles into different adverbial subclasses. See Oxford (2008) for the discussion of Innuaimun and the Ojibwe People's Dictionary for the Ojibwe classifications.
8. See Nichols (1980, 20–22) for noun gender discussion including shifts in gender in a given discourse.
9. Some particles do show certain derivational operations such as lexical preverbs, **chi**-*mewinzha* 'a really long time ago', an often 'optional' locative suffix *jiigaatigong* 'by a tree', and reduplication, **aye**shkam 'gradually.'
10. Many of the demonstrative pronouns are reduced significantly in casual speech. Typically the first syllable is deleted when the demonstrative pronouns occur in running narratives, resulting in forms such as *aw, ow, iw* and *awe, owe, iwe*. Dialect codes here are as follows: GO 'General Ojibwe', WO 'Wisconsin Ojibwe', and BL 'Border Lakes Ojibwe.'

11. Geary (1945, 169n1) appears to have been the first to designate the primary object and secondary object of double-object verbs with these terms. See Rhodes (1990a, 2010a) for a full discussion of ditransitives.
12. Palatalization occurs in a number of Algonquian languages. Brittain (2001) describes languages of the CMN group where all high front vowels trigger palatalization for Naskapi, while Bruening (2001, 46) discusses the same peripheral suffix /-i/ in Passamaquoddy that causes /t/ → /c/ palatalization.
13. The participial suffix can be parsed as follows, where the initial vowel /i/ represents the "participle marker" and the final /g/ or /n/ represents either plurality or obviation.
14. Valentine (1994, 315) identifies /j/ rather than /d/ to be the standard third-person conjunct order suffix for northern Ojibwe.
15. The length distinction between short and long /e/ was still observed in Fox (Meskwaki) somewhat recently (Goddard 1987, 106).
16. See Costa (1996) for full discussion on the vowel system and reconstruction of IC in PA.
17. See Nichols (1980, 270) for rule-based explanations for each example of palatalization in Ojibwe.
18. One such example is the alternation between /-n/ and /zh/, which, according to Valentine, "arose historically because a PA obstruent believed to have the value of θ merged with *l*, which later merged with *n*, though the original PA θ-*sh* palatalization process is still evidenced in the ubiquitous alternations" (1994, 120). He also points out that PA /-n/ does not alternate in Ojibwe.
19. Nichols observes that this most productive process uses "/-n/ in the formation of noun stems from detransitivized TI verbs with the AI final /-ge/. The final /-e/ becomes /-a/, forming a complex noun final /-gan/" (1980, 78). See Nichols (1980, 78–80) for full discussion of *-gan* nominalizations.
20. This is a generalization for General Ojibwe. As will be seen in 3.3.1 and as illustrated in (50) above, some southern speakers use *da-* with personal prefixes as a future definite preverb.
21. Wolvengrey (2006) suggests *prospective* to be a more precise label than *desiderative*, *intentive*, or *voluntative*, since many uses lack meanings associated with desire or want.
22. The reader is urged to consult Nichols (1980) for the morphological shape of imperative verbs and Valentine (2001) for a complete discussion of their usage.
23. The above example was a correction to a previous back-translation attempt at a construction with a changed conjunct (*gaa-wiisiniwaad*), supporting the complementation analysis argued for in this study.
24. See Fairbanks (2008) for a full discussion of *mii* and its nuanced usage.
25. See Fairbanks (2009) for his discussion of conjuncts providing the event-line structure of narratives.

26. Since speaker translations are maintained here, I provide clarification when needed. *Poonjin* is colloquial reservation slang for 'having sex.' The word is common on many Ojibwe reservations and most likely derives from the Ojibwe root *booj*= 'to poke.'
27. The analysis and presentation format here is based largely on that provided by Valentine (2001, 270–78). The reader is referred there for the full discussion of theme signs, including inanimate actors.
28. The terms *actor* and *goal* are traditional terms borrowed from Bloomfield by Hockett (1966) and Valentine (1994, 2001).
29. The attentive Ojibweist will notice the unusual form of the root *nazhike-*, 'to be alone.' This nasal behavior is a characteristic of the Ponemah dialect at Red Lake and is well represented in the Ojibwe People's Dictionary. This will be discussed in 3.3.7.1.4.
30. John Nichols (pers. comm.) points out that *godag* by itself is not an obviative pronoun: he has recorded *godag* 'the other one,' *godagiyag* 'the other ones,' and *godagiyan* 'the other$_{OBV}$ one.' Bruening (2001, 40) provides *kotok*, the Passamaquoddy cognate he glosses as 'the other.' Baraga (1878, 186) lists *kutak* 'other.'
31. Costa (1996, 41) treats IC of /o/ becoming /we/ as the same alternation that the other short vowels /a/ and /i/ undergo, given that "Ojibwa" /o/ originally comes from Proto-Algonquian *we.
32. Costa (1996, 41) points out that verbs consisting of these relative roots and preverbs that exhibit this exceptional IC form largely begin with /t/ across the Algonquian family but points out that it is a voiced /d/ for Ojibwe and Potawatomi.
33. Valentine provides *ogikendaan* **e-gii**-*bakitehozhiyan* 'he knows that you hit me' (1994, 324).
34. Costa (1996) finds the "aorist" *e-* preverb in a number of Algonquian languages including Fox-Kickapoo (Bloomfield 1927 classified the form in this language as a subtype of the conjunct mode), Cheyenne, Potawatomi, and Cree (among others).
35. Brittain (2001, 97) reports two distinct *gaa-* prefixes in Western Naskapi occurring in distinct syntactic environments. Her bimorphemic *kâ-* occurs in complement clauses and some "wh-phrases," while her "reanalyzed *kâ-*" occurs in relative clauses and "focus" constructions. Comparisons can easily be drawn between *kâ-* in that language to *gaa-* discussed here.
36. The same distinction between the *-waa* pluralizer and plural participle marker can be found widely in the Algonquian family, particularly among the southern languages. See Goddard (1987) for Fox, Costa (2003) for Miami-Illinois, Valentine (1994, 2001) and Rhodes (1976, 1996) for Odawa, and Buszard-Welcher (1999) for Potawatomi.
37. Jancewicz (1997) reports a similar strategy of nominalization occurring in Nas-

kapi that is "highly productive," where the *gaa-* prefix attaches to the conjunct third-person form and is subject to all nominal derivational and inflectional processes upon becoming lexicalized by speakers.

38. For examples cited "Clark and Gresczyk 1991" I refer only to the audio that accompanies the book.

39. Nichols and Nyholm (1995) provide *detibisejig* for the participle plural for 'wheel.' This is also given in the Ojibwe People's Dictionary.

40. The plural participle for the dubitative mode shown here in (105) is *-ag*, contrary to that presented by Kaye and Piggott (1973, 357) for Odawa.

41. The example shown above in (105a.) involves a pattern on participle marking undoing a change among modern speakers. This will be discussed in 3.3.13.2 as the negative participle formation appears to be a parameter that shows age-graded variation.

42. Constituent ordering alone cannot serve as the primary diagnostic when differentiating participles from changed conjuncts. After eliciting back-translations for the examples shown above, my consultant reminded me that the singular participle shown above in (113b.) could also be translated (given the right context) as 's/he put it back after s/he used it,' with a changed conjunct interpretation. However, he strongly disliked a participle translation for the changed conjunct example shown above in (113a.).

43. The gloss of *ishkwaa-* 'after' appears here as glossed in Nichols (1980). As treated by Fairbanks (2012), the preverb *ishkwaa-*, commonly taught in L2 classrooms as the go-to strategy for 'after' clauses, is commonly taken literally as 'finish; quit (forever)' by many modern southern speakers.

44. For a full discussion of Ojibwe and Algonquian syntax the reader is referred to the many descriptive works of Rhodes and Dahlstrom, and, for more theoretical generative and minimalist approaches, to Branigan and McKenzie, Déchaine, Brittain, and Bruening.

45. Most Algonquian word order studies are concerned with textual materials, primarily narratives and monologues, for which a stylistic contrast has long been observed (Hockett 1939, 236). Much of the material consulted in such studies is often dated and has typically passed through a series of editors since the original dictation in which they have typically been collected. Goddard (1987, 117n21) mentions an instance with possible problems with data tampering in archived texts, noting Michelson's editing of what he thought were erroneous transcriptions. See Goddard (1984), originally titled, "The Obviative in Fox Narrative Discourse and How Not to Edit It." The title was changed without consultation for publication.

46. The findings from Sullivan (2016) shown here are compiled from Sullivan's A, B, and C groupings. The findings are presented differently here, consolidating those of the published work. The D grouping is relevant to the discussion of the

47. The length of each story can be determined by the total sentences counted. Each story was transcribed and translated with the speaker, who had the liberty of determining how each sentence would be parsed.
48. The sentence is exemplary in that it shows some of the intricacies of Ojibwe verbal morphology and how much meaning verbs can carry, as shown in the more literal glosses provided here: *maajiibizo* VAI 's/he starts off by means of motorized transportation' *maajii*= initial 'start' =*bizo* final 'h/ moves without obstruction, flies, speeds, falls, drives'; *bimibizo* VAI 's/he drives along by means of motorized transportation' *bimi*= initial 'along in space or time' =*bizo* final 'h/ moves without obstruction, flies, speeds, falls, drives'; *baashkijiisijigeyaan* 's/he has a blowout' *baashk*= initial 'burst; broken open (esp. of three-dimensional objects)' =*jii*= medial 'something soft and hollow like a bag or stomach, small round body, belly' =*sid* final 'cause it to fall, lie, impact it' =*ige* final detransitive.
49. Jeanette Gundel (pers. comm.) points out that topic and focus can also move to the left periphery in other VOS languages (for example, Tagalog and other Austronesian languages) and, for that matter, in SVO languages like English, except that there it results in OSV order.
50. Junker's (2004) analysis of East Cree claims that focus as a functional projection is unable to account for the behavior of obviate NPs in her East Cree data. Instead her analysis suggests that focus be treated as an "interpretation rule which is not encoded directly in the syntax" (345).
51. Rosemarie Debungie, pers. comm.
52. Jeanette Gundel (pers. comm.) informs me that indefinite pronouns and quantifiers are always focal crosslinguistically since topics (the portion of the sentence not in focus) must be pragmatically or semantically definite, or at least "uniquely identifiable."
53. Aissen's (1992) study is concerned with Mayan, which she states is also VOS and in which, similar to my analysis of Ojibwe, there is relative freedom of word order and movement operations that are related to discourse functions.

3. Methodology

1. *Boozhoo* 'hello' is a common greeting in many Ojibwe communities, often assumed to be a loan from the French *bonjour*. Local folk etymology challenges this claim, suggesting that the term is derived from Wenabozho, the proper name of a popular cultural hero.
2. Nichols (1988) suspects the document was translated from English into Ojibwe based on some awkward phrases, for example, 'fat trader.' All of Baraga's work was done with the missionary motivation; one can only wonder what attention was paid to what Bowern (2008) refers to as "naturalistic data."

3. Fairbanks (2009) notes the same issue concerning the nature of second position clitics in Ojibwe and how they are best represented in the orthography.
4. The reader is referred to the discussion in 2.3.4 above and Nichols (1980) for the classification of preverbs.
5. The example cited as Mosay (1996) was recorded over twenty years earlier, in February 1975, as part of the Wisconsin Native American Languages Project.
6. In many cases the open mid-back vowel of the first syllable is significantly reduced to schwa, leading some to represent the sound with /i/, for example, *dibwaa-*.
7. Nichols (2011) provides both the long form of demonstratives shown here, along with the short forms identical with those found at Mille Lacs, with the absence of the nasal in the plural animate forms. Speakers consulted from not only Ponemah but also Nett Lake and the Border Lakes will commonly use the short forms in elicitation and in fast speech, but often prefer the longer forms when back-translating and when editing transcriptions. Speakers from the south, however, have only been observed using the longer, more characteristically northern forms when joking or mocking northern speakers.
8. It is worth noting that in written documents, both published and unpublished, it is common for speakers to insist that the initial segment be represented in the written form. As a result many narratives exist with *akina* or *akeyaa* though the speakers pronounce them as *kina* and *keyaa*. A story from Redby from 1987 shows *kina* twice in the text, suggesting this deletion has occurred there for quite some time.
9. I've encountered *ningodwaaso* for the cardinal number 'six' only in one speaker at Ponemah.
10. Angeline Williams was originally from a community near Manistique, Michigan, on the Upper Peninsula; she later relocated to Sault Ste. Marie. Her language is especially interesting due to the relationship between SW Ojibwe and Odawa (pre-syncopation) evident throughout her speech (Bloomfield and Nichols 1991).
11. Pipe Mustache (1904–92), a revered elder from Lac Courte Oreilles, provided both *wagidakamig* and *ogidakamig* in the same narrative, suggesting the varying pronunciations were relevant during his time period.
12. This example appeared in a handwritten story and is spelled here as it occurred in the original text with both glides being represented in the written representation, suggesting that the speaker was conscious of this variation and how to articulate her pronunciation in writing.
13. In accordance with the tradition in Algonquian linguistics I maintain the label /t/ *epenthesis* here for Ojibwe, despite its perceivable status as a misnomer, since the epenthetic consonant for Ojibwe is an orthographic /d/.

14. The reader is referred to Nichols (1980, 43, 132) for the specifics of /o/ stem lengthening and Valentine (1994, 126) for the excrescent nasals of the first-person prefix.
15. One anonymous speaker from a southern community provided unstable inflections, going back and forth between the forms with and without the final *-e*, suggesting this is a variable in transition. Also, one speaker from northern LL (GH) provided the forms lacking the final *-e* in our sessions, though examples can be found on the OPD where she gives both (see OPD entries *baagidoon* and *baagidoone*).
16. Speakers have apparently noticed such variation for quite some time. See Dunigan, Barstow, and Northbird (1988) for a comical account of the variation in "The Animate Pants" story.
17. VTA *-aw* stem contraction is much more complex than suggested here. For communities south of Leech Lake, I have provided full VTA paradigms in the appendix, giving both negative and positive charts showing contractions verified by a speaker from Aazhoomog.
18. Another unrelated variable, mentioned earlier in 1.2.3.3 in regard to VTAs, concerns the strategy for forming benefactives. Nichols (2012) observes variation in regard to the benefactive element *-amaw*, used productively in the north, whereas traditional patterns observed in the south show *-amaw* only for VTI1 and *-aw* on TI2 in south: *ozhitaw* as opposed to the northern variant *ozhitamaw* 'make it for h/' (Nichols 2012, 8). The northern strategy appears to be moving south as instability arises during elicitation with southern speakers.
19. For a discussion on the function of IC and its usage, see 2.6.
20. In one session with Nancy Jones from Nigigoonsiminikaaning (Red Gut), she provided *awenen ayaakozid*, showing IC on /aa/. After testing IC in a number of other /aa/ initial verbs, it was concluded that she does not regularly make the change. For IC on /e/, however, she provided *awenen* **zaye**gizid 'who is scared' and *awegonen* **aye**naabiising 'what has a crack,' showing IC for both.
21. Others working with more northern dialects report that what Fiero (pers. comm.) calls the "situation *gii-*" or "timeless *gii-*" differs from the "completive *gii'-*," where a glottal stop has been recorded. Like *gaa-* shown above in (284), it can co-occur with tense markers: "Timeless *gii-*":

> Whitedog, Ontario *ngoding idash* **gii**-*wii-kizhaatabiyaan*
>   *gishkigwaasonaabik ndaabajitoon*
>   'Sometimes, **when** I want to hurry (in quilting)
>   I use the sewing machine'

22. Data from Pickle Lake and Cat Lake, Ontario, supplied by Chuck Fiero to the author, show obviative participle marking for both singular and plural obvia-

tive participles. When speaking of "the north," I am referring to the northern communities of SW Ojibwe only, in which I have arbitrarily included the Border Lakes communities surveyed.

23. When back-translating this example with another speaker from the south, a "correction" was provided to the form of the participle *gaa-nisinjin*, adding the VTA obviative suffix *-m*: *gaa-nisiminjin*. The obviative *-m* inflection is rare among many modern speakers but is mentioned in the older documentation (Baraga 1850; Nichols 1980).

24. The reader is reminded that, although "Nichols (1988a)" doesn't give the impression of an "old" source, it consists of a document written in Wisconsin c. 1864. The column labeled "Old Ojibwe" represents a generalization, while I am fully aware of the possibility of variation that existed at the time the older sources appeared.

25. Nichols (1980, 215) mistakenly glosses the last two examples as 'had he not been sick' and 'they who are not sick' respectively.

26. The older documentation as well as the more conservative living speakers pronounce the name *Gaa-biboonike*, with no conjunct third-person suffix. Others appear to have replaced the old form by pronouncing the name with the final *-d*.

27. The *gaa-* relativizer is reported at Inger by some of my contemporaries, though I was not able to elicit it from the two speakers I worked with from there.

28. The exact same prompt elicited a similar form *gaa-minwen**im**agin* (obviative *-im*) from a Border Lakes speaker who immediately caught her "mistake" and "corrected" herself, providing the same "corrected" form as above.

29. This example is taken and modified slightly from the Odawa version appearing in Valentine (2001, 303), *Geyaabi go ndeyaawaag giwi(g) mshiimnag gaa-miizhiyinig*. All back-translations were elicited with me providing the Ojibwe prompt.

30. The lack of understanding on the speaker's part can be attributed to two possibly unfamiliar aspects of the construction. The first and perhaps most obvious is the plural participle marker *-in* used with the VTA 2p>1s construction, not attested by any Ponemah speakers. The other concerns the verb itself *ataw*, representing a southern derivation variant where the speaker was most likely more familiar with *atamaw*, the northern variant.

31. Examples taken from Johns (1982, 161–62).

32. Rose "Zhaangweshiban" Tainter (RT), 1939–2014, a native of Ponemah who later relocated to Lac Courte Oreilles and co-founded the Waadookodaading Ojibwe Language Immersion School, would occasionally provide participles, specifically those frequently used in the school setting, such as *egaashiinyijig* 'little ones,' *gekinoo'amaagejig* 'teachers,' and *waabishkiiwejig* 'Caucasians' (no IC). It is assumed that Rose acquired these forms at Lac Courte Oreilles through the

context of her involvement with the school, rather than that they were retained from her original L1 language socialization at Ponemah.

33. 'Boughs.'
34. When providing this generalization Valentine gives an example that, by local SW Ojibwe standards, would not require the obviative participle form that he expects (-*aajin* 3s>3'):

> "*Aapji go jina ngii-gnoonaa wa,*" *gii-kido-sh giiwenh miinwaa bezhig zhmaagnishii-gima wa **gaa-bi-waabmaad niwi**.*
> '"I only spoke to him for a short while," said the other officer, who had come to see him.' (2001, 589)

He later provides an example with the expected participle in the obviative context (590). Other examples (209) and (210) show this same difference in context and participle usage.

4. Relativization in Ojibwe

1. The reader is reminded that Ojibwe has no lexical category preposition. Instead nominals are marked with a locative suffix or verbs with a relative root (*iN-*, *daN-*, or *ond-*). Like Bruening (2001, 53), I "set aside" the issue of whether there is a PP constituent for Ojibwe and Algonquian languages in general.
2. The quirkiness of 'where' questions in Algonquian languages has been observed in many other studies. See Bruening (2001) for Passamaquoddy, Brittain (2001) for Naskapi, Wolfart (1973) for Plains Cree, to name a few.
3. It is not uncommon for linguists to posit theories and make claims based on older forms of a given language. See Ingham (2000) and Radford (2004) for historical comparisons to archaic uses of Middle English, and Benţea (2010) for comparisons to archaic uses of Romanian.
4. See 3.2.1 for the discussion of variation found in regard to the complementizers used.
5. Rizzi's original explanation reflects the nature of C more precisely, as a "C system to express at least two kinds of information, one facing the outside and the other facing the inside" (1997, 283).
6. I do not pursue an analysis at this time concerning the articulation of a split TP involving an AspP head. One could easily assume that features pertaining to aspect are carried by the verb as it moves into the CP layer, eventually winding up in FocP where IC is obtained, satisfying the *wh*-criterion.
7. Rizzi's analysis involves specifier movement, as does Benţea's (2010) depiction of Romanian RCs moving to the spec position of ForceP. For Bianchi (2000), a relativized NP raises only as far as SpecXP, while only the NP head moves further, to a specifier position of a higher head. Benţea (2010, 185) concludes (along

the lines of Rizzi 1997) that the relative DP in Romanian moves to the specifier position of the force phrase. Also, differing from the current approach argued for here, Benţea (2010, 181), in light of Bianchi (1999, 2000), claims the entire relative DP raises to Spec ForceP without passing through an intervening position of the split CP.
8. Valentine (2001, 970) reports how *mii* "can also serve as a focusing device in constructions using relative clauses, rather like English clefted-sentences, such as 'It was a linguist that rescued the cat'" and provides the following template: *mii* + focused item + dem pn + RC.
9. The reader is referred to Valentine (1994, 420) for the nominal character of *mii* in Berens Ojibwe, where examples are provided with obviative and plural markers occurring on *mii*, for example, *mii**wan**/mii**wag***. Such forms, as well as the obviative plural form *miiwa'*, are attested in the speech of Border Lakes speakers.

5. Conclusions

1. For Passamaquoddy, Bruening reports obviative plural demonstratives but states that, as in the more northern varieties of Ojibwe treated here, the conjunct inflections do not make a number distinction and are essentially ambiguous (2001, 45).
2. Costa's (1996) critique of Bloomfield's (1946) reconstruction is supported by the earlier work of Goddard (1979), who notices Bloomfield's version is essentially the same as IC in Menominee, though it is insufficient for the four central languages treated in the sketch.
3. According to Goddard (1978, 585), Miami-Illinois is a name of convenience given to two clusters of dialects having partial speakers as late as the 1960s.
4. Fox-Kickapoo is a language also identified as "Fox," which generally includes Sauk, Fox, and Kickapoo as three dialects of single language (Goddard 1978, 584).
5. The preverb is spelled as *kâ* in Brittain (2001).
6. Bloomfield's (1946) examples shown here in (422c.) and below in (423b.) do not appear to exhibit IC. I have opted to omit IC from the morphological glossing as a result.

REFERENCES

Aissen, Judith. 1992. "Topic and Focus in Mayan." *Language* 68 (1): 43–80.
Andersen, Roger. 1982. "Determining the Linguistic Attributes of Language Attrition." In *The Loss of Language Skills*, edited by R. D. Lambert & B. F. Freed. Rowley MA: Newbury House Publishers.
Andrews, Avery. 2007. "Relative Clauses." In *Language Typology and Syntactic Description*, edited by Timothy Shopen, 206–36. New York: Cambridge University Press.
Bainbridge, Delores. 1997. "Aaniindi da-atooyaan." *Oshkaabewis Native Journal* 4 (1): 54–55.
Baker, Mark. 1985. "The Mirror Principle and Morphosyntactic Explanation." *Linguistic Inquiry* 16: 373–415.
———. 1991. "On Some Subject/Object Non-asymmetries in Mohawk." *Natural Language and Linguistic Theory* 9: 537–76.
———. 1996. *The Polysynthesis Parameter*. New York: Oxford University Press.
Baker, Mark C. 2011. "Degrees of Nominalization: Clause-like Constituents in Sakha." *Lingua* 121: 1164–93.
Baraga, Frederik. 1850. *A Theoretical and Practical Grammar of the Otchipwe Language*. Detroit: Jabez Fox.
———. (1878) 1992. *A Dictionary of the Ojibway Language*. Reprint, St. Paul: Minnesota Historical Society Press.
Benjamin, Millie. 2006. "Elderly Advisory Council." Unpublished story.
Bențea, Anamaria. 2010. "On Restrictive Relatives in Romanian: Towards a Head-raising Analysis." *Generative Grammar in Geneva* 6: 165–90.
Benton, Eddie. 2013. "Manoomin gakinoo'amaagewin." *Dibaajimowinan: Anishinaabe Stories of Culture and Respect*, 161–63. Odanah WI: Great Lakes Indian Fish and Wildlife Commission Press.
Bianchi, Valentina. 1999. *Consequences of Antisymmetry: Headed Relative Clauses*. Berlin: Mouton de Gruyter,.
———. 2000. "The Raising Analysis of Relative Clauses: A Reply to Borsley." *Linguistic Inquiry* 31: 123–40.
Blain, Eleanor. 1999. "Complementizer kâ- in Nêhiyawêwin (Plains Cree)." *MIT Occasional Papers in Linguistics* 17: 1–12.
Bloomfield, Leonard. 1925. "On the Sound-system of Central Algonquian." *Language* 1: 130–56.
———. 1927. "Notes on the Fox Language." *International Journal of American Linguistics* 4: 181–219.

———. "Algonquian." 1946. In *Linguistic Structures of Native America*, edited by Harry Hoijer, 85–129. Viking Fund Publications in Anthropology 6. New York: Wenner-Gren Foundation.

———. 1957. *Eastern Ojibwa Grammatical Sketch, Texts, and Word List*. Ann Arbor: University of Michigan Press.

———. 1958. *Eastern Ojibwa*. Edited by Charles F. Hockett. Ann Arbor: University of Michigan Press.

———. 1962. *The Menomini Language*. Edited by Charles F. Hockett. New Haven CT: Yale University Press.

Bloomfield, Leonard, and John D. Nichols. 1991. *The Dog's Children: Anishinaabe Texts Told by Angeline Williams*. Publications of the Algonquian Text Society. Winnipeg: University of Manitoba Press.

Bowern, Claire. 2008. *Linguistic Fieldwork: A Practical Guide*. New York: Palgrave Macmillan.

Branigan, Phil, and Marguerite McKenzie. 2002. "Word Order Variation at the Left Periphery in Innu-aimun." In *Papers of the Thirty-third Algonquian Conference*, edited by H. C. Wolfart, 110–19. Winnipeg: University of Manitoba Press.

Bresnan, Joan. 1972. "Theory of Complementation in English Syntax." PhD dissertation, MIT.

Brittain, Julie. 2001. *The Morphosyntax of the Algonquian Conjunct Verb*. New York: Garland Publishing.

———. 2003. "A Distributed Morphology Account of the Syntax of the Algonquian Verb." In *Proceedings of the 2003 Annual Conference of the Canadian Linguistic Association*, edited by Stanca Somesfalean and Sophie Burrelle, 25–39. Montreal: Université du Québec à Montréal.

Brittain, Julie, and Marguerite MacKenzie. 2011. "Translating Algonquian Oral Texts." In *Born in the Blood: On Native American Translation*, edited by Brian Swann, 242–74. Lincoln: University of Nebraska Press.

Bruening, Benjamin. 2001. "Syntax at the Edge: Cross-Clausal Phenomena and the Syntax of Passamaquoddy." PhD dissertation, MIT.

Buszard-Welcher, Laura. 1999. *Topics in Potawatomi Grammar*. Hannahville MI: Potawatomi Language Scholars' College.

Campana, Mark. 1996. "The Conjunct Order in Algonquian." *The Canadian Journal of Linguistics* 41: 201–34.

Campbell, Lyle. 1997. *American Indian Languages: The Historical Linguistics of Native America*. Oxford: Oxford University Press.

Campbell, Lyle, and Martha C. Muntzel. 1989. "The Structural Consequences of Language Death." In Dorian, *Investigating Obsolescence*, 181–96.

Chambers, J. K., and Peter Trudgill. 1998. *Dialectology*. 2nd ed. Cambridge: Cambridge University Press.

Chomsky, Noam. 1973. "Conditions on Transformations." In *A Festschrift for Morris*

Halle, edited by Stephen Anderson and Paul Kiparsky, 232–86. New York: Holt, Rinehart & Winston.
———. 1977. "On Wh-movement." In *Formal Syntax*, edited by P. W. Culicover, T. Wasow, and A. Akmajian, 71–132. New York: Academic Press.
———. 1993. "A Minimalist Program for Linguistic Theory." In *The View from Building 20: Essays in Honor of Sylvain Bromberger*, edited by K. Hale and S. J. Keyser, 1–52. Cambridge MA: MIT Press.
———. 1995. *The Minimalist Program*. Cambridge MA: MIT Press.
———. 1998. "Minimalist Inquiries: The Framework." *MIT Occasional Papers in Linguistics* 15. Cambridge MA: MIT Press.
———. 1999. "Derivation by Phase." *MIT Occasional Papers in Linguistics* 18. Cambridge MA: MIT.
———. 2000. "Minimalist Inquiries." In *Step by Step: Essays on Minimalist Syntax in Honor of Howard Lasnik*, edited by Roger Martin, David Michaels, and Juan Uriagereka, 89–155. Cambridge MA: MIT Press.
———. 2001. "Derivation by Phase." In *Ken Hale: A Life in Language*, edited by M. Kenstowicz, 1–50. Cambridge MA: MIT Press.
———. 2005. "On Phases." Unpublished manuscript.
———. 2008. "On Phases." In *Foundational Issues in Linguistic Theory*, edited by R. Freidin, C. Otero, and M. Zubizarreta, 133–67. Cambridge MA: MIT Press.
Clark, Jim, and Rick Gresczyk. 1991. *Traveling with Ojibwe: A Phrasebook in the Chippewa Language with Emphasis on the Contemporary, with 6 CDs accompanying the Text*. Minneapolis: Eagle Works.
Clark, James. 2001. "Jiigibiig Nenaandago-ziibing." In *Living Our Language*, edited by Anton Treuer, 65–68. St. Paul: Minnesota Historical Society Press.
Comrie, Bernard. 1989. *Language Universals and Linguistic Typology*. 2nd ed. Chicago: University of Chicago.
Cook, Clare. 2008. "The Syntax and Semantics of Clause-typing in Plains Cree." PhD dissertation, University of British Columbia.
Costa, David. 1996. "Reconstructing Initial Change in Algonquian." *Anthropological Linguistics* 38: 39–72.
———. 2003. *The Miami-Illinois Language*. Lincoln: University of Nebraska Press.
Crystal, David. 2000. *Language Death*. Cambridge: Cambridge University Press.
Dahlstrom, Amy. 1991. *Plains Cree Morphosyntax*. New York: Garland.
———. 1993. "The Syntax of Discourse Functions in Fox." In *Proceedings of the Nineteenth Annual Meeting of the Berkeley Linguistics Society: Special Session on Syntactic Issues in Native American Languages*, 11–21.
———. 1995. *Topic, Focus and Other Word Order Problems in Algonquian*. Winnipeg: Voices of Rupert's Land.
———. 2004. "External and Internal Topics in Meskwaki." Handout from presentation read at Thirty-sixth Algonquian Conference, Madison, Wisconsin.

DeBungie, Rosemarie, and Rose Tainter. 2014. "Bepeshinidiwin." In *Wiijikiiwending*, 22–23. Minneapolis: Wiigwaas Press.

Dorian, Nancy. 1973. "Grammatical Change in a Dying Dialect." *Language* 49: 413–38.

———, ed. 1989. *Investigating Obsolescence: Studies in Contraction and Death*. Cambridge: Cambridge University Press.

Dressler, Wolfgang. 1972. "On the Phonology of Language Death." *Papers from the 8th Regional Meeting of the Chicago Linguistic Society*, 448–57. Chicago: Chicago Linguistic Society.

Dunigan, Timothy, Rose Barstow, and Angeline Northbird. 1988. "Ojibwe Texts: Language Mixing and Humor in the Mille Lacs and Red Lake Dialects." In *An Ojibwe Text Anthology*, edited by John D. Nichols, 1–32. London, Ontario: Centre for the Research and Teaching of Canadian Native Languages, University of Western Ontario.

Fairbanks, Brendan. 2008. "All about Mii." In *Papers of the Thirty-ninth Algonquian Conference*, edited by Regna Darnell & Karl S. Hele, 166–221. London: University of Western Ontario.

———. 2009. "Ojibwe Discourse Markers." PhD dissertation, University of Minnesota.

———. 2016. "The Ojibwe Changed Conjunct Verb as Completive Aspect." In *Papers of the Forty-fourth Algonquian Conference*, edited by Monica Macaulay, Margaret Noodin, and J. Randolph Valentine, 51–66. Albany: SUNY Press.

Fillmore, Charles J., and Paul Kay. 1995. "Construction Grammar." Unpublished manuscript.

Foster, Michael. 1996. "Language and the Cultural History of North America." In *Languages*, edited by Ives Goddard, 64–110. Vol. 17 of *Handbook of North American Indians*, edited by William C. Sturtevant. Washington DC: Smithsonian Institution.

Frantz, Donald. 2009. *Blackfoot Grammar*. 2nd ed. Toronto: University of Toronto Press.

Geary, James. 1945. "The Changed Conjunct Verb (without *-ni*) in Fox." *International Journal of American Linguistics* 11: 169–81.

Gilstrap, Roger. 1978. *Algonquin Dialect Relationships in Northwestern Quebec*. National Museum of Man, Mercury Series, Canadian Ethnology Service Paper 44. Ottawa: National Museums of Canada.

Goddard, Ives. 1974. "Remarks on the Algonquian Independent Indicative." *International Journal of American Linguistics* 40 (4): 317–27.

———. 1978. "Central Algonquian Languages." In *Northeast*, edited by Bruce G. Trigger, 583–87. Vol. 15 of *Handbook of North American Indians*, edited by William C. Sturtevant. Washington DC: Government Printing Office.

———. 1979. "Comparative Algonquian." In *The Languages of Native America: His-*

torical and Comparative Assessment, edited by Lyle Campbell and Marianne Mithun, 70–132. Austin: University of Texas Press.

———. 1984. "The Obviative in Fox Narrative Discourse." *Papers of the Fifteenth Annual Algonquian Conference*, edited by William Cowan, 273–86. Ottawa: Carleton University.

———. 1987. "Fox Participles." In *Native American Languages and Grammatical Typology*, edited by Paul Kroeber and Robert Moore, 105–18. Bloomington: University of Indiana Linguistics Club.

———. 1990. "Primary and Secondary Stem Derivation in Algonquian." *International Journal of American Linguistics* 56 (4): 449–83.

———. 1996a. "Introduction." In *Languages*, edited by Ives Goddard, 1–16. Vol. 17 of *The Handbook of North American Indians*, edited by William C. Sturtevant. Washington DC: Smithsonian Institution.

———. 1996b. "The Description of the Native Languages of North America before Boas." In *Languages*, edited by Ives Goddard, 17–42. Vol. 17 of *The Handbook of North American Indians*, edited by William C. Sturtevant. Washington DC: Smithsonian Institution.

———. 2002. "Grammatical Gender in Algonquian." In *Papers of the Thirty-third Algonquian Conference*, edited by H. C. Wolfart, 195–231. Winnipeg: University of Manitoba.

Greenberg, Joseph. 1960. "General Classification of Central and South American Languages." In *Men and Cultures: Fifth International Congress of Anthropological and Ethnological Sciences*, edited by A. Wallace, 791–94. Philadelphia: University of Pennsylvania Press.

Gundel, Jeanette K. 1988. *The Role of Topic and Comment in Linguistic Theory*. New York: Garland.

Gundel, Jeanette K., and Thorstein Fretheim. 2004. "Topic and Focus." In *Handbook of Pragmatics*, edited by Laurence Horn and Gregory Ward. Oxford and Malden MA: Blackwell.

Guile, Timothy. 2001. "Sketch of Menominee Grammar." In *An Anthology of Menominee Sayings, with Translations, Annotations, and Grammatical Sketch*, 452–501. München: LINCOM Europa.

Hale, Kenneth. 1983. "Warlpiri and the Grammar of Non-configurational Languages." *Natural Language and Linguistic Theory* 1: 5–47.

Henderson, Brent. 2006. "The Syntax and Typology of Bantu Relative Clauses." PhD dissertation, University of Illinois at Urbana-Champaign.

Hill, Jane. 1989. "The Social Functions of Relativization in Obsolescent and Non-obsolescent Languages." In Dorian, *Investigating Obsolescence*, 149–64.

Hockett, Charles. 1939. "Potawatomi Syntax." *Language* 15: 235–48.

———. 1950. "The Conjunct Modes in Ojibwa and Potawatomi." *Language* 26 (2): 278–82.

———. 1966. "What Algonquian Is Really Like." *International Journal of American Linguistics* 32 (1): 59–73.

Hoenigswald, Henry. 1989. "Language Obsolescence and Language History: Matters of Linearity, Leveling, Loss, and the Like." In Dorian, *Investigating Obsolescence*, 347–54.

Ingham, Richard. 2000. "Negation and OV Order in Late Middle English." *Journal of Linguistics* 36: 13–38.

James, Deborah. 1991. *Preverbs and the function of clauses in Moose Cree*. Winnipeg: Voices of Rupert's Land.

Jancewicz, Bill. 1997. "Nominalizations in Naskapi: Production and Inflection." In *Papers of the Twenty-Eighth Algonquian Conference*, edited by David Pentland, 181–99. Winnipeg: University of Manitoba.

Jelinek, Eloise. 1984. "Empty Categories, Case, and Configurationality." *Natural Language and Linguistic Theory* 2: 39–76.

———. 1989a. "The Case Split and Argument Type in Choctaw." In *Configurationality: The Typology of Asymmetries*, edited by Lazlo Maracz and Pieter Muysken, 189–213. Dordrecht: Foris.

———. 1989b. "The Bi-construction and Pronominal Arguments in Apachean." In *Athapaskan Linguistics*, edited by Eung-Do Cook and Keren D. Rice, 41–68. New York: Mouton de Gruyter.

Johansson, Sara. 2010. "Phi-feature Concord on Blackfoot Relative Clauses." Paper presented at the Forty-second Algonquian Conference, Memorial University of Newfoundland.

———. 2011. "Towards a Typology of Algonquian Relative Clauses." *UBCWPL: Proceedings of the 16th Annual Workshop on the Structure and Constituency of Languages of the Americas*, edited by Meagan Louie and Alexis Black, 92–104. Vancouver: University of British Columbia.

———. 2012. "Relative Clauses, or Clause-sized Nominalizations? A Consideration of Blackfoot." *Working Papers of the Linguistics Circle of the University of Victoria* 21 (2): 1–15.

———. 2013. "A Participle Account of Blackfoot Relative Clauses." *The Canadian Journal of Linguistics* 58 (2): 217–38.

Johns, Alana. 1982. "A Unified Analysis of Relative Clauses and Questions in Rainy River Ojibwe." *Papers of the Thirteenth Algonquian Conference*, edited by William Cowan, 161–68. Ottawa: Carleton University.

Johnson, Meredith, Monica Macaulay, Bryan Rosen, and Rachel Wang. 2015. "A Survey of Menominee Word Order." In *Papers of the Forty-third Algonquian Conference 2011*, edited by Monica Macaulay and J. Randolph Valentine, 154–78. Albany: SUNY Press.

Jones, Nancy. 2013a. "Makoons giigoonyiked." In Jones et al., *Naadamaading*, 11–21..

———. 2013b. "Waawaashkeshiins." In Jones et al., *Naadamaading*, 23–37.

———. 2013c. "Migiziins omawidisaa' ookomisa'." In *Mino-doodaading: Dibaajimowinan ji-mino-ayaang*, 39–53. Minneapolis: Wiigwaas Press.

Jones, Nancy, Eugene Stillday, Rose Tainter, Anna Gibbs, Marlene Stately, Anton Treuer, Keller Paap, et al. 2013. *Naadamaading: Dibaajimowinan ji-nisidotaading*. Minneapolis: Wiigwaas Press.

Jones, William. 1919. *Ojibwe Texts*, vol. 7, part 2, edited by Truman Michelson. New York: American Ethnological Society.

Josselin de Jong, Jan Petrus Benjamin de. 1913. *Original Odžibwe-texts, with English Translation, Notes and Vocabulary*. Leipzig: B. G. Teubner.

Junker, Marie-Odile. 2004. "Focus, Obviation, and Word Order in East Cree." *Lingua* 114: 345–65.

Kaye, J. D., and G. L. Piggott. 1973. "On the Cyclical Nature of Ojibwa T-Palatalization." *Linguistic Inquiry* 4 (3): 345–62.

Kayne, Richard S. 1994. *The Antisymmetry of Syntax*. Cambridge MA: MIT Press.

Keenan, Edward. 1985. "Relative Clauses." In *Language Typology and Syntactic Description: Complex Constructions*, edited by Timothy Shopen, 141–70. Cambridge: Cambridge University Press.

Kegg, Maude. 1991. *Portage Lake: Memories of an Ojibwe Childhood*. Edited by John D. Nichols. Edmonton: University of Alberta Press.

Lees, James. 1979. "A Mini Grammar of Cree-Montagnais." *Montreal Working Papers in Linguistics* 12: 109–48.

LeSourd, Phil. 2001. "The Maliseet-Passamaquoddy Quantifier *Tan* 'How; Such': A Preliminary Report." Paper presented at the Society for the Study of the Indigenous Languages of the Americas annual meeting.

Lochbihler, Bethany, and Eric Mathieu. 2013. "Wh-agreement in Ojibwe Relative Clauses: Evidence for CP Structure." *The Canadian Journal of Linguistics* 58 (2): 293–318.

McBride, Elizabeth. 1987a. *The Horseback Riding Owl*. Edited by Charles Fiero, recorded at the SIL, Grand Forks, North Dakota.

———. 1987b. *Gii-agaashiinyiyaan*. Edited by Charles Fiero, recorded at the SIL, Grand Forks, North Dakota.

McNally, Michael. 2009. *Ojibwe Singers: Hymns, Grief, and a Native American Culture in Motion*. Minneapolis: University of Minnesota Press.

Michelson, Truman. 1935. "Phonetic Shifts in Algonquian Languages." *International Journal of American Linguistics* 8 (3/4): 132–71.

Mitchell, Sam. "Anangoowininiwag." *Oshkaabewis Native Journal* 4 no. 2 edited by John D. Nichols, (1997): 38–39. Bemidji: Bemidji State University.

Mithun, Marianne. 1989. "The Incipient Obsolescence of Polysynthesis: Cayuga in Ontario and Oklahoma." In Dorian, *Investigating Obsolescence*, 243–58.

———. 1999. *The Languages of Native North America*. Cambridge: Cambridge University Press.

Mosay, Archie. 1996. "Gaagiigidowin ji-gikinoo'amaageng." *Oshkaabewis Native Journal* 3 (2): 36–45.

Motapanyane, Virginia. 1998. "C/T Merge Locations for Focus." *Linguistica Atlantica* 20: 109–22.

Mühlbauer, Jeffrey. 2003. "Word-order and the Interpretation of Nominals in Plains Cree." Unpublished manuscript, University of British Columbia.

Nichols, John D. 1976. *Survey of Inland Dialects in Northwestern Ontario*. Unpublished report submitted to the Department of Indian Affairs and Northern Development, Ontario Region.

———. 1980. "Ojibwe Morphology." PhD dissertation, Harvard University.

———. 1988a. *Statement Made by the Indians: A Bilingual Petition of the Chippewas of Lake Superior*. Text series Number 1, Studies in the Interpretation of Canadian Native Languages and Cultures. London: University of Western Ontario.

———. 1988b. *An Ojibwe Text Anthology*. London, Ontario: Centre for the Research and Teaching of Canadian Native Languages, University of Western Ontario.

———. 2011. "The Ojibwe Language of Obaashiing (Ponemah, Minnesota)." Presented to the Forty-third Algonquian Conference, Ann Arbor, University of Michigan.

———. 2012. "Notes on Variation in Minnesota Ojibwa (Chippewa [CIW])." Unpublished report to the National Science Foundation.

Nichols, John D., and Catherine Price. 2002. *Native Languages: A Support Document for the Teaching of Language Patterns, Ojibwe and Cree*. Toronto: Ontario Ministry of Education.

Nichols, John D., and Earl Nyholm. 1995. *A Concise Dictionary of Minnesota Ojibwe*. Minneapolis: University of Minnesota Press.

Ningwance, Patricia. 1993. *Survival Ojibwe: Learning Conversational Ojibwe in Thirty Lessons*. Winnipeg: Mazinaate Press.

Oakgrove, Collins. 1997. "Wenji-nibwaakaad Nenabozho." *Oshkaabewis Native Journal* 4 (2):32–35. Bemidji MN: Bemidji State University.

Oxford, Will. 2008. "A Grammatical Study of Innu-aimun Particles." *Algonquian and Iroquoian Linguistics Memoir 20*. Winnipeg: Algonquian and Iroquoian Linguistics.

Pagotto, Louise. 1980. "On Complementizer Adjuncts in the Rapid Lake Dialect of Algonquin." In *Papers of the Eleventh Algonquian Conference*, edited by William Cowan, 231–46. Ottawa: Carleton University.

Payne, Thomas. 1997. *Describing Morphosyntax: A Guide for Field Linguists*. Cambridge: Cambridge University Press.

Petesky, David. 1982. "Paths and Categories." PhD dissertation, MIT.

Piggott, Glyne. 1978. "Algonquin and Other Ojibwa Dialects: A Preliminary Report." In *Papers of the Ninth Algonquian Conference*, edited by William Cowan, 160–87. Ottawa: Carleton University.

Proulx, Paul. 1980. "The Linguistic Evidence on Algonquian Prehistory." *Anthropological Linguistics* 22 (1): 1–21.

Radford, Andrew. 2004. *Minimalist Syntax: Exploring the Structure of English*. Cambridge: Cambridge University Press.

Reinhart, Tanya. 1982. *Pragmatics and Linguistics: An Analysis of Sentence Topics*. Bloomington: Indiana University Linguistics Club.

Rhodes, Richard A. 1978. "The Morphosyntax of the Central Ojibwa Verb." PhD dissertation, University of Michigan.

———. 1979. "Some Aspects of Ojibwa Discourse." In *Papers of the Tenth Algonquian Conference*, edited by William Cowan, 102–17. Ottawa: Carleton University.

———. 1982. "Algonquian Trade Languages." In *Papers of the Thirteenth Algonquian Conference*, edited by William Cowan, 1–10. Ottawa: Carleton University.

———. 1985. "The Consequential Future in Cree and Ojibwa." *International Journal of American Linguistics* 51 (4): 547–49.

———. 1990a. "Ojibwa Secondary Objects." In *Grammatical Relations: A Crosstheoretical Perspective*, edited by Katarzyna Dziwirek, Patrick Farrell, and Errapel Mejias-Bikandi, 401–14. Stanford: CSLI Publications.

———. 1990b. "Relative Root Complements in Ojibwa." Unpublished manuscript, University of California, Berkeley.

———. 1996. "Relative Clauses in Ottawa." Paper presented to the Twenty-eighth Algonquian Conference, Toronto, Ontario.

———. 2008. "Ojibwe in the Cree of Métchif." In *Papers in the Thirty-ninth Algonquian Conference*, edited by Karl S. Hele and Regna Darnell, 569–80. London: University of Western Ontario.

———. 2010a. "Ditransitive Constructions in Ojibwe." In *Studies in Ditransitive Constructions: A Comparative Handbook*, edited by Andrej Malchuko, Martin Haspelmath, and Bernard Comrie, 626–50. Berlin: Mouton de Gruyter.

———. 2010b. "Relative Root Complement: A Unique Grammatical Relation in Algonquian Syntax." In *Rara and Rarissima: Documenting the Fringes of Linguistic Diversity*, edited by Jan Wohlgemuth and Michael Cysouw, 305–24. Berlin: Mouton de Gruyter.

———. 2012. "Algonquian Trade Languages Revisited." In *Papers of the Fortieth Algonquian Conference*, edited by Karl Hele and J. R. Valentine, 358–69. Albany: SUNY Press.

Rhodes, Richard A., and Evelyn M. Todd. 1981. "Subarctic Algonquian Languages." In *Subarctic*, edited by June Helm, 52–66. Vol. 6 of *Handbook of North American Indians*, edited by William C. Sturtevant. Washington DC: Smithsonian Institution.

Richards, Norvin W. 2004. "The Syntax of the Conjunct and Independent Orders in Wampanoag." *International Journal of American Linguistics* 70 (4): 327–68.

Ritter, Elizabeth, and Martina Wiltschko. 2009. "Varieties of INFL: Tense, Location, and Person." In *Alternatives to Cartography*, edited by Jeroen van Craenenbroeck, 153–202. Berlin: Mouton de Gruyter.

Ritzenthaler, Robert. 1978. "Southwestern Chippewa." In *Northeast*, edited by Bruce G. Trigger, 743–59. Vol. 15 of *Handbook of North American Indians*, edited by William C. Sturtevant. Washington DC: Smithsonian Institution.

Rizzi, Luigi. 1997. "The Fine Structure of the Left Periphery." In *Elements of Grammar*, edited by L. Haegeman, 281–337. Dordrecht: Kluwer.

Rochment, Michael. 1978. "A Theory of Stylistic Rules in English." PhD dissertation, University of Massachusetts.

———. 1986. *Focus in Generative Grammar*. Amsterdam: John Benjamins.

Rogers, Benny. 2013. "Jiisikewinini miinawaa binesiiwag." In *Dibaajimowinan: Anishinaabe Stories of Culture and Respect*, edited by H. James St. Arnold and Wesley Ballinger, 126–27. Odanah WI: Great Lakes Indian Fish and Wildlife Commission Press.

Rogers, Jean. 1978. "Differential Focusing in Ojibwa Conjunct Verbs: On Circumstance, Participants, or Events." *International Journal of American Linguistics* 44: 167–79.

Sapir, Edward. 1913. "Wiyot and Yurok, Algonkin Languages of California." *American Anthropologist* 15: 617–46.

———. 1921. *Language: An Introduction to the Study of Speech*. New York: Harcourt, Brace.

Schoolcraft, Henry. 1851. *Historical and Statistical Information respecting the History, Condition and Prospects of the Indian Tribes of the United States*, vol. 6. Washington DC: Historical American Indian Press.

Shields, Rebecca. 2004. "Word Order and Discourse in Menominee." In *Proceedings of the Thirty-fifth Algonquian Conference*, edited by H. C. Wolfart, 373–88.

Smallwood, Larry. 2013a. "Gidinwewininaan miinawaa gidizhitwaawininaan." In *Dibaajimowinan: Anishinaabe Stories of Culture and Respect*, edited by H. James St. Arnold and Wesley Ballinger, 13–15. Odanah WI: Great Lakes Indian Fish and Wildlife Commission Press.

———. 2013b. "Mayagi-manidoonsag." In *Dibaajimowinan: Anishinaabe Stories of Culture and Respect*, edited by H. James St. Arnold and Wesley Ballinger, 111–13. Odanah WI: Great Lakes Indian Fish and Wildlife Commission Press.

———. 2013c. "Nimanidookewininaanan." *Dibaajimowinan: Anishinaabe Stories of Culture and Respect*, edited by H. James St. Arnold and Wesley Ballinger, 116–17. Odanah WI: Great Lakes Indian Fish and Wildlife Commission Press.

Staples, Lee, and Chato Gonzalez. 2015. *Aanjikiing: Changing Worlds, an Anishinaabe Traditional Funeral*. Winnepeg: Algonquian and Iroquoian Linguistics.

Starks, Donna. 1992. "Aspects of Woods Cree Syntax." PhD dissertation, University of Manitoba.

Stillday, Eugene. 2013a. "Bagida'wewin." In Jones et al., *Naadamaading*, 53–65.

———. 2013b. "Andabineshiinyiwewag." In *Mino-doodaading: Dibaajimowinan ji-mino-ayaang*, 55–65. Minneapolis: Wiigwaas Press.

———. 2014. "Gichi-bikwaakwad." In *Wiijikiiwending*, 58–63. Minneapolis: Wiigwaas Press.

Sullivan, Michael. 2016. "Making Statements in Ojibwe: A Survey of Word Order in Spontaneous Sentences." In *Papers of the Forty-fourth Algonquian Conference*, edited by Monica Macaulay, Margaret Noodin, and J. Randolph Valentine, 329–47. Albany: SUNY Press.

Swart, Henriëtte de, and Helen de Hoop. 1995. "Topic and Focus." *Glot International* 1 (7): 3–7.

Tainter, Rose. 2013a. "Gii-mawinzowaad Makoons miinawaa Nigigoons." In Jones et al., *Naadamaading*, 39–51.

———. 2013b. "Gii-wewebanaabiiwaad Nigigoons miinawaa Makoons." In Jones et al., *Naadamaading*, 66–81.

Teeter, Karl. 1967. "Genetic Classification in Algonquian." In *Proceedings of the First Algonquian Conference*, 1–6. National Museum of Canada: Contributions to Anthropology Series.

Todd, Evelyn. 1970. *A Grammar of the Ojibwa Language*. Ann Arbor MI: University Microfilms, Inc.

Tomlin, Russ, and Richard Rhodes. 1979. "An Introduction to Information Distribution in Ojibwa." In *Papers from the Fifteenth Regional Meeting of the Chicago Linguistic Society: April 19–20, 1979*, edited by Paul R. Clyne, 307–21.

Travis, Lisa. 1984. "Parameters and Effects of Word Order Variation." PhD dissertation, MIT.

Treuer, Anton. 2010. *Ojibwe in Minnesota*. St. Paul: Minnesota Historical Society Press.

Treuer, Anton, and Keller Paap. 2009. *Aaniin Ekidong: Ojibwe Vocabulary Project*. St. Paul: Minnesota Humanities Center.

Valentine, J. Randolph. 1994. "Ojibwe Dialect Relationships." PhD dissertation, University of Texas-Austin.

———. 1996. "Phonological Parameters of Ojibwe Dialect Variation." In *Papers of the Twenty-seventh Algonquian Conference*, edited by David H. Pentland, 287–323. Winnipeg: University of Manitoba.

———. 2001. *Nishnaabemwin Reference Grammar*. Toronto: University of Toronto Press.

———. 2002. "Variation in Body-part Verbs in Ojibwe Dialects." *International Journal of American Linguistics* 68 (1): 81–119.

Voorhis, Paul. 1974. *Introduction to the Kickapoo Language*. Bloomington: Indiana University.

Vries, Mark de. 2002. "The Syntax of Relativization." PhD dissertation, Landelijke Onderzoekschool Taalwetenschap, Utrecht.

Whipple, Dorothy. 2015. *Chi-mewinzha: Ojibwe Stories from Leech Lake*. Edited by Wendy Genuisz and Brendan Fairbanks. Minneapolis: University of Minnesota Press.

Wilson, Edward. 1870. *The Ojebway Language: A Manual for Missionaries and Others Employed among the Ojebway Indians*. Toronto: Roswell & Hutchison.

Wolfart, Hans Christoph. 1973. *Plains Cree: A Grammatical Study*. Philadelphia: American Philosophical Society.

Wolvengrey, Arok. 2006. "ēkosi wī-ispayin. (kwayāciho!): Prospective Aspect in the Western Dialects of Cree." *International Journal of American Linguistics* 73 (3): 397–407.

INDEX

The letter t appended to a page locator indicates table.

Aadizookaanan, 128t30, 129–30, 131t31, 134

Aazhoomog MN: animacy status of nouns at, 212; articulation of glides /y/ and /w/ at, 195; disjunctive personal pronouns at, 170; final nasals at, 178, 180; inanimate plural in conjunct at, 158; initial change at, 123; initial /g/ at, 186; initial nasals at, 43, 173; *ji-/da-* complementizer at, 155; lack of identification with Mille Lacs, 36; lexical variants at, 206; participial forms at, 236; preterit peripheral suffixes at, 157; syncope at, 204; /t/ epenthesis at, 199; vocative forms at, 197, 198; vowel height at, 190. *See also* Mille Lacs reservation MN

Aissen, Judith, 136, 335n53

Albany River Ojibwe, 34

Alberta, 31

Algic languages, 28, 329n13

Algonquian languages: aorist prefix in, 45, 109, 110, 286, 290, 316, 333n34; core vs. relative root arguments in, 22, 264, 269; dependent verbs in, 99; determination of clause type in, 282–83; dialectology of, 28–29; first-language acquisition of, 323; independent vs. conjunct verbs in, 68, 274–75; initial change in, 108–10, 256, 270, 315–17, 333n32; "Lake Eastern" grouping, 320, 322; morphological leveling in, 140; nonconfigurationality of, 55, 124; palatalization in, 332n12; participles in, 17, 317–19, 320, 333n36; and pronominal argument hypothesis, 56–58, 124; proximate/obviative distinction in, 10, 65, 104–7; relative clauses in, 46, 49–52, 231, 239, 303; tense interpretation of embedded clauses in, 277; /t/ epenthesis in, 198; topicality hierarchy in, 102–7; transcription systems for, 76; unanalyzable stems from, 77; uninterpretable features in, 63–64; verb types in, 9, 26; "where" questions in, 339n2; word order in, 124–25, 130, 334n45. *See also individual languages*

Algonquin: age-graded variation in, 151; as dialect of Ojibwe, 38, 72; *giji-* complementizer in, 152; inanimate plural in conjunct in, 160–61; labialization and rounding in, 188; lexical variants in, 207; liquids in, 331n4; Old, 30; participial forms in, 318; preterit peripheral suffix in, 156; voicing and strength distinction in, 76

Amos, George, 33

Andersen, Roger, 59

Andrews, Avery, 6, 25

Arapahoan, 28, 29

archival data: audio recordings, 149–50, 322; on demonstrative pronouns, 168, 254, 329–30n14; on final nasals, 176; handwritten stories, 149, 186,

archival data (*continued*)
188, 199–200, 336n12; on initial /g/, 185–86; on initial nasals, 173; on iterative mode, 268; on *ji-/da-* complementizer, 154; on labialization, 188; on obviative plural, 164; on participial forms, 227, 231–32, 234, 236; post-treaty petitions, 329–30n14; on /t/ epenthesis, 200, 255–56. *See also* fieldwork methods

Bad River reservation WI, 5, 35
Baker, Mark C., 51, 56–57, 59–60, 64
Bantu languages, 49, 82, 287
Baraga, Frederik: on demonstratives, 168; on final nasal in negation suffix *-sii(n)*, 175; findings on variation, 42, 43; influence of Odawa in work of, 329–30n14; on initial change, 109, 111, 121, 216, 256, 281; on initial /g/, 187; on initial /n/, 174; on labialized stops, 187; on "Michigan Chippewa," 33; missionary motivation in work of, 335n2; on neutralization of inanimate plural in conjunct, 158; on obviative forms, 333n30; and other dialect studies, 38; on participial forms, 229–30, 314; on preterit peripheral suffixes, 156; on relative clauses, 46; on vowel height, 189, 190t35
Bențea, Anamaria, 7, 283, 339–40n7
Berens River Ojibwe, 34, 162, 340n9. *See also* Saulteaux
Bianchi, Valentina, 339n7
Big Trout Lake First Nation ON, 30
Blackfoot: as Algonquian language, 28, 29; initial change in, 54; participial forms in, 17, 50; relative clauses in, 49, 50, 52, 330n25
Bloomfield, Leonard: on animacy status of nouns, 73; on "Chippewa" label, 33; classification of verbs, 81, 95; on initial change, 109, 315; reconstruction of Proto-Algonquian, 28, 314, 315, 319, 320–21, 340n2; and transcription practices, 76
Bois Forte reservation MN: animacy status of nouns at, 43, 210, 211; changed conjunct forms at, 222; "correction" data from, 251; establishment and ties to other communities, 35, 244; *gaa-* participles at, 241; influence of Saulteaux at, 243; initial change at, 41, 217, 218; initial /n/ at, 42, 172, 173; lexical variants at, 205–6; number under obviation at, 164; TA *-aw* stem contraction at, 214. *See also* Lake Vermilion MN; Nett Lake reservation MN
Border Lakes Ojibwe: absence of core vs. relative root distinction in, 25; animacy status of nouns at, 147, 210, 211, 212; demonstrative pronouns in, 168, 336n7; in dialect studies, 41; initial change at, 217, 218; initial /g/ in, 186; initial /n/ in, 173, 174; *ji-* complementizer in, 152; labialized stops in, 189; lexical variants in, 204, 206, 208; number under obviation in, 162, 340n9; relative clause formation in, 46–48; and Saulteaux, 3, 31, 243; in southern dialect grouping, 38; and speech of other communities, 244, 251; and SW Ojibwe, 40, 140–41; TA *-aw* stem contraction at, 215; as "transitional area," 2, 39; vowel height in, 191
Bowern, Claire, 139, 142, 257, 335n2
Boy Lake MN, 168, 171, 174, 217, 245
Brittain, Julie: C checks VCJ hypothesis, 62, 68, 125, 270, 273, 274–75, 277, 289; on dialectal differences, 151; on

e- and *gaa*- prefixes, 316–17, 333n35; on initial change, 54, 110, 280; and mirror principle, 64; on palatalization, 332n12; and pronominal hypothesis argument, 57, 306; and proximate/obviative distinction, 67

Bruening, Benjamin: cyclic movement analysis of Passamaquoddy, 285; on demonstratives, 45, 340n1; on ditransitive verbs, 82; feature-checking approach, 270; on initial change, 54, 108; on nonconfigurationality, 55; on palatalization, 332n12; on proximate/obviative distinction, 63, 65–66, 67, 104, 106, 333n30

Campana, Mark, 54, 68
Campbell, Lyle, 310, 312–13
Cape Croker ON, 32
Cat Lake ON, 337n22
Cayuga, 310
Central Southern Ojibwe. *See* Southwestern (SW) Ojibwe
Chambers, J. K., 142, 143, 245, 256
Cheyenne, 28, 29, 316, 320, 333n34
Chippewa, 31–34, 38, 41, 204. *See also* Southwestern (SW) Ojibwe
Chomsky, Noam, 52–53, 62, 69, 282–83, 285
Chosa, Joe, 329n3
Cook, Clare, 99
Costa, David, 99, 110, 315–16, 333nn31–32, 340n2
Cree: aorist prefix in, 316, 333n34; contact with Ojibwe, 37–38, 311, 330n15; *ga*- preverb in, 199; independent vs. conjunct order in, 99; initial change in, 110; participial forms in, 318, 319, 320, 322; relative clause formation in, 49; and Saulteaux, 243; VTA inflection in, 216; word order in, 125, 130, 136

Cree-Montagnais-Naskapi (CMN): bimorphemic *kâ* in, 317; and Brittain's C checks VCJ hypothesis, 68, 274; initial change in, 110; palatalization in, 332n12; Proto-Algonquian as ancestor of, 28; relative clause formation in, 49. *See also* Cree
Crystal, David, 143–44
Curve Lake ON, 207

Dahlstrom, Amy, 125, 131, 132–33, 135, 136
DeBungie, Rosemarie, 254
dialectology, 28, 141–44, 243, 249
Dorian, Nancy, 311
Dressler, Wolfgang, 311

East Cree, 125, 130, 335n50. *See also* Cree
Eastern Algonquian, 315
Eastern Ojibwe, 30, 32, 38
East Lake MN, 36, 236
Emo ON, 39
English: conditional clauses in, 11, 68; as contact language in fieldwork, 131, 145, 148; finiteness in, 277; function of *that* in, 7, 19, 262, 329n5; perceived higher status of, 4; split-CP approach to, 287, 289; use in Ojibwe communities, 5, 313

Fairbanks, Brendan, 97–98, 121–24, 136, 300, 301, 336n3
feature-checking theory, 61–62, 67
fieldwork methods: back-translation and grammaticality judgments, 249–53, 334n42, 338n23, 338n28; "direct" and "indirect" elicitation, 145–46; and free variation, 256; and language obsolescence, 142–43,

fieldwork methods (*continued*) 150–51, 312, 313; naturalistic data collection, 142; and notion of linguistic "purity," 140, 142; picture elicitation tasks, 126, 128, 131, 147, 148; speaker fluency and, 139, 150; survey questionnaire, 144–49. *See also* archival data

Fiero, Charles, 337nn21–22

focus, 132–34

Fond du Lac reservation MN, 3, 5, 35

Fort William First Nation ON, 314

Fox: obviative plural in, 314; participial forms in, 49, 318–19, 320, 322; vowel length distinctions in, 332n15; word order in, 125, 132, 133

Fox-Kickapoo, 316, 333n34, 340n4

Frantz, Donald, 50

gaa- relativizing prefix: co-occurring with tense markers, 218–19, 224, 252; and definiteness, 47; in free variation with southern forms, 248–49; and IC form of "potential" *gii-$_2$*, 220, 239, 240; northern distribution, 27, 223, 239–40, 241–42, 269–70, 306; and place-name prefix *gaa-*, 110, 241; as "reanalyzed *kâ*," 316–17, 333n35; similarity to IC form of past tense *gii-*, 40, 47, 218–20, 252–53; southern speakers' back-translations of, 252–53; in syntax of relative clauses, 49, 286, 290, 292

Geary, James, 332n11

Gii-paashkijiisijigeyaan, 128t30, 129, 131t31

Goddard, Ives: on Central Algonquian languages, 29; on classification of native languages, 28; on data tampering, 334n45; on decline of native languages, 4; on "Miami-Illinois," 340n3; on noun gender in Ojibwe, 73; on oblique arguments, 264; on Ojibweyan language family, 29–30; on participial forms in Fox, 318; on participle, 26, 49, 99; on work of Bloomfield, 340n2

Golden Lake ON, 32

Grand Portage reservation MN, 35, 314

Greenberg, Joseph, 329n12

Gundel, Jeannette, 335n49, 335n52

Hale, Kenneth, 55

Hill, Jane, 311

Hockett, Charles, 102, 319, 320

Hoenigswald, Henry, 311

Inger MN: animacy status of nouns at, 212–13; "correction" and back-translation data from, 251, 252–53; demonstrative pronouns at, 168, 248; divergence from other Leech Lake speech, 36, 245, 248; *gaa-* participles at, 241, 338n27; inanimate plural in conjunct at, 158, 159; initial change at, 41, 217; initial /g/ at, 186; initial nasals at, 171, 175–76; lexical variants at, 207. *See also* Leech Lake reservation MN

initial change (IC), 108–24, 216–20; in Algonquian languages, 108–10, 256, 270, 315–17, 322; and aorist prefix, 110, 286, 290, 292; association with focus, 279–81, 284, 289; in Border Lakes Ojibwe, 47; and completive aspect, 121–24, 272, 281; and conjunct verbs, 99, 279, 283, 284; and *daN-* relative root, 267; as dialectal marker, 41–42, 48, 217–18, 269–70; elicitation of forms showing, 146;

functioning as complementizer, 19, 25; and indefiniteness, 47, 48; and language obsolescence, 312; and participle formation, 45, 112–21, 201–2, 210; on specific vowels, 11t2, 333n31, 337n20; and use of *gaa*- complementizer, 218–20, 239–42, 290, 292; and *wh*-agreement, 52–54, 111–12, 267, 279–82, 283, 286, 299. *See also* Ojibwe phonology

Innu people, 73
Isle MN, 36
Italian, 282

Jancewicz, Bill, 333n37
Jelinek, Eloise, 56–57, 124
Johansson, Sara, 17, 49–52, 330n25
Johns, Alana, 46–48, 330n24
Johnson, Meredith, 132, 134, 136, 137
Jones, Nancy, 337n20
Jones, William, 164, 173, 256
Josselin de Jong, Jan Petrus Benjamin de, 168, 254, 255, 256
Junker, Marie-Odile, 125, 130, 335n50

Kansas, 310
Kaye, J. D., 322, 334n40
Kayne, Richard S., 292
Keenan, Edward, 6
Kegg, Maude, 195
Kingfisher Lake ON, 168

Labov, William, 142
Labrador, 73
Lac Courte Oreilles reservation WI: animacy status of nouns at, 212; articulation of glides /y/ and /w/ at, 193, 194, 336n11; demonstrative pronouns at, 168; establishment and settlement, 35, 244; immersion school in, 5; initial change at, 109; initial /g/ at, 186; initial nasals at, 171, 173; interaction with other communities, 3; *ji-/da*- complementizer at, 153; labialized stops in, 188; lexical variants in, 204, 206; participial forms at, 236, 338–39n32; preterit peripheral suffixes at, 156; /t/ epenthesis at, 199–200, 201, 255–56; vowel height at, 40, 189, 190, 191

Lac du Flambeau reservation WI: animacy status of nouns at, 210; articulation of glides /y/ and /w/ at, 193; attitudes to "Chippewa" at, 33; demonstrative pronouns at, 168; establishment, 35; initial change at, 109; initial nasals at, 171, 173; interaction with other communities, 3; participial forms at, 236; vowel height at, 40, 189

Lac La Croix First Nation ON: Bois Forte band and, 41; final nasals at, 177, 178; *gaa*- participles at, 241; inanimate plural in conjunct at, 158; initial nasals at, 171; as part of Border Lakes region, 2, 141; and Red Lake Ojibwe, 34; ties to Lake Vermilion, 244

Lac Seul Ojibwe, 34
Lake Lena MN. *See* Aazhoomog MN
Lake of the Woods Ojibwe, 34
Lake Vermilion MN: animacy status of nouns at, 210, 211; initial change at, 217; initial /g/ at, 186; initial /n/ at, 171; number under obviation at, 164, 165; participial forms at, 252; TA -*aw* stem contraction at, 214; ties to Lac La Croix First Nation, 244. *See also* Bois Forte reservation MN; Nett Lake reservation MN

358 Index

Leech Lake reservation MN: agreement suffixes used in, 1; animacy status of nouns at, 43, 147, 209, 211, 212; articulation of glides /y/ and /w/ at, 194, 195; changed conjunct forms at, 222; demonstrative pronouns at, 168; dialectal variation within, 36; establishment and settlement, 35, 243, 249; final nasal in negation suffix *-sii(n)* at, 180; immersion school in, 5; initial change at, 41, 217, 218, 248; initial /n/ at, 172, 173; interaction with other communities, 3; *ji-* complementizer in, 152; lexical variants in, 205, 206, 207–8, 337n15; neutralization of inanimate plural in conjunct at, 158; participial forms at, 223, 225, 235, 239, 241, 251; preterit peripheral suffixes at, 157; TA *-aw* stem contraction at, 214, 215; as transitional area, 245–49; vocative forms at, 197; vowel height at, 191. *See also* Inger MN

Le Jeune, Paul, 73

linguistic variable, defined, 141

Lochbihler, Bethany, 52–54

Macaulay, Monica, 132, 134, 136, 137

Manitoba, 3, 31, 201

Manitoulin Island, 30

Maniwaki QC, 32

Mathieu, Eric, 52

Mayagi-manidoonsag, 128t30, 131t31

Mayan, 335n53

McBride, Elizabeth, 185

Menominee: as Algonquian language, 28; Bloomfield's classification of verbs in, 81; participial forms in, 319, 320; word order in, 132, 133, 136, 137

Menominee people, 35

Meskwaki. *See* Fox

Miami-Illinois, 28, 315, 320, 340n3

Michelson, Truman, 319, 334n45

Michif, 330n15

Michigan, 1, 34–35, 156, 160, 310

Micmac, 320

Mille Lacs reservation MN: animacy status of nouns at, 43, 212; articulation of glides /y/ and /w/ at, 194, 195; back-translation of *gaa-* participles at, 252; benefactive verbs at, 42; demonstrative pronouns at, 167, 168, 336n7; establishment, 35, 36; final nasals at, 175, 176, 183; and "General Ojibwe," 72; initial change at, 41, 109, 123, 216, 217; initial /n/ at, 171, 172, 173; interaction with other communities, 3, 243–44; *ji-/da-* complementizer in, 152, 155; labialized stops in, 188; lexical variants at, 207–8; neutralization of inanimate plural in conjunct at, 158; number of Ojibwe speakers in, 4; participial forms at, 223, 234–35, 236; preterit peripheral suffix at, 156; and southern Leech Lake communities, 245; syncope at, 201, 204; /t/ epenthesis at, 199, 255–56; vocative forms at, 197; vowel height at, 191. *See also* Aazhoomog MN

minimalist program, 60, 61

Minnesota: dialectal variation in, 1, 41; future tense marker *da-* in, 155; inanimate number neutralization in conjunct in, 160; language revitalization efforts in, 5; obviative plural in, 164; as part of SW Ojibwe range, 34–35; phonological features found in, 39, 76, 156; reservations in, 35; vowel height in, 189

mirror principle, 59–60, 64, 288

Mole Lake reservation WI, 35

Montagnais, 73
Mosay, Archie, 336n5
Mühlbauer, Jeffrey, 58, 125, 136, 306
Muntzel, Martha C., 310, 312–13
Mustache, James "Pipe," 336n11

Nahua, 310
Naskapi, 151, 316, 333–34n37. *See also* Cree-Montagnais-Naskapi (CMN)
Nett Lake reservation MN: animacy status of nouns at, 210, 211; Bois Forte band and, 41; demonstrative pronouns at, 168, 336n7; final nasals at, 178; initial change at, 217, 218; initial nasals at, 171, 175; interaction with other communities, 3; and Lake Vermilion speakers, 244; obviation at, 164, 165, 252; and Red Lake Ojibwe, 34; TA -*aw* stem contraction at, 215. *See also* Bois Forte reservation MN; Lake Vermilion MN
Nichols, John: on benefactive verbs, 337n18; classification of verbs, 81, 152, 239; on conjunct negative suffix, 236; on "core demonstratives," 167, 168, 336n7; dialect study of SW Ojibwe, 41–43; on "disjunctive personal pronouns," 170; on final nasals, 175, 182–83; on initial change, 109, 110–11, 122, 216–17, 218, 256, 315; on initial /n/, 171, 172, 173, 174; on labialized stops, 188; on lexical variation, 205, 207, 208; on nasal spreading, 184–85; on neutralization of inanimate plural in conjunct, 158; on obviative forms, 164, 333n30; and Ojibwe People's Dictionary, 148; and other dialect studies, 38, 144, 151; on participles, 99, 113, 114, 118, 222, 227, 234; on preterit mode, 100, 156; on preverbs, 88, 91, 93, 94; on relative clauses, 46; on restructuring of dependent noun stems, 166; on TA -*aw* stem contraction, 213; on /t/ epenthesis, 199; transcription system for Ojibwe, 76; use of term "root," 77; on vocative forms, 197; on work of Baraga, 329–30n14, 331n1, 335n2
Nigigoonsiminikaaning (Red Gut), 2, 141, 216, 241, 337n20
Niigaane school, 5
Ningwance, Patricia, 201
Nipissing ON, 156, 160
nonconfigurationality, 55–56
North Bay ON, 166
North Dakota, 31, 35
Northern Algonquin, 207
Northern East Cree, 49. *See also* Cree
Northern Ojibwe, 29, 207, 216, 318
north-south SW Ojibwe distinctions: in animacy status of nouns, 209–13; articulation of glides /y/ and /w/, 192; in benefactive verbs, 42; in demonstrative pronouns, 336n7; difficulties in drawing, 244; in future tense marker *da*-, 156; in inanimate plural in conjunct, 157–61, 272–73; initial change and, 41–42, 306; in lexical variation, 205–8; in lexicon, 43; in naming conventions, 42–43, 196–98; in number under obviation, 161–65; in participles, 1, 15, 25–27, 41–42, 114, 221–36, 244–45; and relative clause formation, 2, 269–70; and settlement patterns, 3; in stem-forming morphemes, 42; in syncope, 203; TA -*aw* stem contraction, 213–16
Northwestern Ojibwe, 160

Odawa: aorist prefix in, 45, 54, 109, 316; conjunct verb forms in, 41, 314; demonstrative pronouns in, 168,

Odawa (*continued*)
329n14; inanimate number neutralization in conjunct in, 160; initial vowels in, 39–40; labeled as "Chippewa," 31–32; lexical variants in, 207; linguistic variation within, 32–33; loss of final nasals in, 181; orthography of, 331n2; participial forms in, 318, 334n40; relative clauses in, 43–46; restructuring of dependent noun stems in, 166; as Southern Ojibwe language, 30, 38–39; syncope in, 201; vowel height in, 189

Odawa people, 3, 35

Ojibwe: as Algonquian language, 28, 314; decline of, 4–5, 36, 139–40, 311–13; *Ethnologue* classification of, 34; kinship terms, 107, 165–67; language change in, 2–3, 140, 150–51, 236–39, 245, 253–54; naming conventions, 42–43, 110, 196–98, 241; revitalization efforts, 2, 3–4, 5, 311, 313; second-language study of, 2, 3–4, 141, 164, 313–14; spelling and transcription of, 76, 85, 331n2; typological classification, 8, 25, 73, 77. *See also* Border Lakes Ojibwe; Ojibwe dialects; Ojibwe morphosyntax; Ojibwe people; Ojibwe phonology; Red Lake Ojibwe; Severn Ojibwe; Southwestern (SW) Ojibwe

Ojibwe dialects: indicators vs. markers in, 143; and isogloss distribution, 141–42, 243; major groupings, 29–31, 38–39; mutual intelligibility across, 249; obviation and number in, 105; preterit peripheral suffixes in, 156; in relation to Cree-Montaignais-Naskapi, 37–38; "relic" features in, 142, 170, 256; and speaker identification, 148–49, 203; studies of, 37–43; variation in pronouns across, 78

Ojibwe morphosyntax, 77–138

— complementizers: and conjunct order, 68, 270–71, 273, 306; *gaa-* prefix as, 47, 217–20, 239–42; initial change as, 19–20, 54, 272; *ji-/da-*, 152–56, 271, 278, 288–89, 293, 336n6; null, 261, 262, 270–71, 278, 284, 289, 293; in relative clause formation, 7, 25, 260–62

— demonstrative pronouns: across dialects and varieties, 167–70, 254, 336n7; in case-marking analysis, 67; in casual speech, 331n10, 336n7; and nonconfigurationality, 56; range of variation in, 78, 79t13, 209

— nouns: animacy status, 43, 73–74, 146–47, 209–13; derivational processes, 85–87; final nasals in plural suffixes of, 182–83; inflection, 17, 77–78, 79tt11–12; restructuring of dependent stems, 165–67

— other pronouns, 78–80: "clitic," 57; dubitative, 43, 172; indefinite, 131, 133; interrogative *wh-*, 19, 48, 111–12; null, 55, 59; personal, 63, 170

— participles: and changed conjunct verbs, 12–13, 41, 95, 99, 119–20, 222t37, 259–60; defined, 12, 45, 49, 112–13, 221–22; dialectal variation in, 25–27, 40, 221, 222–36, 307; differentiation from nominalizations, 50–52; and ditransitive verbs, 116, 231–32, 234, 250; and indefinite actor morphology, 233–35; initial change in, 45, 112–21, 201–2, 210, 283; and iterative suffix, 221, 298; as linguistic marker, 143, 149; morphology, 12–16, 41, 95; under negation, 236–39; in neologisms, 14, 15t5, 115–16; nominalized character, 12, 14, 16t6, 17, 99, 113, 222; palatalization and, 83–85, 223, 224, 233, 237, 239; plural, 113–14, 117, 236, 251, 269, 272; and plural inanimate agreement morphology, 158; and Proto-Algonquian forms, 320–22; in syntax of relative clauses, 18, 117, 120–21, 223, 257–58; in *wh*-constructions, 48, 301–2

— preverbs: and articulation of glides /y/ and /w/, 195; and dependent noun stems, 167; and derivations from particles, 331n9; *ga-*, 199; initial change in, 108–9, 239; and *ji-/da-* complementizers, 154; overview, 87–95; past tense marker *gii-*, 40, 47, 87–88, 218–20, 252–53; "potential" marker *gii-$_2$*, 88, 220, 239, 240; "timeless" marker *gii-*, 337n21

— relative clauses: core vs. relative root arguments in, 22–25, 89–90, 263–69, 270, 295–97, 306; cyclic head movement analysis of, 283–84, 285–87, 288; discontinuous, 21; externally vs. internally headed, 21–22, 263, 303–6, 310; headless, 20–21; and language loss, 310–11; locative, 266–67, 296–97; manner, 264–66, 299; multiple, 262–63; and mutual intelligibility, 37; northern vs. southern, 27, 223, 239–40, 241–42, 269–70; plural inanimate agreement morphology and, 158–59, 160; postnominal vs. prenominal, 20, 262, 304–6; preverbs and, 89–91; pronominal vs. complementizer, 7, 19–20, 260–62; role of participles in, 17–20, 117, 120, 223, 269; temporal, 268, 297–98; types of, 45–46; and *wh*-agreement, 52–54, 291

— verbs: -*aadage*/-*aadagaa*, 208; benefactive, 42, 337n18; body-part-incorporating, 42, 205–7, 331n5; ditransitive, 81–82, 116; four aspectual modes of, 99–102; four types of, 9, 81; initial change and, 108–11, 121–24; loss of final /n/ and, 181–82; medials in, 77; morphology, 8–9, 80–82; *ngwaam(i)*, 207–8; orders of inflection, 10–12, 95–99, 270, 274–75, 287, 314; preterit peripheral suffixes, 156–57; proximate/obviative distinction in, 10; in split-CP structure, 289

— word order: and changed conjunct/participle distinction, 120, 334n42; data for determining, 126–30; and obviation, 105; in relative clauses, 294–301, 303–6, 304, 310; and split-CP hypothesis, 130–38, 276–94, 307; in *wh*-questions, 301–3. See also *gaa-* relativizing prefix

Ojibwe people: bilingualism, 311, 313; forced surrender of children, 5, 35–36; migration history, 2; self-identification as Anishinaabe, 32; settlement in reservations, 35, 243

Ojibwe People's Dictionary (OPD): on articulation of glides /y/ and /w/, 194; on body-part-incorporating suffix -*e*, 337n15; fieldwork for, 37, 144, 148; on nasals, 333n29; on *ngwaam(i)* verbs, 208; on participial forms, 334n39

Ojibwe phonology, 170–204; final nasal in negation suffix -*sii(n)*, 174–80; glides /y/ and /w/, 192–96; initial /g/, 185–87, 336n8; initial /n/, 171–74; inventory of vowels and consonants, 74–77; labialization and rounding, 187–89; loss of final /n/, 180–84;

Ojibwe phonology (*continued*)
nasal spreading, 184–85; prosody, 170; syncope, 201–4; TA -*aw* stem contraction, 213–16, 251, 255, 326–28; /t/ epenthesis, 198–201, 336n13; vowel height, 189–91. *See also* initial change (IC); palatalization

Oji-Cree, 311. *See also* Severn Ojibwe

Oklahoma, 310

Onigum MN: animacy status of nouns at, 147; aorist prefix at, 109; demonstrative pronouns at, 168, 248; *gaa-* participles at, 241; initial change at, 217; initial nasals at, 171, 173–74; participial forms at, 236, 248–49, 257; as part of Leech Lake reservation, 36, 245

Ontario (ON): Algonquin speakers in, 318; archival data from, 255; Cayuga speakers in, 310; dialects of Ojibwe in, 34; obviative forms in, 162, 337–38n22; Ojibwe as trade language in, 35; preterit peripheral suffixes in, 156; in voicing and strength distinctions, 76

Osnaburgh ON, 156

Ottawa. *See* Odawa

Paap, Keller, 4–5

palatalization: in Algonquian languages, 332n12; in animate plural participles, 113, 223, 291; in ForceP, 284, 291t42, 298; in inverse participles, 233; and iterative suffix, 221, 298; in *ji-/da-* complementizer, 155; in negative participles, 237; in obviative participles, 13t3, 83–84, 115, 223–24, 239, 291; of third-person suffix /d/, 286. *See also* Ojibwe phonology

Passamaquoddy: demonstrative pronouns in, 45; ditransitive verbs in, 82; obviative forms in, 314, 319, 333n30, 340n1; palatalization in, 332n12; participial forms in, 319; word order in, 54, 125, 285

Petesky, David, 274

phase theory, 285

Pickle Lake ON, 337n22

Piggott, Glyne L., 74, 322, 334n40

Plains Cree, 49, 99, 110, 125, 170. *See also* Cree

Plains Ojibwe. *See* Saulteaux

Ponemah MN: animacy status of nouns at, 210, 211, 212; articulation of glides /y/ and /w/ at, 194, 195; benefactive verbs at, 42; characteristics of speakers from, 3, 4, 36, 244, 245, 250, 251; demonstrative pronouns at, 168, 169, 254, 336n7; dependent noun stems at, 166; final nasals at, 175, 179–80, 183; *gaa-* participles at, 241, 254–55; initial change at, 41, 217, 218; initial /g/ at, 187; initial /n/ at, 171–72, 173, 333n29; labialized stops at, 188–89; lexical variants in, 204, 205, 206, 207, 208; nasal spreading at, 184–85; negative suffixes at, 257; neutralization of inanimate plural in conjunct at, 158; TA -*aw* stem contraction at, 214, 215, 255; /t/ epenthesis at, 199; vocative forms at, 198; vowel height at, 191. *See also* Red Lake reservation MN

Potawatomi: absence of obviative plural in, 314; as Algonquian language, 28; aorist prefix in, 316, 333n34; initial change in, 315, 333n32; north-south variation within, 310; in Ojibweyan family, 30; participial forms in, 318, 320

Potawatomi people, 3, 31, 35

pronominal argument hypothesis (PAH), 56–59, 62, 306, 323
Proto-Algic, 329n13
Proto-Algonquian (PA): initial change in, 315; and Ojibwe *ga-* preverb, 199; participles in, 319–22; proposed as ancestor of Yurok and Wiyot, 329n13; reconstruction of, 28, 314; vowels in, 85, 333n31
Proto-Eastern Algonquian, 28
Proulx, Paul, 320, 322

Quebec (QC), 73, 156, 318

Radford, Andrew, 278
Rainy River Ojibwe, 34. *See also* Border Lakes Ojibwe
Rapid Lake QC, 331n4
Redby MN, 194, 204, 254, 336n8
Red Cliff reservation WI, 5, 35
Red Lake Ojibwe: animacy status of nouns in, 43; articulation of glides /y/ and /w/ in, 194; changed conjunct forms in, 222; closest subdialects, 34; inclusion in Valentine's study, 38; initial change in, 41, 217; initial /n/ in, 172, 173; *ji-* complementizer in, 152; preterit peripheral suffixes in, 156, 157; restructuring of dependent noun stems in, 166; and Saulteaux, 31, 36–37, 243; stem-forming morphemes in, 42; /t/ epenthesis in, 256
Red Lake reservation MN, 3, 4, 35
Rhodes, Richard A.: on adjunct vs. term relative clauses, 25, 303; on age-graded variation, 151; on Baraga's grammar of Southwestern Ojibwe, 329–30n14; on "Chippewa" vs. "Ojibwe," 33; classification of relative clauses, 45–46; on conjunct verbs, 97–98; on dialects of Ojibwe, 37–38, 151; on *ga-* preverb, 199; on *ji-* complementizer, 152; on linguistic designations, 31; on noun phrases, 126; on Odawa, 30, 43–46, 99, 126; on participles, 120–21; on "partitive constructions," 330n21
Ritter, Elizabeth, 52
Ritzenthaler, Robert, 34–35
Rizzi, Luigi, 276, 277, 283, 339n5. *See also* split-CP hypothesis
Rocky Boy MT, 31, 330n15
Rogers, Jean, 110–11, 278
Romanian, 262, 287, 339–40n7
Rosen, Bryan, 132, 134, 136, 137
Round Lake WI, 168, 189

Sandy Lake MN, 36
Sapir, Edward, 329n13
Sarnia ON, 32
Saskatchewan, 31, 34
Sauk-Fox-Kickapoo, 28, 340n4. *See also* Fox
Saulteaux: contact with Ojibwe, 2, 31, 36–37, 244; in dialect classifications, 30, 38–39; geographic distribution, 3, 31; neutralization of inanimate plural in conjunct in, 160; obviative plural in, 162; self-designated term for, 32; treatment of /wa/ as vowel, 201
Schoolcraft, Henry, 33, 168, 256, 297, 298t43
Severn Ojibwe: final nasals in, 175; and "General Ojibwe," 72; inanimate plural in conjunct in, 160; initial /n/ in, 174; lexical variants in, 207; in northern dialectal grouping, 38; participial forms, 40, 318, 322; vowel height in, 189
Shawnee, 28, 316, 320

Smallwood, Larry "Amik," 127–30
Southern Ojibwe, 29–30
Southwestern (sw) Ojibwe: age-graded variation within, 153, 166, 172, 253–56; aligned with other southern Ojibwe dialects, 39; articulation of glides /y/ and /w/ in, 193; dialect studies of, 37–43; ditransitive verbs in, 82; *Ethnologue* classification of, 34; final nasals in, 175, 180, 183; *gaa-* prefix in, 27, 40, 47, 49, 110, 220; geographical range, 34–35; initial change in, 216–17, 256; initial /n/ in, 174; labialized stops in, 187–89; lexical variation in, 205t36, 207; nongeographic variation in, 151, 165, 167, 172, 183; noun phrase structure, 44–45; and Odawa, 30, 38, 39–40, 336n10; other terms for, 1; participial forms, 12, 25–27, 222–24, 242, 246–47t40; rarity of aorist prefix in, 45, 109; and religious practices, 3; subdialect groupings, 3; syncope in, 201–4; /t/ epenthesis in, 198; as trade language, 35; voicing and strength contrasts in, 76; word order in, 133. *See also* north-south sw Ojibwe distinctions; *and individual locales and varieties*
split-CP hypothesis: applied to Ojibwe, 283–84, 288–303; approach to clause structure, 69–70, 276–77, 288, 307; and cyclic movement analysis, 285–87; and locus of *wh-*agreement, 54, 279–82, 290–91; and movement to left periphery, 58–59; and particle *mii*, 300–301; and syntactic environments of conjunct, 125, 277–79
Staples, Lee, 330n22
St. Croix reservation WI: demonstrative pronouns at, 168; establishment and settlement, 35, 244; initial change at, 109; initial nasal at, 173; interactions with other communities, 3; *ji-/da-* complementizer at, 154; linguistic variation within, 36; participial forms at, 236
St. Germaine, Thomas Leo, 33–34
Stillday, Eugene, 197–98, 254
Sullivan, Michael, 126, 127, 128, 131–32, 134, 137

Tainter, Rose "Zhaangweshiban," 254, 338n32
Todd, Evelyn M., 30, 31, 33, 37–38, 151
Tomlin, Russ, 126, 127
topic, 134–38
Travis, Lisa, 278
Treuer, Anton, 4–5
Trudgill, Peter, 142, 143, 245, 256
Turtle Mountain ND, 31, 330n15

Upper Peninsula MI, 1, 34

Valentine, J. Randolph: on age-graded variation, 151; on Algonquian comparative linguistics, 314, 332n18; on Algonquin, 331n4; on animacy status in nouns, 73; on articulation of glides /y/ and /w/, 193, 195; on Border Lakes region, 2, 38, 39, 204; on "Chippewa," 33, 204; classification of verbs, 81; on decline of Ojibwe, 311; on demonstrative pronouns, 168; on dialectal variation in Ojibwe, 1, 30, 36–41, 108, 141, 170, 243; on direct elicitation of forms, 146; on final nasals, 174–75, 180, 181; on "General Ojibwe," 72; on *giji-* complementizer, 152; on influence of Odawa on Ojibwe, 329–30n14; on initial change, 108, 109; on initial /g/, 185;

Index   365

on initial /n/, 174, 330n18; on iterative suffix, 220, 221; on labialized stops, 188, 189; on language prestige, 31, 310; on Leech Lake, 245; on lexical variation, 204, 205, 206, 207; on *mii* particle, 340n8; on neutralization of inanimate plural in conjunct, 157–58, 160; on obviation, 105, 106; on Ojibwe phonemic inventory, 74, 76; on "paralinguistic/exclamatory forms," 331n2; on participles, 12, 40, 115, 257–58, 317–18, 332n14; on perception of dialectal difference, 143; on peripheral suffixes, 78; on preterit dubitative mode, 101; on relative clause formation, 22, 262, 303; on relative root complements, 23; on restructuring of dependent noun stems, 166; on "rusty speakers," 139; on Saulteaux, 243; on syncope, 201, 202; on TA -*aw* stem contraction, 213, 216; on topicality hierarchy, 102; on vowel height, 189
Viereck, Wolfgang, 142

Waadookodaading Ojibwe Language Immersion School, 5, 338n32
Walpole Island ON, 30, 32
Western Algonquin, 156, 166. *See also* Algonquin
Western Naskapi, 49, 68, 110, 274, 306, 333n35. *See also* Cree-Montagnais-Naskapi (CMN)
Wheeler, Burton K., 33

White Earth reservation MN, 3, 35, 41, 194, 243
Whitefish Bay ON, 39, 156
Wikwemikong ON, 30, 168
Williams, Angeline, 189–90, 336n10
Wilson, Edward, 109, 113, 256
Wiltschko, Martina, 52
Wisconsin: animacy status of nouns in, 43; articulation of glides /y/ and /w/ in, 193, 195; demonstrative pronouns in, 329–30n14; final nasal in negation suffix -*sii(n)* in, 179; influence of Odawa in, 30; initial /g/ in, 186; *ji-/da-* complementizer in, 152, 154, 155; labialized stops in, 188; language revitalization efforts in, 5; number of Ojibwe speakers in, 4; optional lack of initial /w/, 39; participial forms in, 227, 231, 234, 235, 237; as part of SW Ojibwe range, 34–35; Potawatomi in, 310; reservations in, 35; and southern Leech Lake communities, 245; syncope in, 204; TA -*aw* stem contraction in, 215–16; /t/ epenthesis in, 199, 200, 255–56; vowel height in, 189, 190
Wisconsin Native American Languages Project, 149, 336n5
Wiyot, 329n13
Wolfart, Hans Christoph, 110, 317, 318
Wolvengrey, Arok, 332n21

Yurok, 329n13

www.ingramcontent.com/pod-product-compliance
Lightning Source LLC
Chambersburg PA
CBHW030332240426
43661CB00052B/1604